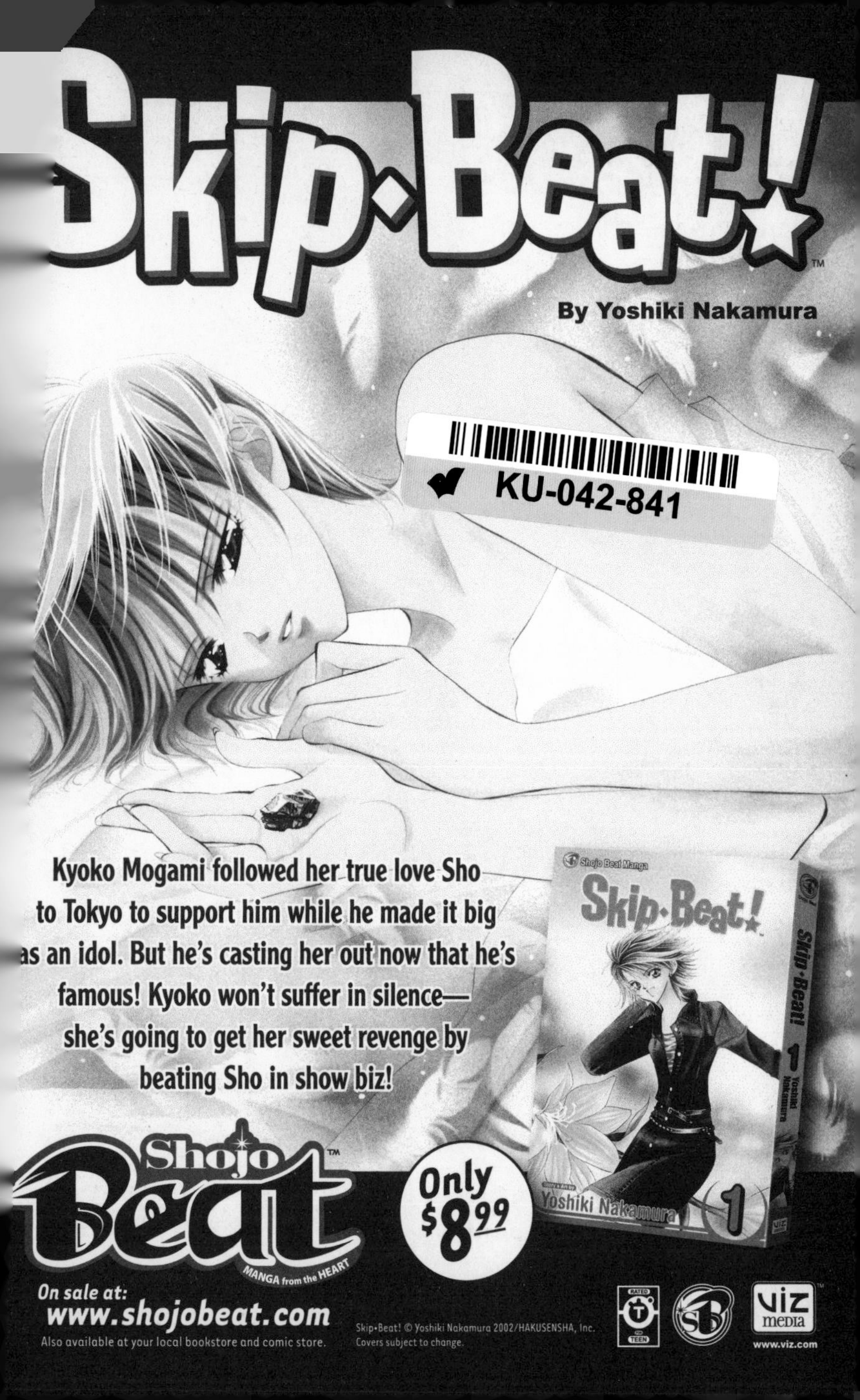
Skip·Beat!™
By Yoshiki Nakamura
Kyoko Mogami followed her true love Sho to Tokyo to support him while he made it big as an idol. But he's casting her out now that he's famous! Kyoko won't suffer in silence— she's going to get her sweet revenge by beating Sho in show biz!
Shojo Beat Manga
Skip·Beat!
1
Yoshiki Nakamura
Shojo Beat™
MANGA from the HEART
Only $8.99
On sale at:
www.shojobeat.com
Also available at your local bookstore and comic store.
Skip•Beat! © Yoshiki Nakamura 2002/HAKUSENSHA, Inc.
Covers subject to change.
RATED T TEEN
VIZ media
www.viz.com

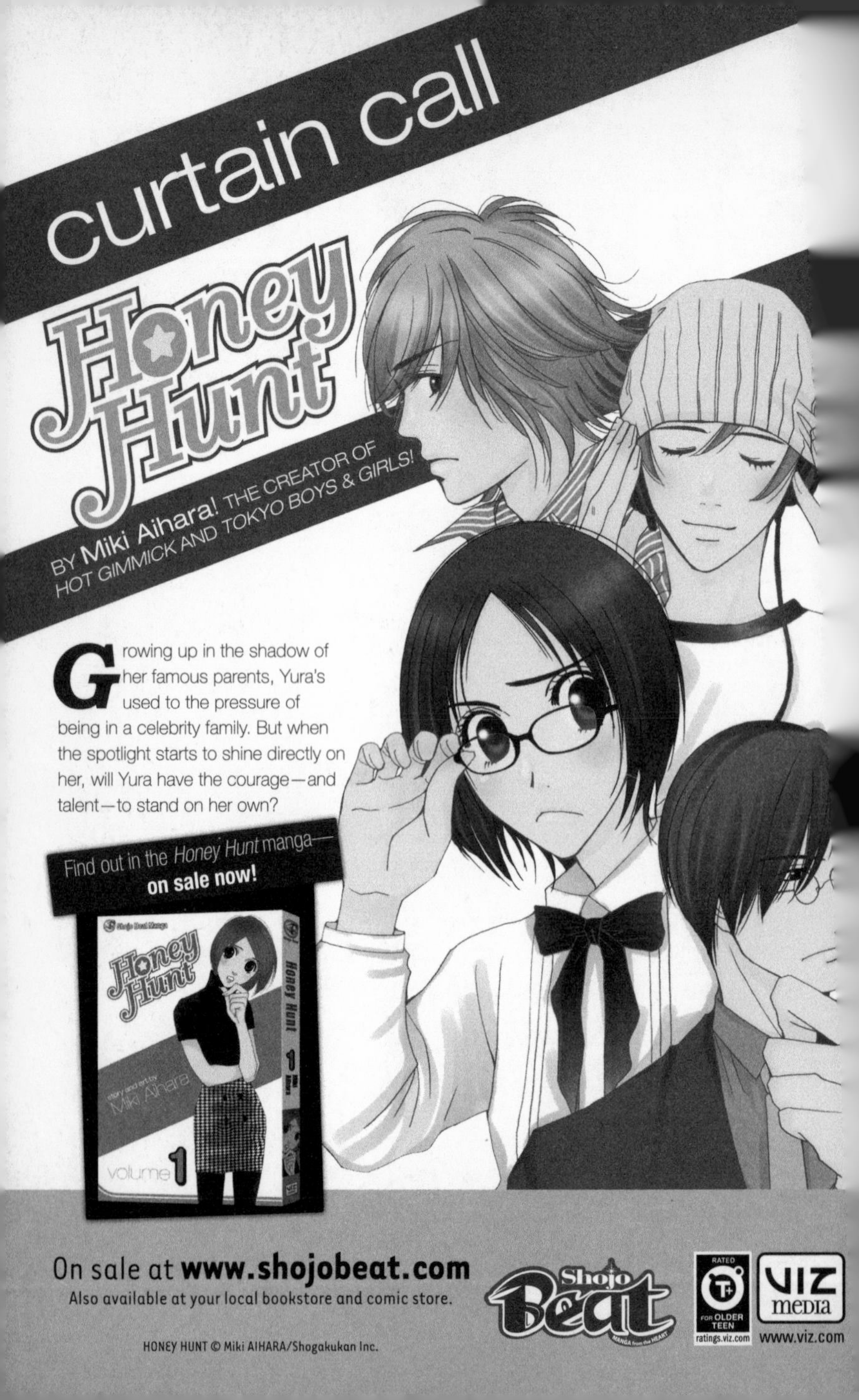
curtain call
Honey Hunt
BY Miki Aihara! THE CREATOR OF HOT GIMMICK AND TOKYO BOYS & GIRLS!
Growing up in the shadow of her famous parents, Yura's used to the pressure of being in a celebrity family. But when the spotlight starts to shine directly on her, will Yura have the courage—and talent—to stand on her own?
Find out in the Honey Hunt manga— on sale now!
Honey Hunt
story and art by Miki Aihara
volume 1
On sale at www.shojobeat.com
Also available at your local bookstore and comic store.
Shojo Beat
RATED T+ FOR OLDER TEEN
ratings.viz.com
VIZ media
www.viz.com
HONEY HUNT © Miki AIHARA/Shogakukan Inc.

Tell us what you think about Shojo Beat Manga!

Our survey is now available online. Go to:

shojobeat.com/mangasurvey

Help us make our product offerings better!

THE REAL DRAMA BEGINS IN...

FULL MOON WO SAGASHITE © 2001 by Arina Tanemura/SHUEISHA Inc.
Fushigi Yûgi: Genbu Kaiden © 2004 Yuu WATASE/Shogakukan Inc.
Ouran Koko Host Club © Bisco Hatori 2002/HAKUSENSHA, Inc.

Love and Leftovers

Mixed Vegetables

by Ayumi Komura

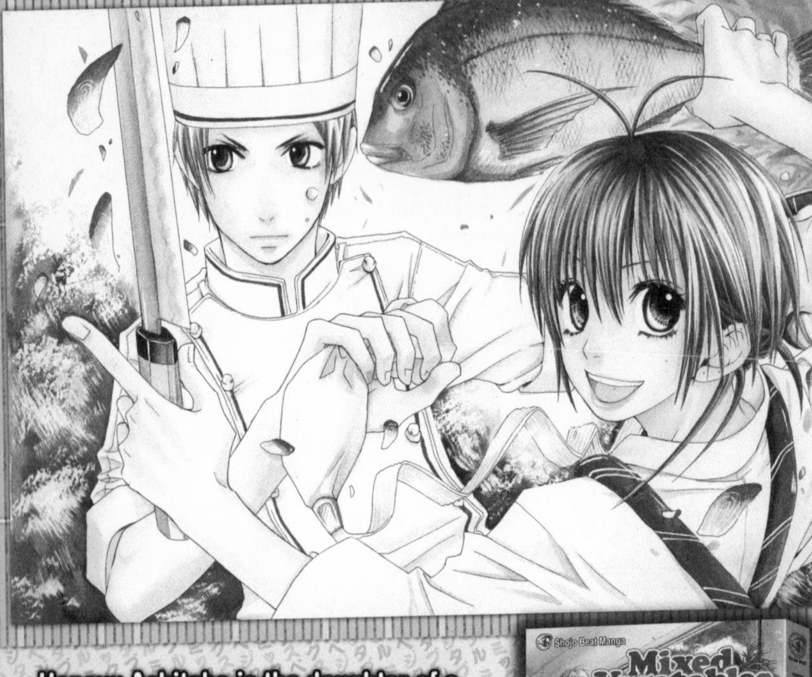

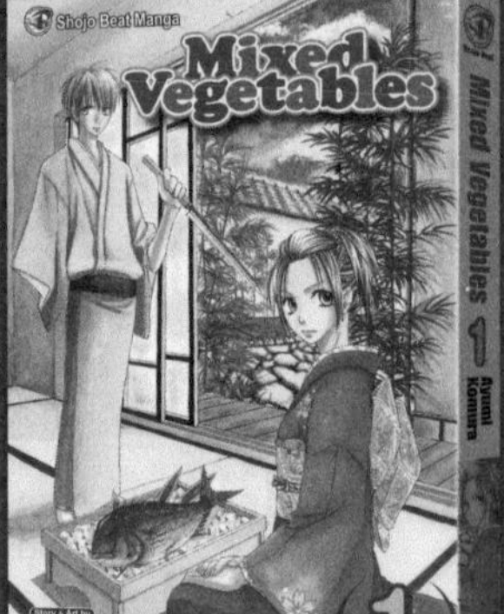
Shojo Beat Manga
Mixed Vegetables
Mixed Vegetables 1 Ayumi Komura
Story & Art by
Ayumi Komura
1

Hanayu Ashitaba is the daughter of a celebrated baker but dreams of being a sushi chef. Hayato Hyuga is the son of a sushi master and wants to become a pastry chef! Will these star-crossed gourmands fulfill their cuisine dreams?

Find out in *Mixed Vegetables*—manga available now!

Shojo Beat MANGA from the HEART

On sale at www.shojobeat.com

Also available at your local bookstore and comic store.

RATED T FOR TEEN ratings.viz.com

VIZ media www.viz.com

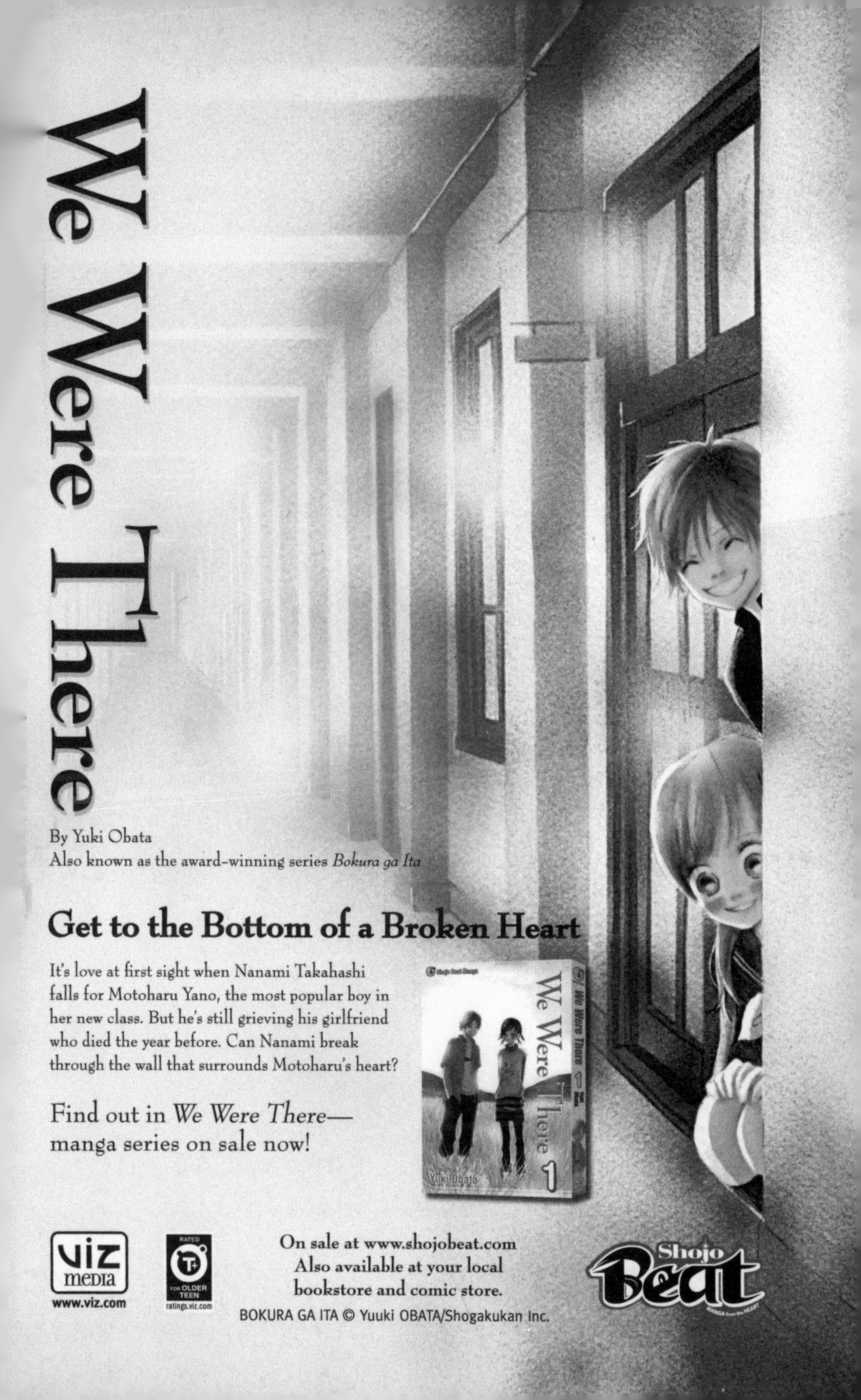
We Were There
By Yuki Obata
Also known as the award-winning series Bokura ga Ita
Get to the Bottom of a Broken Heart
It's love at first sight when Nanami Takahashi falls for Motoharu Yano, the most popular boy in her new class. But he's still grieving his girlfriend who died the year before. Can Nanami break through the wall that surrounds Motoharu's heart?
Find out in We Were There—
manga series on sale now!
We Were There 1
Yuki Obata
viz media
www.viz.com
RATED T+ FOR OLDER TEEN
ratings.viz.com
On sale at www.shojobeat.com
Also available at your local bookstore and comic store.
BOKURA GA ITA © Yuuki OBATA/Shogakukan Inc.
Shojo Beat
MANGA from the HEART

honey and clover

Where unrequited love is a masterpiece

13 uncut episodes on 3 discs

honey and clover
BOX 1

A story of five art school friends and two very complicated love triangles. With so much love to go around, why is everyone still single?

Original and uncut anime now available in collectible DVD box sets

On sale at honeyandclover.viz.com and at your local DVD retailer

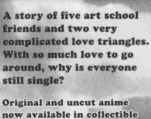

VIZ MEDIA
www.viz.com

Shojo Beat
www.shojobeat.com

Available on iTunes

hulu

©2005 CHICA UMINO/SHUEISHA•Honey and Clover committee

DVD VIDEO

RATED T+ FOR OLDER TEEN
ratings.viz.com

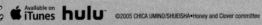

HONEY AND CLOVER
VOL. 9
Shojo Beat Edition

STORY AND ART BY CHICA UMINO

English Translation & Adaptation/Akemi Wegmuller
Touch-up Art & Lettering/Sabrina Heep
Design/Yukiko Whitley
Editor/Pancha Diaz

VP, Production/Alvin Lu
VP, Sales & Product Marketing/Gonzalo Ferreyra
VP, Creative/Linda Espinosa
Publisher/Hyoe Narita

HONEY AND CLOVER © 2000 by Chica Umino. All rights reserved.
First published in Japan in 2000 by SHUEISHA Inc., Tokyo.
English translation rights arranged by SHUEISHA Inc.

The rights of the author(s) of the work(s) in this publication to be so identified
have been asserted in accordance with the Copyright, Designs and Patents Act
1988. A CIP catalogue record for this book is available from the British Library.

The stories, characters and incidents mentioned in this publication are
entirely fictional.

No portion of this book may be reproduced or transmitted in any form or by any
means without written permission from the copyright holders.

Printed in Canada

Published by VIZ Media, LLC
P.O. Box 77010
San Francisco, CA 94107

10 9 8 7 6 5 4 3 2 1
First printing, March 2010

www.viz.com   www.shojobeat.com

PARENTAL ADVISORY
HONEY AND CLOVER is rated T+ for Older Teen and is
recommended for ages 16 and up. This volume contains
adult situations.
ratings.viz.com

Honey and Clover is going to be made into a movie this summer!! The first time I saw a preview screening, I felt like my children had gone off on a big journey, and I was getting to see a film of them having a great time somewhere far away. It brought tears to my eyes to realize that they'd all grown up to be stronger and healthier than I thought they were. I'd like to thank the director, staff and all the cast from the bottom of my heart.

-Chica Umino

Chica Umino was born in Tokyo and started out as a product designer and illustrator. Her beloved *Honey and Clover* debuted in 2000 and received the Kodansha Manga Award in 2003. *Honey and Clover* was also nominated for the Tezuka Culture Prize and an award from the Japan Media Arts Festival. The *Honey and Clover* movie is available in the U.S. from VIZ Pictures, and the anime is available in the U.S. from VIZ Media.

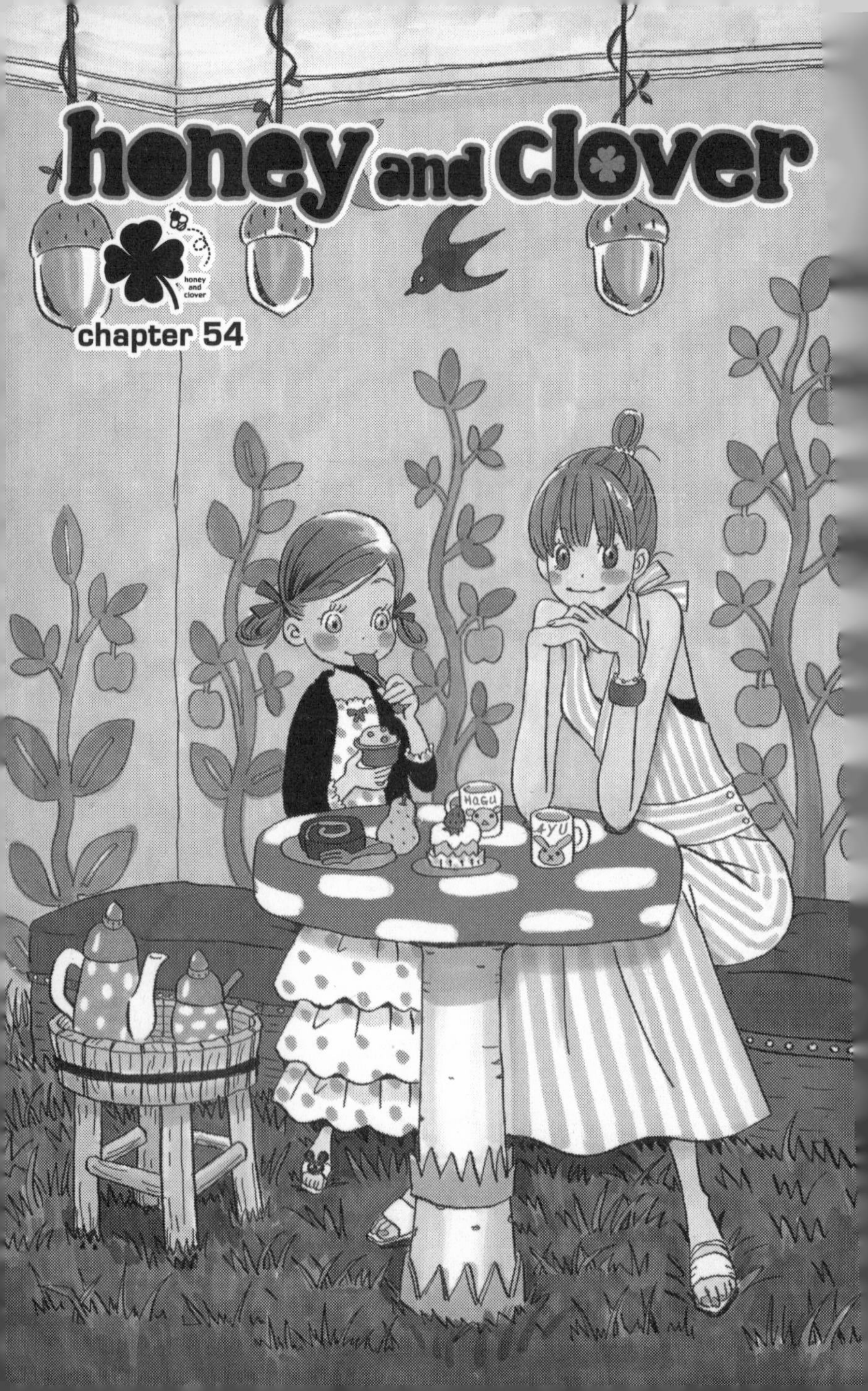
honey and clover
honey and clover
chapter 54
HAGU
AYU

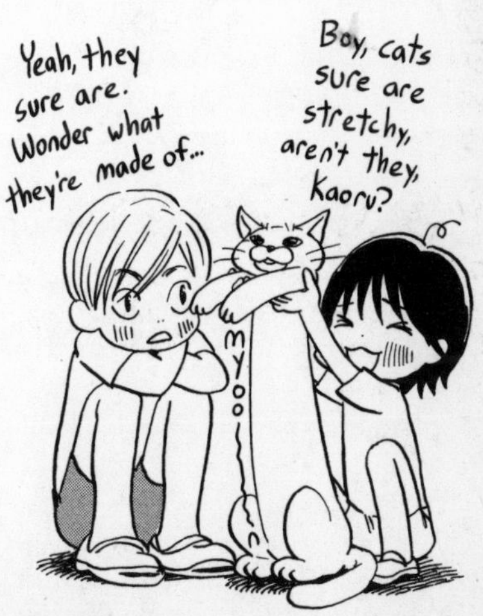
Boy, cats sure are stretchy, aren't they, Kaoru?
Yeah, they sure are. Wonder what they're made of...
MYOOO

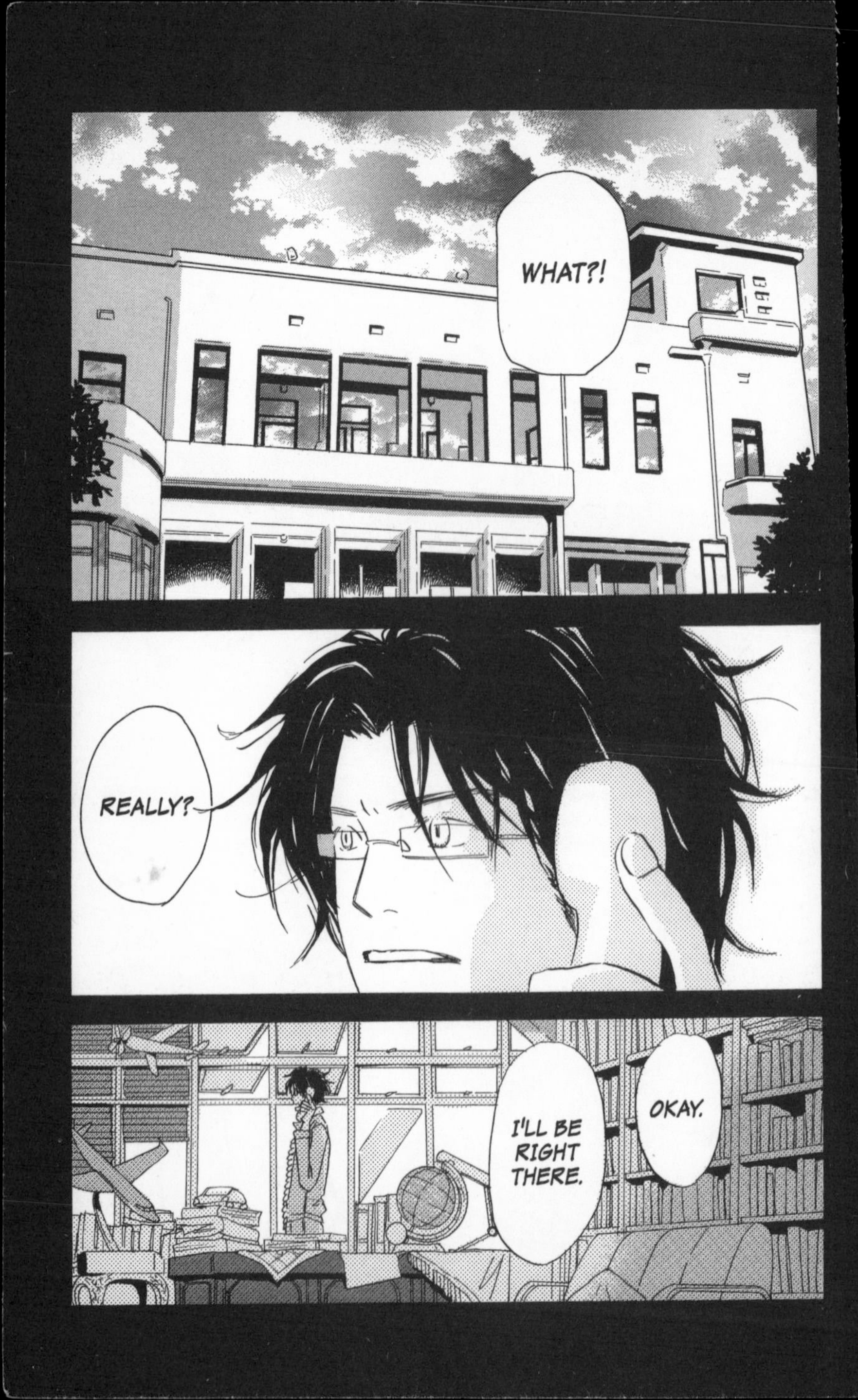
WHAT?!
REALLY?
OKAY.
I'LL BE RIGHT THERE.

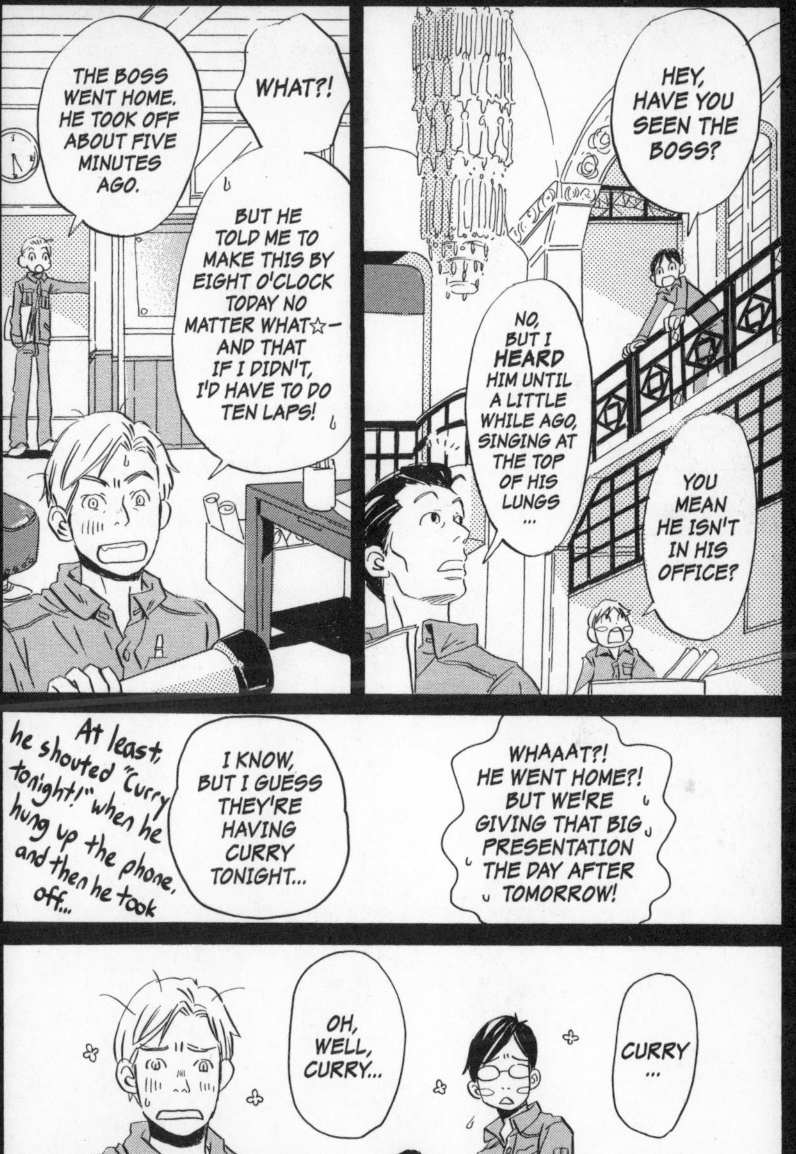
HEY, HAVE YOU SEEN THE BOSS?
NO, BUT I HEARD HIM UNTIL A LITTLE WHILE AGO, SINGING AT THE TOP OF HIS LUNGS...
YOU MEAN HE ISN'T IN HIS OFFICE?
THE BOSS WENT HOME. HE TOOK OFF ABOUT FIVE MINUTES AGO.
WHAT?!
BUT HE TOLD ME TO MAKE THIS BY EIGHT O'CLOCK TODAY NO MATTER WHAT☆— AND THAT IF I DIDN'T, I'D HAVE TO DO TEN LAPS!
WHAAAT?! HE WENT HOME?! BUT WE'RE GIVING THAT BIG PRESENTATION THE DAY AFTER TOMORROW!
I KNOW, BUT I GUESS THEY'RE HAVING CURRY TONIGHT...
At least, he shouted "Curry tonight!" when he hung up the phone, and then he took off...
CURRY...
OH, WELL, CURRY...

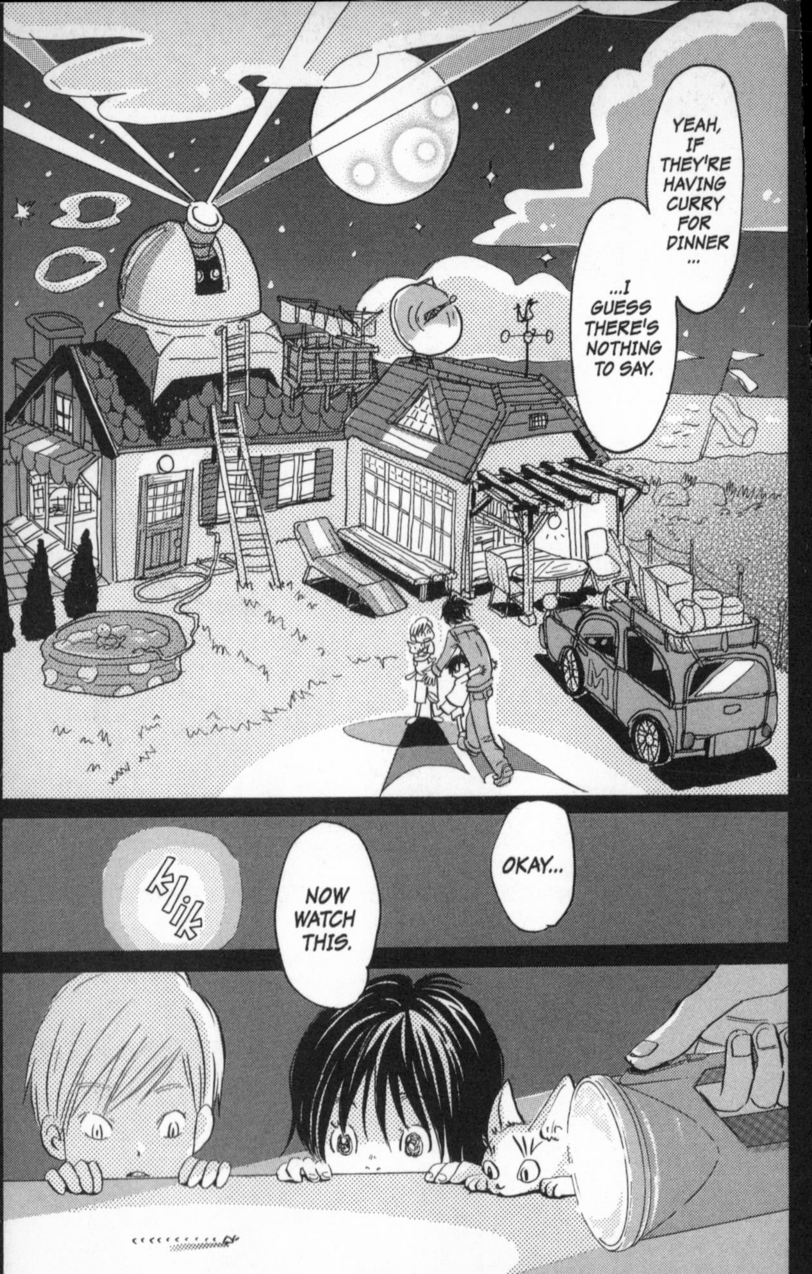
YEAH, IF THEY'RE HAVING CURRY FOR DINNER...
...I GUESS THERE'S NOTHING TO SAY.
OKAY...
NOW WATCH THIS.
klik

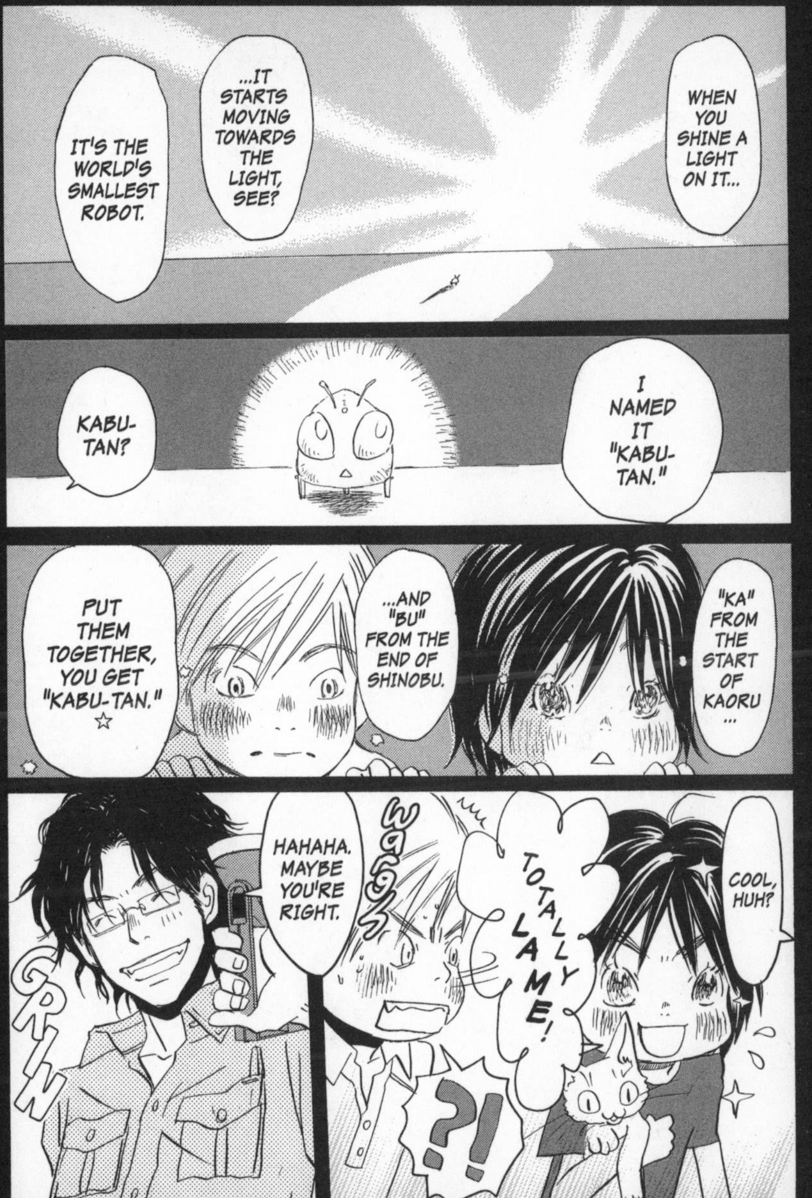
WHEN YOU SHINE A LIGHT ON IT...
...IT STARTS MOVING TOWARDS THE LIGHT, SEE?
IT'S THE WORLD'S SMALLEST ROBOT.
I NAMED IT "KABU-TAN."
KABU-TAN?
"KA" FROM THE START OF KAORU ...
...AND "BU" FROM THE END OF SHINOBU.
PUT THEM TOGETHER, YOU GET "KABU-TAN." ☆
COOL, HUH?
TOTALLY LAME!
?!
WARGH
HAHAHA. MAYBE YOU'RE RIGHT.
GRIN

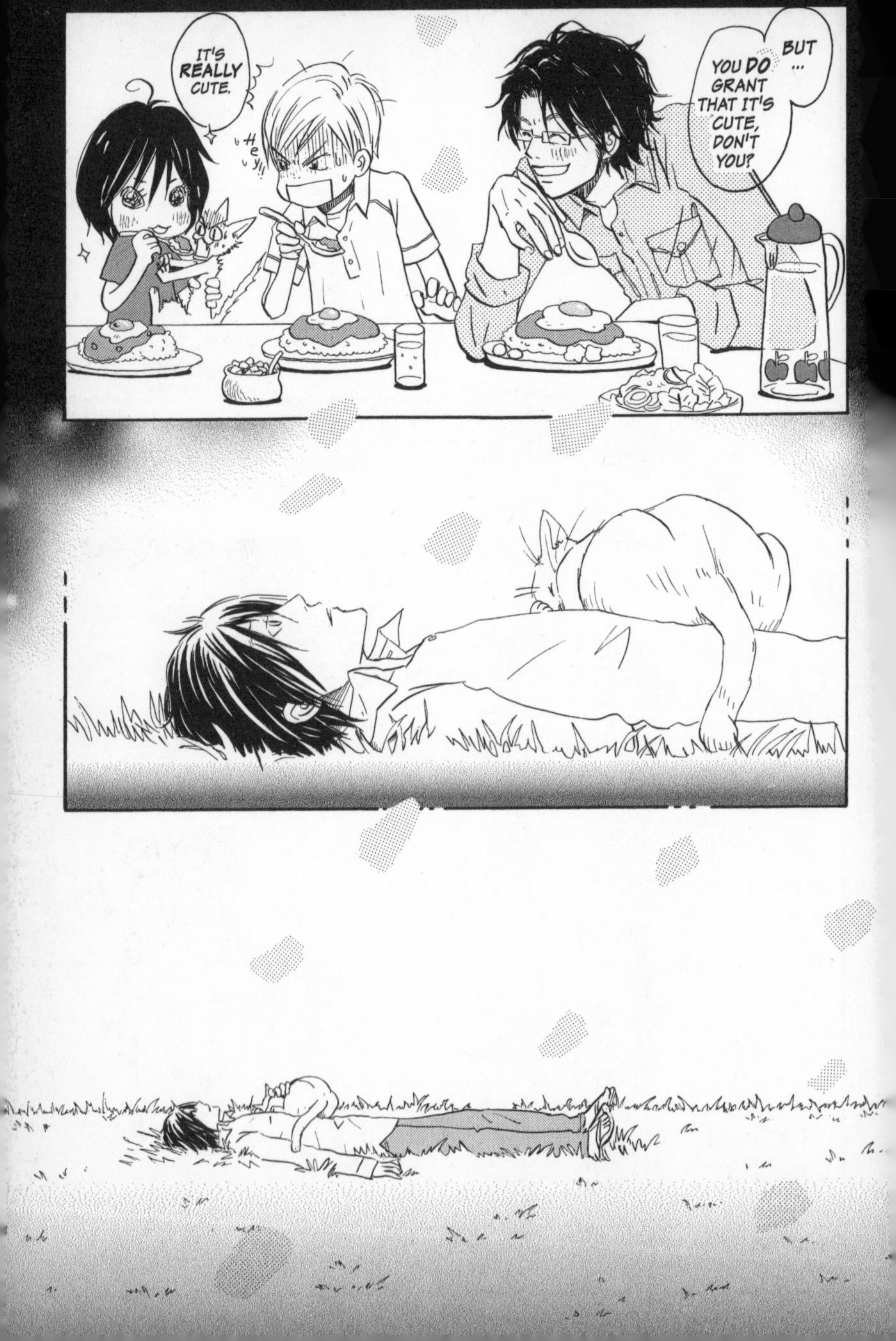
BUT ... YOU DO GRANT THAT IT'S CUTE, DON'T YOU?
Hey!!
IT'S REALLY CUTE.

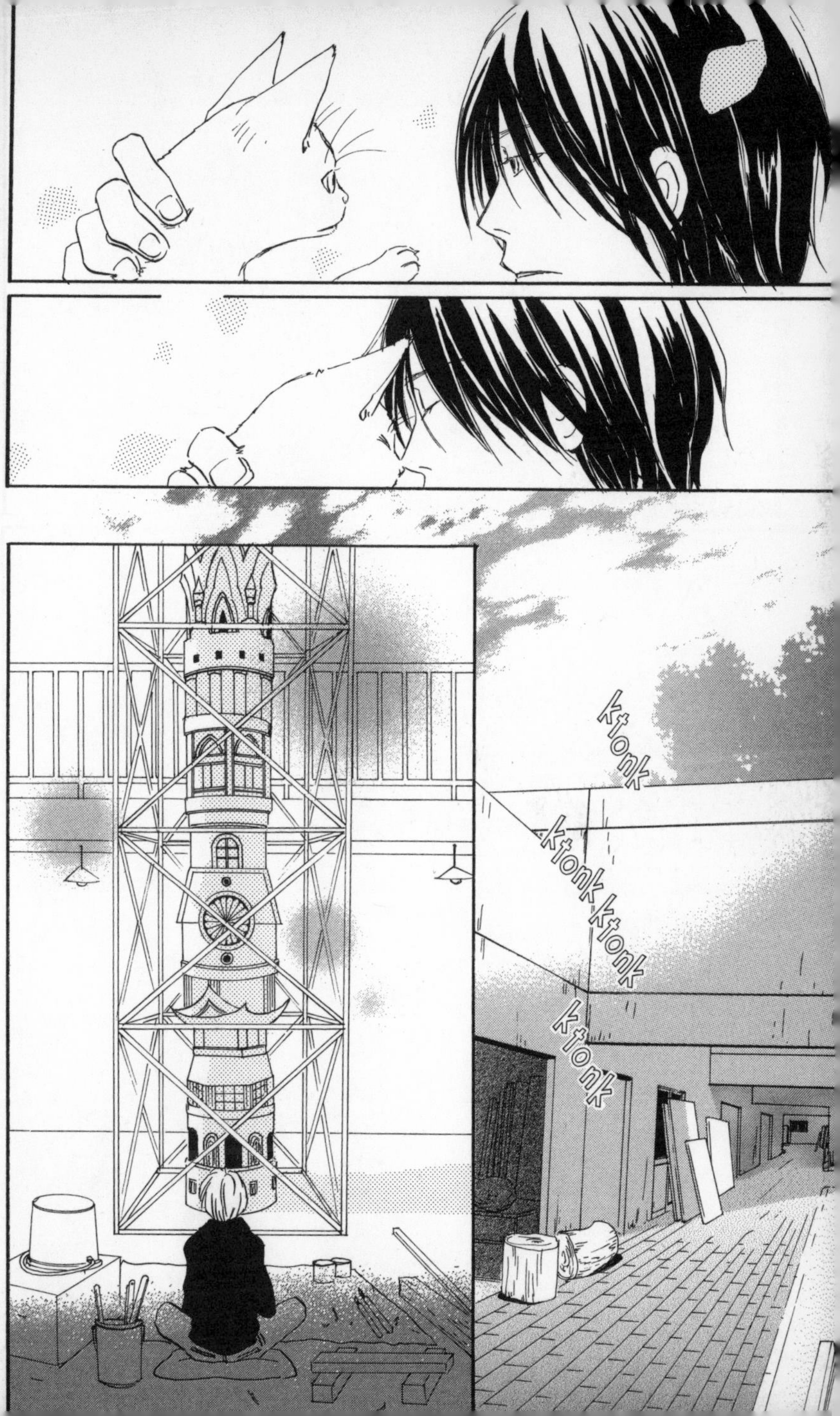
ktonk
ktonk ktonk
ktonk

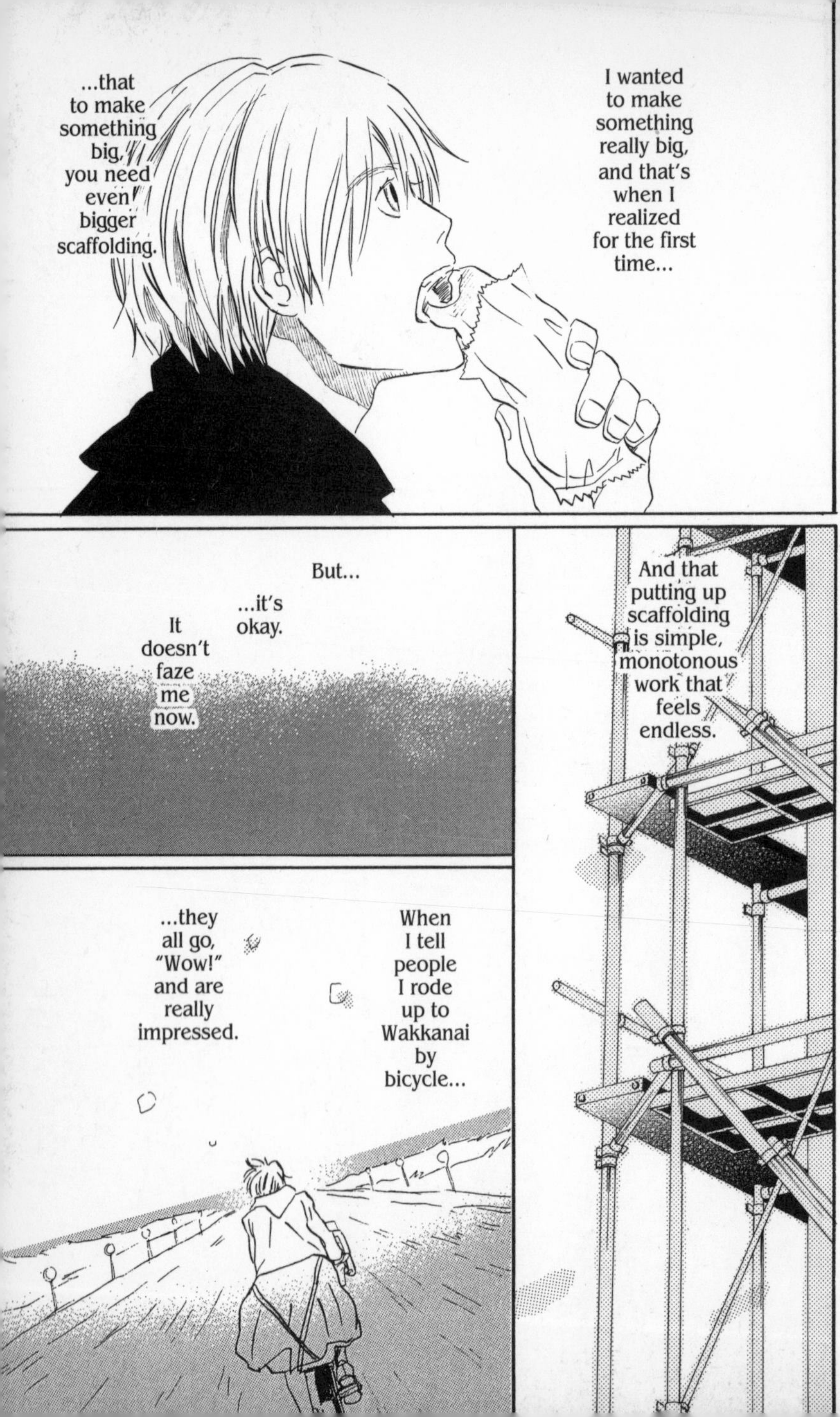
I wanted to make something really big, and that's when I realized for the first time...
...that to make something big, you need even bigger scaffolding.
And that putting up scaffolding is simple, monotonous work that feels endless.
But...
...it's okay.
It doesn't faze me now.
When I tell people I rode up to Wakkanai by bicycle...
...they all go, "Wow!" and are really impressed.

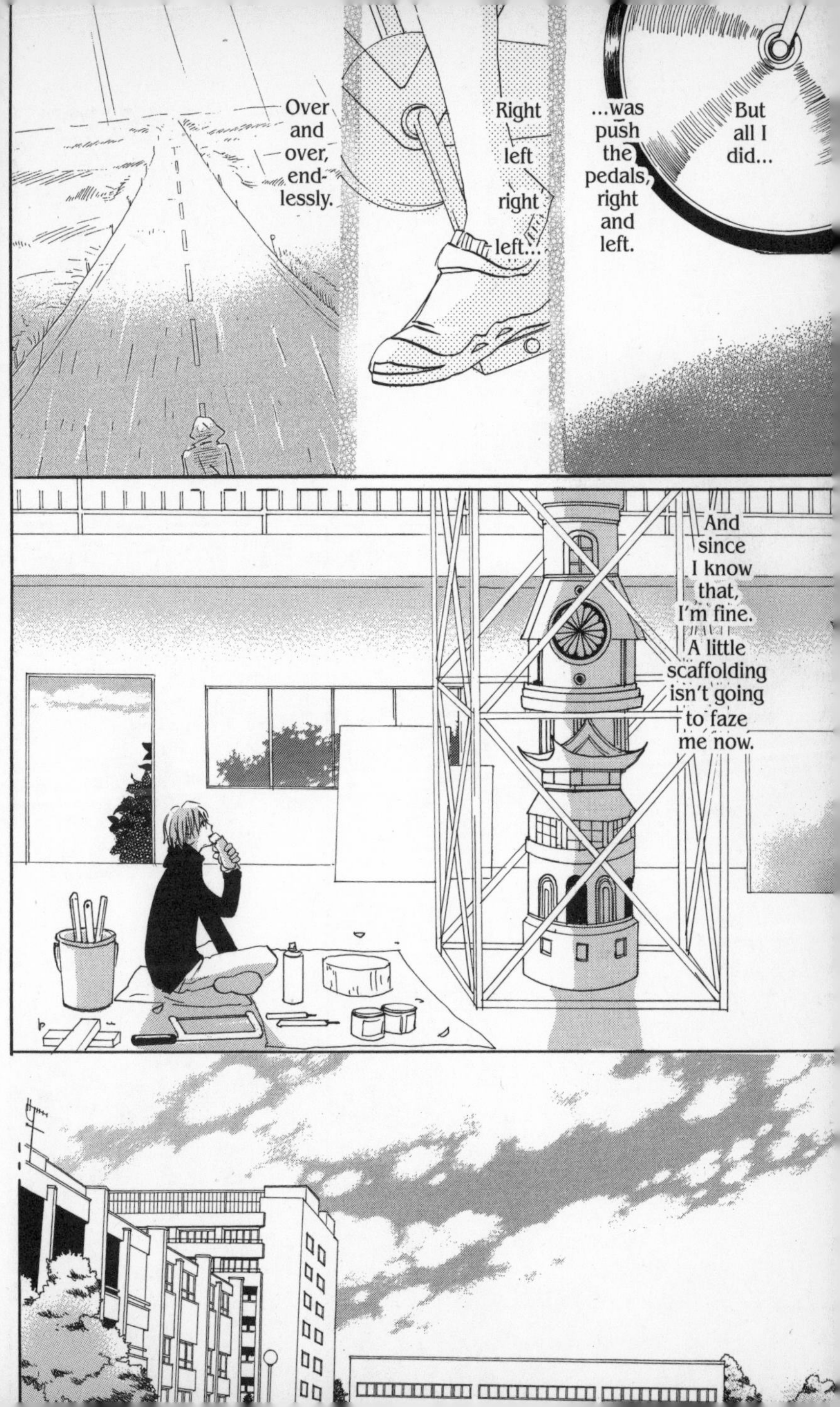
But all I did...
...was push the pedals, right and left.
Right left right left...
Over and over, endlessly.
And since I know that, I'm fine.
A little scaffolding isn't going to faze me now.

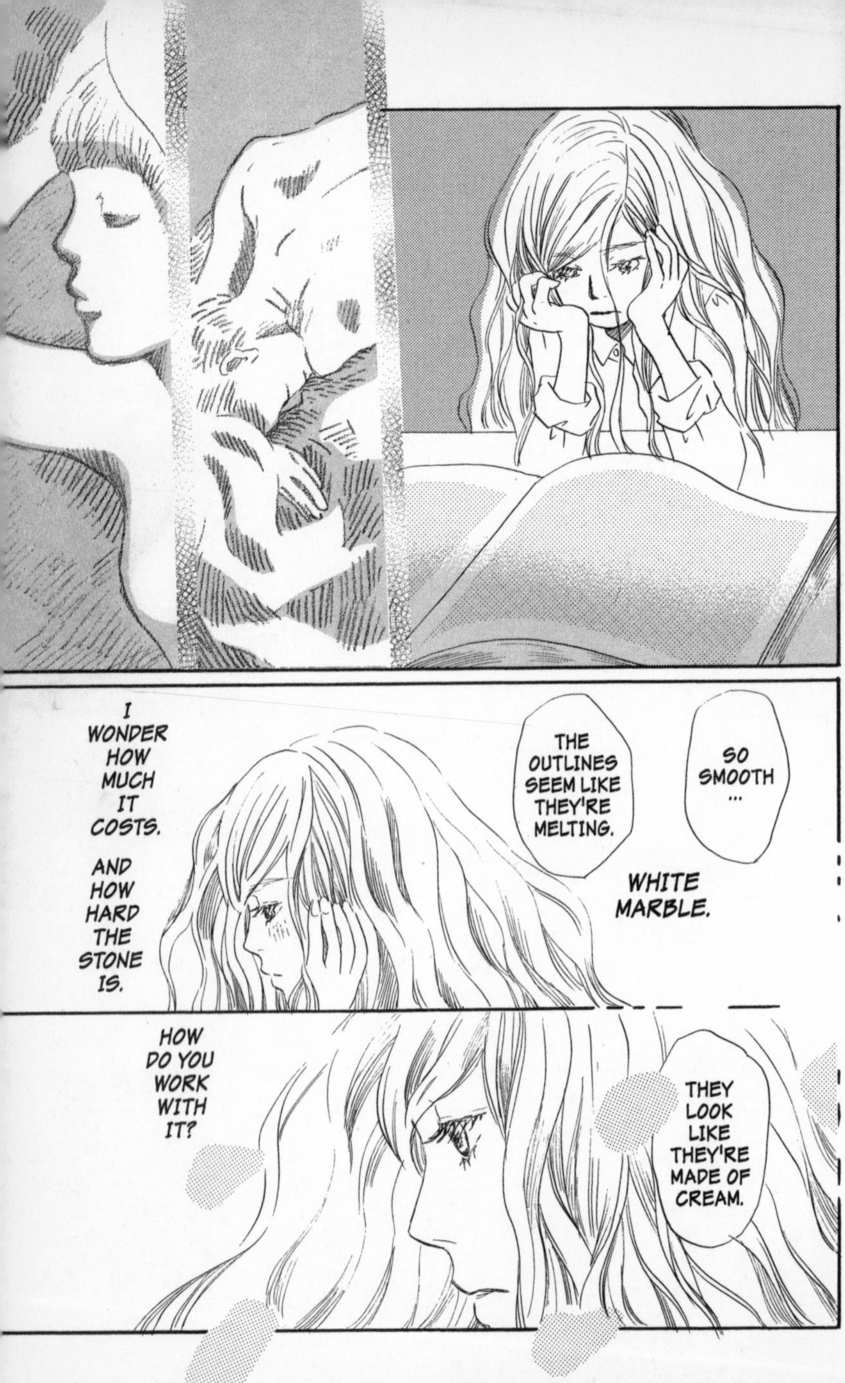
SO SMOOTH ...
THE OUTLINES SEEM LIKE THEY'RE MELTING.
WHITE MARBLE.
I WONDER HOW MUCH IT COSTS.
AND HOW HARD THE STONE IS.
THEY LOOK LIKE THEY'RE MADE OF CREAM.
HOW DO YOU WORK WITH IT?

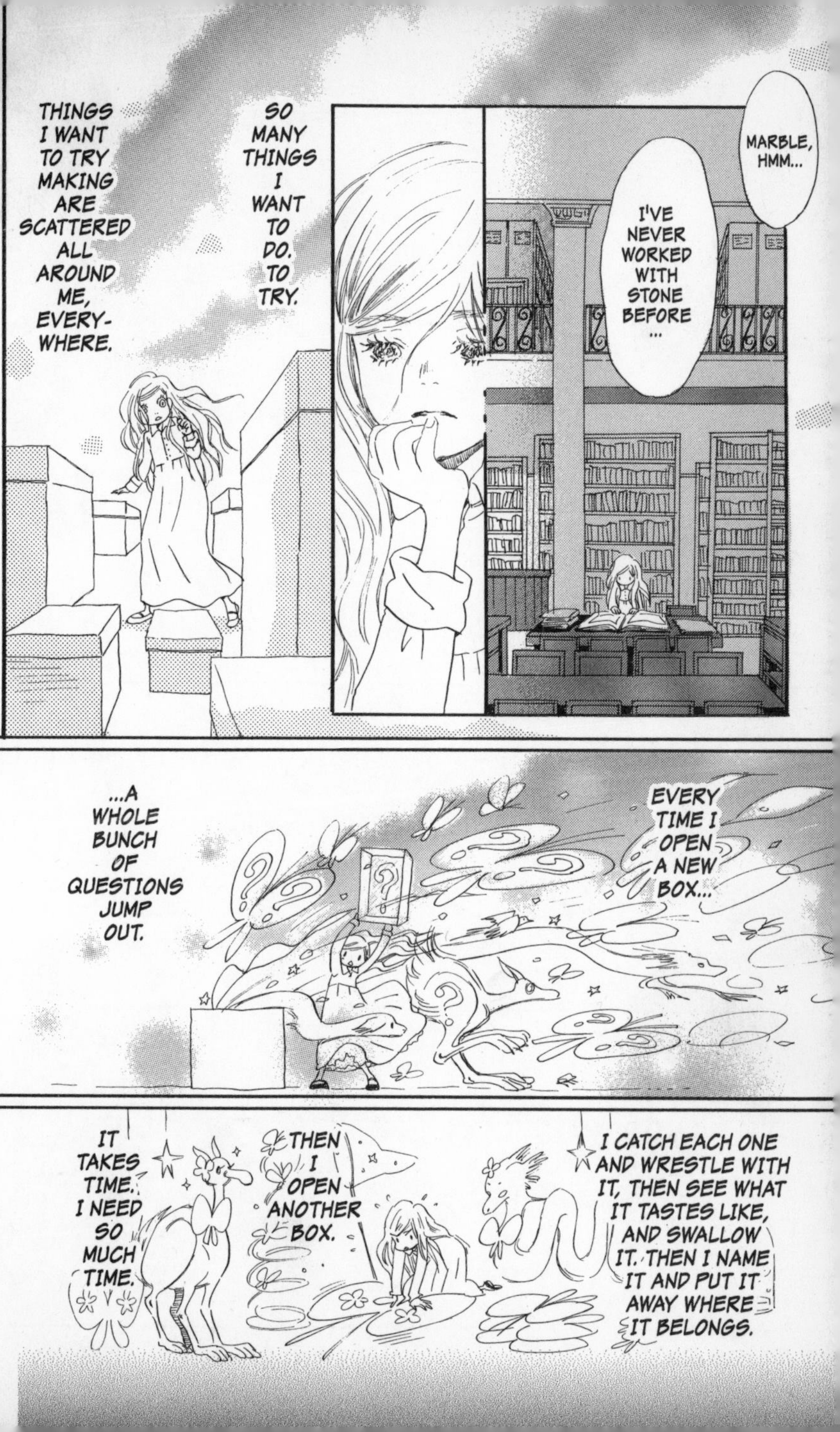
MARBLE, HMM...
I'VE NEVER WORKED WITH STONE BEFORE...
SO MANY THINGS I WANT TO DO. TO TRY.
THINGS I WANT TO TRY MAKING ARE SCATTERED ALL AROUND ME, EVERYWHERE.
EVERY TIME I OPEN A NEW BOX...
...A WHOLE BUNCH OF QUESTIONS JUMP OUT.
I CATCH EACH ONE AND WRESTLE WITH IT, THEN SEE WHAT IT TASTES LIKE, AND SWALLOW IT. THEN I NAME IT AND PUT IT AWAY WHERE IT BELONGS.
THEN I OPEN ANOTHER BOX.
IT TAKES TIME. I NEED SO MUCH TIME.

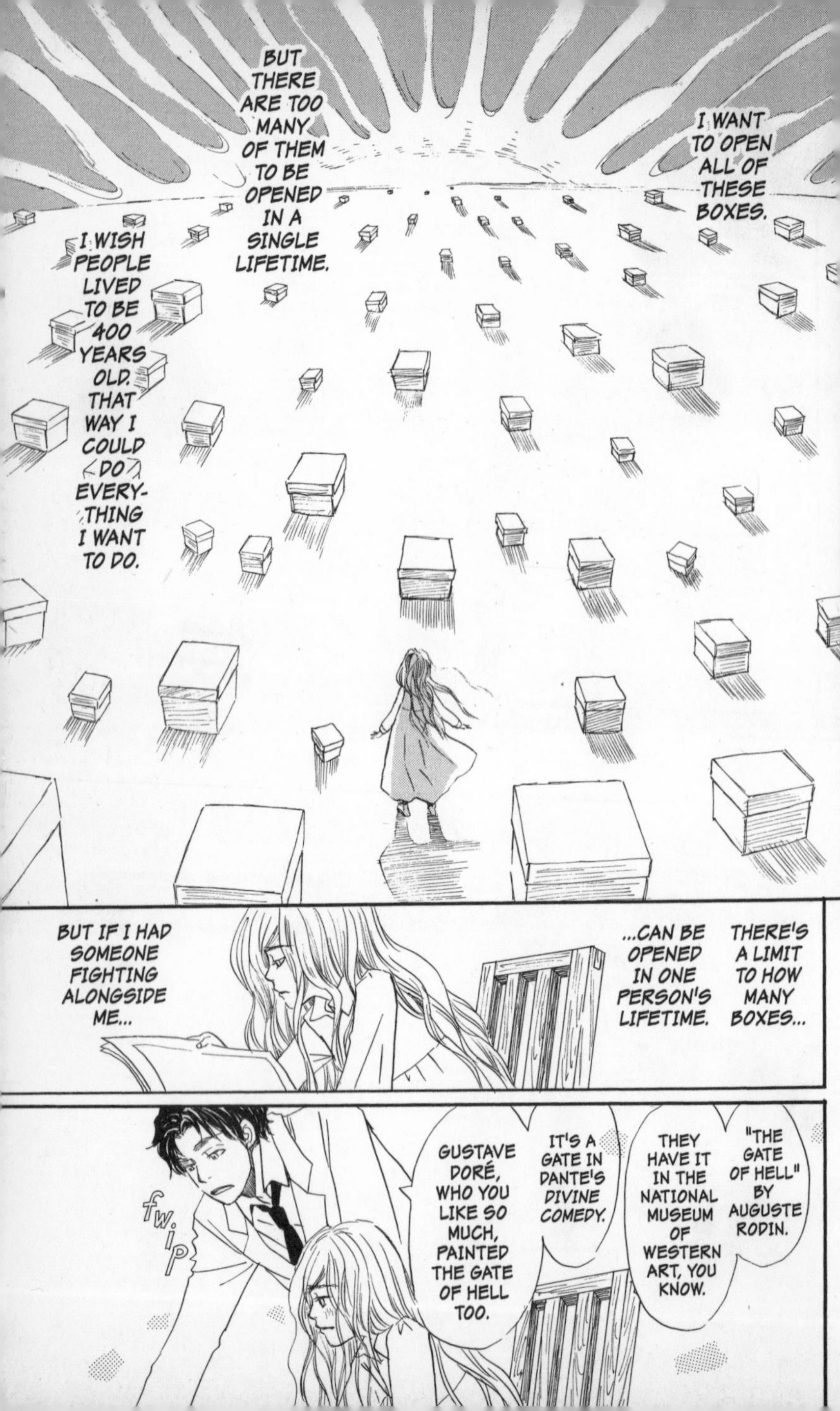

I WANT TO OPEN ALL OF THESE BOXES.
BUT THERE ARE TOO MANY OF THEM TO BE OPENED IN A SINGLE LIFETIME.
I WISH PEOPLE LIVED TO BE 400 YEARS OLD. THAT WAY I COULD DO EVERYTHING I WANT TO DO.
THERE'S A LIMIT TO HOW MANY BOXES...
...CAN BE OPENED IN ONE PERSON'S LIFETIME.
BUT IF I HAD SOMEONE FIGHTING ALONGSIDE ME...
"THE GATE OF HELL" BY AUGUSTE RODIN.
THEY HAVE IT IN THE NATIONAL MUSEUM OF WESTERN ART, YOU KNOW.
IT'S A GATE IN DANTE'S DIVINE COMEDY.
GUSTAVE DORÉ, WHO YOU LIKE SO MUCH, PAINTED THE GATE OF HELL TOO.
fwip

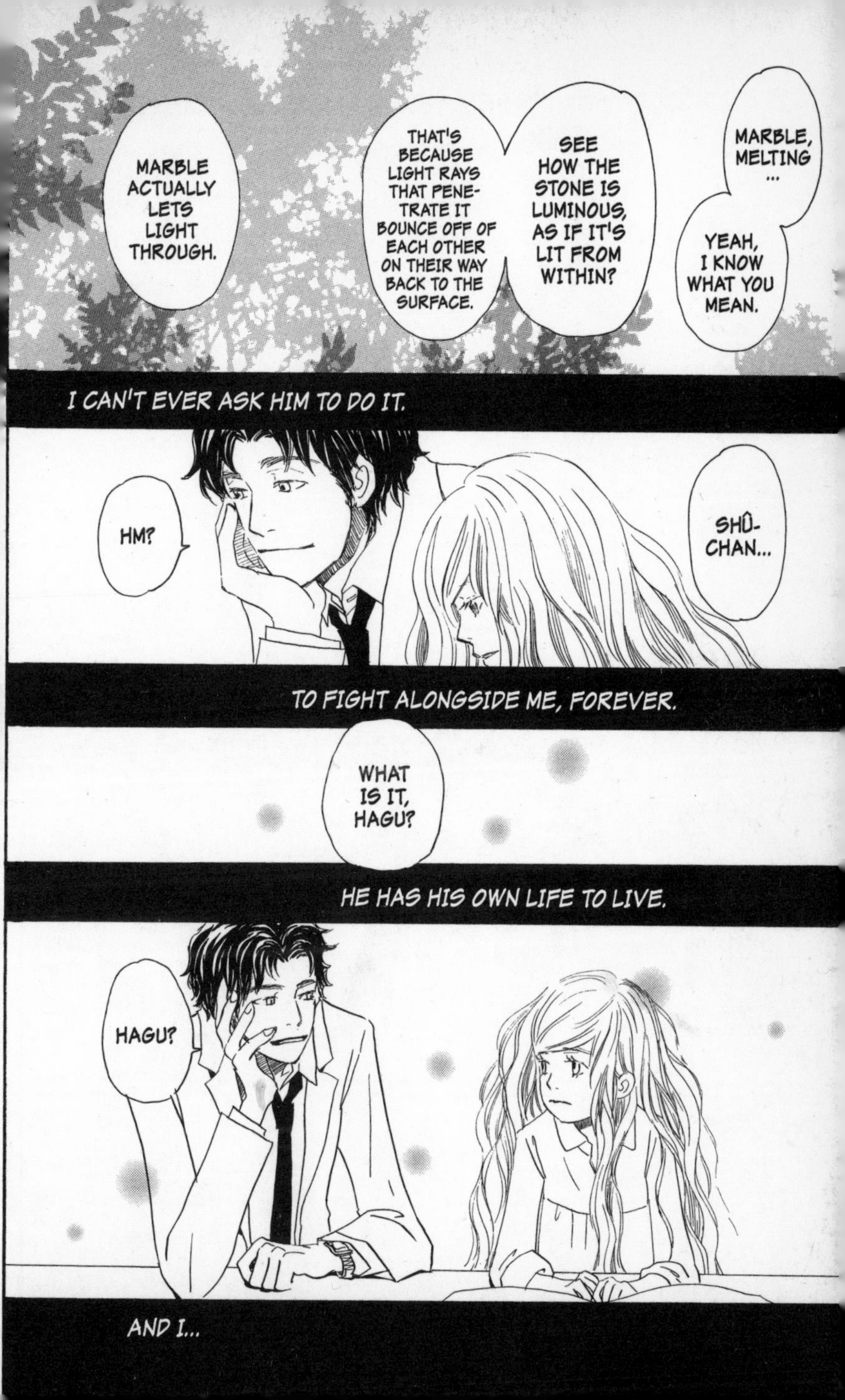
MARBLE, MELTING...
YEAH, I KNOW WHAT YOU MEAN.
SEE HOW THE STONE IS LUMINOUS, AS IF IT'S LIT FROM WITHIN?
THAT'S BECAUSE LIGHT RAYS THAT PENETRATE IT BOUNCE OFF OF EACH OTHER ON THEIR WAY BACK TO THE SURFACE.
MARBLE ACTUALLY LETS LIGHT THROUGH.
I CAN'T EVER ASK HIM TO DO IT.
SHÛ-CHAN...
HM?
TO FIGHT ALONGSIDE ME, FOREVER.
WHAT IS IT, HAGU?
HE HAS HIS OWN LIFE TO LIVE.
HAGU?
AND I...

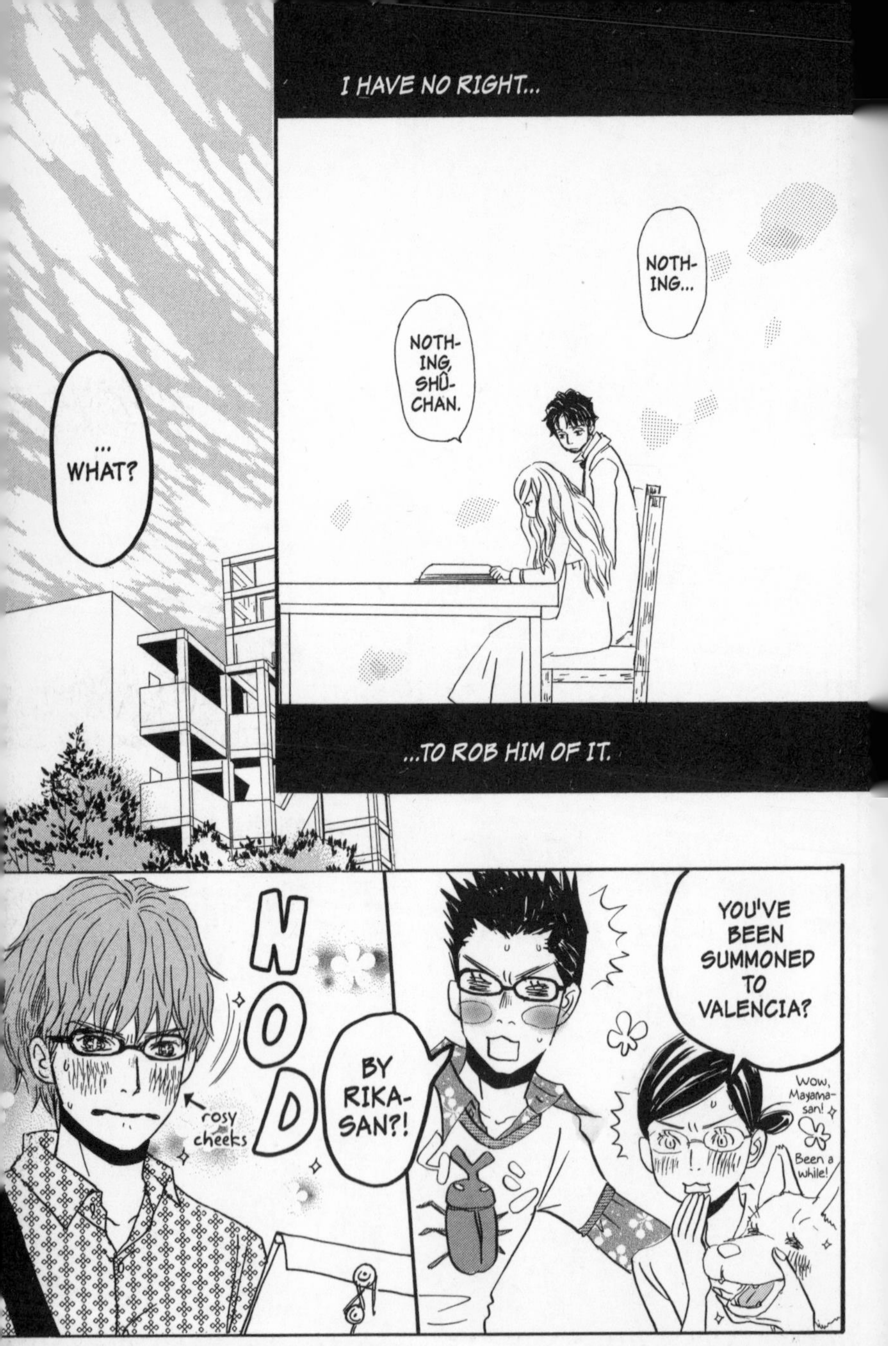
I HAVE NO RIGHT...
NOTH-ING...
NOTH-ING, SHŪ-CHAN.
...TO ROB HIM OF IT.
... WHAT?
YOU'VE BEEN SUMMONED TO VALENCIA?
BY RIKA-SAN?!
Wow, Mayama-san!
Been a while!
NOD
rosy cheeks

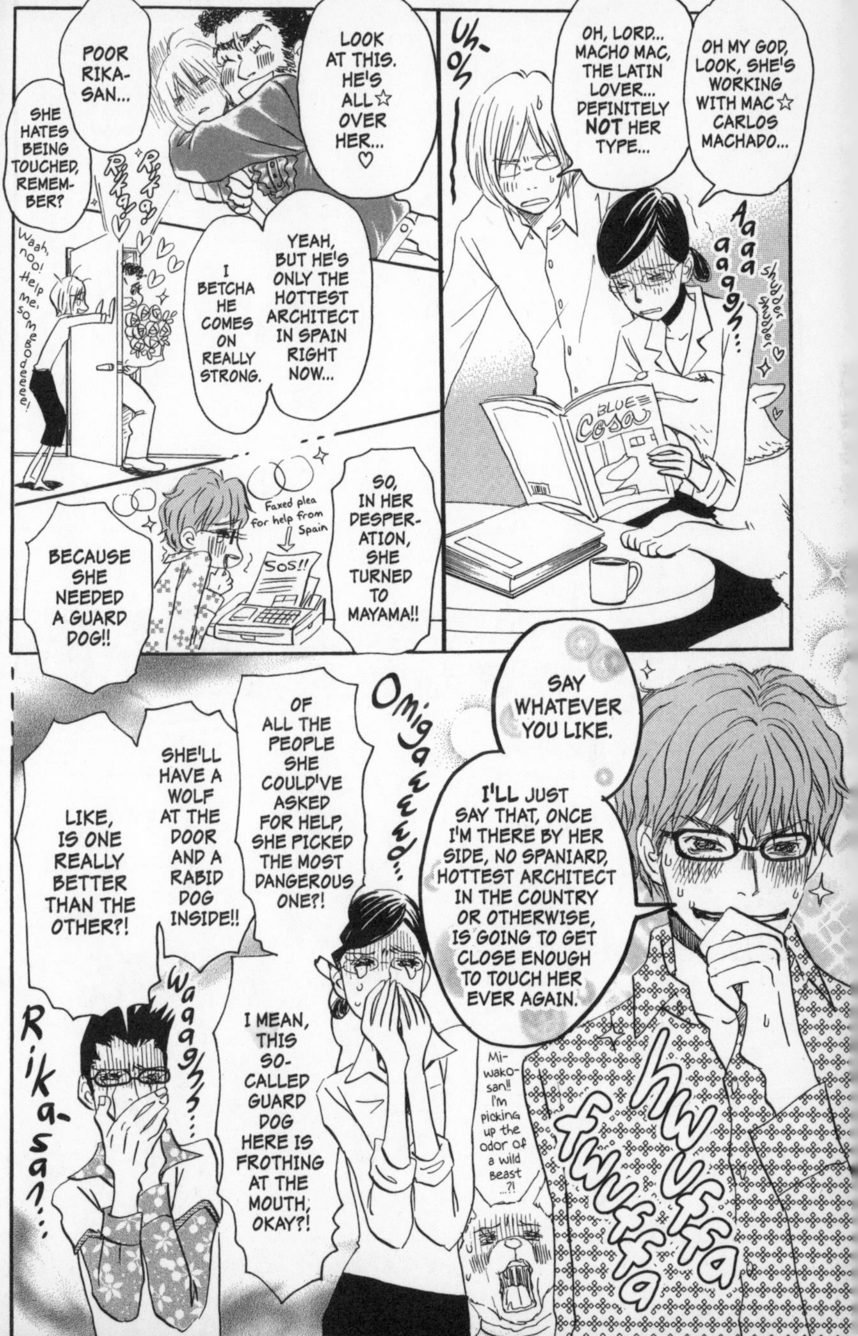
OH MY GOD, LOOK, SHE'S WORKING WITH MAC☆ CARLOS MACHADO...
OH, LORD... MACHO MAC, THE LATIN LOVER... DEFINITELY **NOT** HER TYPE...
Uh-oh
Aaaaaagh...
shudder shudder♡
BLUE Cosa
LOOK AT THIS. HE'S ALL☆ OVER HER...♡
POOR RIKA-SAN...
SHE HATES BEING TOUCHED, REMEMBER?
YEAH, BUT HE'S ONLY THE HOTTEST ARCHITECT IN SPAIN RIGHT NOW...
I BETCHA HE COMES ON REALLY STRONG.
Waah, nooo! Help me, somebodeeee!
SO, IN HER DESPERATION, SHE TURNED TO MAYAMA!!
Faxed plea for help from Spain
SOS!!
BECAUSE SHE NEEDED A GUARD DOG!!
SAY WHATEVER YOU LIKE.
I'LL JUST SAY THAT, ONCE I'M THERE BY HER SIDE, NO SPANIARD, HOTTEST ARCHITECT IN THE COUNTRY OR OTHERWISE, IS GOING TO GET CLOSE ENOUGH TO TOUCH HER EVER AGAIN.
hwuffa fwuffa
Omigawwwd...
OF ALL THE PEOPLE SHE COULD'VE ASKED FOR HELP, SHE PICKED THE MOST DANGEROUS ONE?!
SHE'LL HAVE A WOLF AT THE DOOR AND A RABID DOG INSIDE!!
LIKE, IS ONE REALLY BETTER THAN THE OTHER?!
Mi-wako-san!! I'm picking up the odor of a wild beast...?!
I MEAN, THIS SO-CALLED GUARD DOG HERE IS FROTHING AT THE MOUTH, OKAY?!
Waaaghhh...
Rika-san...

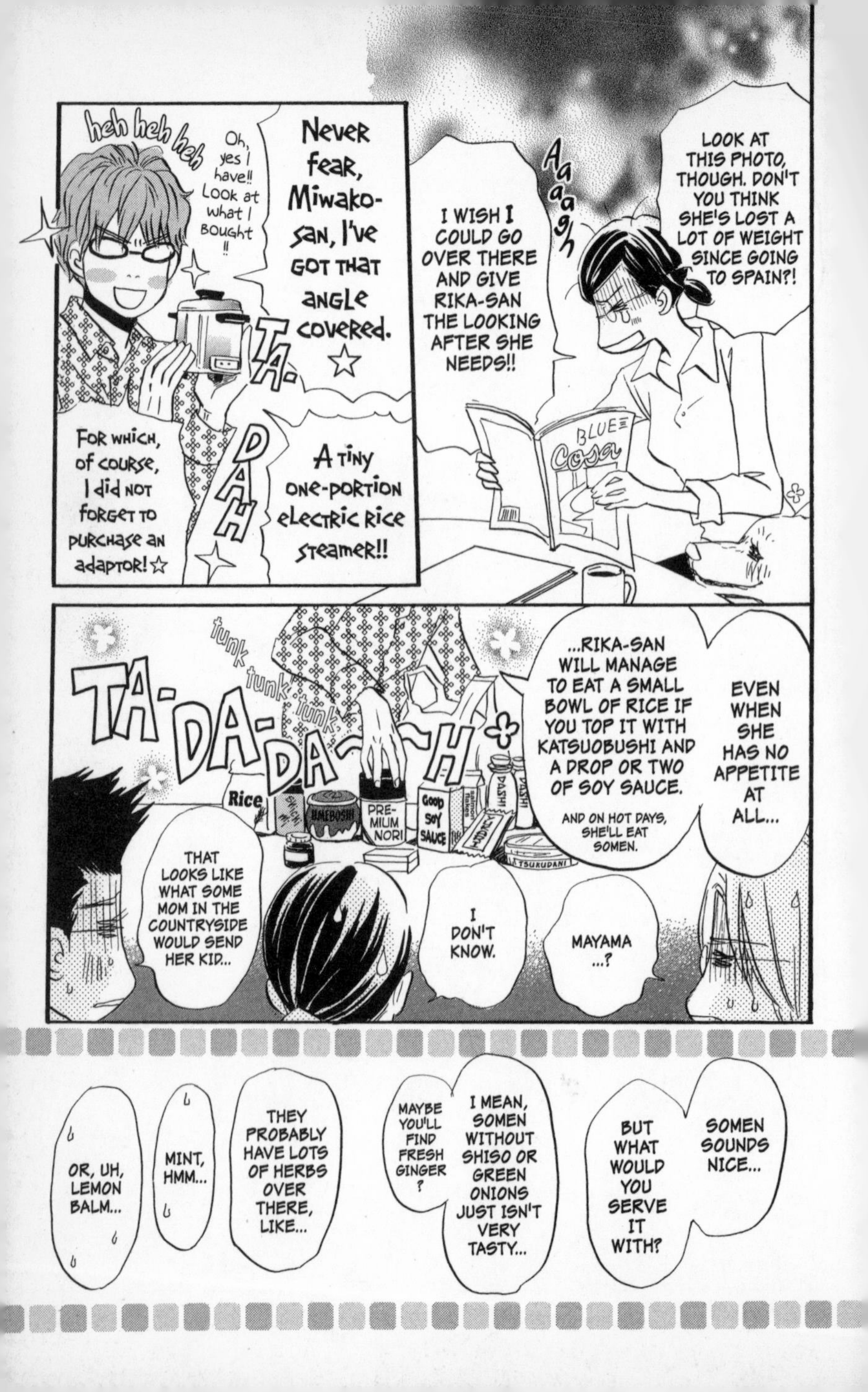
LOOK AT THIS PHOTO, THOUGH. DON'T YOU THINK SHE'S LOST A LOT OF WEIGHT SINCE GOING TO SPAIN?!
Aaaagh
I WISH I COULD GO OVER THERE AND GIVE RIKA-SAN THE LOOKING AFTER SHE NEEDS!!
BLUE Cosa
Never fear, Miwako-san, I've got that angle covered. ☆
Oh, yes I have!! Look at what I bought!!
heh heh heh
TA-DAH
A tiny one-portion electric rice steamer!!
For which, of course, I did not forget to purchase an adaptor! ☆
EVEN WHEN SHE HAS NO APPETITE AT ALL...
...RIKA-SAN WILL MANAGE TO EAT A SMALL BOWL OF RICE IF YOU TOP IT WITH KATSUOBUSHI AND A DROP OR TWO OF SOY SAUCE.
AND ON HOT DAYS, SHE'LL EAT SOMEN.
tunk tunk tunk
TA-DA-DA~~H
Rice
UMEBOSHI
PREMIUM NORI
GOOD SOY SAUCE
DASHI
DASHI
TSUKUDANI
MAYAMA ...?
I DON'T KNOW.
THAT LOOKS LIKE WHAT SOME MOM IN THE COUNTRYSIDE WOULD SEND HER KID...
SOMEN SOUNDS NICE...
BUT WHAT WOULD YOU SERVE IT WITH?
I MEAN, SOMEN WITHOUT SHISO OR GREEN ONIONS JUST ISN'T VERY TASTY...
MAYBE YOU'LL FIND FRESH GINGER?
THEY PROBABLY HAVE LOTS OF HERBS OVER THERE, LIKE...
MINT, HMM...
OR, UH, LEMON BALM...

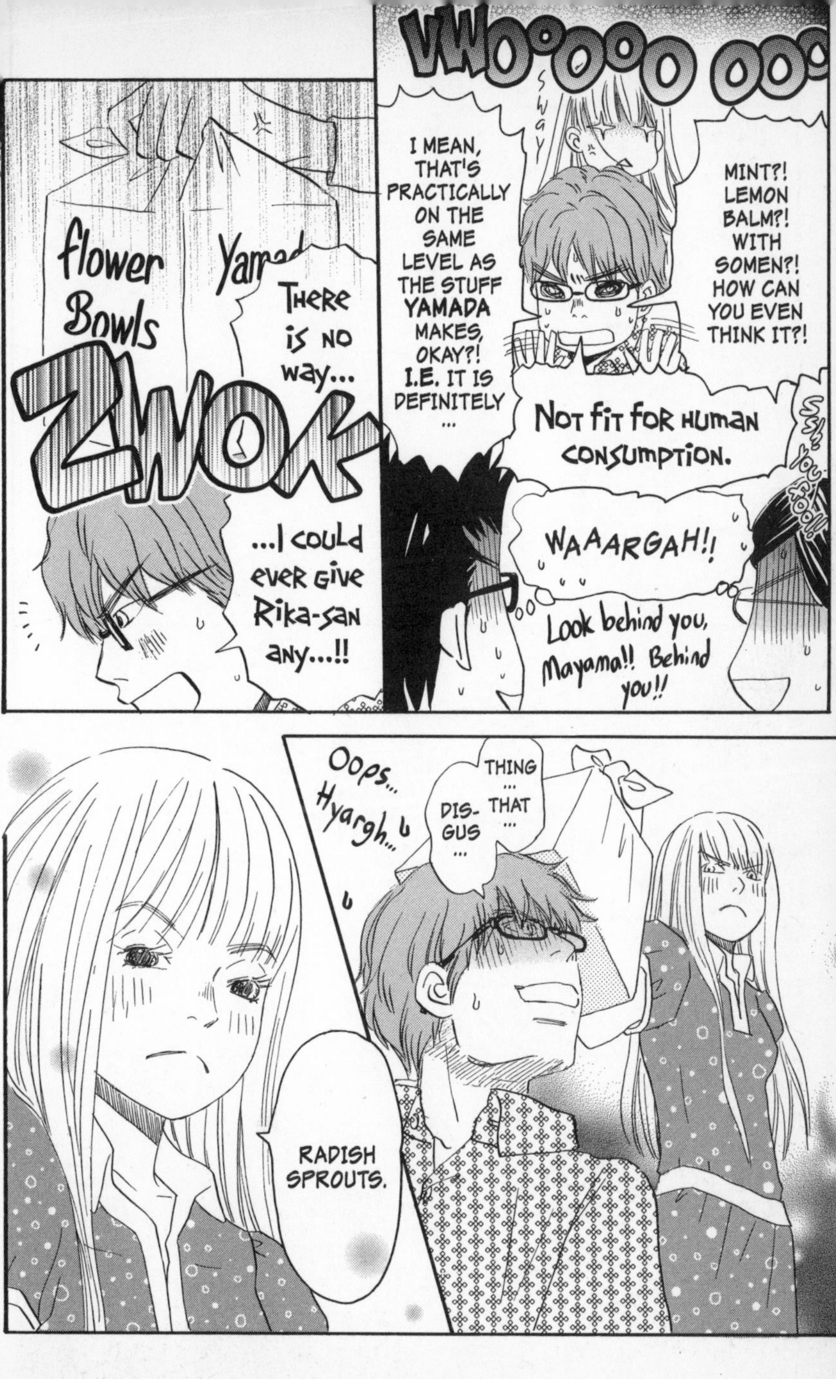

VWOOOOO OOO
sway
MINT?! LEMON BALM?! WITH SOMEN?! HOW CAN YOU EVEN THINK IT?!
I MEAN, THAT'S PRACTICALLY ON THE SAME LEVEL AS THE STUFF YAMADA MAKES, OKAY?! I.E. IT IS DEFINITELY ...
Not fit for human consumption.
Ssh you fool!!
WAAARGAH!!
Look behind you, Mayama!! Behind you!!
flower Bowls
There is no way...
ZWOK
...I could ever give Rika-san any...!!
THING ... THAT ...
DIS-GUS ...
Oops... Hyargh...
RADISH SPROUTS.

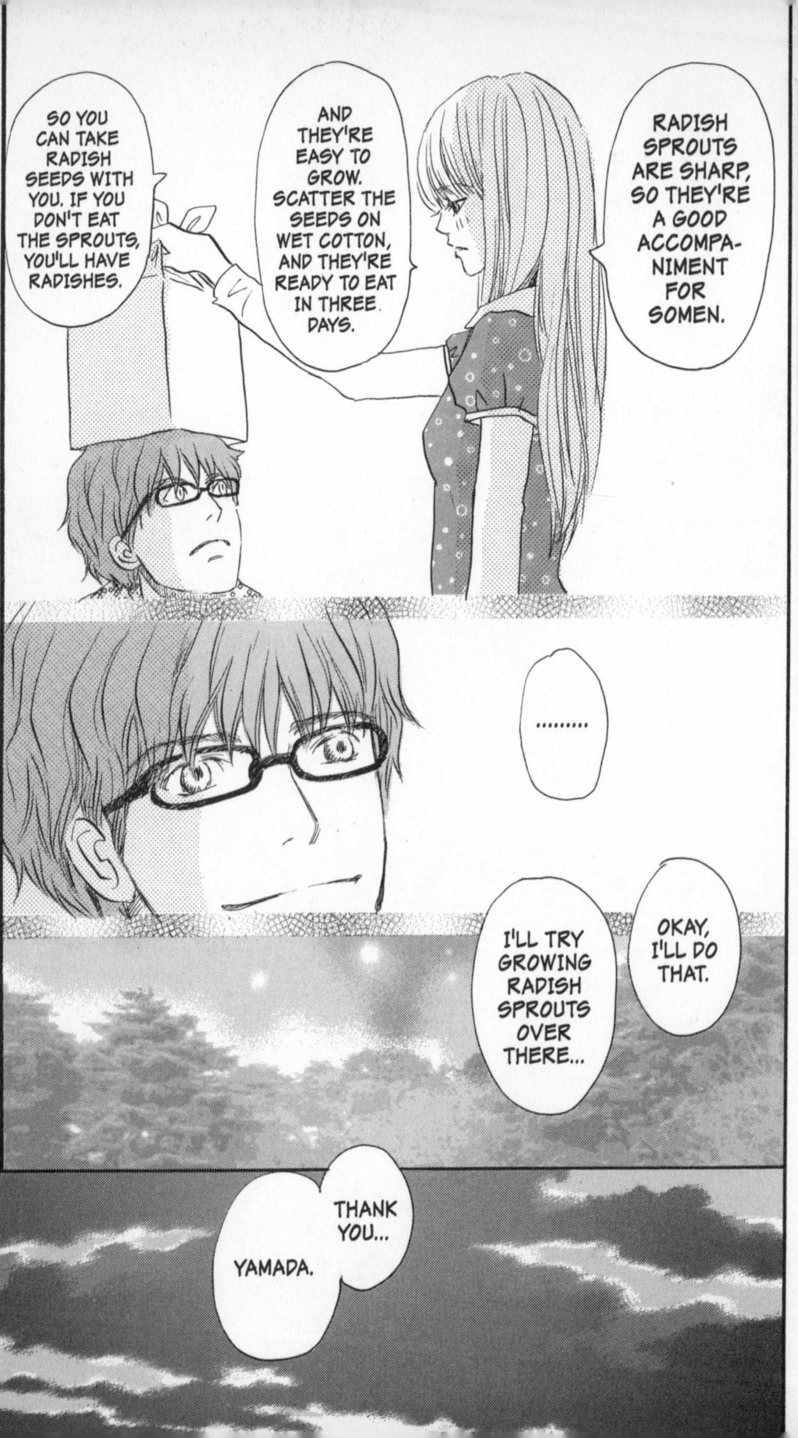
RADISH SPROUTS ARE SHARP, SO THEY'RE A GOOD ACCOMPANIMENT FOR SOMEN.
AND THEY'RE EASY TO GROW. SCATTER THE SEEDS ON WET COTTON, AND THEY'RE READY TO EAT IN THREE DAYS.
SO YOU CAN TAKE RADISH SEEDS WITH YOU. IF YOU DON'T EAT THE SPROUTS, YOU'LL HAVE RADISHES.
....
OKAY, I'LL DO THAT.
I'LL TRY GROWING RADISH SPROUTS OVER THERE...
THANK YOU...
YAMADA.

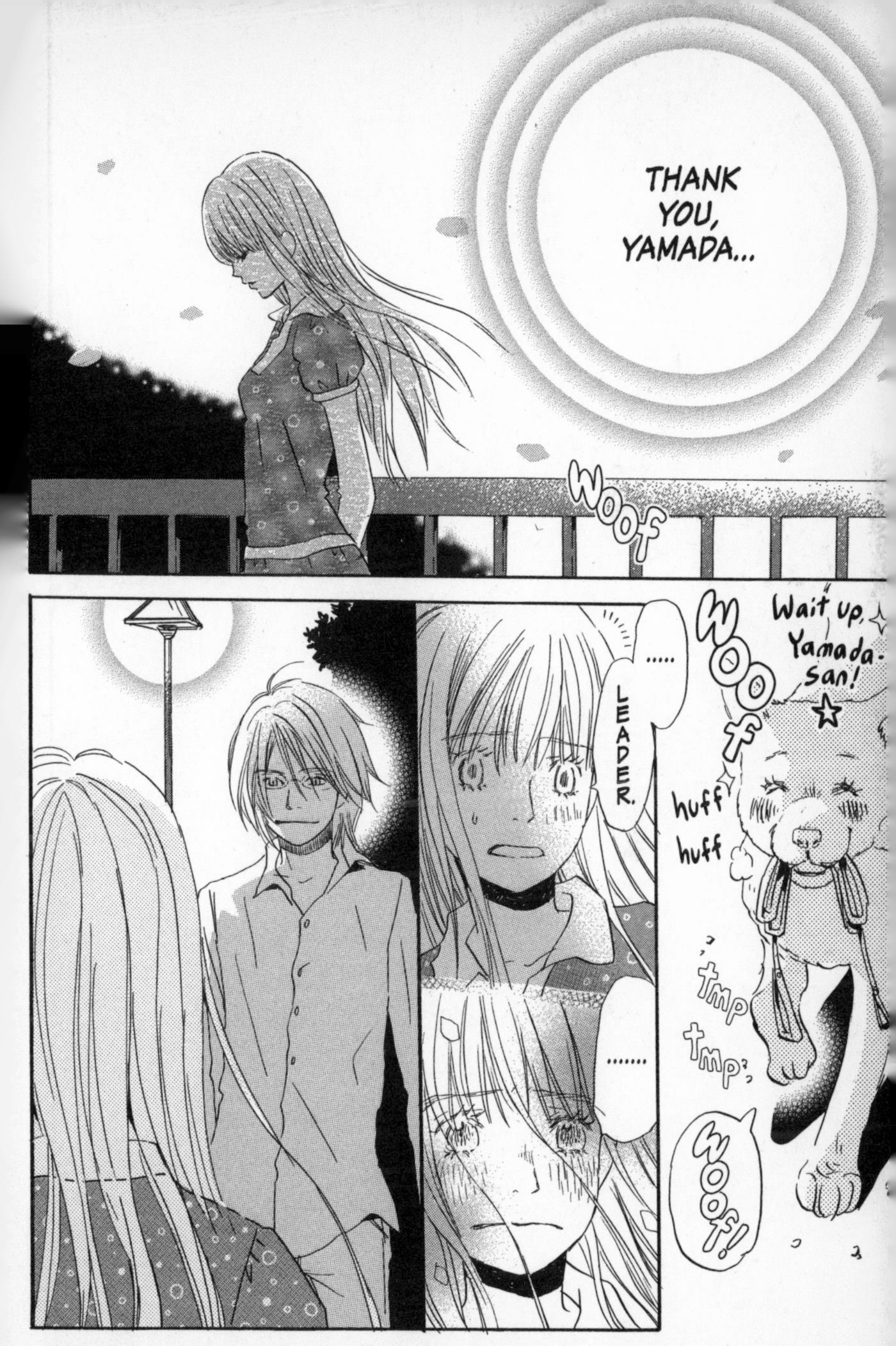
THANK YOU, YAMADA...
WOOF
Wait up, Yamada-san!
WOOF
huff huff
tmp tmp
WOOF!
.....
LEADER.
....

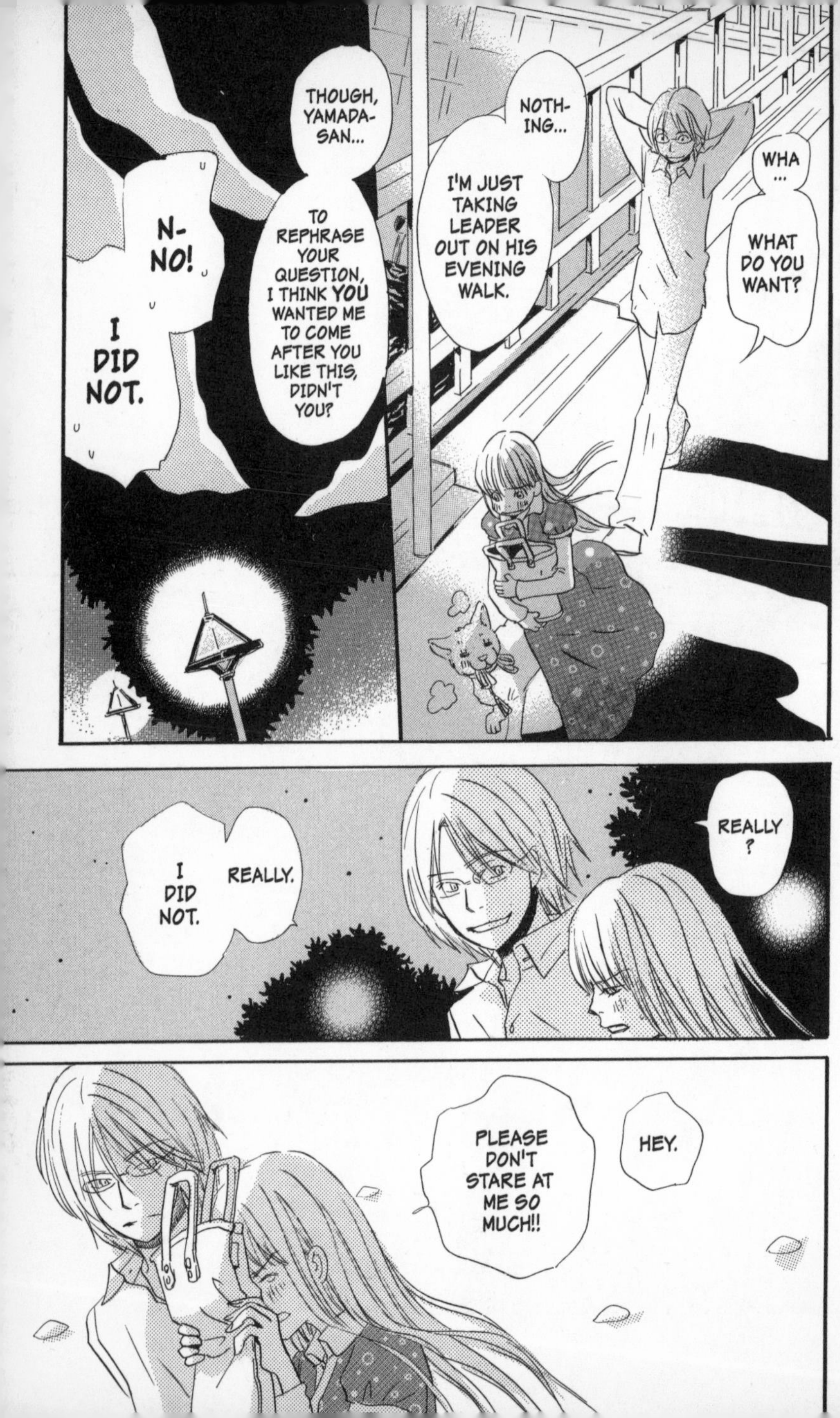
WHA...
WHAT DO YOU WANT?
NOTH-ING...
I'M JUST TAKING LEADER OUT ON HIS EVENING WALK.
THOUGH, YAMADA-SAN...
TO REPHRASE YOUR QUESTION, I THINK YOU WANTED ME TO COME AFTER YOU LIKE THIS, DIDN'T YOU?
N-NO!
I DID NOT.
REALLY?
REALLY.
I DID NOT.
HEY.
PLEASE DON'T STARE AT ME SO MUCH!!

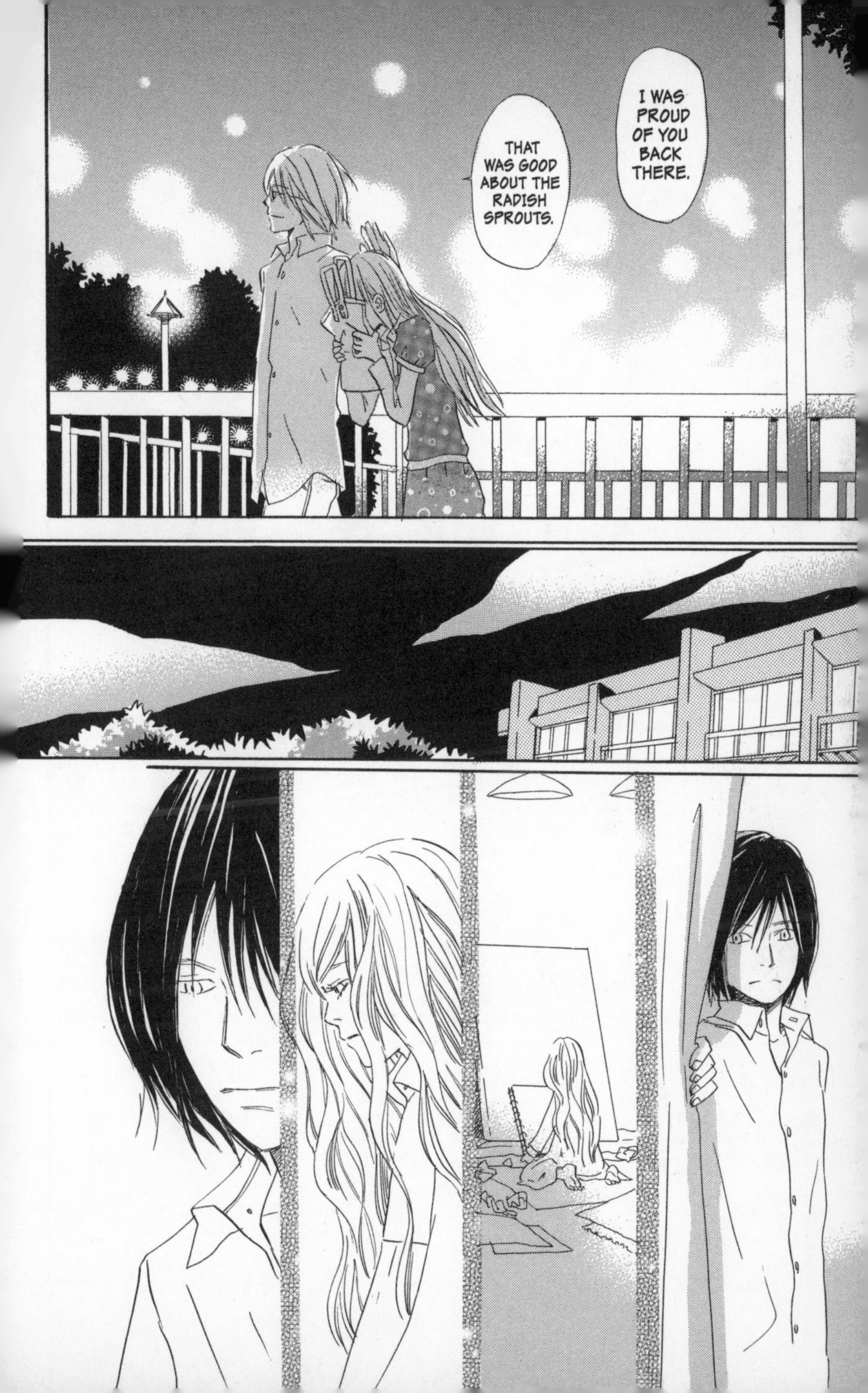
I WAS PROUD OF YOU BACK THERE.
THAT WAS GOOD ABOUT THE RADISH SPROUTS.

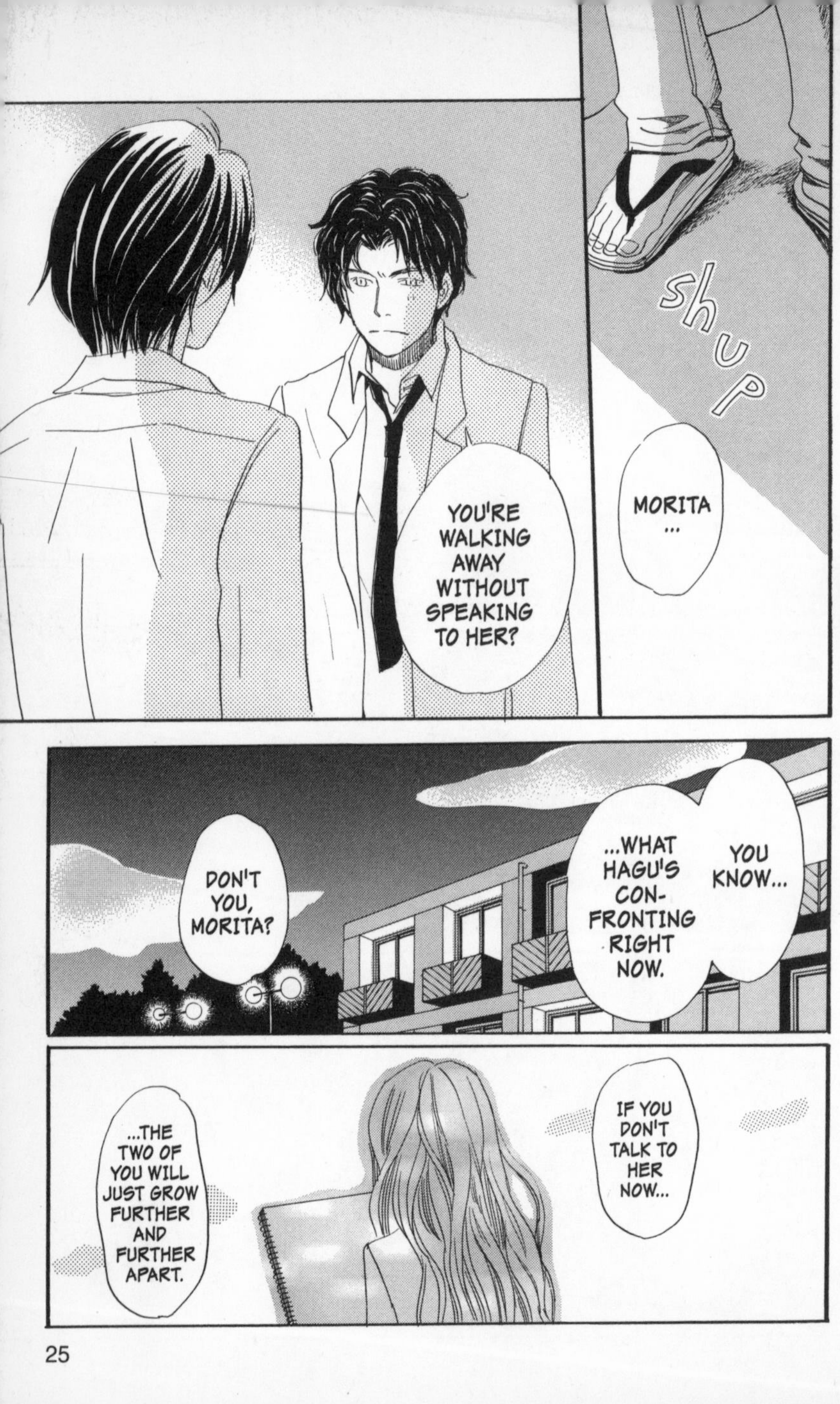
SHUP
MORITA...
YOU'RE WALKING AWAY WITHOUT SPEAKING TO HER?
YOU KNOW...
...WHAT HAGU'S CON-FRONTING RIGHT NOW.
DON'T YOU, MORITA?
IF YOU DON'T TALK TO HER NOW...
...THE TWO OF YOU WILL JUST GROW FURTHER AND FURTHER APART.

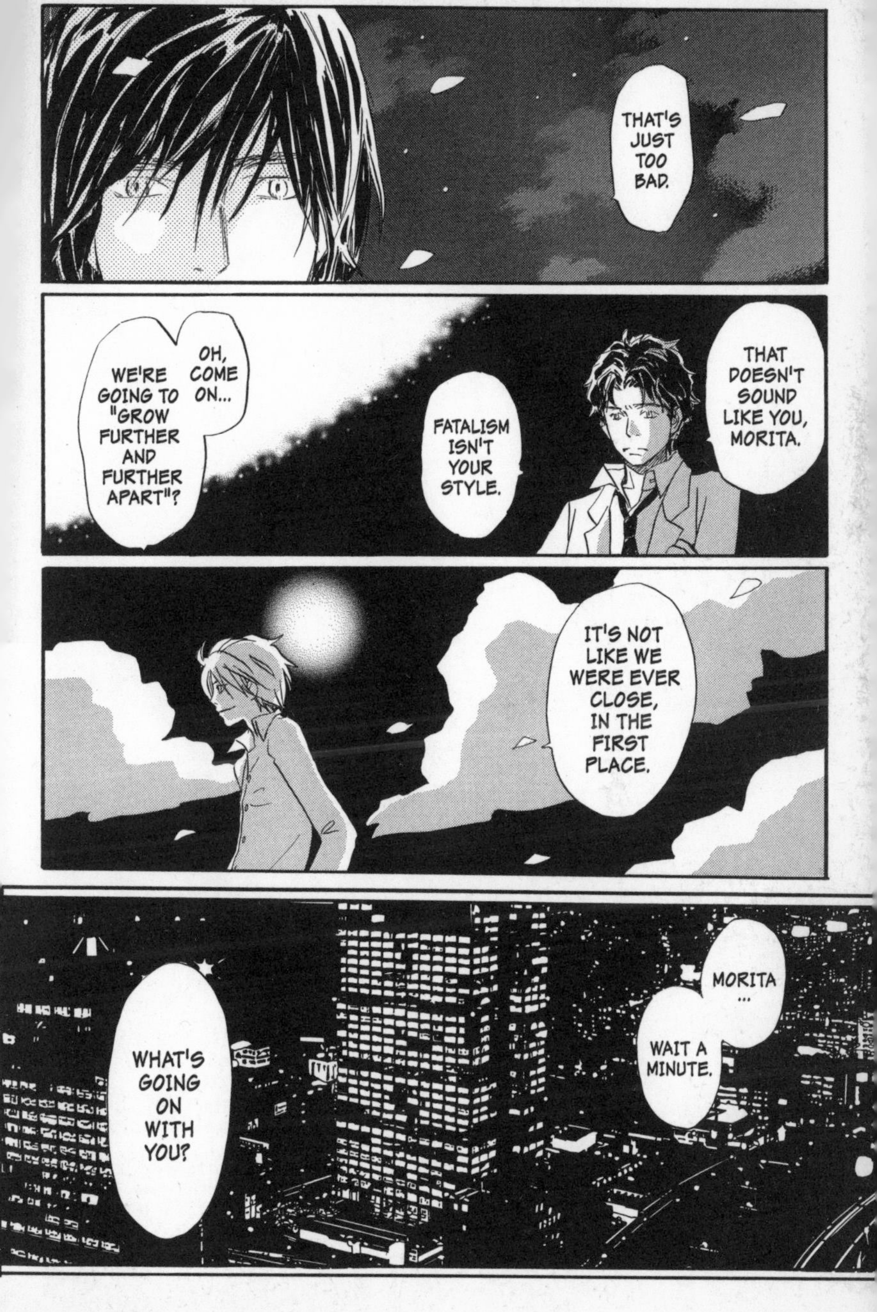
THAT'S JUST TOO BAD.
THAT DOESN'T SOUND LIKE YOU, MORITA.
FATALISM ISN'T YOUR STYLE.
OH, COME ON...
WE'RE GOING TO "GROW FURTHER AND FURTHER APART"?
IT'S NOT LIKE WE WERE EVER CLOSE, IN THE FIRST PLACE.
MORITA...
WAIT A MINUTE.
WHAT'S GOING ON WITH YOU?

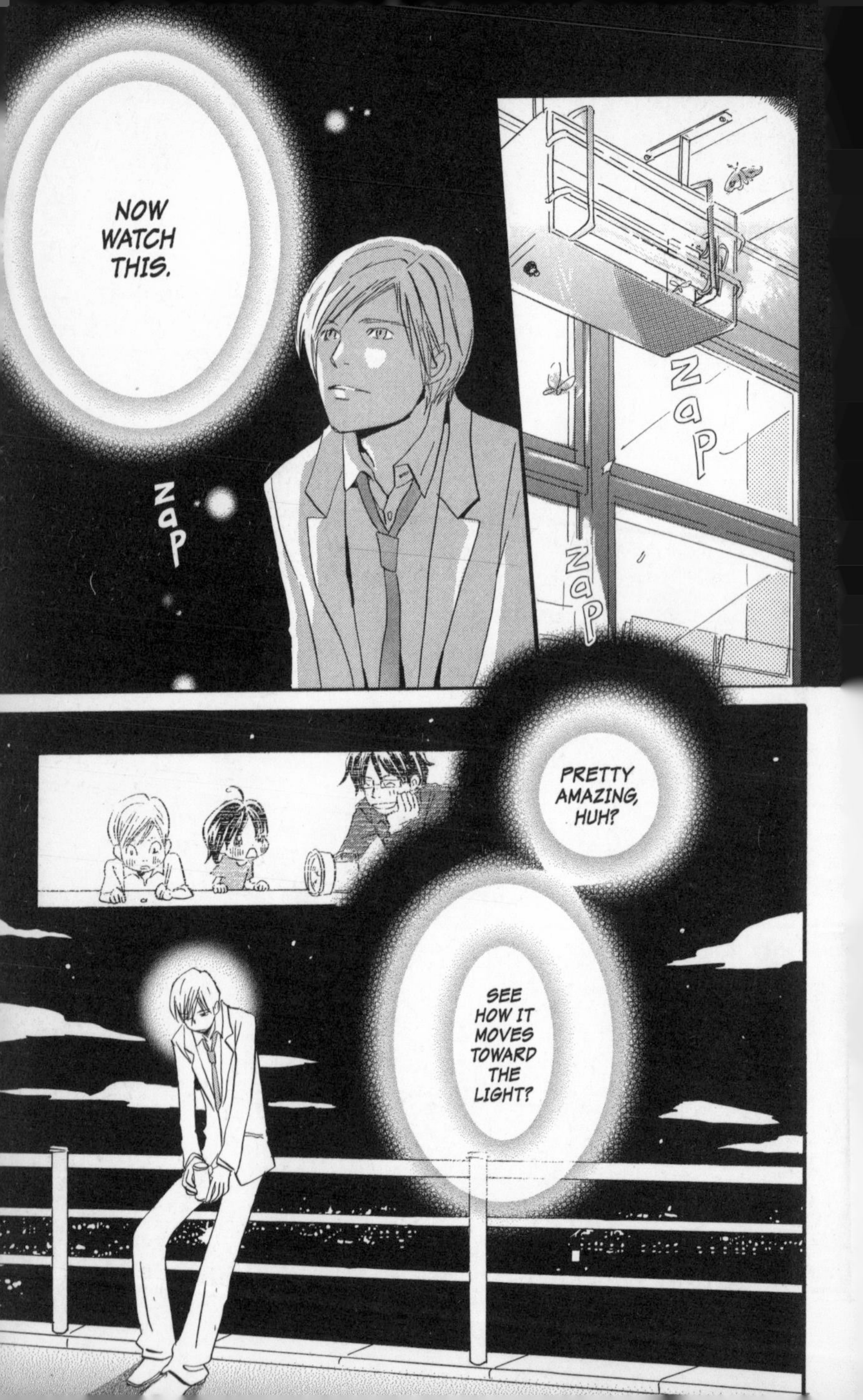
ZAP
ZAP
NOW WATCH THIS.
ZAP
PRETTY AMAZING, HUH?
SEE HOW IT MOVES TOWARD THE LIGHT?

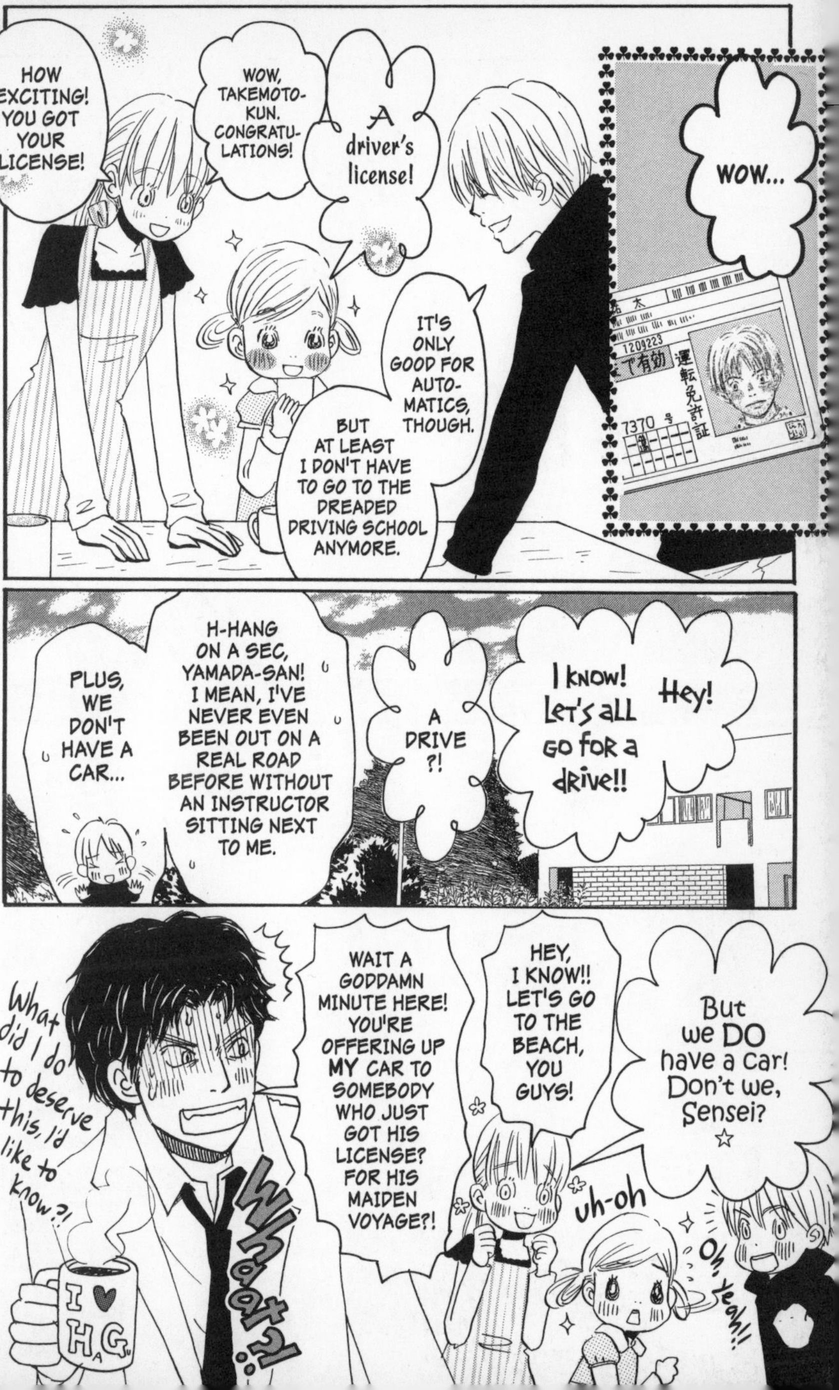
WOW...
運転免許証
A driver's license!
WOW, TAKEMOTO-KUN. CONGRATULATIONS!
HOW EXCITING! YOU GOT YOUR LICENSE!
IT'S ONLY GOOD FOR AUTOMATICS, THOUGH.
BUT AT LEAST I DON'T HAVE TO GO TO THE DREADED DRIVING SCHOOL ANYMORE.
Hey!
I know! Let's all go for a drive!!
A DRIVE?!
H-HANG ON A SEC, YAMADA-SAN! I MEAN, I'VE NEVER EVEN BEEN OUT ON A REAL ROAD BEFORE WITHOUT AN INSTRUCTOR SITTING NEXT TO ME.
PLUS, WE DON'T HAVE A CAR...
But we DO have a car! Don't we, Sensei? ☆
Oh, yeah!!
HEY, I KNOW!! LET'S GO TO THE BEACH, YOU GUYS!
uh-oh
WAIT A GODDAMN MINUTE HERE! YOU'RE OFFERING UP MY CAR TO SOMEBODY WHO JUST GOT HIS LICENSE? FOR HIS MAIDEN VOYAGE?!
What?!
What did I do to deserve this, I'd like to know?!
I ♥ HG

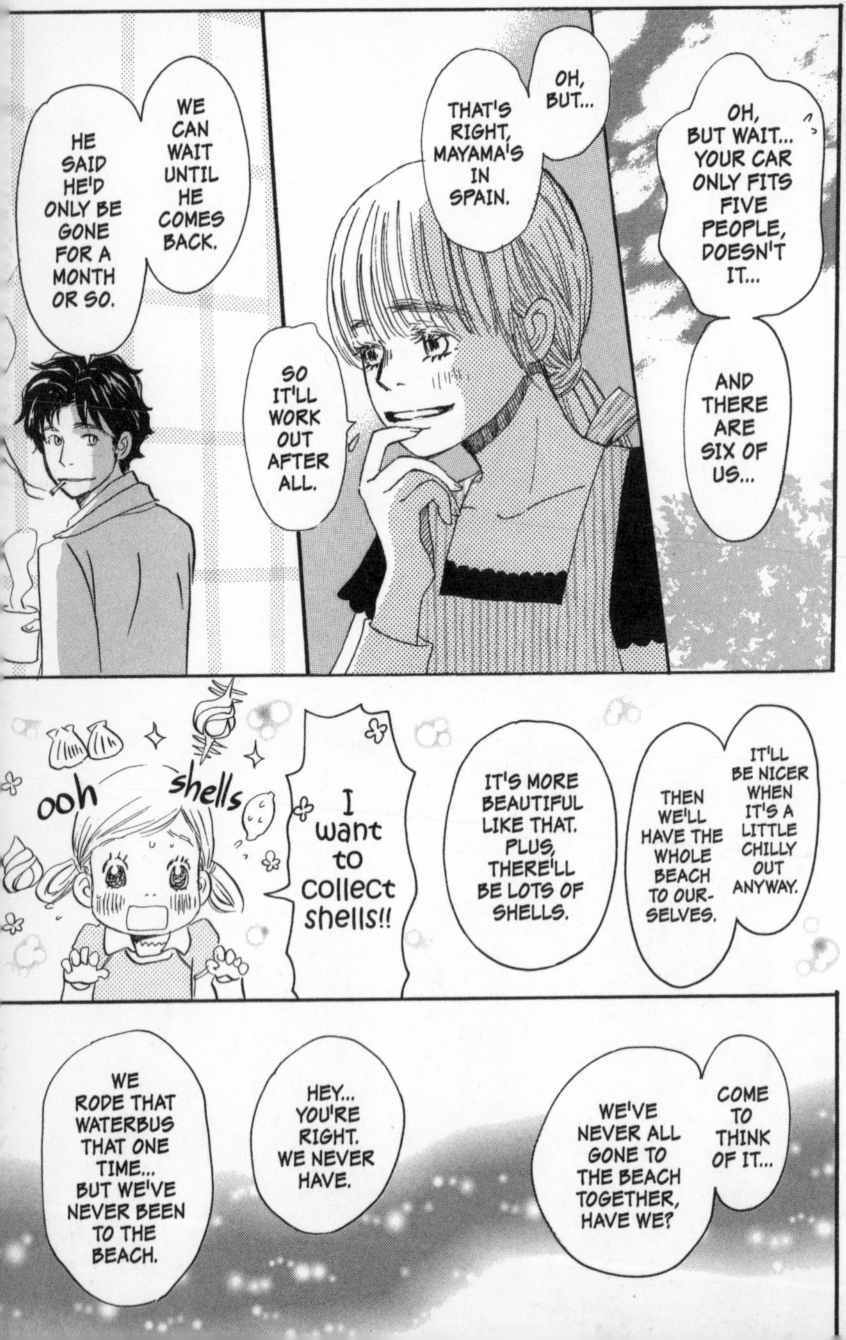
OH, BUT WAIT... YOUR CAR ONLY FITS FIVE PEOPLE, DOESN'T IT...
AND THERE ARE SIX OF US...
OH, BUT...
THAT'S RIGHT, MAYAMA'S IN SPAIN.
SO IT'LL WORK OUT AFTER ALL.
WE CAN WAIT UNTIL HE COMES BACK.
HE SAID HE'D ONLY BE GONE FOR A MONTH OR SO.
IT'LL BE NICER WHEN IT'S A LITTLE CHILLY OUT ANYWAY.
THEN WE'LL HAVE THE WHOLE BEACH TO OUR-SELVES.
IT'S MORE BEAUTIFUL LIKE THAT. PLUS, THERE'LL BE LOTS OF SHELLS.
I want to collect shells!!
shells
ooh
COME TO THINK OF IT...
WE'VE NEVER ALL GONE TO THE BEACH TOGETHER, HAVE WE?
HEY... YOU'RE RIGHT. WE NEVER HAVE.
WE RODE THAT WATERBUS THAT ONE TIME... BUT WE'VE NEVER BEEN TO THE BEACH.

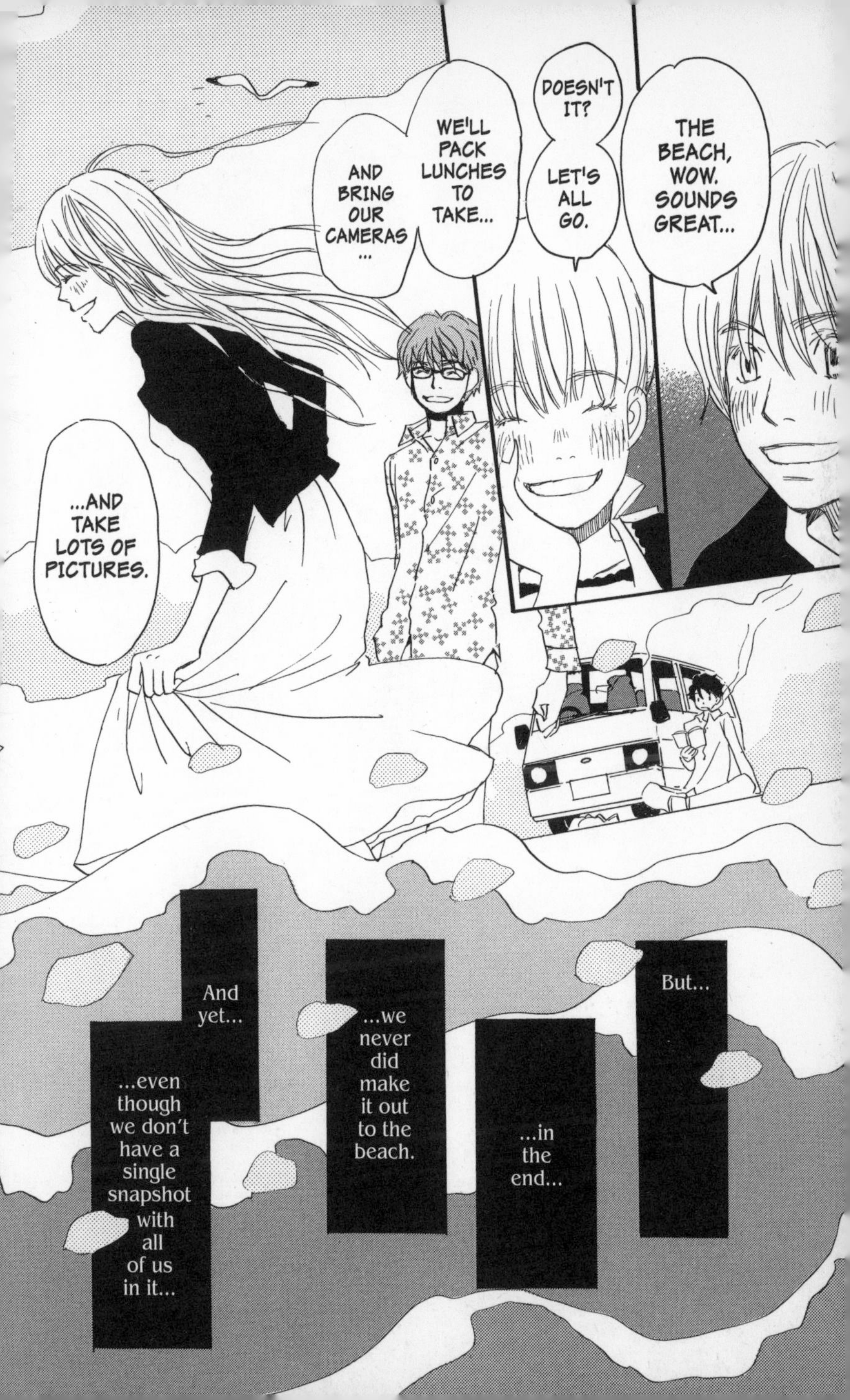
THE BEACH, WOW. SOUNDS GREAT...
DOESN'T IT?
LET'S ALL GO.
WE'LL PACK LUNCHES TO TAKE...
AND BRING OUR CAMERAS...
...AND TAKE LOTS OF PICTURES.
But...
...in the end...
...we never did make it out to the beach.
And yet...
...even though we don't have a single snapshot with all of us in it...

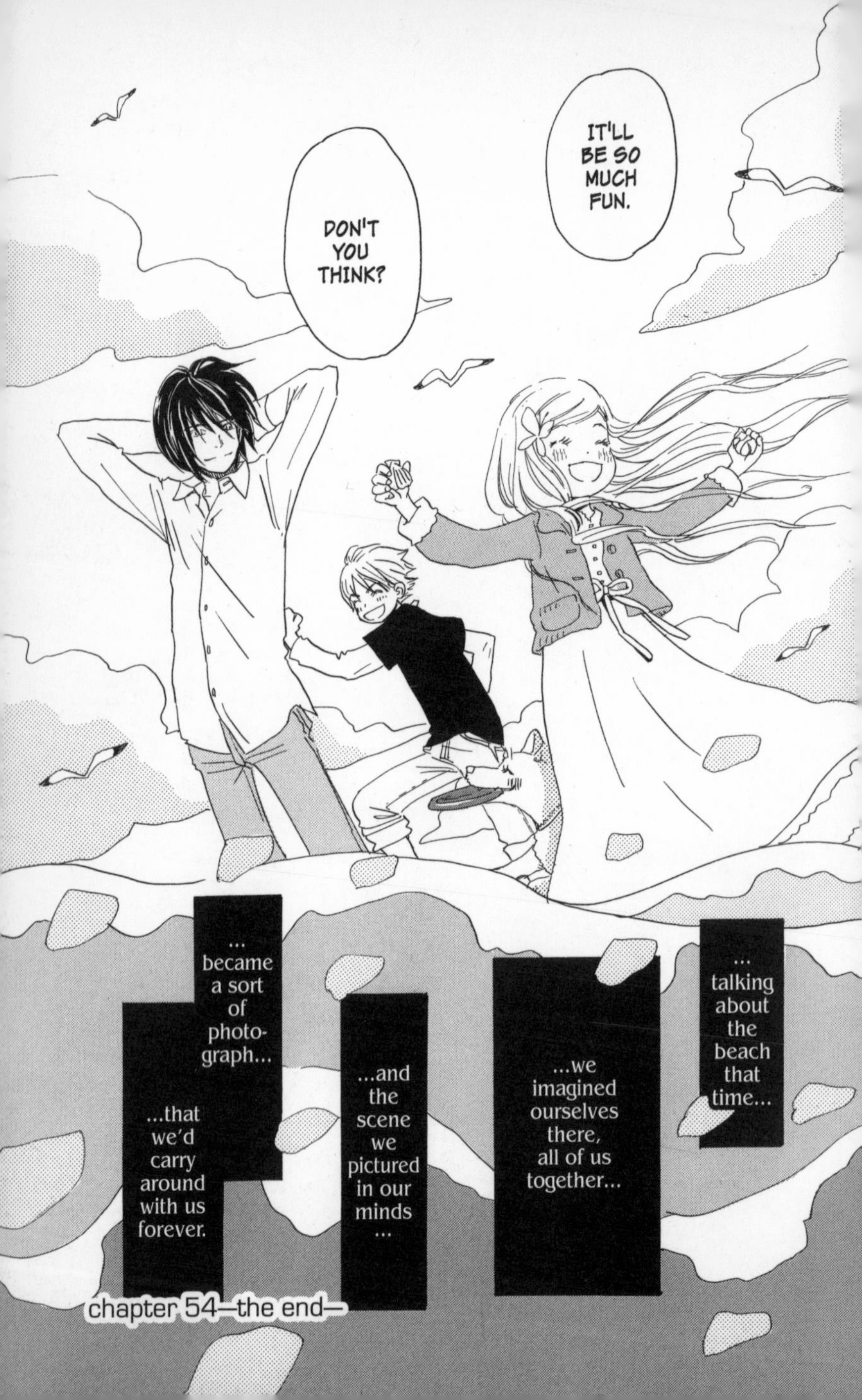
IT'LL BE SO MUCH FUN.
DON'T YOU THINK?
... talking about the beach that time...
...we imagined ourselves there, all of us together...
...and the scene we pictured in our minds ...
... became a sort of photo-graph...
...that we'd carry around with us forever.
chapter 54—the end—

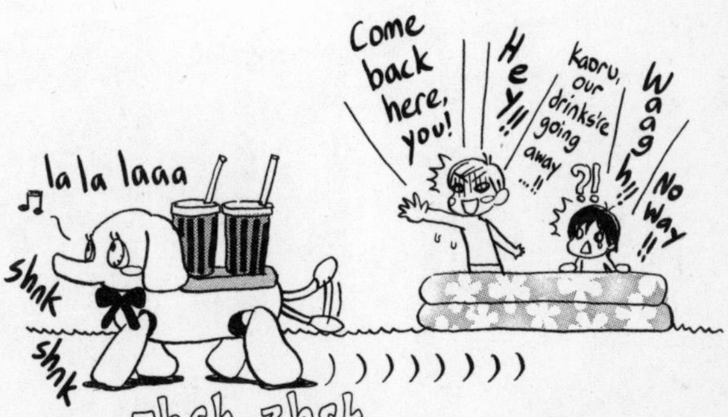
No way!!
Waagh!!
?!
Kaoru, our drinks're going away...!!
Hey!!
Come back here, you!
la la laaa
shnk
shnk
zhrk zhrk

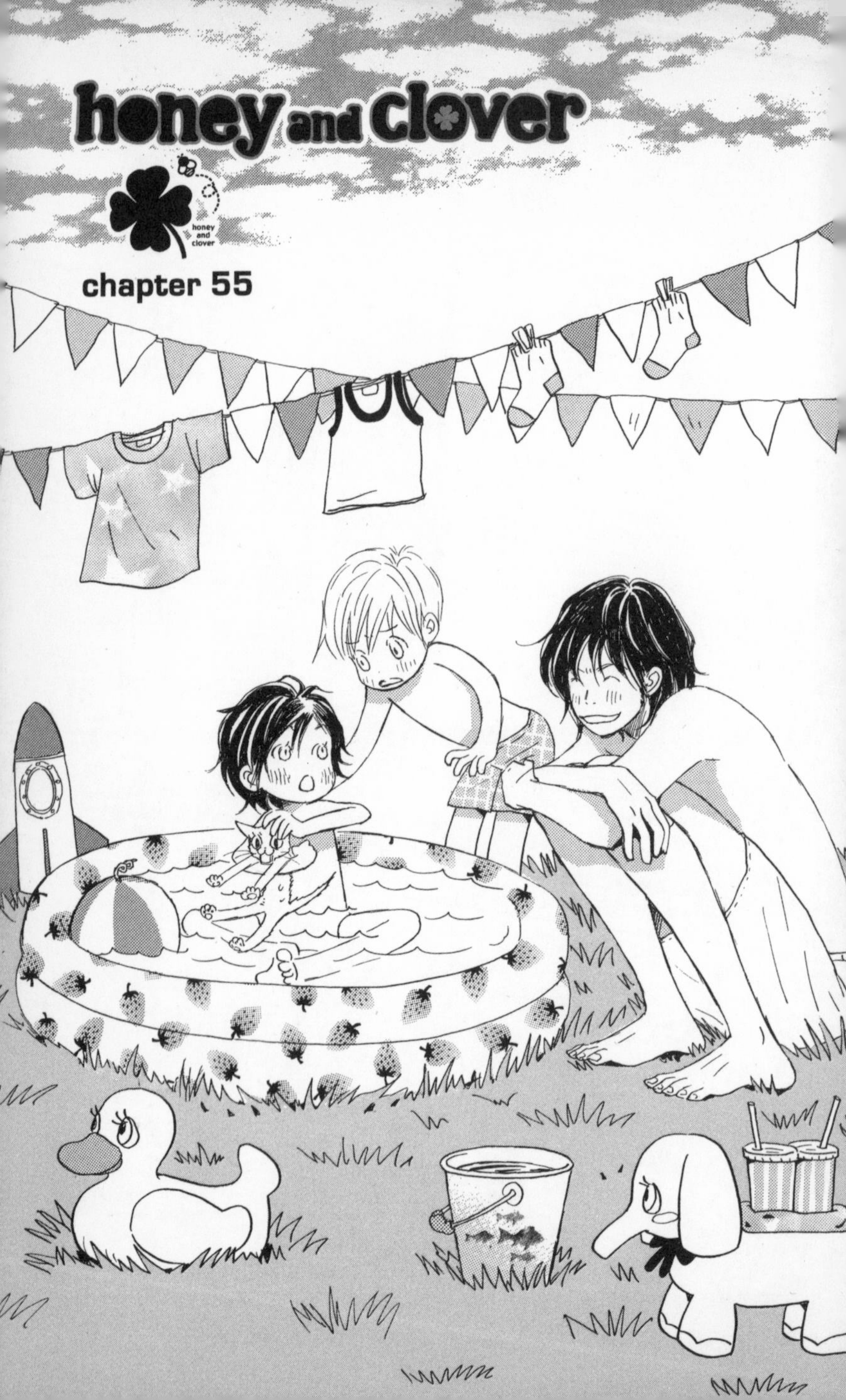
honey and clover
honey and clover
chapter 55

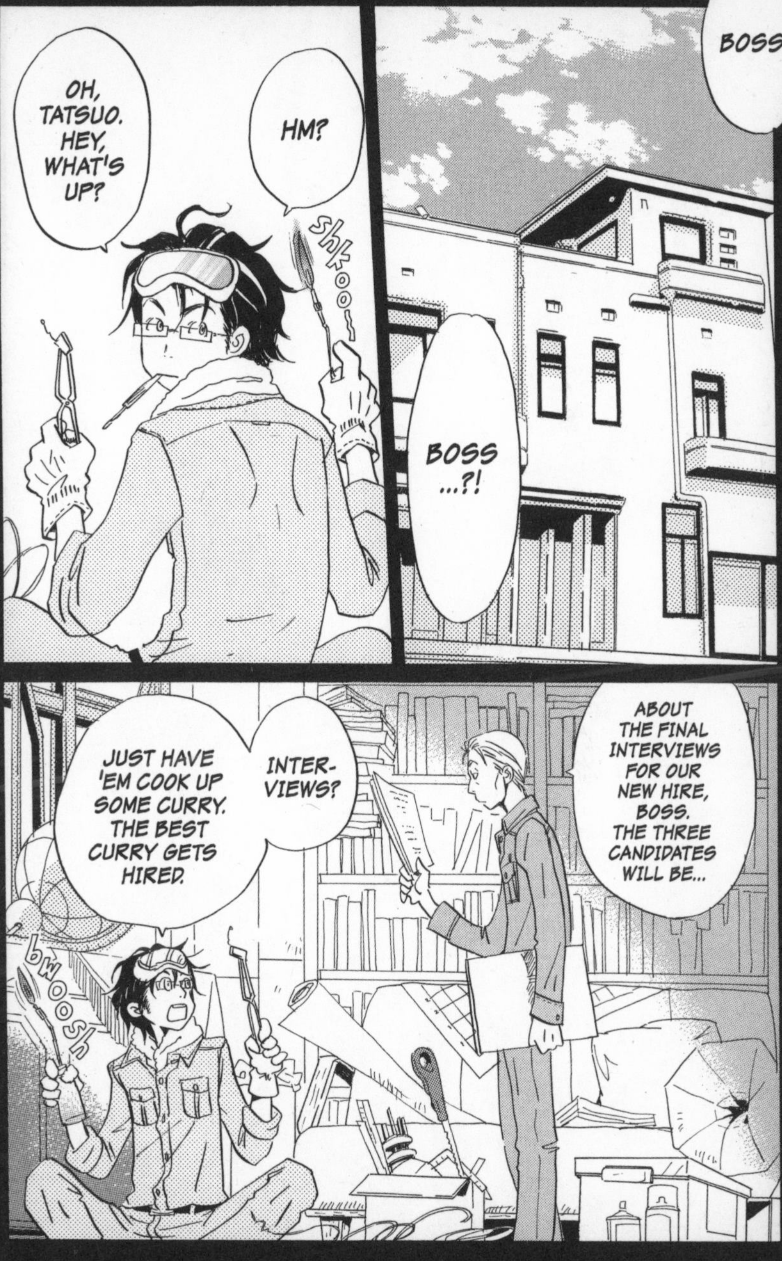
BOSS.
BOSS ...?!
HM?
OH, TATSUO. HEY, WHAT'S UP?
shkoo~
ABOUT THE FINAL INTERVIEWS FOR OUR NEW HIRE, BOSS. THE THREE CANDIDATES WILL BE...
INTER-VIEWS?
JUST HAVE 'EM COOK UP SOME CURRY. THE BEST CURRY GETS HIRED.
bwoosh

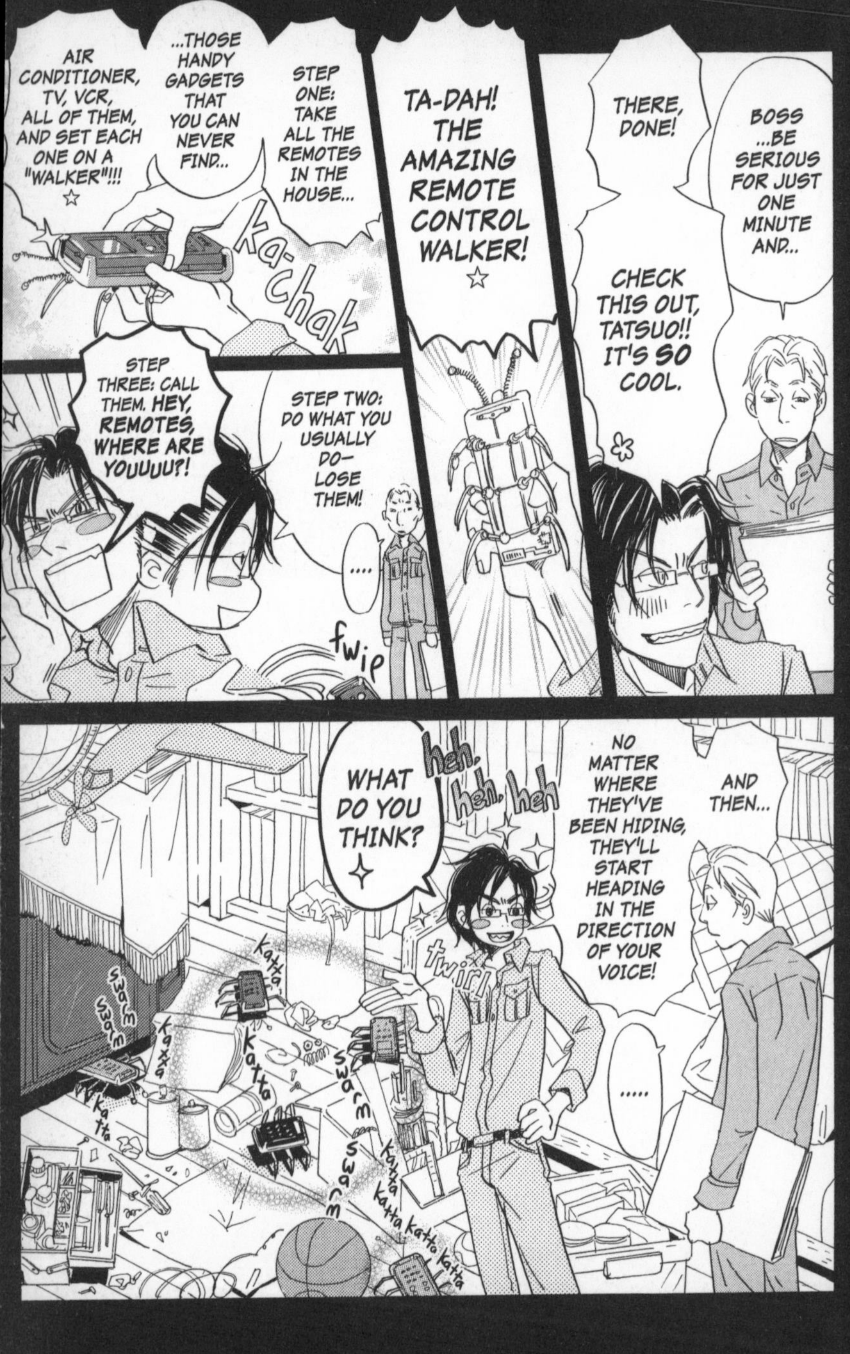
THERE, DONE!
BOSS ...BE SERIOUS FOR JUST ONE MINUTE AND...
CHECK THIS OUT, TATSUO!! IT'S SO COOL.
TA-DAH! THE AMAZING REMOTE CONTROL WALKER! ☆
STEP ONE: TAKE ALL THE REMOTES IN THE HOUSE...
...THOSE HANDY GADGETS THAT YOU CAN NEVER FIND...
AIR CONDITIONER, TV, VCR, ALL OF THEM, AND SET EACH ONE ON A "WALKER"!!! ☆
ka-chak
STEP TWO: DO WHAT YOU USUALLY DO— LOSE THEM!
.....
STEP THREE: CALL THEM. HEY, REMOTES, WHERE ARE YOUUUU?!
fwip
AND THEN...
NO MATTER WHERE THEY'VE BEEN HIDING, THEY'LL START HEADING IN THE DIRECTION OF YOUR VOICE!
heh. heh. heh
WHAT DO YOU THINK?
twirl
.....
swarm swarm
katta katta katta
swarm swarm swarm
katta katta katta katta

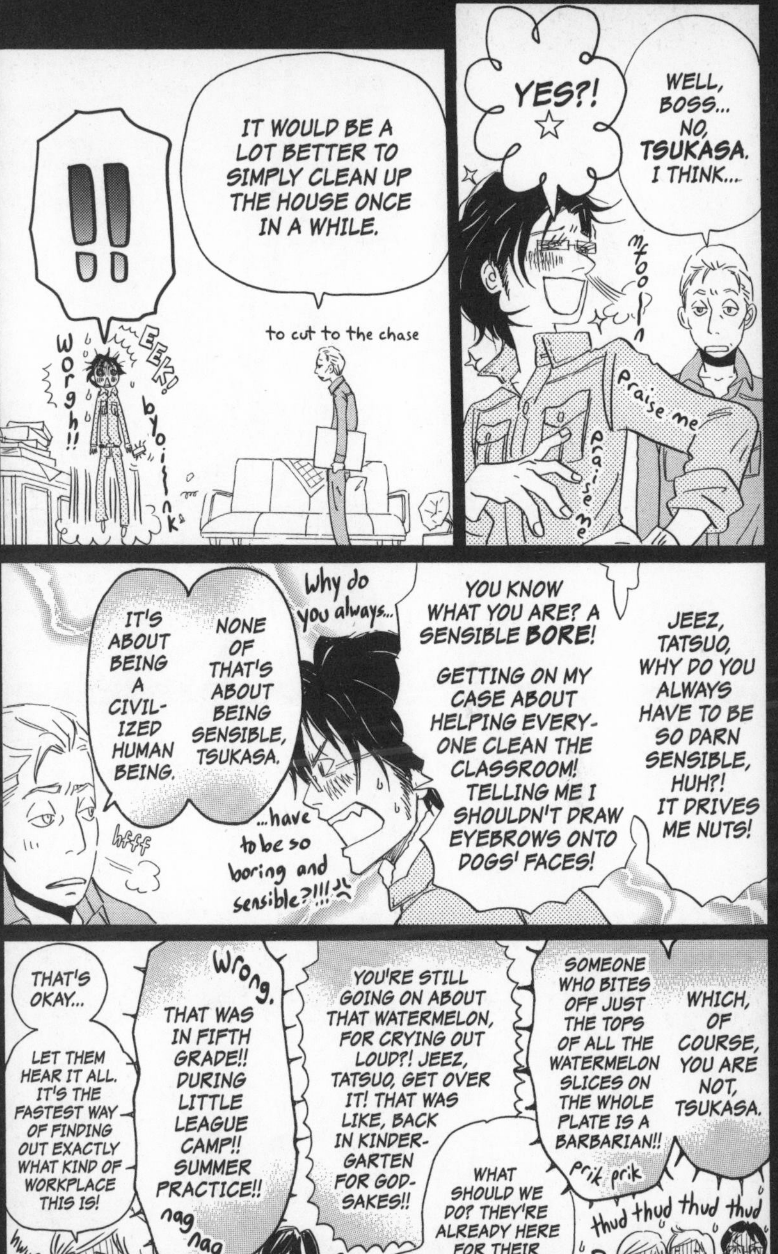
WELL, BOSS... NO, TSUKASA. I THINK...
YES?! ☆
mfoo~n
Praise me
Praise me
IT WOULD BE A LOT BETTER TO SIMPLY CLEAN UP THE HOUSE ONCE IN A WHILE.
to cut to the chase
!!
EEK!
Worgh!!
byoi~nk
JEEZ, TATSUO, WHY DO YOU ALWAYS HAVE TO BE SO DARN SENSIBLE, HUH?! IT DRIVES ME NUTS!
YOU KNOW WHAT YOU ARE? A SENSIBLE BORE!
GETTING ON MY CASE ABOUT HELPING EVERY-ONE CLEAN THE CLASSROOM! TELLING ME I SHOULDN'T DRAW EYEBROWS ONTO DOGS' FACES!
Why do you always...
...have to be so boring and sensible?!!!
NONE OF THAT'S ABOUT BEING SENSIBLE, TSUKASA.
IT'S ABOUT BEING A CIVIL-IZED HUMAN BEING.
hfff
WHICH, OF COURSE, YOU ARE NOT, TSUKASA.
SOMEONE WHO BITES OFF JUST THE TOPS OF ALL THE WATERMELON SLICES ON THE WHOLE PLATE IS A BARBARIAN!!
prik prik
thud thud thud thud
YOU'RE STILL GOING ON ABOUT THAT WATERMELON, FOR CRYING OUT LOUD?! JEEZ, TATSUO, GET OVER IT! THAT WAS LIKE, BACK IN KINDER-GARTEN FOR GOD-SAKES!!
WHAT SHOULD WE DO? THEY'RE ALREADY HERE FOR THEIR INTERVIEWS.
psst psst
Wrong.
THAT WAS IN FIFTH GRADE!! DURING LITTLE LEAGUE CAMP!! SUMMER PRACTICE!!
nag nag
THAT'S OKAY...
LET THEM HEAR IT ALL. IT'S THE FASTEST WAY OF FINDING OUT EXACTLY WHAT KIND OF WORKPLACE THIS IS!

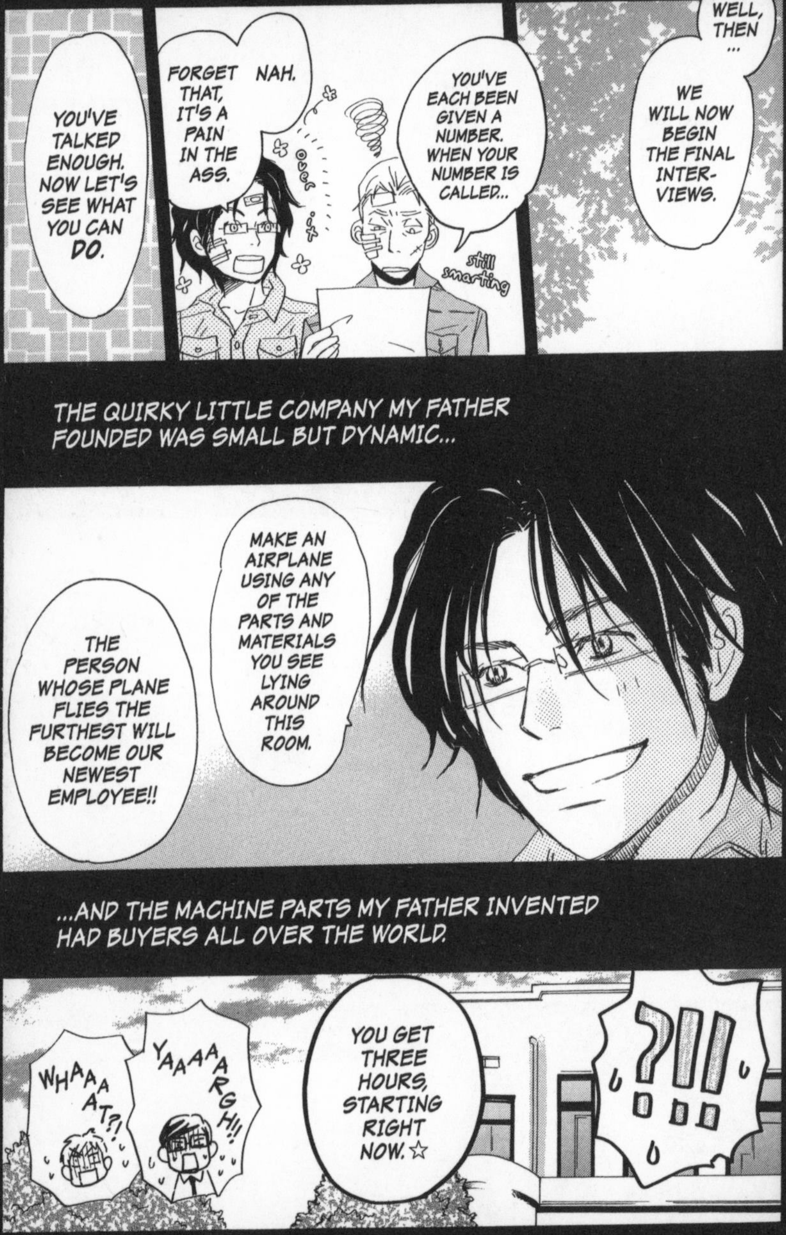
WELL, THEN ...
WE WILL NOW BEGIN THE FINAL INTER-VIEWS.
YOU'VE EACH BEEN GIVEN A NUMBER. WHEN YOUR NUMBER IS CALLED...
still smarting
over it
NAH.
FORGET THAT, IT'S A PAIN IN THE ASS.
YOU'VE TALKED ENOUGH. NOW LET'S SEE WHAT YOU CAN DO.
THE QUIRKY LITTLE COMPANY MY FATHER FOUNDED WAS SMALL BUT DYNAMIC...
MAKE AN AIRPLANE USING ANY OF THE PARTS AND MATERIALS YOU SEE LYING AROUND THIS ROOM.
THE PERSON WHOSE PLANE FLIES THE FURTHEST WILL BECOME OUR NEWEST EMPLOYEE!!
...AND THE MACHINE PARTS MY FATHER INVENTED HAD BUYERS ALL OVER THE WORLD.
?!!
YOU GET THREE HOURS, STARTING RIGHT NOW.☆
YAAAAARGH!!
WHAAAAT?!

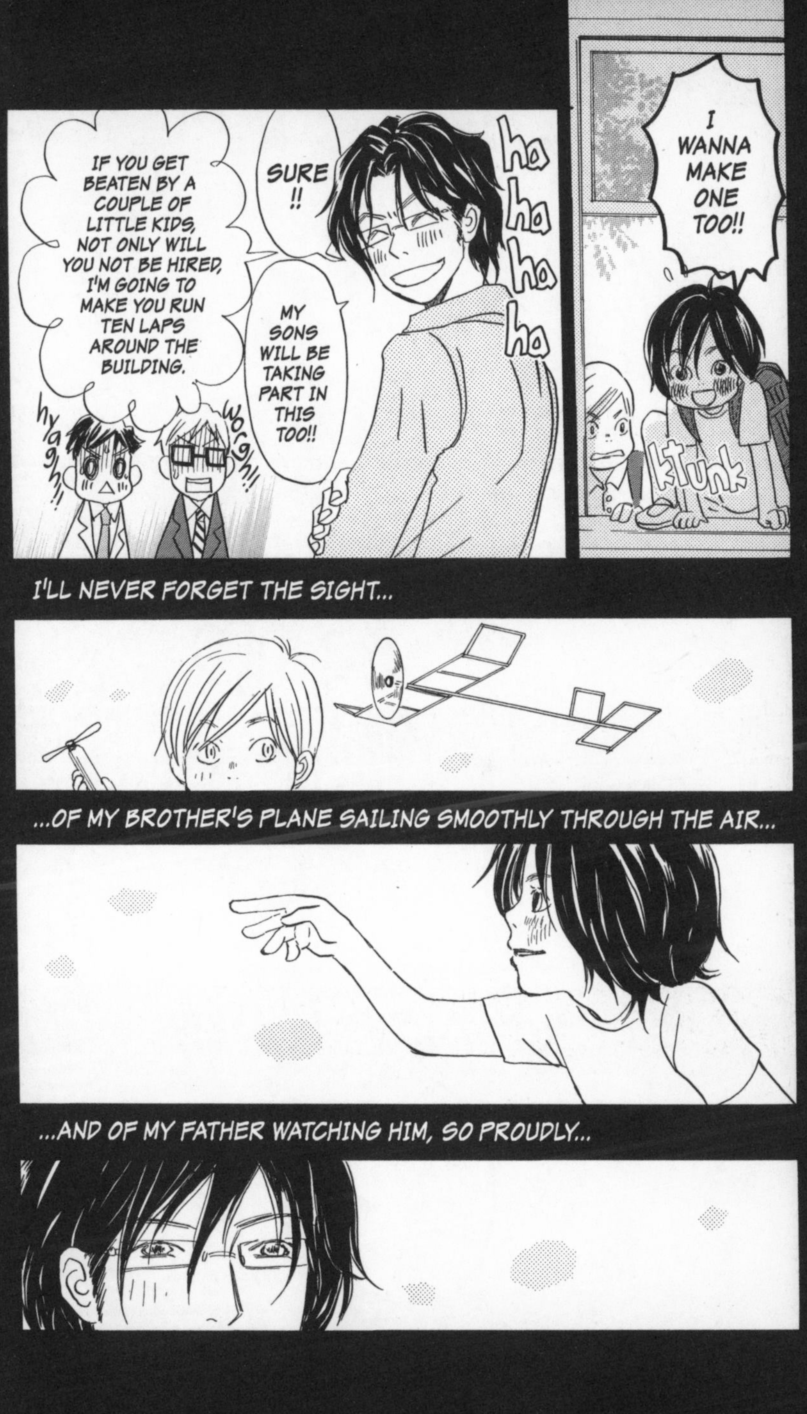
I WANNA MAKE ONE TOO!!
ktunk
ha ha ha ha ha
SURE!!
MY SONS WILL BE TAKING PART IN THIS TOO!!
IF YOU GET BEATEN BY A COUPLE OF LITTLE KIDS, NOT ONLY WILL YOU NOT BE HIRED, I'M GOING TO MAKE YOU RUN TEN LAPS AROUND THE BUILDING.
worgh!!
hyagh!!
I'LL NEVER FORGET THE SIGHT...
...OF MY BROTHER'S PLANE SAILING SMOOTHLY THROUGH THE AIR...
...AND OF MY FATHER WATCHING HIM, SO PROUDLY...

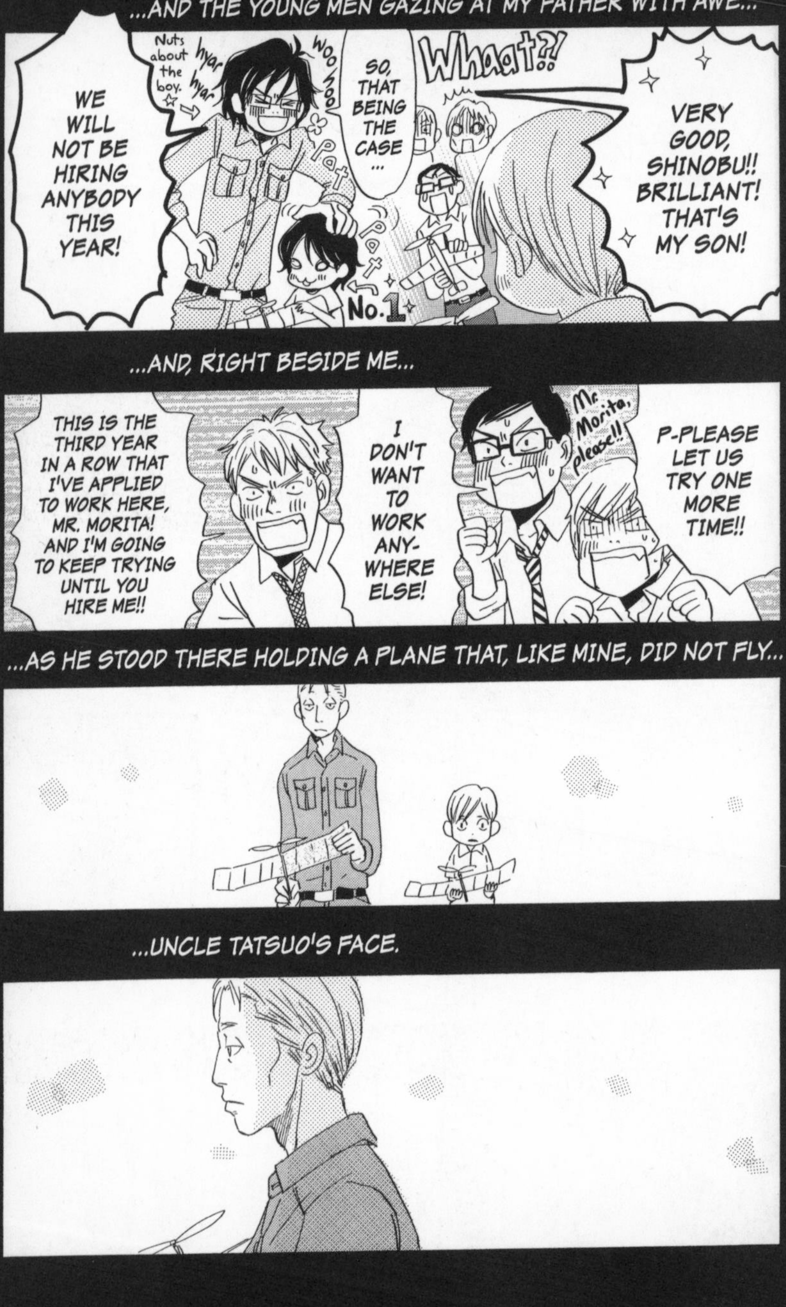
...AND THE YOUNG MEN GAZING AT MY FATHER WITH AWE...
VERY GOOD, SHINOBU!! BRILLIANT! THAT'S MY SON!
Whaat?!
SO, THAT BEING THE CASE...
woo hoo
hyar hyar
Nuts about the boy.
WE WILL NOT BE HIRING ANYBODY THIS YEAR!
pat pat
No.1
...AND, RIGHT BESIDE ME...
P-PLEASE LET US TRY ONE MORE TIME!!
Mr. Morita, please!!
I DON'T WANT TO WORK ANY-WHERE ELSE!
THIS IS THE THIRD YEAR IN A ROW THAT I'VE APPLIED TO WORK HERE, MR. MORITA! AND I'M GOING TO KEEP TRYING UNTIL YOU HIRE ME!!
...AS HE STOOD THERE HOLDING A PLANE THAT, LIKE MINE, DID NOT FLY...
...UNCLE TATSUO'S FACE.

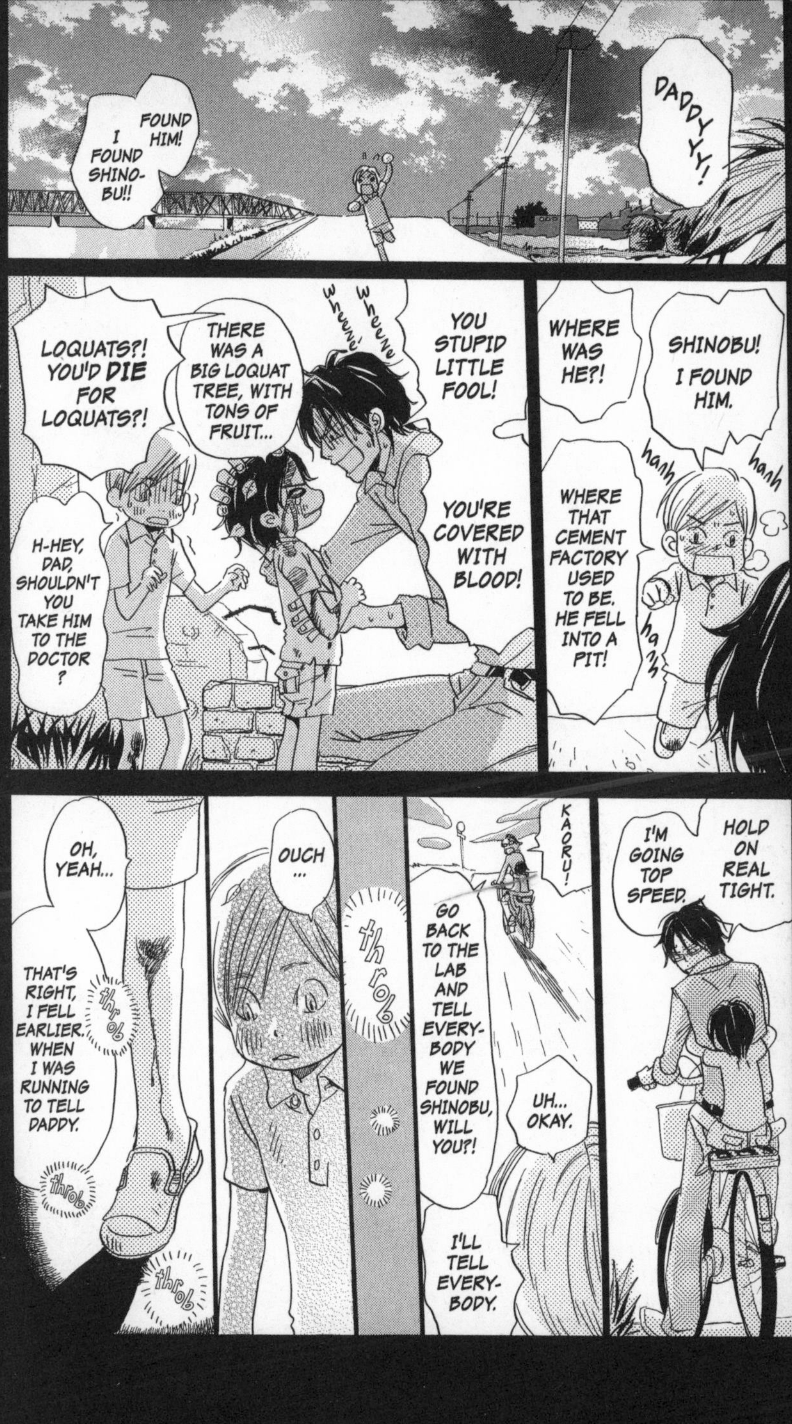
DADDYYY!
I FOUND HIM! I FOUND SHINOBU!!
SHINOBU! I FOUND HIM.
hanh hanh
WHERE WAS HE?!
WHERE THAT CEMENT FACTORY USED TO BE. HE FELL INTO A PIT!
hanh
YOU STUPID LITTLE FOOL!
wheeze wheeze
THERE WAS A BIG LOQUAT TREE, WITH TONS OF FRUIT...
LOQUATS?! YOU'D DIE FOR LOQUATS?!
YOU'RE COVERED WITH BLOOD!
H-HEY, DAD, SHOULDN'T YOU TAKE HIM TO THE DOCTOR?
HOLD ON REAL TIGHT.
I'M GOING TOP SPEED.
KAORU!
GO BACK TO THE LAB AND TELL EVERYBODY WE FOUND SHINOBU, WILL YOU?!
UH... OKAY.
I'LL TELL EVERYBODY.
throb
OUCH...
OH, YEAH...
THAT'S RIGHT, I FELL EARLIER WHEN I WAS RUNNING TO TELL DADDY.
throb
throb
throb

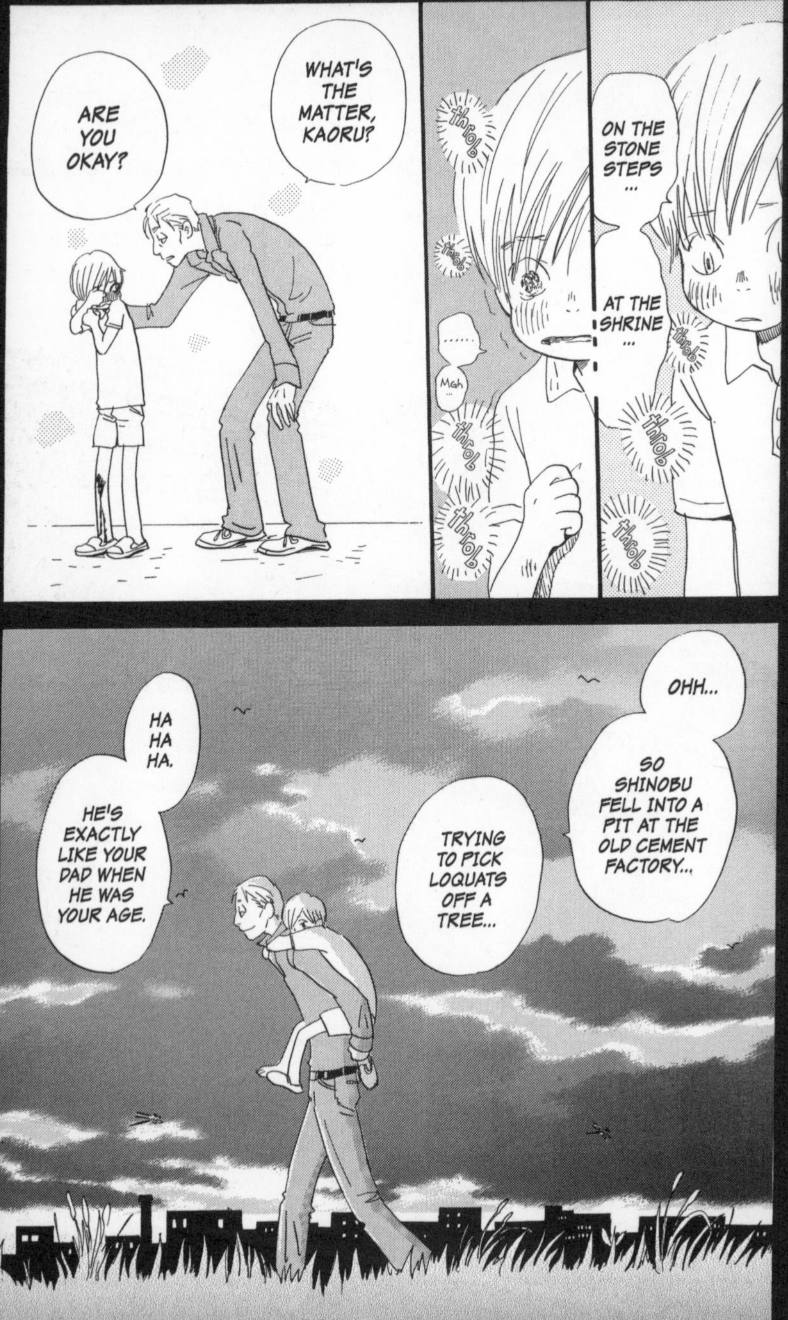
ON THE STONE STEPS ...
AT THE SHRINE ...
throb
throb
throb
throb
throb
......
Mgh ...
throb
throb
WHAT'S THE MATTER, KAORU?
ARE YOU OKAY?
OHH...
SO SHINOBU FELL INTO A PIT AT THE OLD CEMENT FACTORY...
TRYING TO PICK LOQUATS OFF A TREE...
HA HA HA.
HE'S EXACTLY LIKE YOUR DAD WHEN HE WAS YOUR AGE.

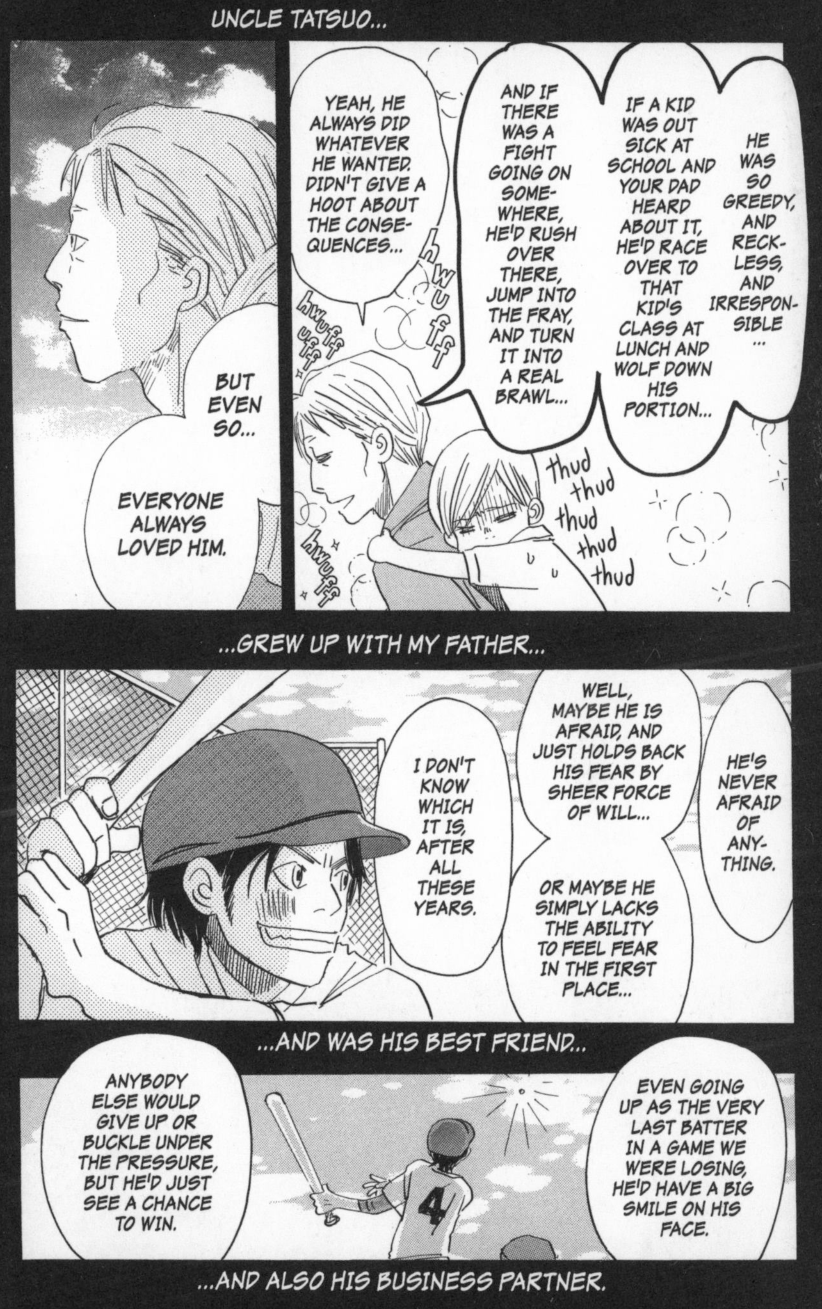
UNCLE TATSUO...
HE WAS SO GREEDY, AND RECKLESS, AND IRRESPONSIBLE...
IF A KID WAS OUT SICK AT SCHOOL AND YOUR DAD HEARD ABOUT IT, HE'D RACE OVER TO THAT KID'S CLASS AT LUNCH AND WOLF DOWN HIS PORTION...
AND IF THERE WAS A FIGHT GOING ON SOME-WHERE, HE'D RUSH OVER THERE, JUMP INTO THE FRAY, AND TURN IT INTO A REAL BRAWL...
YEAH, HE ALWAYS DID WHATEVER HE WANTED. DIDN'T GIVE A HOOT ABOUT THE CONSE-QUENCES...
hwuff
hwuff uff
thud thud thud thud thud
hwuff
BUT EVEN SO...
EVERYONE ALWAYS LOVED HIM.
...GREW UP WITH MY FATHER...
HE'S NEVER AFRAID OF ANY-THING.
WELL, MAYBE HE IS AFRAID, AND JUST HOLDS BACK HIS FEAR BY SHEER FORCE OF WILL...
OR MAYBE HE SIMPLY LACKS THE ABILITY TO FEEL FEAR IN THE FIRST PLACE...
I DON'T KNOW WHICH IT IS, AFTER ALL THESE YEARS.
...AND WAS HIS BEST FRIEND...
EVEN GOING UP AS THE VERY LAST BATTER IN A GAME WE WERE LOSING, HE'D HAVE A BIG SMILE ON HIS FACE.
ANYBODY ELSE WOULD GIVE UP OR BUCKLE UNDER THE PRESSURE, BUT HE'D JUST SEE A CHANCE TO WIN.
...AND ALSO HIS BUSINESS PARTNER.

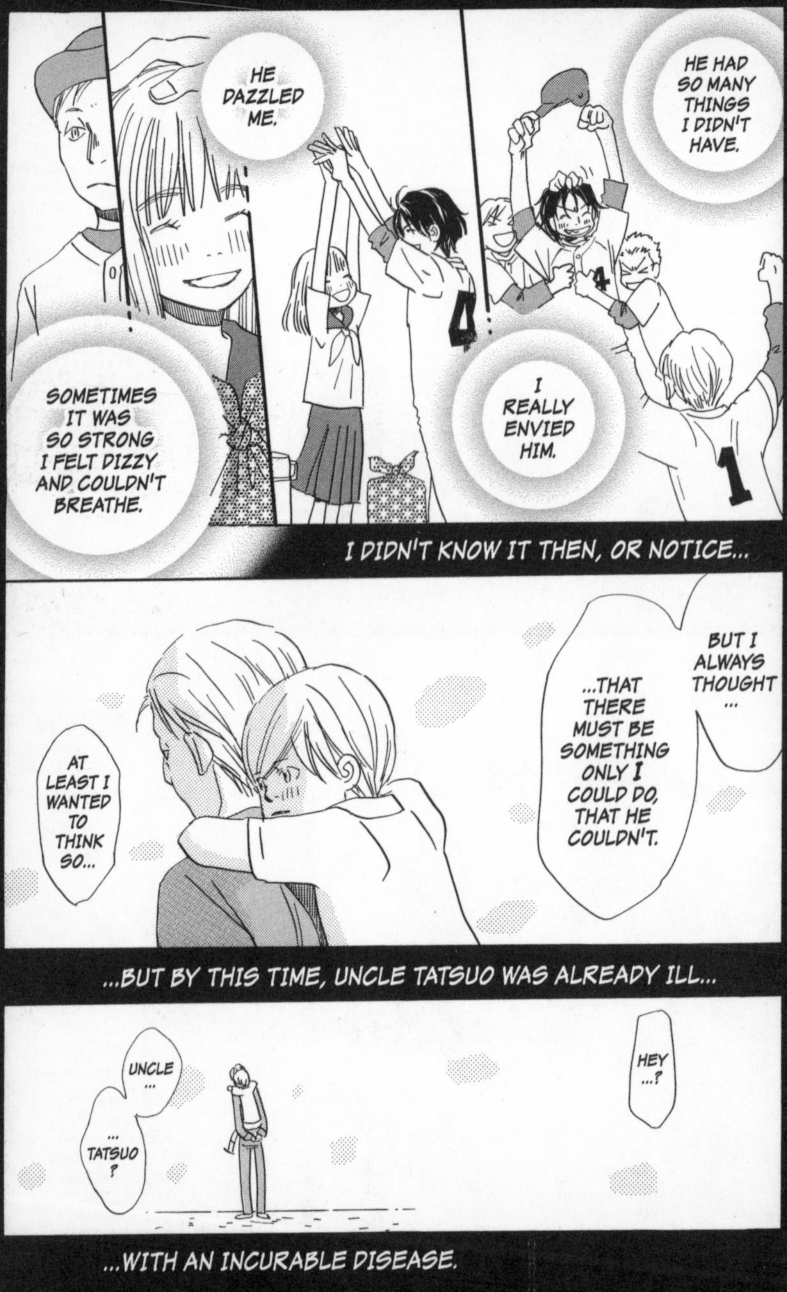
HE HAD SO MANY THINGS I DIDN'T HAVE.
I REALLY ENVIED HIM.
HE DAZZLED ME.
SOMETIMES IT WAS SO STRONG I FELT DIZZY AND COULDN'T BREATHE.
I DIDN'T KNOW IT THEN, OR NOTICE...
BUT I ALWAYS THOUGHT...
...THAT THERE MUST BE SOMETHING ONLY I COULD DO, THAT HE COULDN'T.
AT LEAST I WANTED TO THINK SO...
...BUT BY THIS TIME, UNCLE TATSUO WAS ALREADY ILL...
HEY ...?
UNCLE ...
... TATSUO ?
...WITH AN INCURABLE DISEASE.

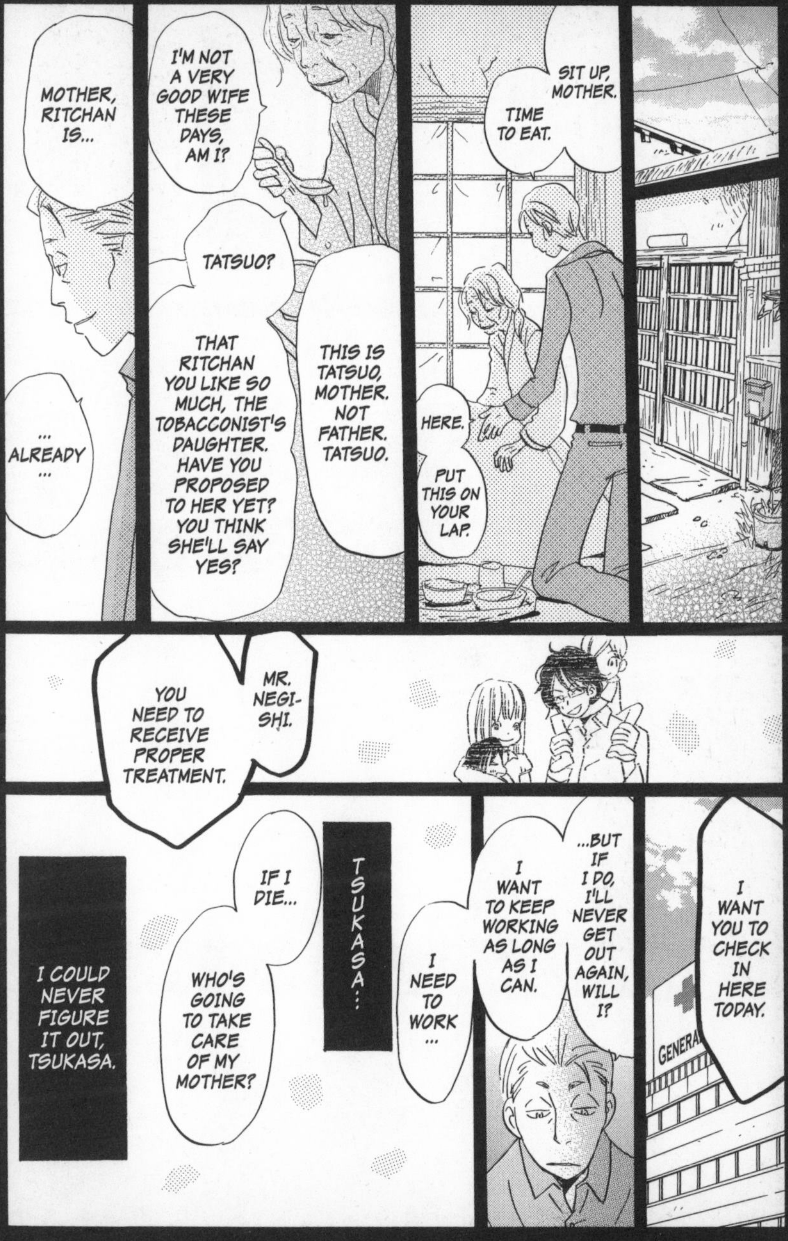
SIT UP, MOTHER.
TIME TO EAT.
HERE.
PUT THIS ON YOUR LAP.
I'M NOT A VERY GOOD WIFE THESE DAYS, AM I?
THIS IS TATSUO, MOTHER. NOT FATHER. TATSUO.
TATSUO?
THAT RITCHAN YOU LIKE SO MUCH, THE TOBACCONIST'S DAUGHTER. HAVE YOU PROPOSED TO HER YET? YOU THINK SHE'LL SAY YES?
MOTHER, RITCHAN IS...
... ALREADY ...
MR. NEGISHI.
YOU NEED TO RECEIVE PROPER TREATMENT.
I WANT YOU TO CHECK IN HERE TODAY.
...BUT IF I DO, I'LL NEVER GET OUT AGAIN, WILL I?
I WANT TO KEEP WORKING AS LONG AS I CAN.
I NEED TO WORK ...
TSUKASA...
IF I DIE...
WHO'S GOING TO TAKE CARE OF MY MOTHER?
I COULD NEVER FIGURE IT OUT, TSUKASA.

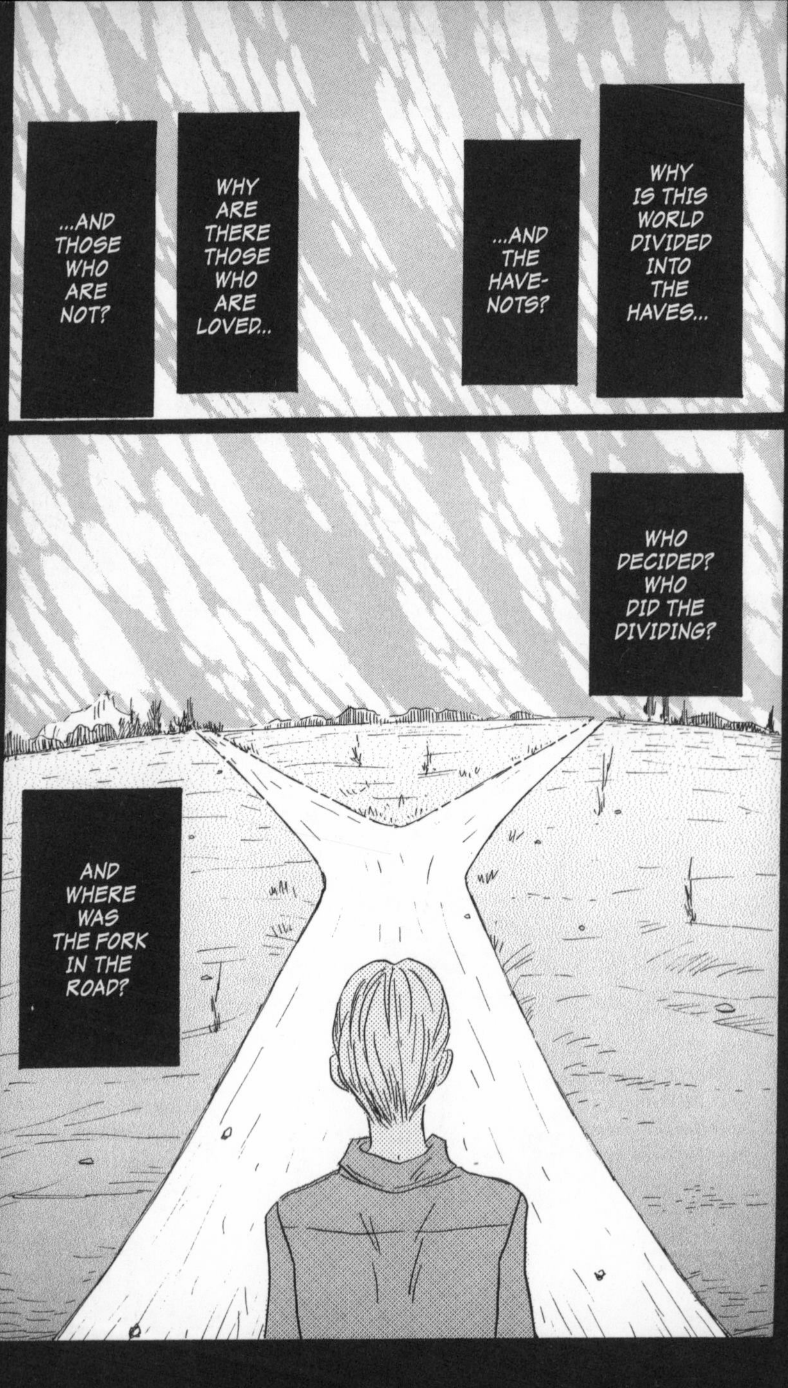
WHY IS THIS WORLD DIVIDED INTO THE HAVES...
...AND THE HAVE-NOTS?
WHY ARE THERE THOSE WHO ARE LOVED...
...AND THOSE WHO ARE NOT?
WHO DECIDED? WHO DID THE DIVIDING?
AND WHERE WAS THE FORK IN THE ROAD?

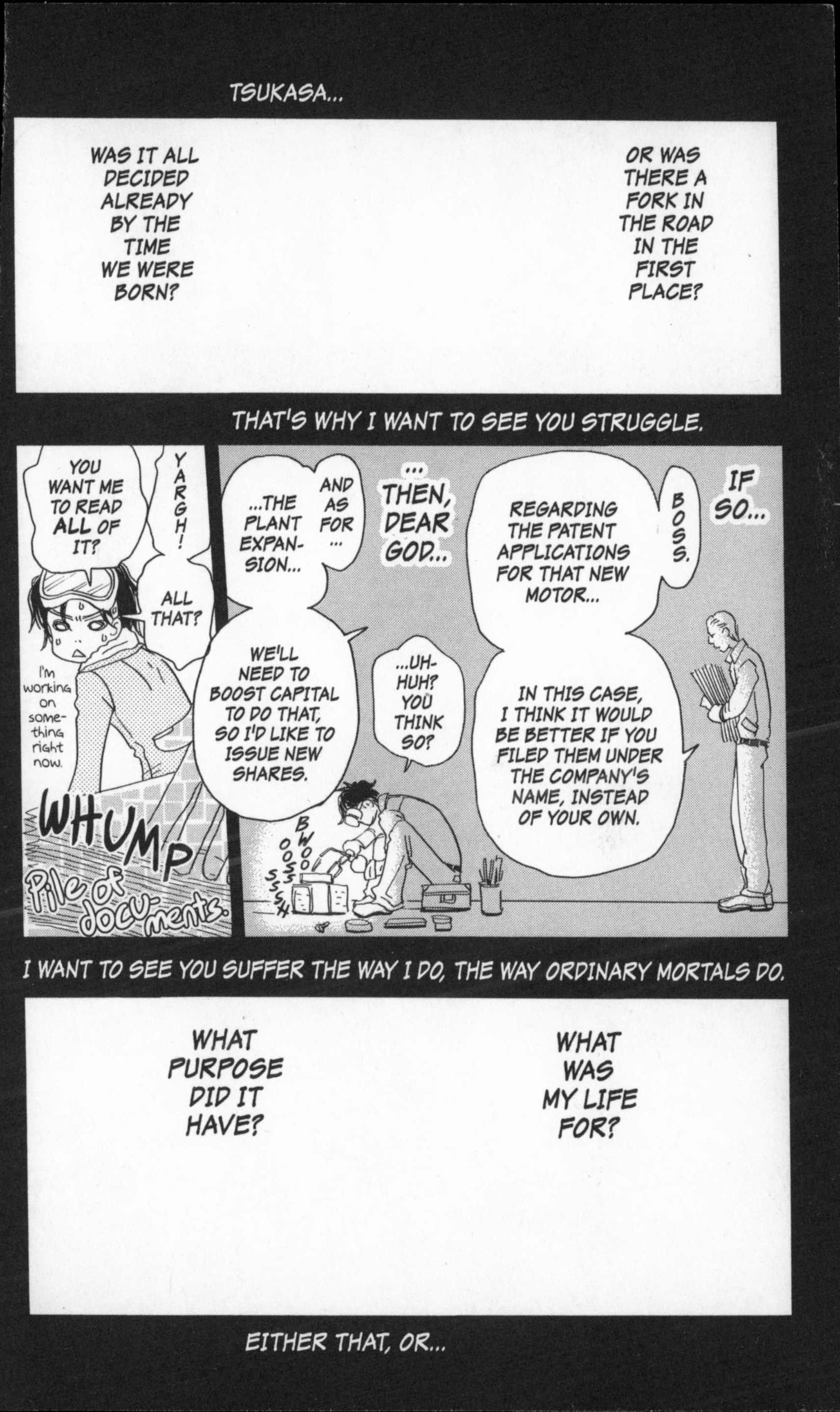
TSUKASA...
OR WAS THERE A FORK IN THE ROAD IN THE FIRST PLACE?
WAS IT ALL DECIDED ALREADY BY THE TIME WE WERE BORN?
THAT'S WHY I WANT TO SEE YOU STRUGGLE.
IF SO...
BOSS.
REGARDING THE PATENT APPLICATIONS FOR THAT NEW MOTOR...
IN THIS CASE, I THINK IT WOULD BE BETTER IF YOU FILED THEM UNDER THE COMPANY'S NAME, INSTEAD OF YOUR OWN.
...THEN, DEAR GOD...
...UH-HUH? YOU THINK SO?
AND AS FOR...
...THE PLANT EXPANSION...
WE'LL NEED TO BOOST CAPITAL TO DO THAT, SO I'D LIKE TO ISSUE NEW SHARES.
BWOOOOSSSSSH
YARGH!
YOU WANT ME TO READ ALL OF IT?
ALL THAT?
I'm working on something right now.
WHUMP
Pile of documents.
I WANT TO SEE YOU SUFFER THE WAY I DO, THE WAY ORDINARY MORTALS DO.
WHAT WAS MY LIFE FOR?
WHAT PURPOSE DID IT HAVE?
EITHER THAT, OR...

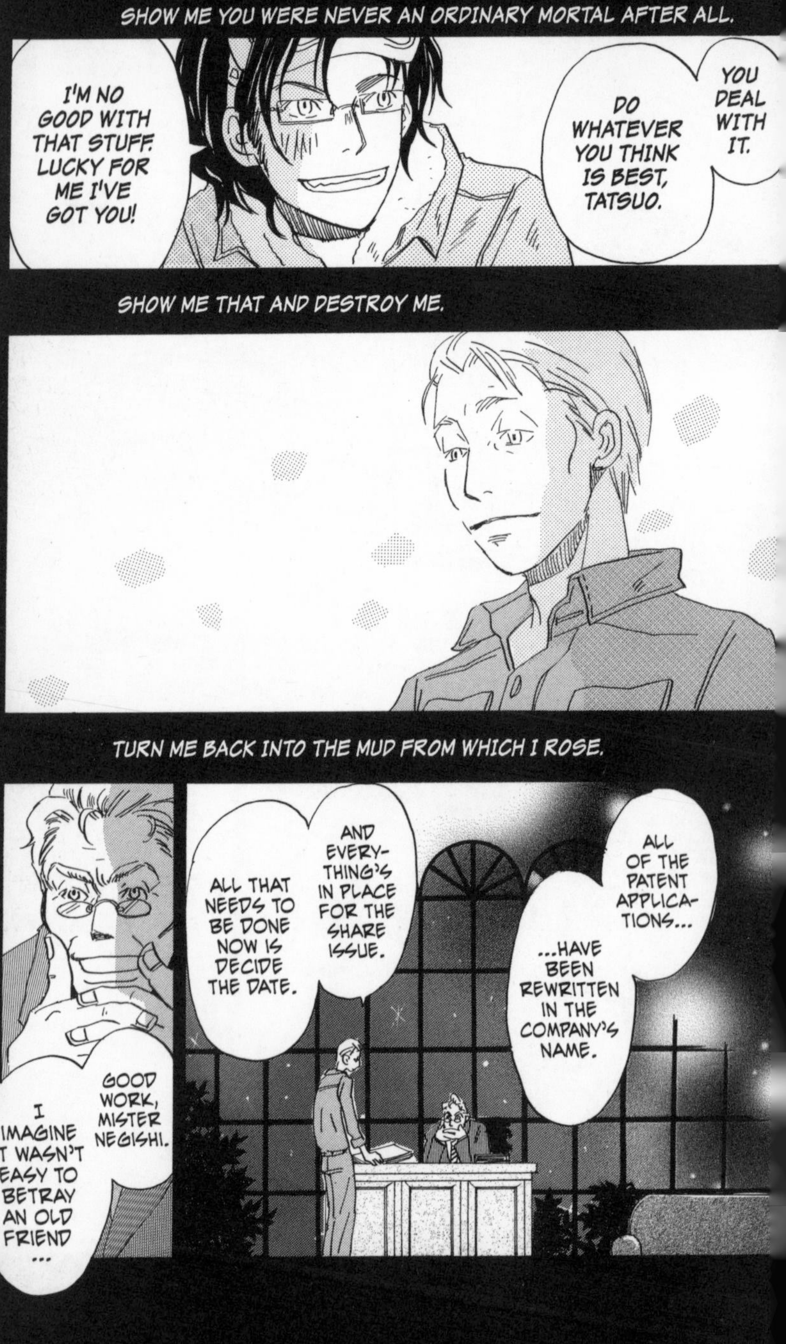
SHOW ME YOU WERE NEVER AN ORDINARY MORTAL AFTER ALL.
YOU DEAL WITH IT.
DO WHATEVER YOU THINK IS BEST, TATSUO.
I'M NO GOOD WITH THAT STUFF. LUCKY FOR ME I'VE GOT YOU!
SHOW ME THAT AND DESTROY ME.
TURN ME BACK INTO THE MUD FROM WHICH I ROSE.
ALL OF THE PATENT APPLICATIONS...
...HAVE BEEN REWRITTEN IN THE COMPANY'S NAME.
AND EVERYTHING'S IN PLACE FOR THE SHARE ISSUE.
ALL THAT NEEDS TO BE DONE NOW IS DECIDE THE DATE.
GOOD WORK, MISTER NEGISHI.
I IMAGINE IT WASN'T EASY TO BETRAY AN OLD FRIEND...

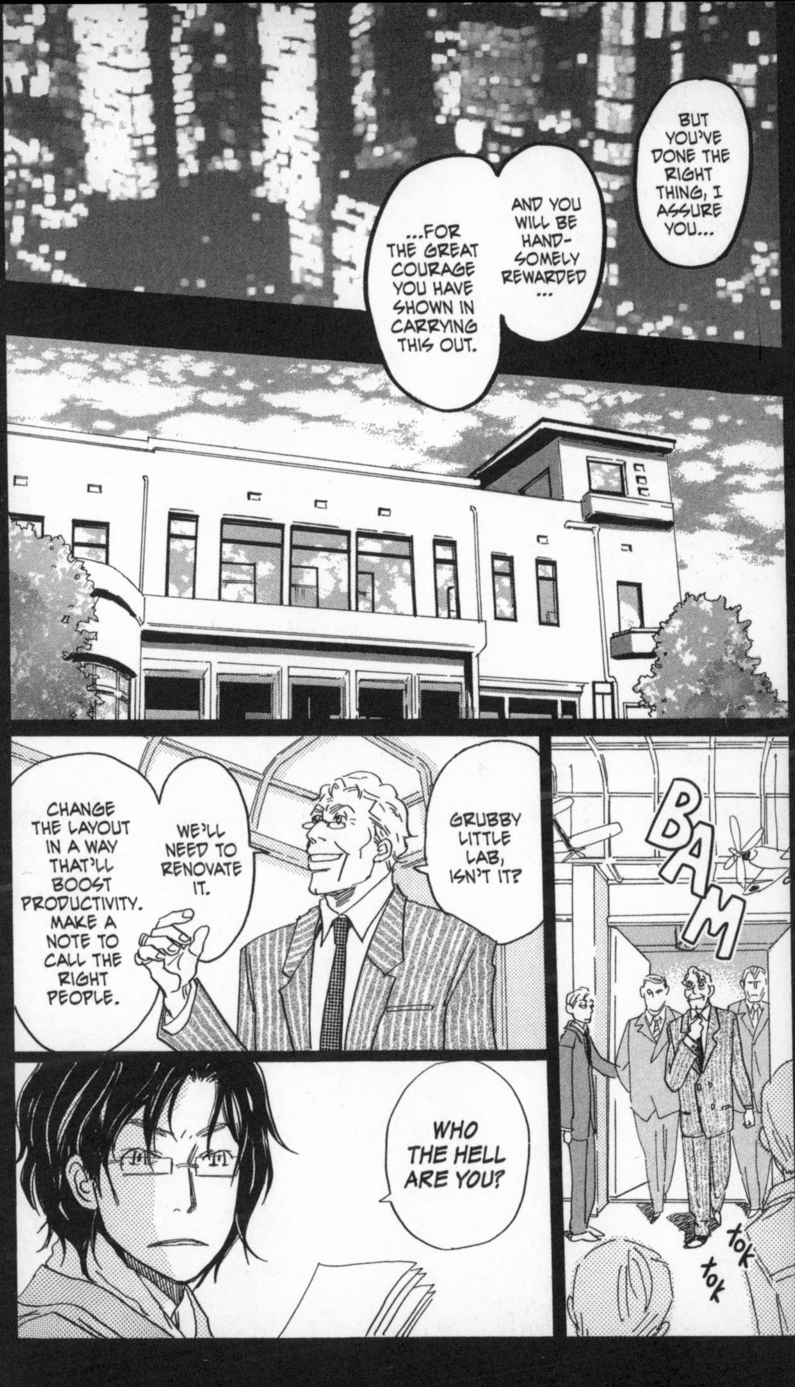
BUT YOU'VE DONE THE RIGHT THING, I ASSURE YOU...
AND YOU WILL BE HAND-SOMELY REWARDED...
...FOR THE GREAT COURAGE YOU HAVE SHOWN IN CARRYING THIS OUT.
BAM
tok tok
GRUBBY LITTLE LAB, ISN'T IT?
WE'LL NEED TO RENOVATE IT.
CHANGE THE LAYOUT IN A WAY THAT'LL BOOST PRODUCTIVITY. MAKE A NOTE TO CALL THE RIGHT PEOPLE.
WHO THE HELL ARE YOU?

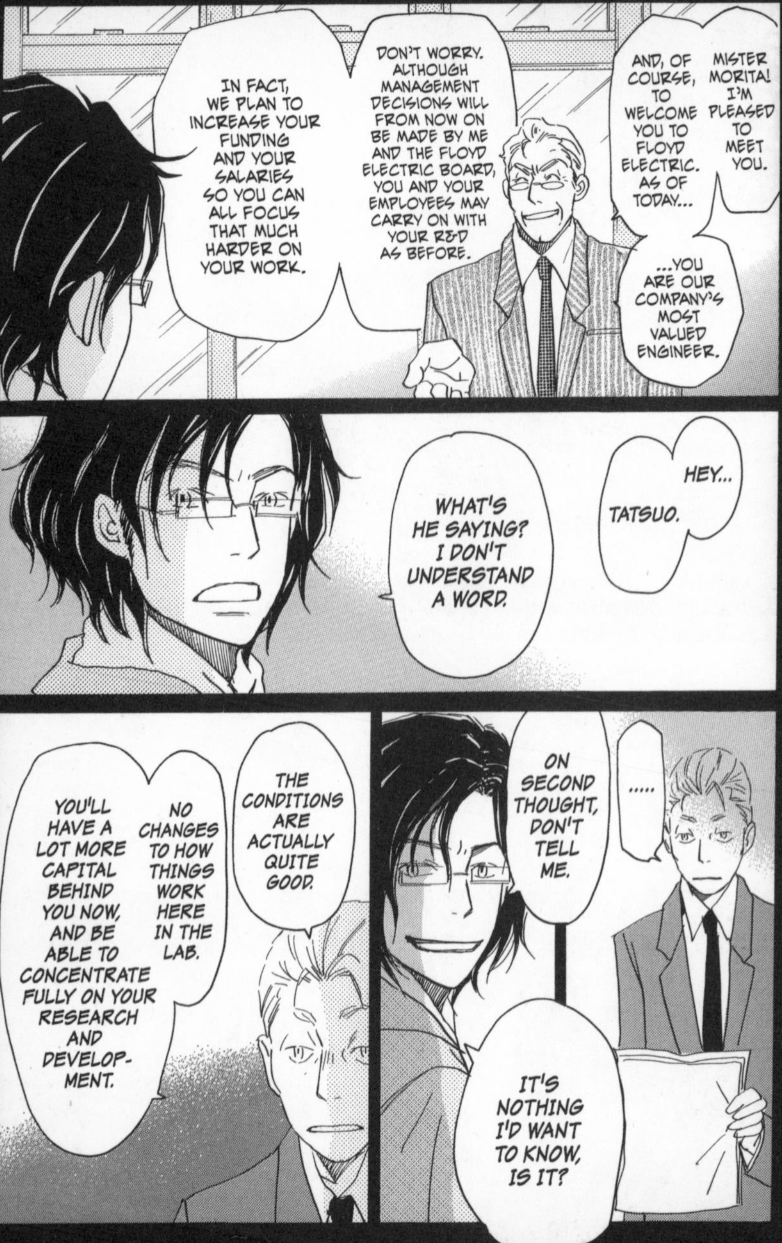
MISTER MORITA! I'M PLEASED TO MEET YOU.
AND, OF COURSE, TO WELCOME YOU TO FLOYD ELECTRIC. AS OF TODAY...
...YOU ARE OUR COMPANY'S MOST VALUED ENGINEER.
DON'T WORRY. ALTHOUGH MANAGEMENT DECISIONS WILL FROM NOW ON BE MADE BY ME AND THE FLOYD ELECTRIC BOARD, YOU AND YOUR EMPLOYEES MAY CARRY ON WITH YOUR R&D AS BEFORE.
IN FACT, WE PLAN TO INCREASE YOUR FUNDING AND YOUR SALARIES SO YOU CAN ALL FOCUS THAT MUCH HARDER ON YOUR WORK.
HEY... TATSUO.
WHAT'S HE SAYING? I DON'T UNDERSTAND A WORD.
.....
ON SECOND THOUGHT, DON'T TELL ME.
IT'S NOTHING I'D WANT TO KNOW, IS IT?
THE CONDITIONS ARE ACTUALLY QUITE GOOD.
NO CHANGES TO HOW THINGS WORK HERE IN THE LAB.
YOU'LL HAVE A LOT MORE CAPITAL BEHIND YOU NOW, AND BE ABLE TO CONCENTRATE FULLY ON YOUR RESEARCH AND DEVELOPMENT.

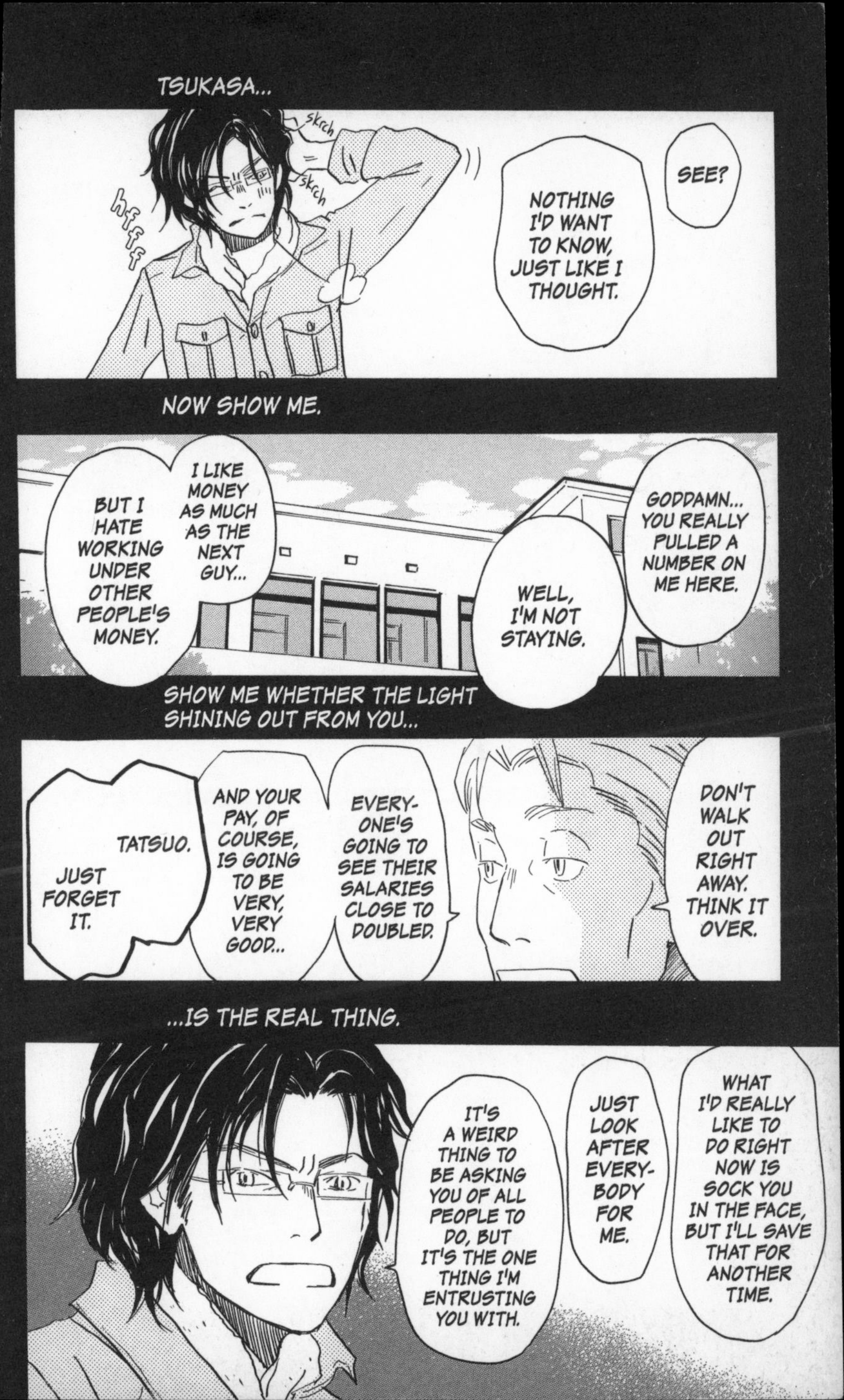
TSUKASA...
SEE?
NOTHING I'D WANT TO KNOW, JUST LIKE I THOUGHT.
skrch
skrch
hfff
NOW SHOW ME.
GODDAMN... YOU REALLY PULLED A NUMBER ON ME HERE.
WELL, I'M NOT STAYING.
I LIKE MONEY AS MUCH AS THE NEXT GUY...
BUT I HATE WORKING UNDER OTHER PEOPLE'S MONEY.
SHOW ME WHETHER THE LIGHT SHINING OUT FROM YOU...
DON'T WALK OUT RIGHT AWAY. THINK IT OVER.
EVERY-ONE'S GOING TO SEE THEIR SALARIES CLOSE TO DOUBLED.
AND YOUR PAY, OF COURSE, IS GOING TO BE VERY, VERY GOOD...
TATSUO.
JUST FORGET IT.
...IS THE REAL THING.
WHAT I'D REALLY LIKE TO DO RIGHT NOW IS SOCK YOU IN THE FACE, BUT I'LL SAVE THAT FOR ANOTHER TIME.
JUST LOOK AFTER EVERY-BODY FOR ME.
IT'S A WEIRD THING TO BE ASKING YOU OF ALL PEOPLE TO DO, BUT IT'S THE ONE THING I'M ENTRUSTING YOU WITH.

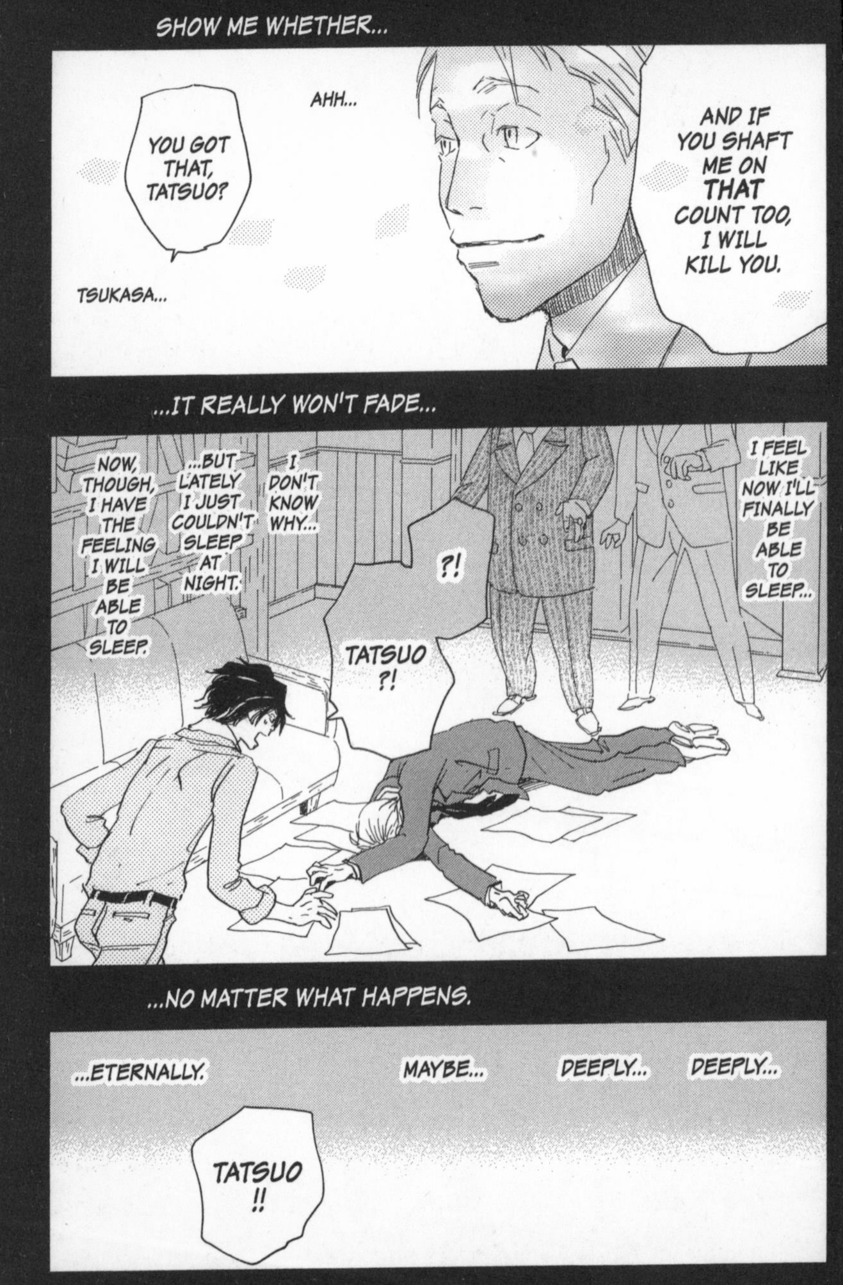

SHOW ME WHETHER...
AND IF YOU SHAFT ME ON THAT COUNT TOO, I WILL KILL YOU.
AHH...
YOU GOT THAT, TATSUO?
TSUKASA...
...IT REALLY WON'T FADE...
I FEEL LIKE NOW I'LL FINALLY BE ABLE TO SLEEP...
?!
I DON'T KNOW WHY...
...BUT LATELY I JUST COULDN'T SLEEP AT NIGHT.
NOW, THOUGH, I HAVE THE FEELING I WILL BE ABLE TO SLEEP.
TATSUO ?!
...NO MATTER WHAT HAPPENS.
DEEPLY...
DEEPLY...
MAYBE...
...ETERNALLY.
TATSUO !!

AND SO, THE THREE OF US...

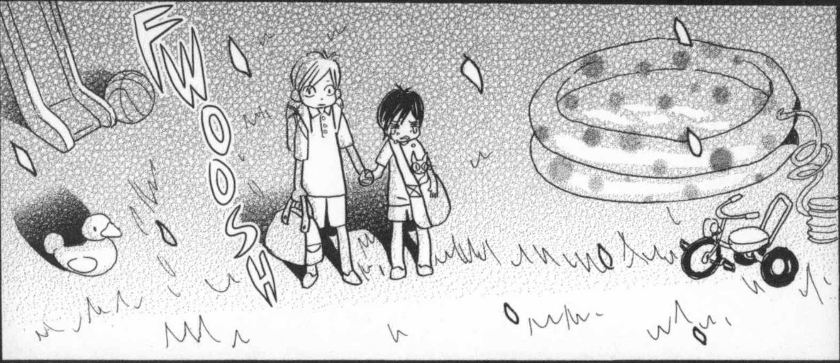
FWOOSH

...HAD TO PUT OUR PARADISE BEHIND US...

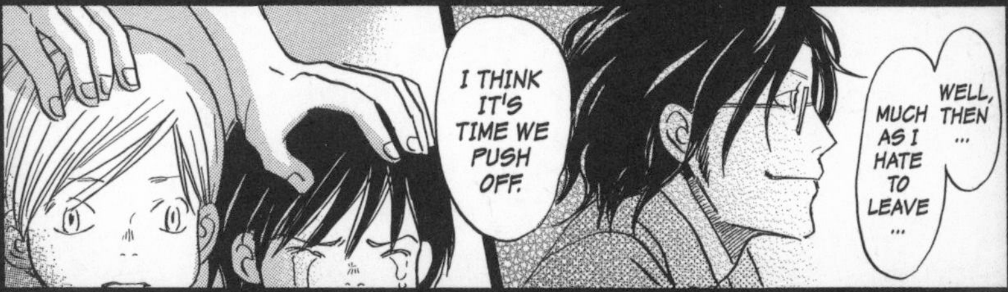
WELL, THEN... MUCH AS I HATE TO LEAVE...
I THINK IT'S TIME WE PUSH OFF.

...AND SET OUT INTO THE BOTTOMLESS NIGHT.

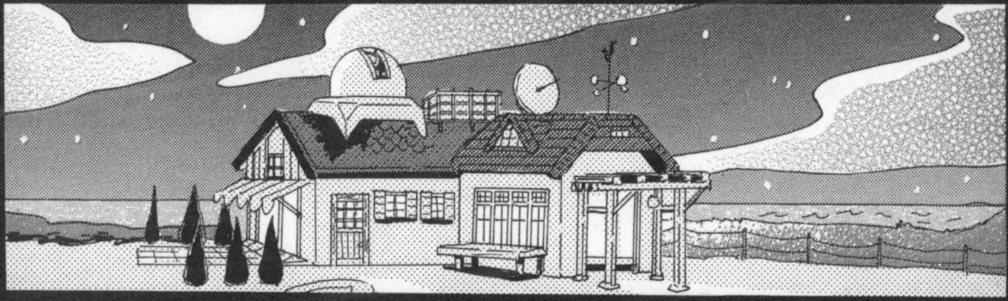

WITHOUT EVEN KNOWING...

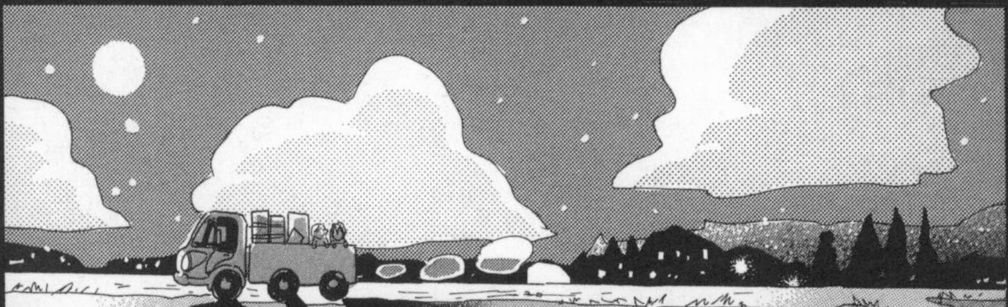

...WHO TO BLAME FOR OUR PLIGHT.

chapter 55—the end—

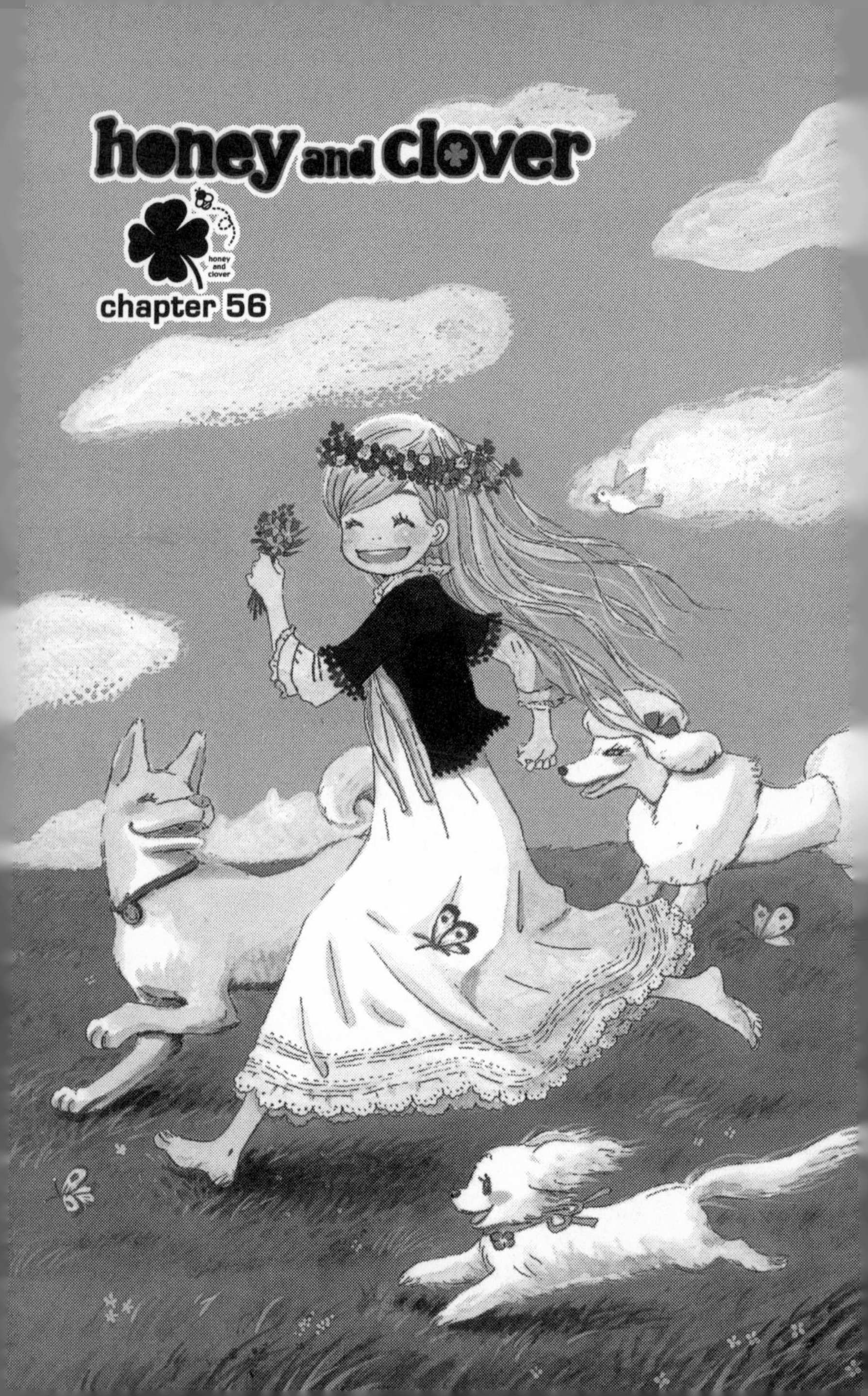
honey and clover
honey and clover
chapter 56

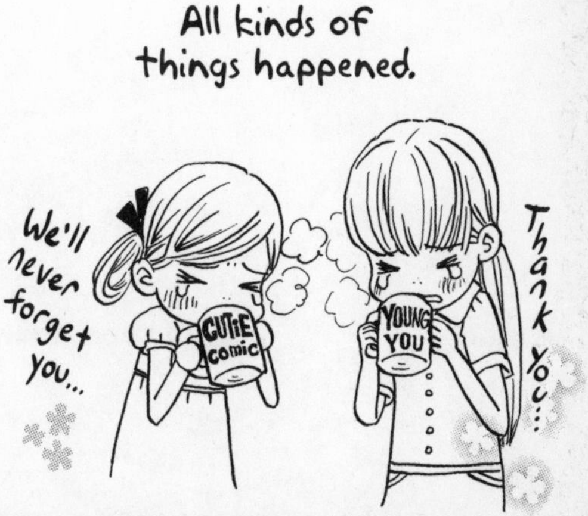
All kinds of things happened.
Thank you...
YOUNG YOU
CUTiE comic
We'll never forget you...

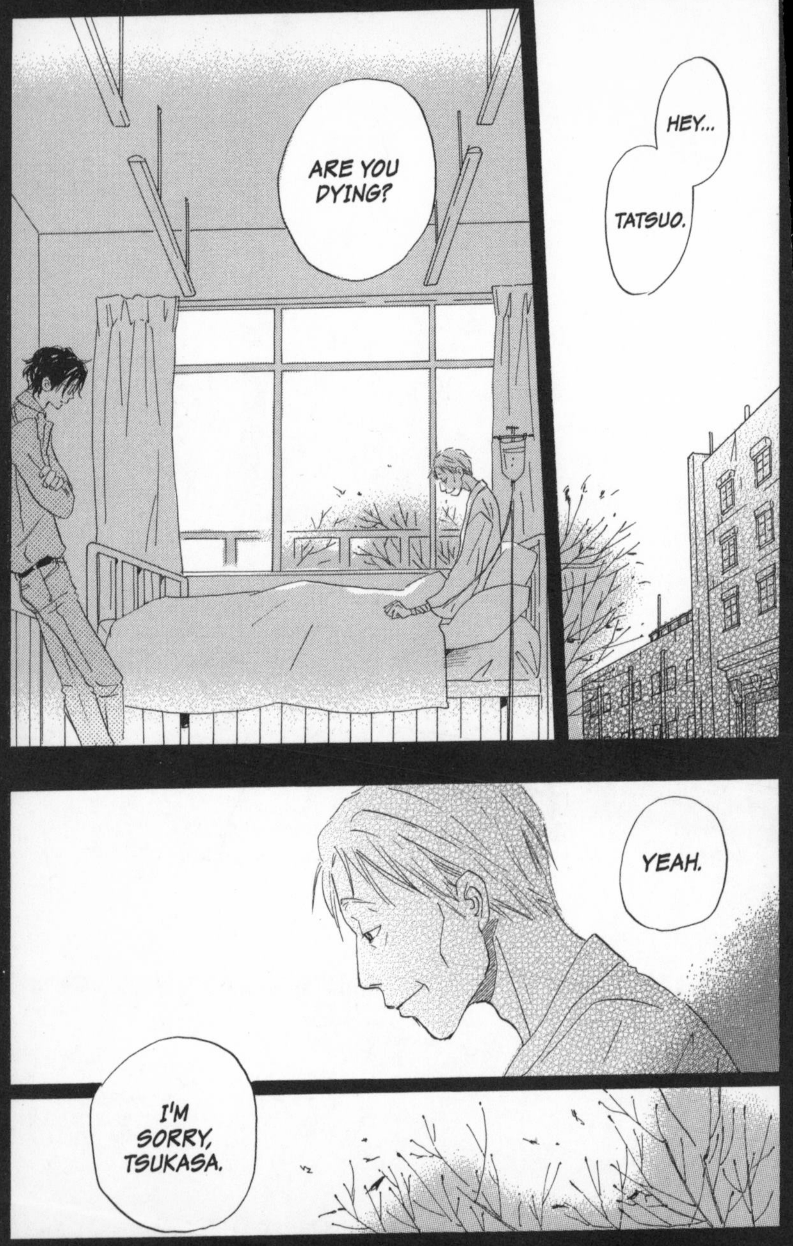
HEY...
TATSUO.
ARE YOU DYING?
YEAH.
I'M SORRY, TSUKASA.

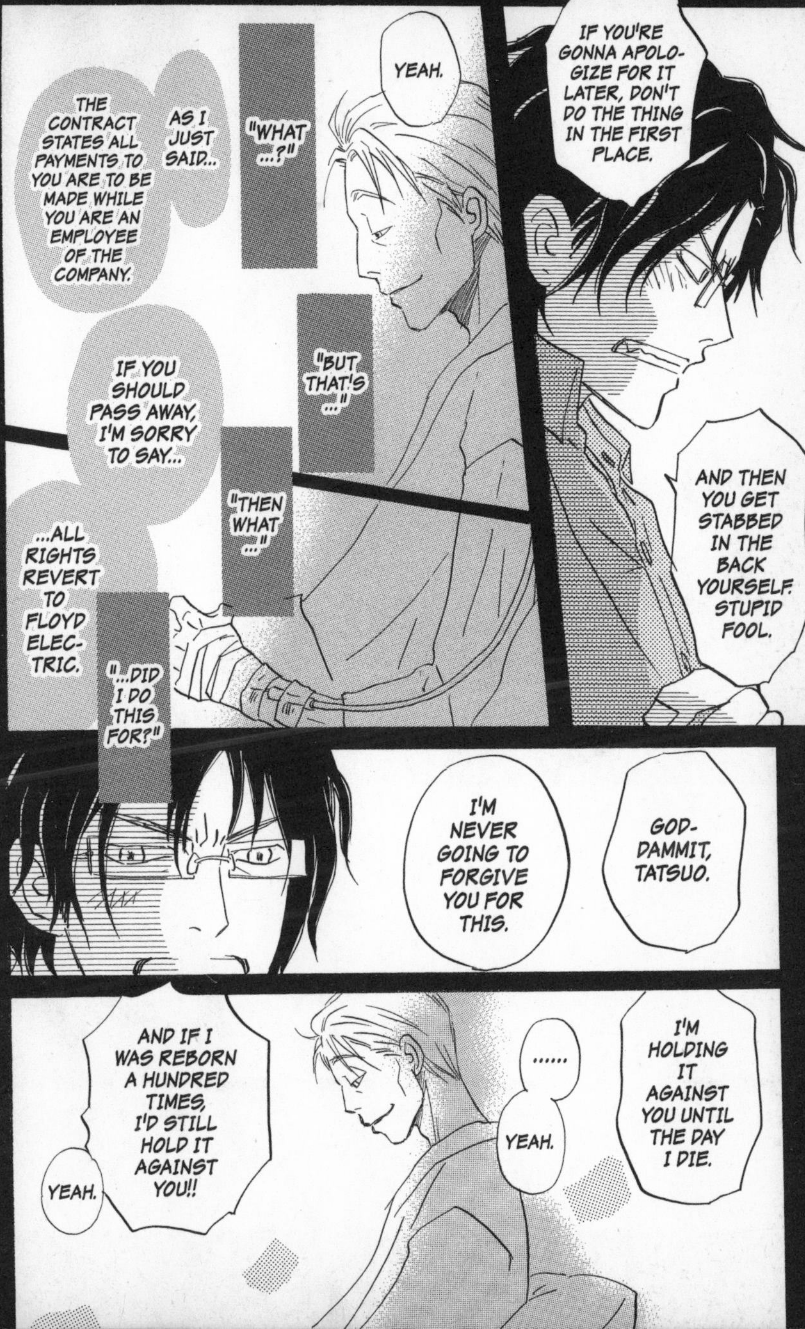
IF YOU'RE GONNA APOLOGIZE FOR IT LATER, DON'T DO THE THING IN THE FIRST PLACE.
AND THEN YOU GET STABBED IN THE BACK YOURSELF. STUPID FOOL.
YEAH.
"WHAT ...?"
AS I JUST SAID...
THE CONTRACT STATES ALL PAYMENTS TO YOU ARE TO BE MADE WHILE YOU ARE AN EMPLOYEE OF THE COMPANY.
"BUT THAT'S ..."
IF YOU SHOULD PASS AWAY, I'M SORRY TO SAY...
"THEN WHAT ..."
...ALL RIGHTS REVERT TO FLOYD ELECTRIC.
"...DID I DO THIS FOR?"
GOD-DAMMIT, TATSUO.
I'M NEVER GOING TO FORGIVE YOU FOR THIS.
I'M HOLDING IT AGAINST YOU UNTIL THE DAY I DIE.
......
YEAH.
AND IF I WAS REBORN A HUNDRED TIMES, I'D STILL HOLD IT AGAINST YOU!!
YEAH.

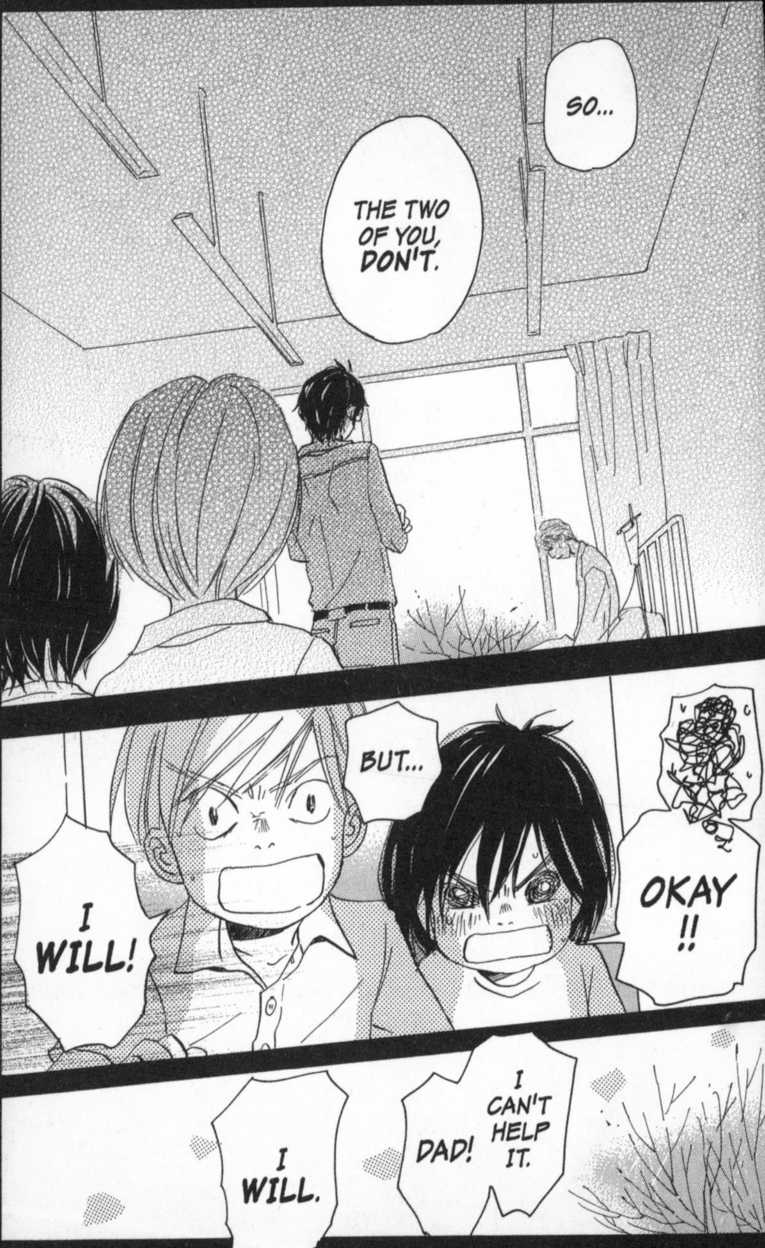
SO...
THE TWO OF YOU, DON'T.
OKAY !!
BUT...
I WILL!
I CAN'T HELP IT.
DAD!
I WILL.

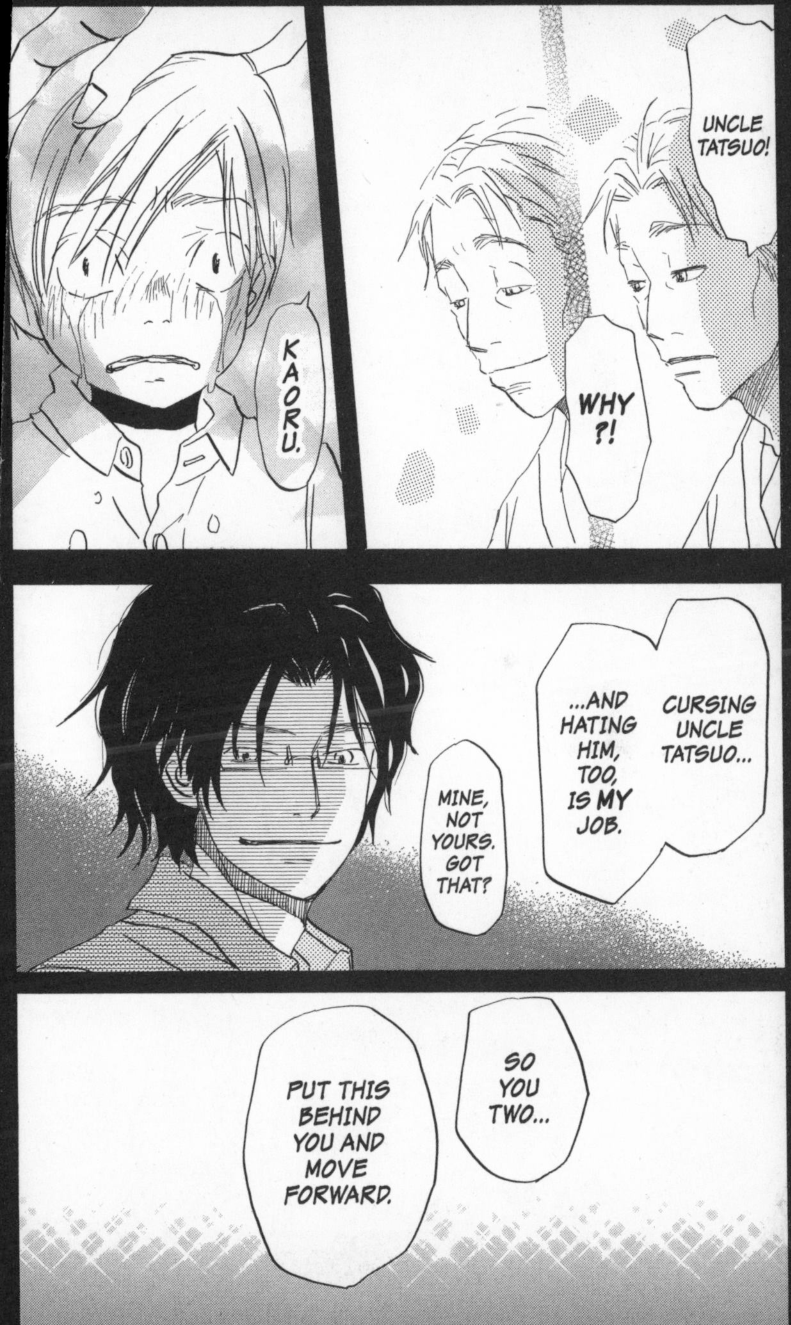
UNCLE TATSUO!
WHY ?!
KAORU.
CURSING UNCLE TATSUO...
...AND HATING HIM, TOO, IS MY JOB.
MINE, NOT YOURS. GOT THAT?
SO YOU TWO...
PUT THIS BEHIND YOU AND MOVE FORWARD.

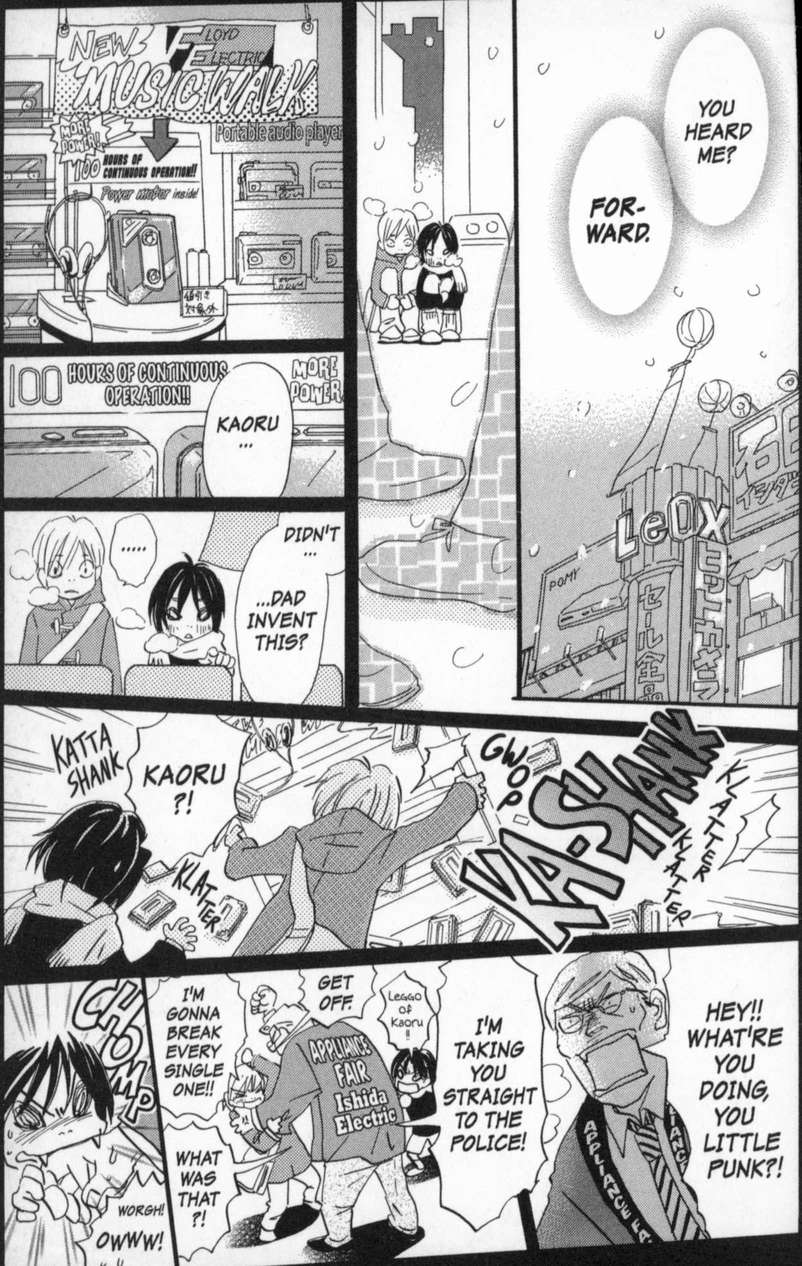
YOU HEARD ME?
FOR-WARD.
LeOX
POMY
NEW FLOYD ELECTRIC MUSIC WALK
MORE POWER!
100 HOURS OF CONTINUOUS OPERATION!!
Portable audio player
Power motor inside!
値引き対象外
100 HOURS OF CONTINUOUS OPERATION!!
MORE POWER!
KAORU ...
DIDN'T ...
...DAD INVENT THIS?
......
KA-SHANK
KLATTER
KLATTER
GWOOP
KAORU ?!
KATTA SHANK
KLATTER
HEY!! WHAT'RE YOU DOING, YOU LITTLE PUNK?!
I'M TAKING YOU STRAIGHT TO THE POLICE!
Leggo of Kaoru!!
GET OFF.
I'M GONNA BREAK EVERY SINGLE ONE!!
APPLIANCE FAIR Ishida Electric
WHAT WAS THAT?!
CHOMP
WORGH!
OWWW!

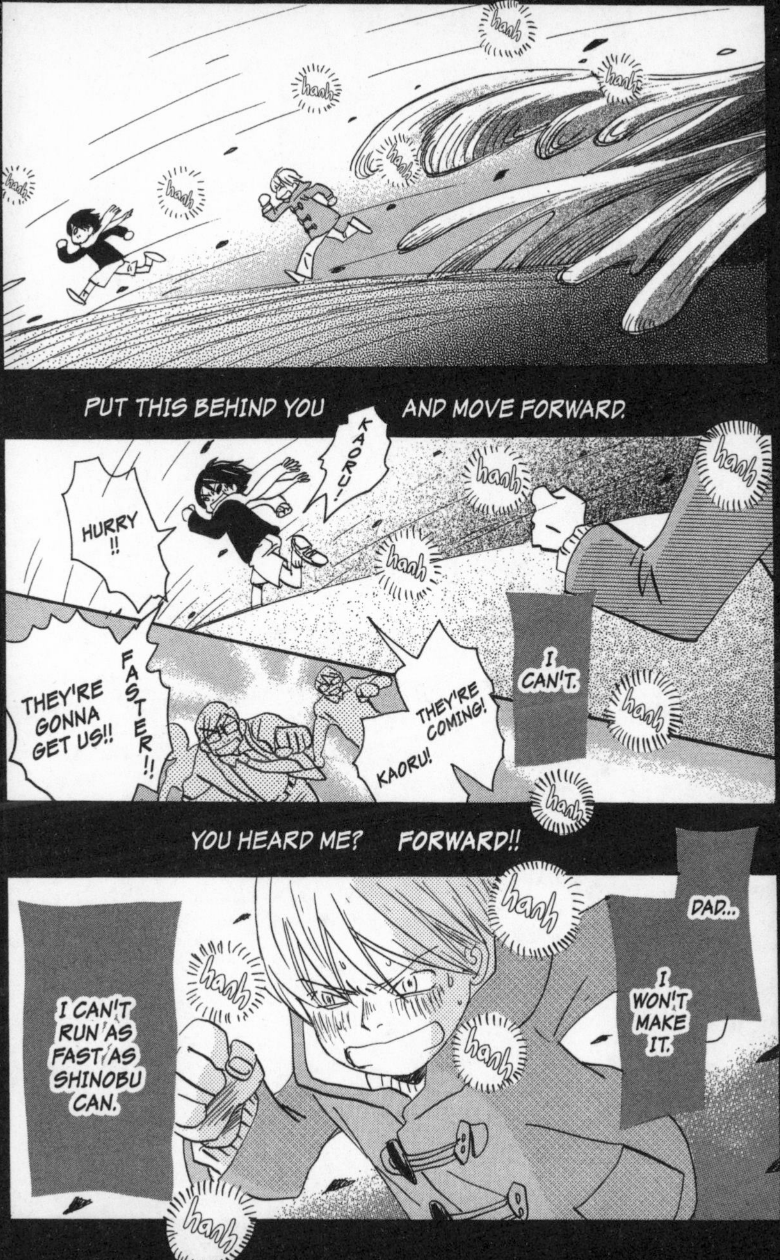
hanh
hanh
hanh
hanh
hanh
hanh
PUT THIS BEHIND YOU
AND MOVE FORWARD.
hanh
hanh
KAORU!
HURRY!!
hanh
I CAN'T.
hanh
THEY'RE COMING!
KAORU!
FASTER!!
THEY'RE GONNA GET US!!
hanh
YOU HEARD ME?
FORWARD!!
DAD...
I WON'T MAKE IT.
hanh
hanh
hanh
I CAN'T RUN AS FAST AS SHINOBU CAN.
hanh

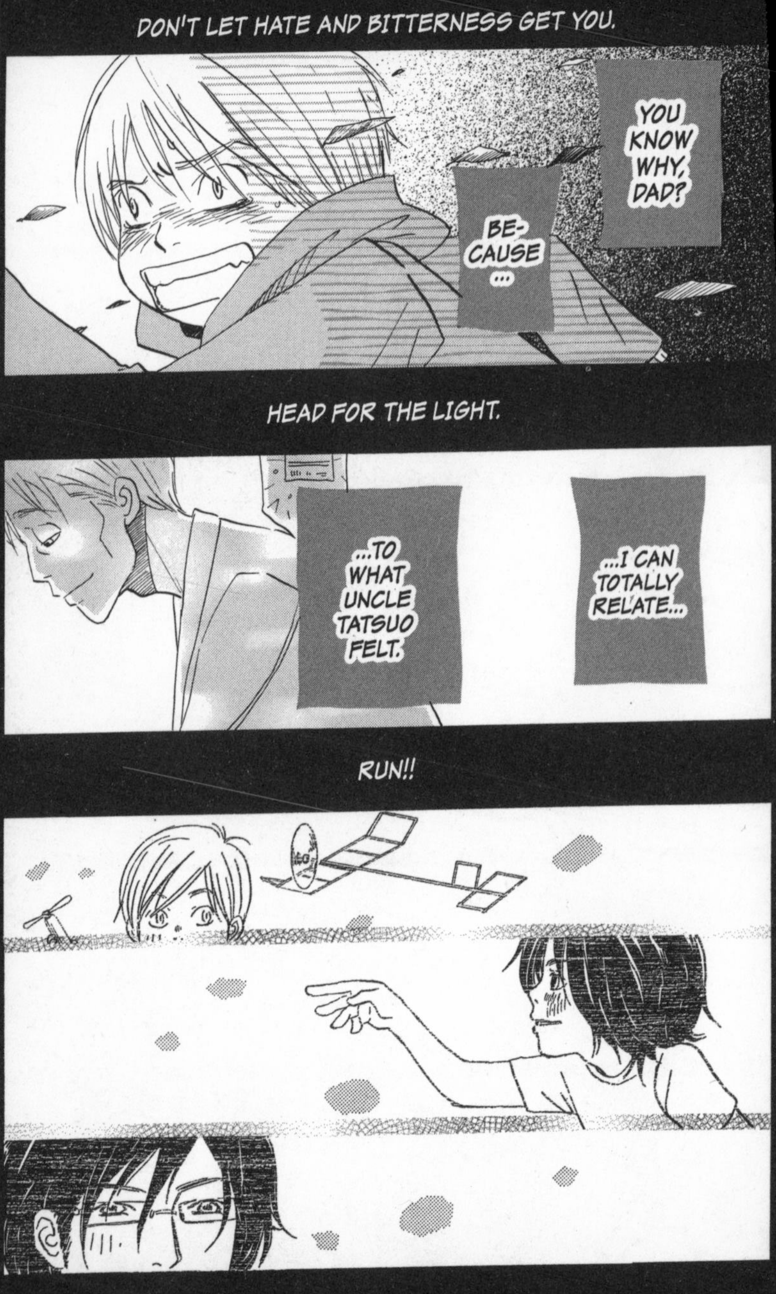
DON'T LET HATE AND BITTERNESS GET YOU.
YOU KNOW WHY, DAD?
BE-CAUSE...
HEAD FOR THE LIGHT.
...I CAN TOTALLY RELATE...
...TO WHAT UNCLE TATSUO FELT.
RUN!!

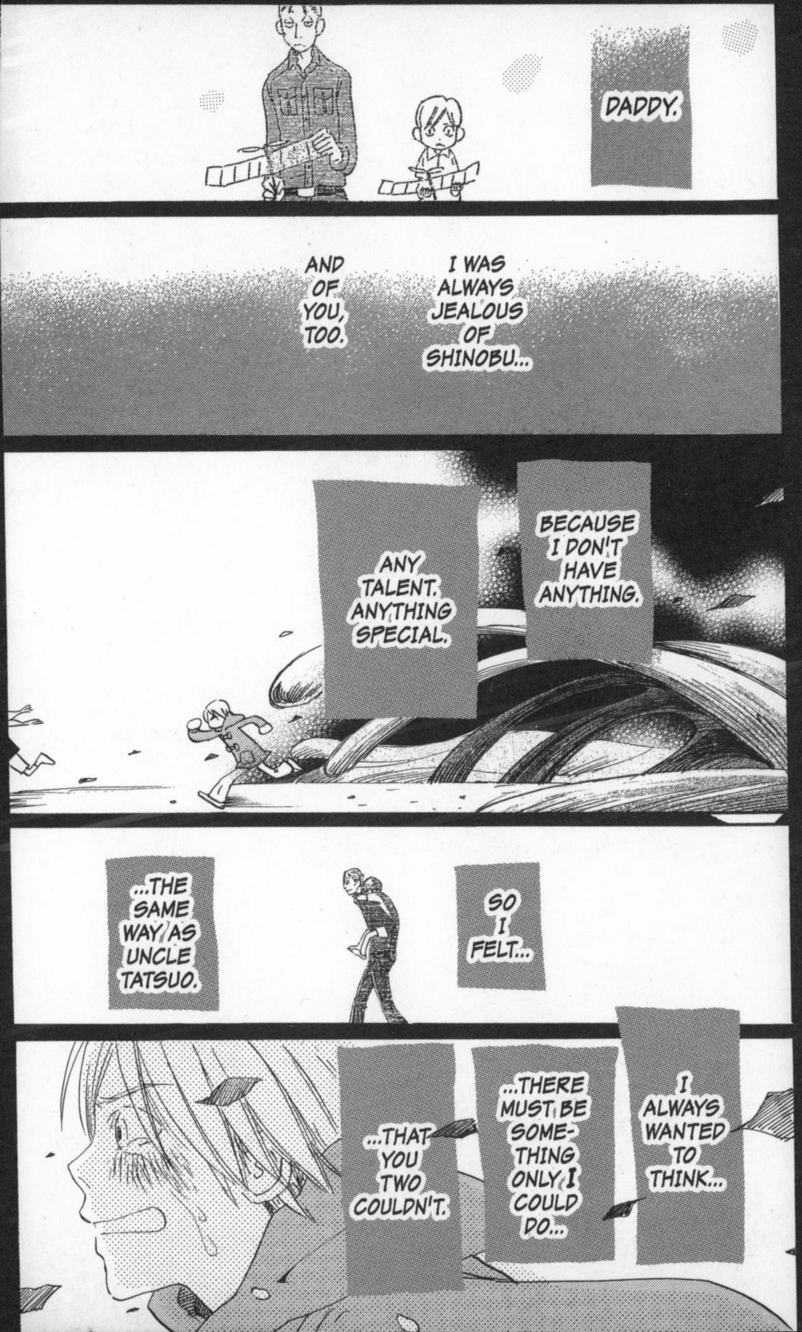
DADDY.
I WAS ALWAYS JEALOUS OF SHINOBU...
AND OF YOU, TOO.
BECAUSE I DON'T HAVE ANYTHING.
ANY TALENT. ANYTHING SPECIAL.
SO I FELT...
...THE SAME WAY AS UNCLE TATSUO.
I ALWAYS WANTED TO THINK...
...THERE MUST BE SOMETHING ONLY I COULD DO...
...THAT YOU TWO COULDN'T.

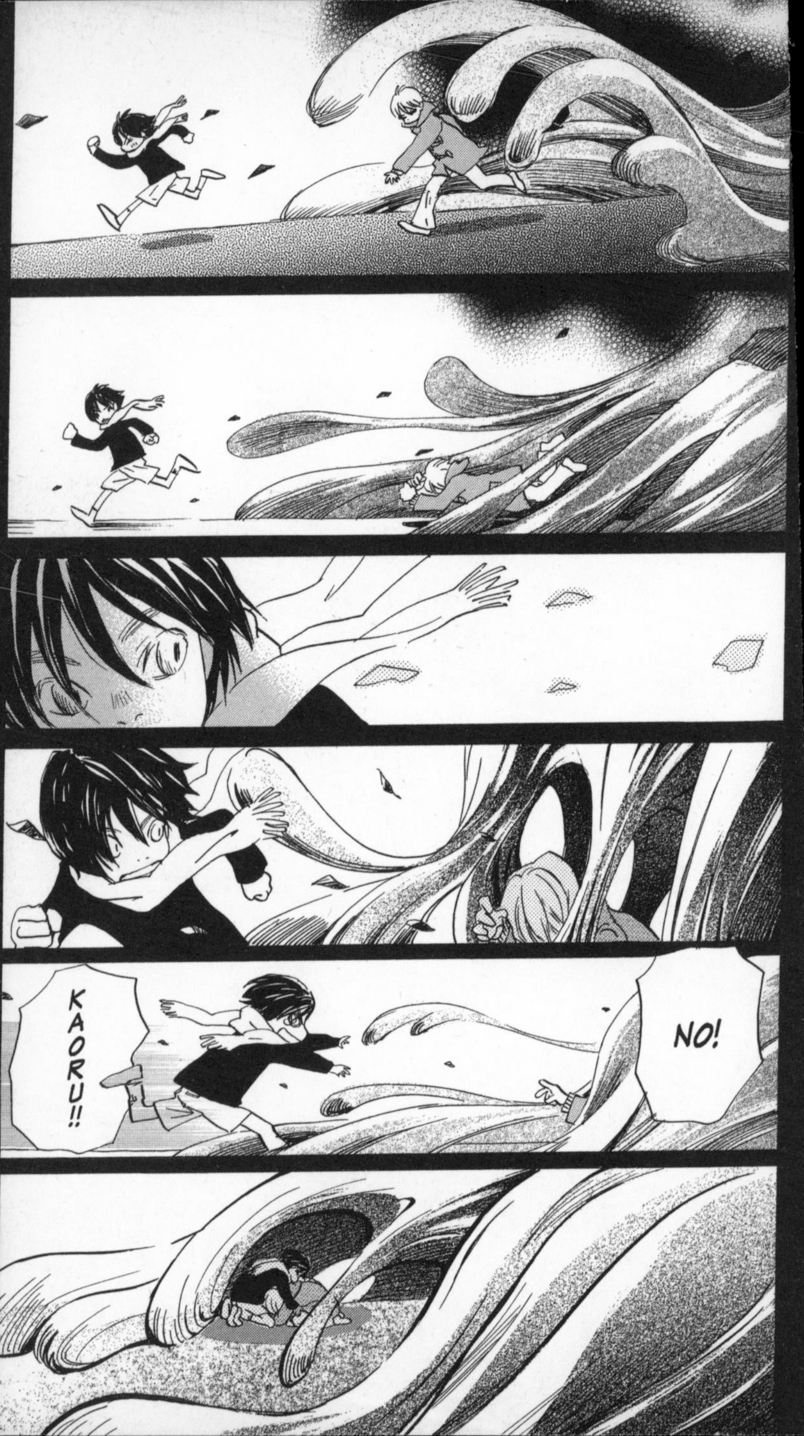
NO!
KAORU!!

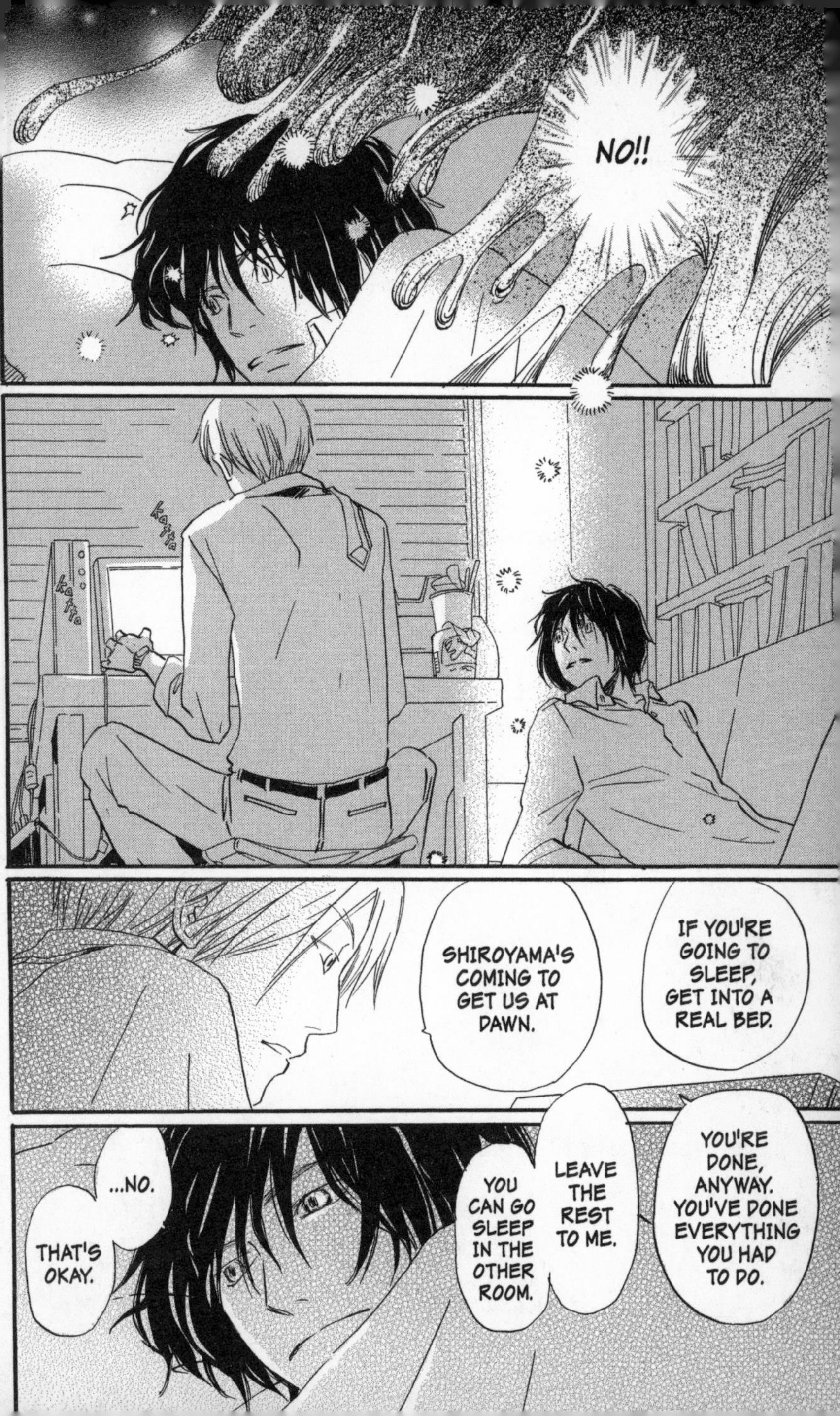
NO!!
katta
katta
IF YOU'RE GOING TO SLEEP, GET INTO A REAL BED.
SHIROYAMA'S COMING TO GET US AT DAWN.
YOU'RE DONE, ANYWAY. YOU'VE DONE EVERYTHING YOU HAD TO DO.
LEAVE THE REST TO ME.
YOU CAN GO SLEEP IN THE OTHER ROOM.
...NO.
THAT'S OKAY.

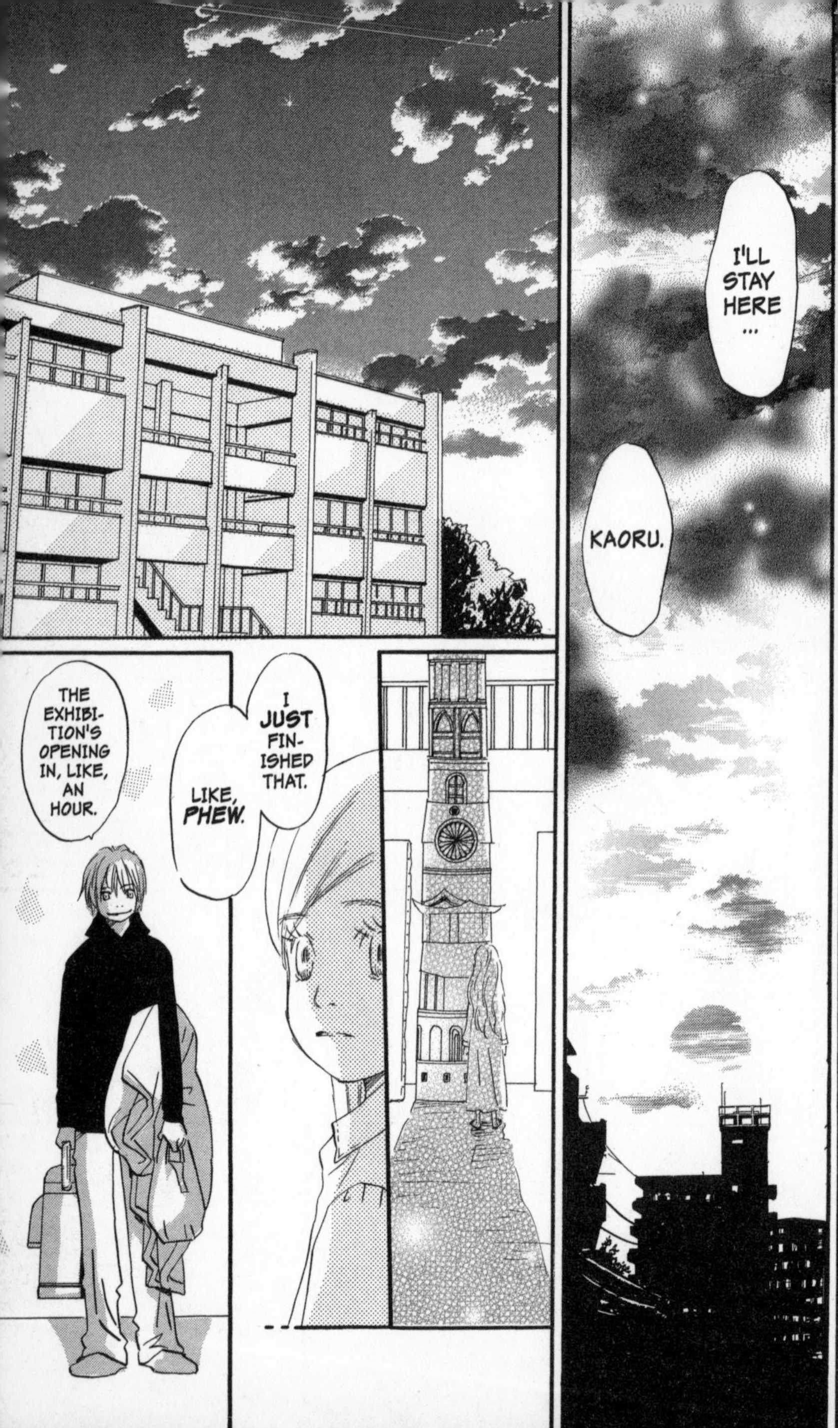
I'LL STAY HERE ...
KAORU.
I JUST FINISHED THAT.
LIKE, PHEW.
THE EXHIBITION'S OPENING IN, LIKE, AN HOUR.

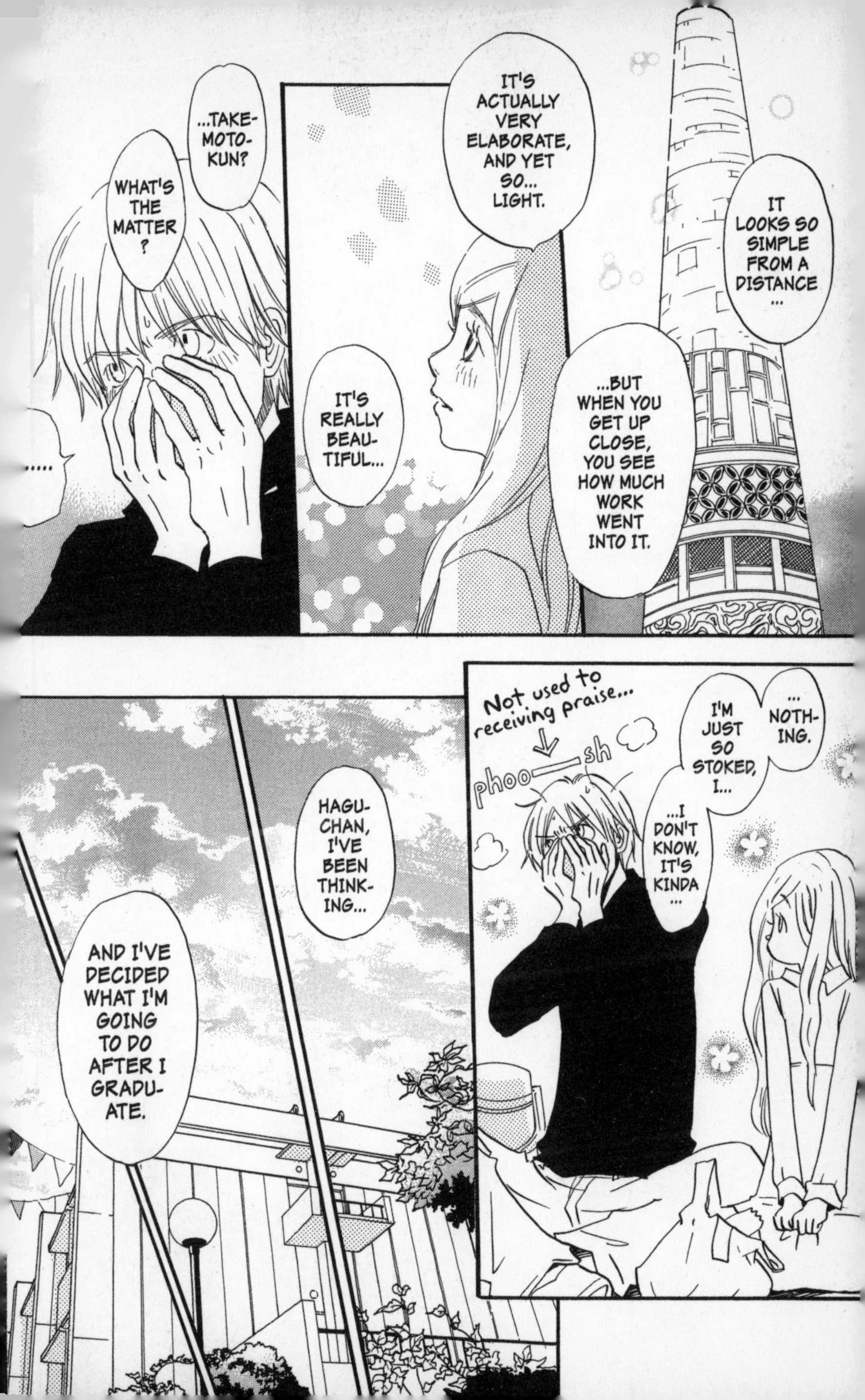
IT LOOKS SO SIMPLE FROM A DISTANCE...
...BUT WHEN YOU GET UP CLOSE, YOU SEE HOW MUCH WORK WENT INTO IT.
IT'S ACTUALLY VERY ELABORATE, AND YET SO... LIGHT.
IT'S REALLY BEAUTIFUL...
...TAKEMOTO-KUN?
WHAT'S THE MATTER?
.....
... NOTHING.
I'M JUST SO STOKED, I...
...I DON'T KNOW, IT'S KINDA...
Not used to receiving praise...
phoo—sh
HAGU-CHAN, I'VE BEEN THINKING...
AND I'VE DECIDED WHAT I'M GOING TO DO AFTER I GRADUATE.

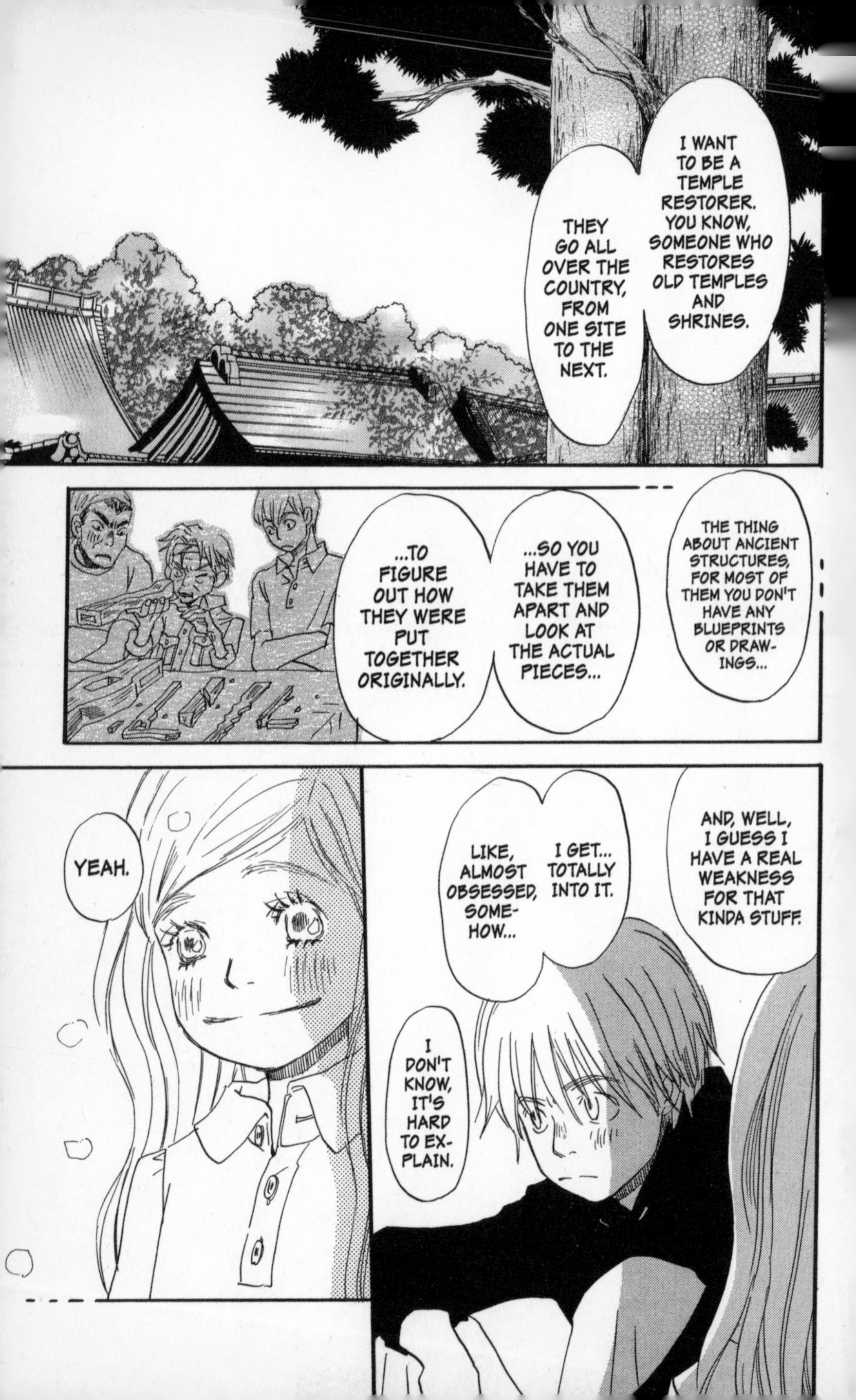
I WANT TO BE A TEMPLE RESTORER. YOU KNOW, SOMEONE WHO RESTORES OLD TEMPLES AND SHRINES.
THEY GO ALL OVER THE COUNTRY, FROM ONE SITE TO THE NEXT.
THE THING ABOUT ANCIENT STRUCTURES, FOR MOST OF THEM YOU DON'T HAVE ANY BLUEPRINTS OR DRAW-INGS...
...SO YOU HAVE TO TAKE THEM APART AND LOOK AT THE ACTUAL PIECES...
...TO FIGURE OUT HOW THEY WERE PUT TOGETHER ORIGINALLY.
AND, WELL, I GUESS I HAVE A REAL WEAKNESS FOR THAT KINDA STUFF.
I GET... TOTALLY INTO IT.
LIKE, ALMOST OBSESSED, SOME-HOW...
I DON'T KNOW, IT'S HARD TO EX-PLAIN.
YEAH.

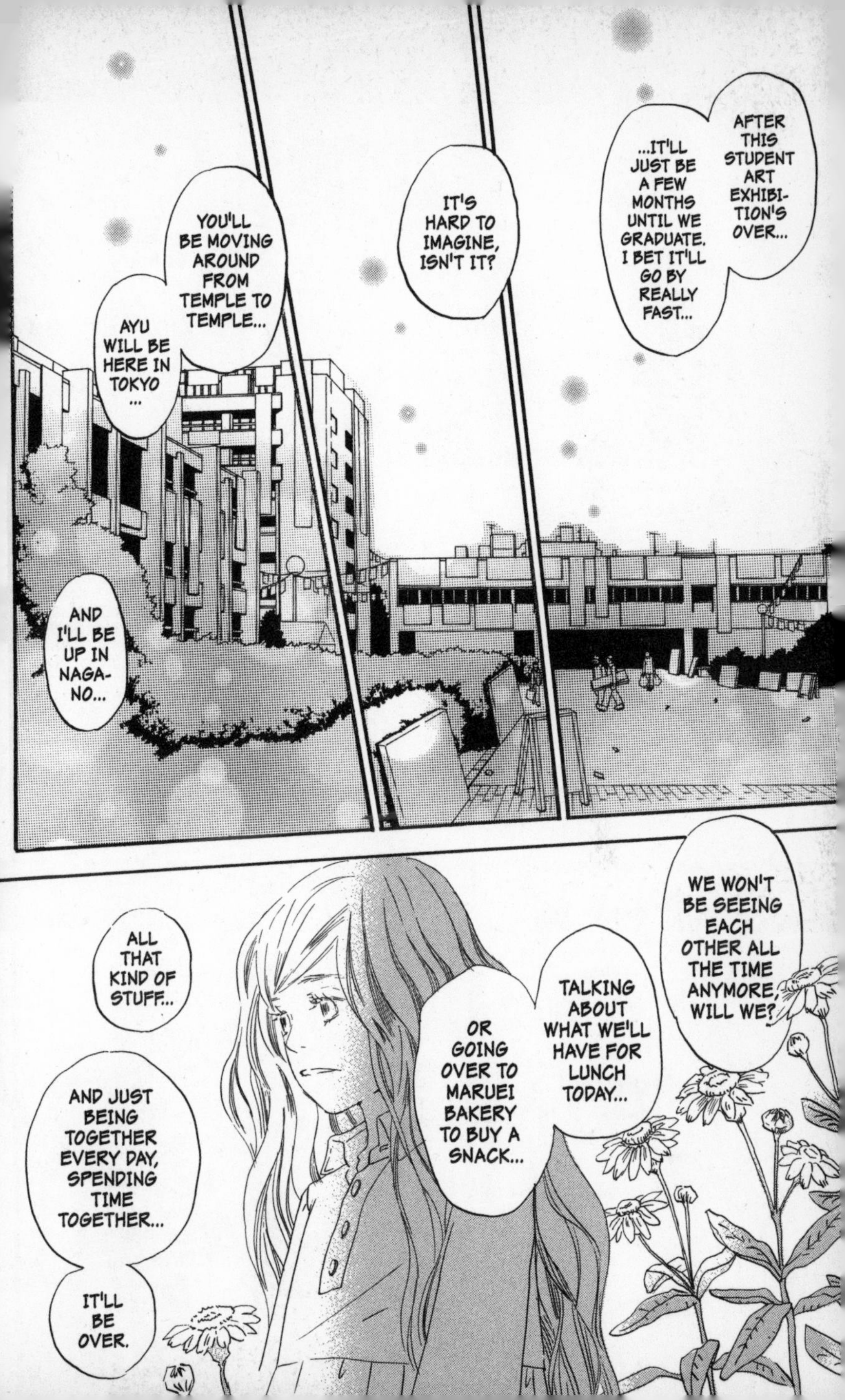
AFTER THIS STUDENT ART EXHIBITION'S OVER...
...IT'LL JUST BE A FEW MONTHS UNTIL WE GRADUATE. I BET IT'LL GO BY REALLY FAST...
IT'S HARD TO IMAGINE, ISN'T IT?
YOU'LL BE MOVING AROUND FROM TEMPLE TO TEMPLE...
AYU WILL BE HERE IN TOKYO ...
AND I'LL BE UP IN NAGANO...
WE WON'T BE SEEING EACH OTHER ALL THE TIME ANYMORE, WILL WE?
TALKING ABOUT WHAT WE'LL HAVE FOR LUNCH TODAY...
OR GOING OVER TO MARUEI BAKERY TO BUY A SNACK...
ALL THAT KIND OF STUFF...
AND JUST BEING TOGETHER EVERY DAY, SPENDING TIME TOGETHER...
IT'LL BE OVER.

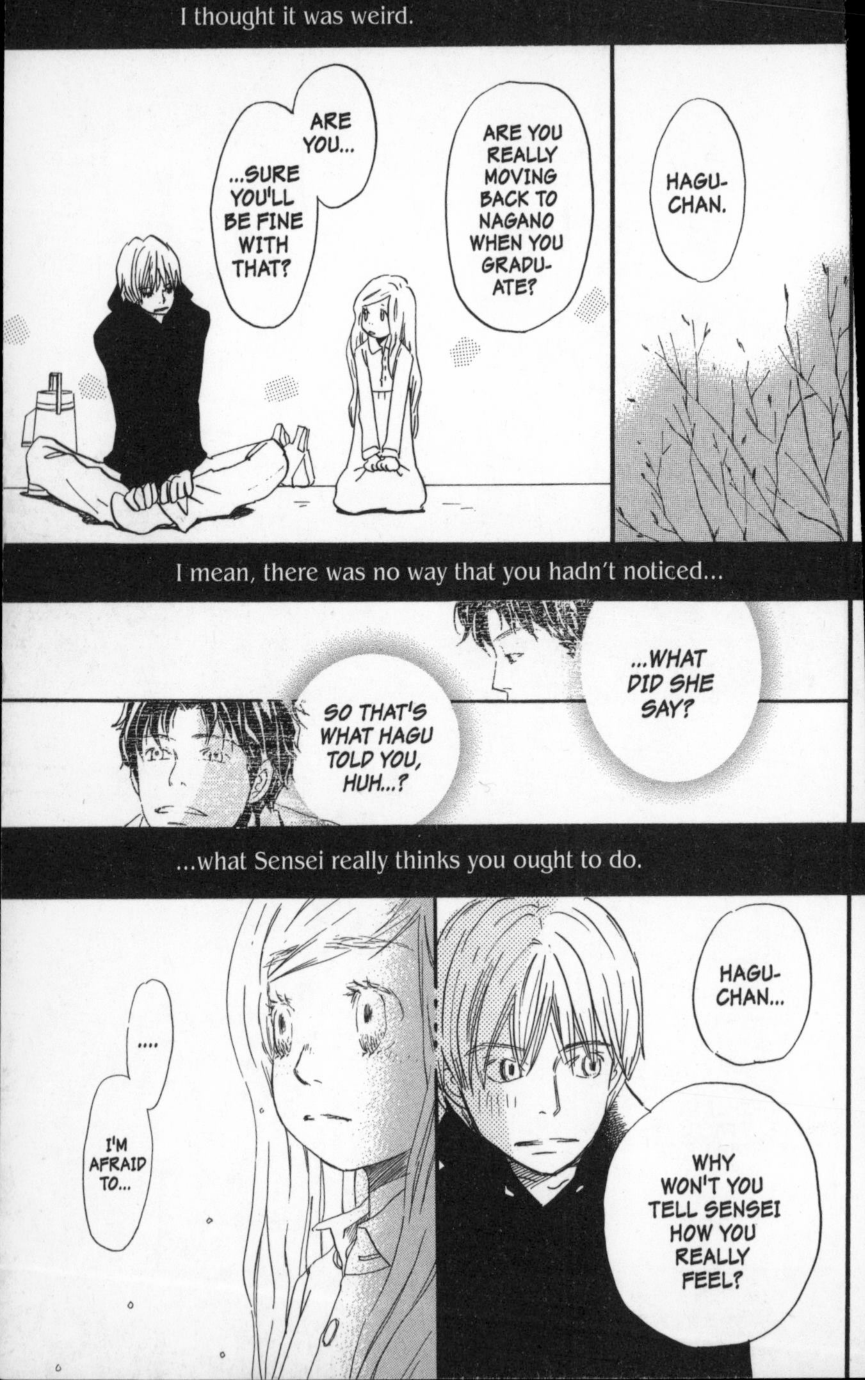
I thought it was weird.
HAGU-CHAN.
ARE YOU REALLY MOVING BACK TO NAGANO WHEN YOU GRADUATE?
ARE YOU...
...SURE YOU'LL BE FINE WITH THAT?
I mean, there was no way that you hadn't noticed...
...WHAT DID SHE SAY?
SO THAT'S WHAT HAGU TOLD YOU, HUH...?
...what Sensei really thinks you ought to do.
HAGU-CHAN...
WHY WON'T YOU TELL SENSEI HOW YOU REALLY FEEL?
....
I'M AFRAID TO...

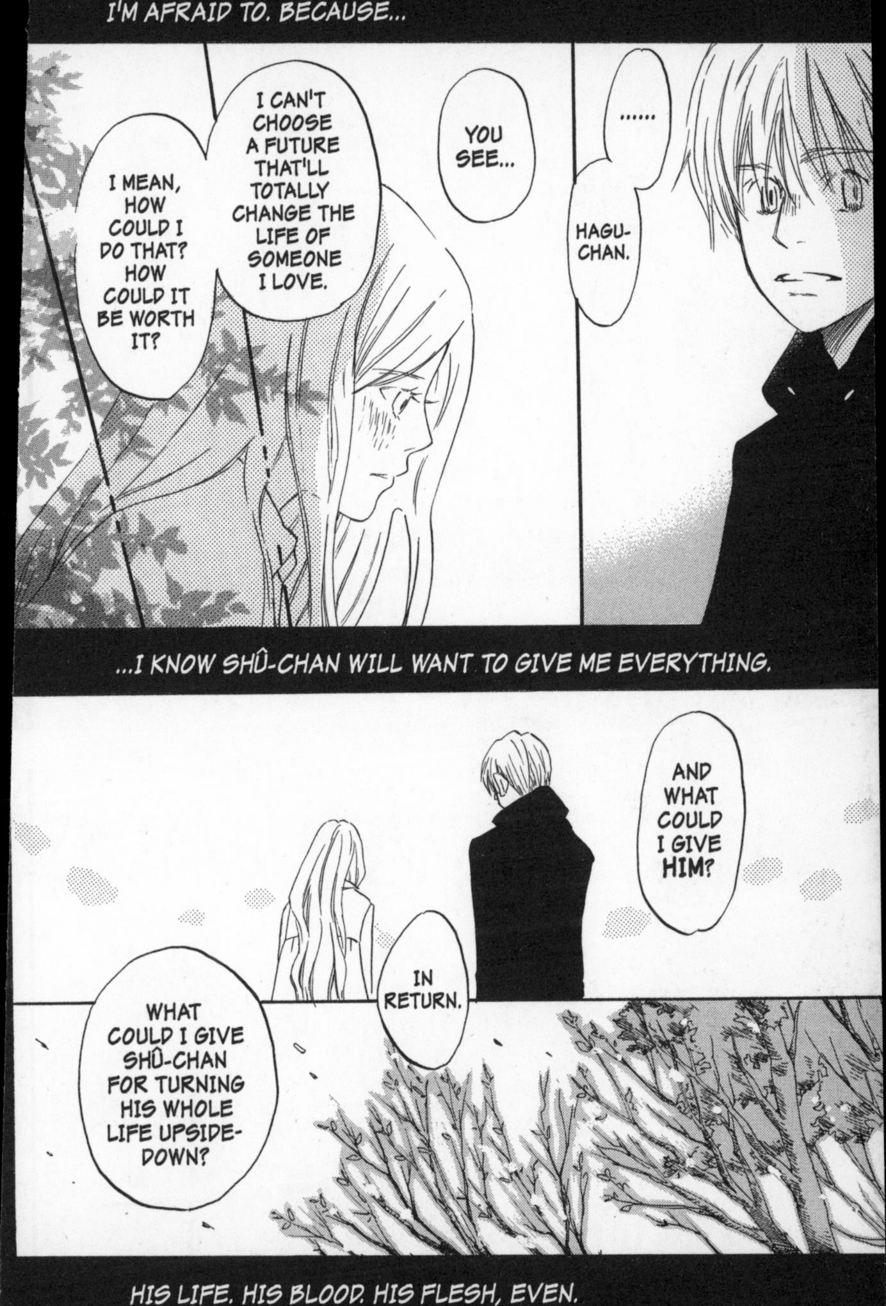
I'M AFRAID TO. BECAUSE...
......
HAGU-CHAN.
YOU SEE...
I CAN'T CHOOSE A FUTURE THAT'LL TOTALLY CHANGE THE LIFE OF SOMEONE I LOVE.
I MEAN, HOW COULD I DO THAT? HOW COULD IT BE WORTH IT?
...I KNOW SHÛ-CHAN WILL WANT TO GIVE ME EVERYTHING.
AND WHAT COULD I GIVE HIM?
IN RETURN.
WHAT COULD I GIVE SHÛ-CHAN FOR TURNING HIS WHOLE LIFE UPSIDE-DOWN?
HIS LIFE. HIS BLOOD. HIS FLESH, EVEN.

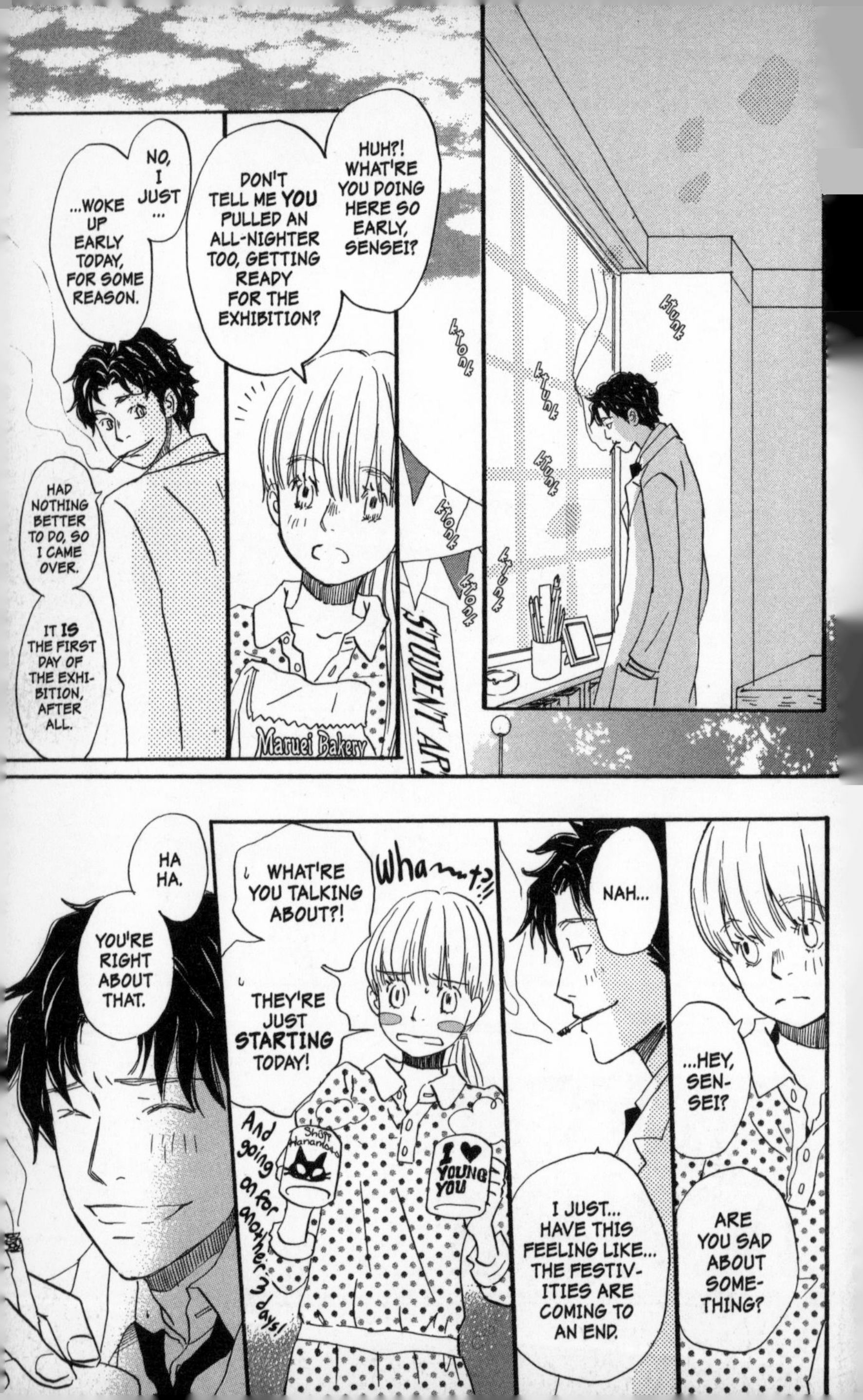
ktunk
ktunk
ktunk
ktunk
ktunk
ktunk
ktunk
HUH?! WHAT'RE YOU DOING HERE SO EARLY, SENSEI?
DON'T TELL ME YOU PULLED AN ALL-NIGHTER TOO, GETTING READY FOR THE EXHIBITION?
Maruei Bakery
NO, I JUST...
...WOKE UP EARLY TODAY, FOR SOME REASON.
HAD NOTHING BETTER TO DO, SO I CAME OVER.
IT IS THE FIRST DAY OF THE EXHIBITION, AFTER ALL.
...HEY, SEN-SEI?
ARE YOU SAD ABOUT SOME-THING?
NAH...
I JUST... HAVE THIS FEELING LIKE... THE FESTIV-ITIES ARE COMING TO AN END.
Whaaat?!
WHAT'RE YOU TALKING ABOUT?!
THEY'RE JUST STARTING TODAY!
And going on for another 3 days!
I ♥ YOUNG YOU
HA HA.
YOU'RE RIGHT ABOUT THAT.

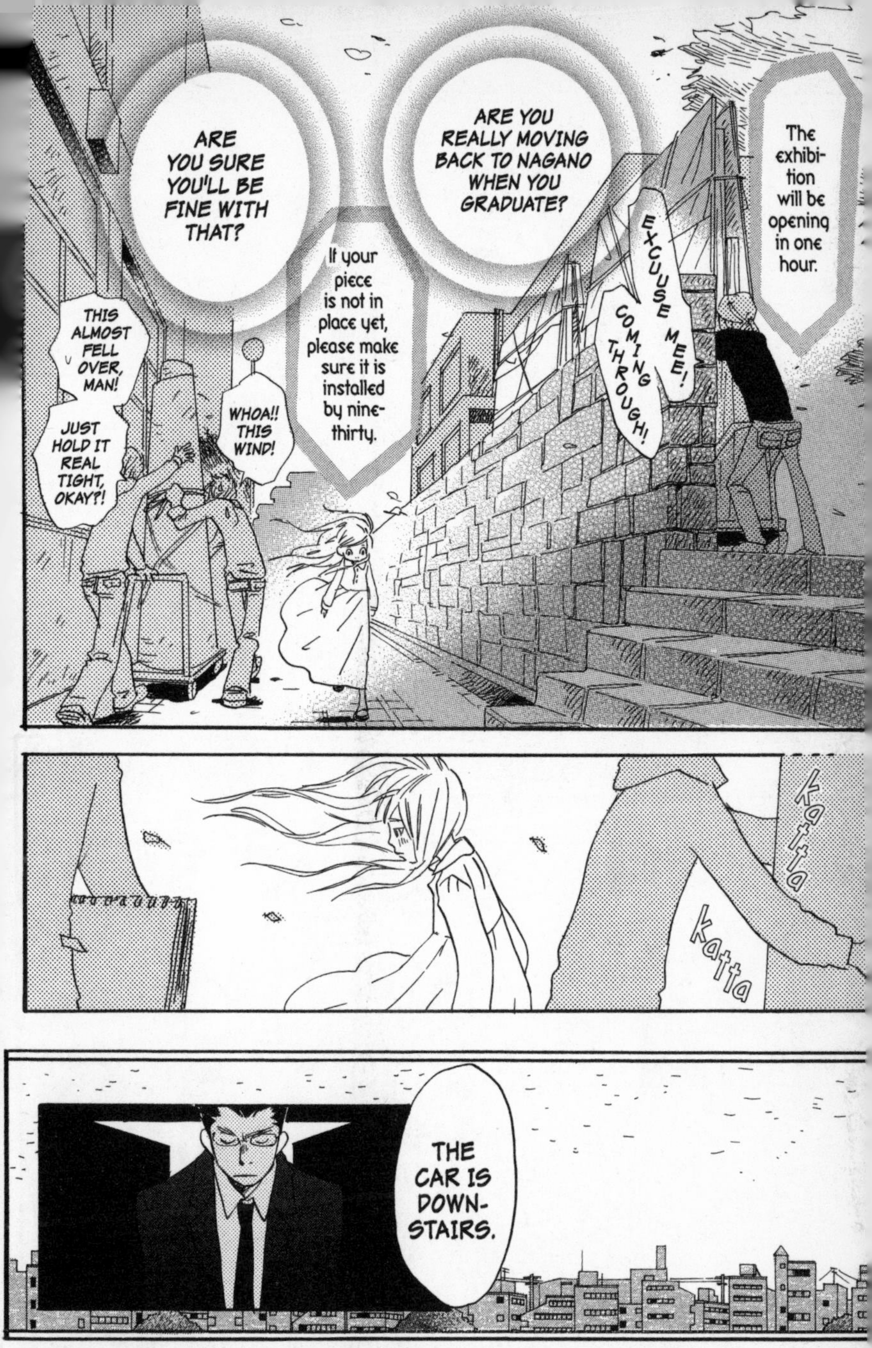
The exhibition will be opening in one hour.
EXCUSE MEE! COMING THROUGH!
ARE YOU REALLY MOVING BACK TO NAGANO WHEN YOU GRADUATE?
If your piece is not in place yet, please make sure it is installed by nine-thirty.
ARE YOU SURE YOU'LL BE FINE WITH THAT?
WHOA!! THIS WIND!
THIS ALMOST FELL OVER, MAN!
JUST HOLD IT REAL TIGHT, OKAY?!
katta
katta
THE CAR IS DOWNSTAIRS.

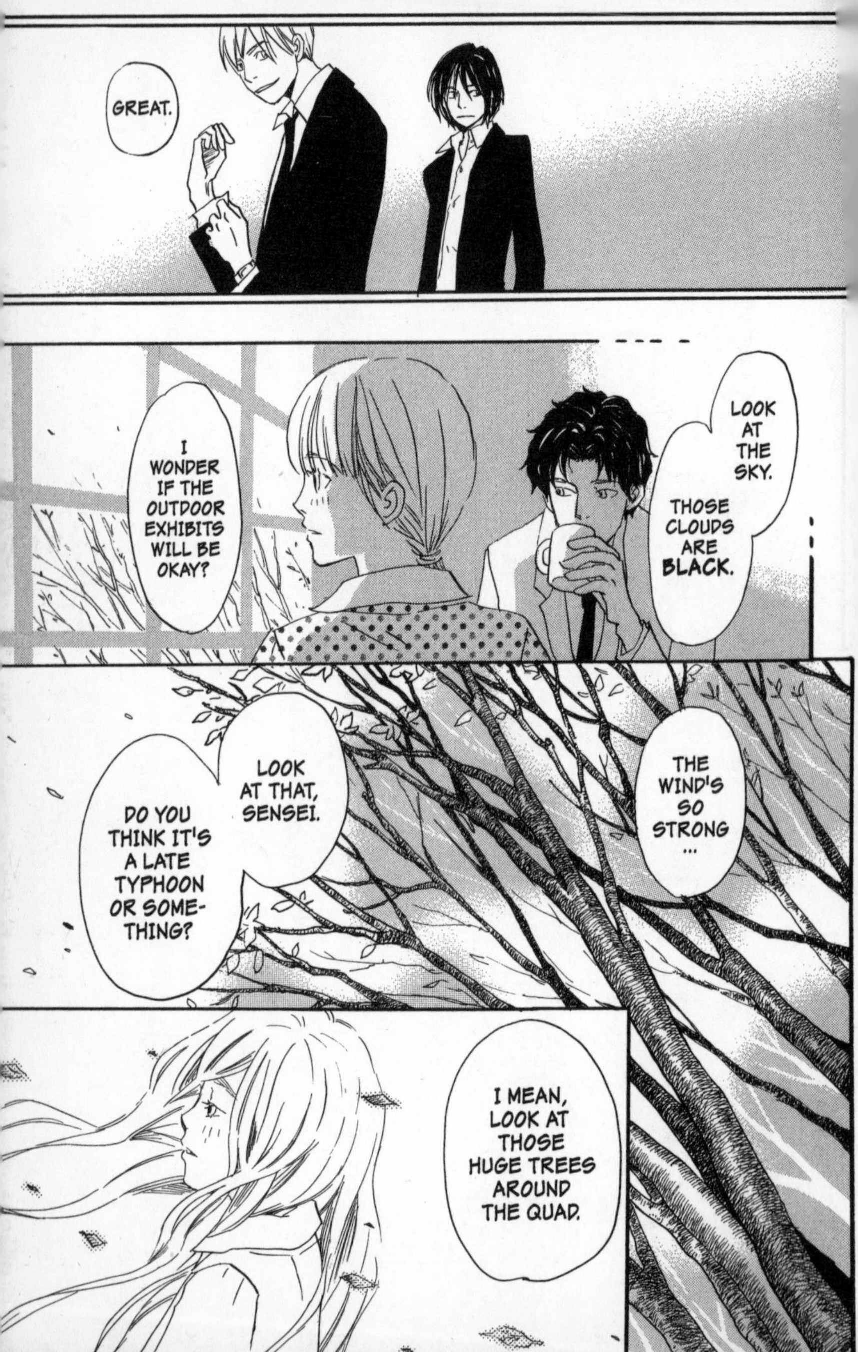
GREAT.
LOOK AT THE SKY.
THOSE CLOUDS ARE BLACK.
I WONDER IF THE OUTDOOR EXHIBITS WILL BE OKAY?
THE WIND'S SO STRONG ...
LOOK AT THAT, SENSEI.
DO YOU THINK IT'S A LATE TYPHOON OR SOME-THING?
I MEAN, LOOK AT THOSE HUGE TREES AROUND THE QUAD.

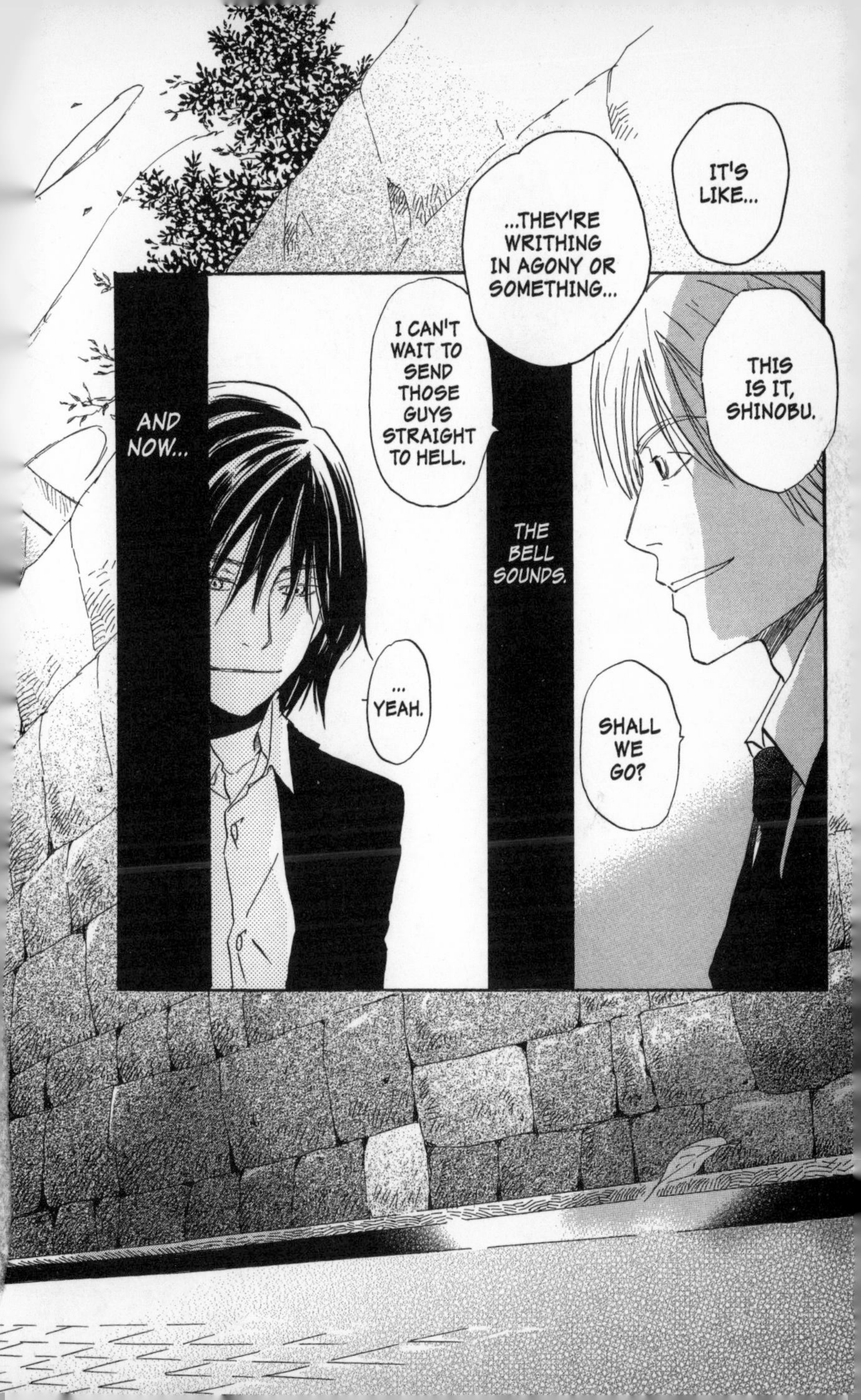
IT'S LIKE...
...THEY'RE WRITHING IN AGONY OR SOMETHING...
THIS IS IT, SHINOBU.
SHALL WE GO?
THE BELL SOUNDS.
I CAN'T WAIT TO SEND THOSE GUYS STRAIGHT TO HELL.
... YEAH.
AND NOW...

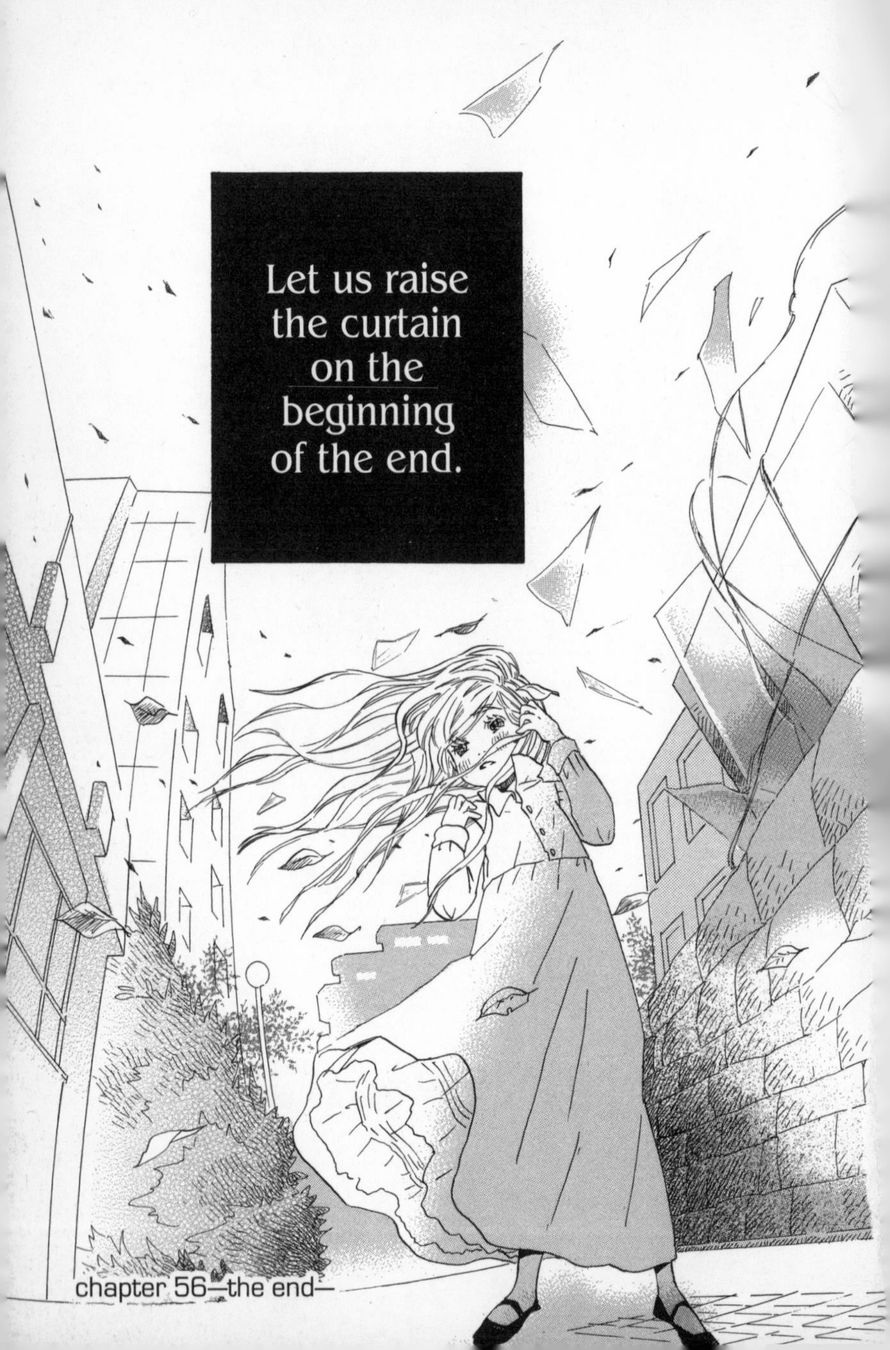
Let us raise the curtain on the beginning of the end.
chapter 56—the end—

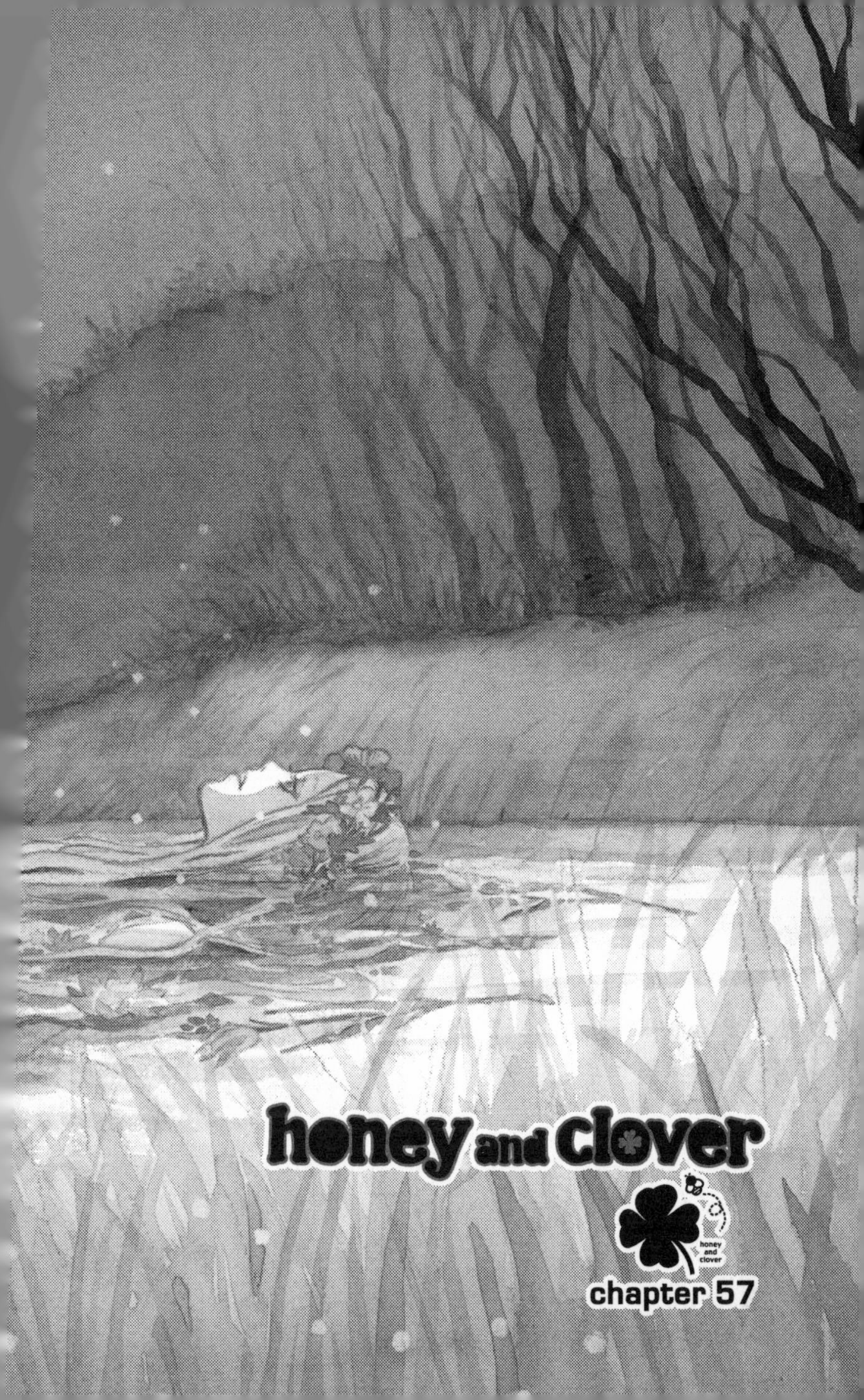
honey and clover
honey and clover
chapter 57

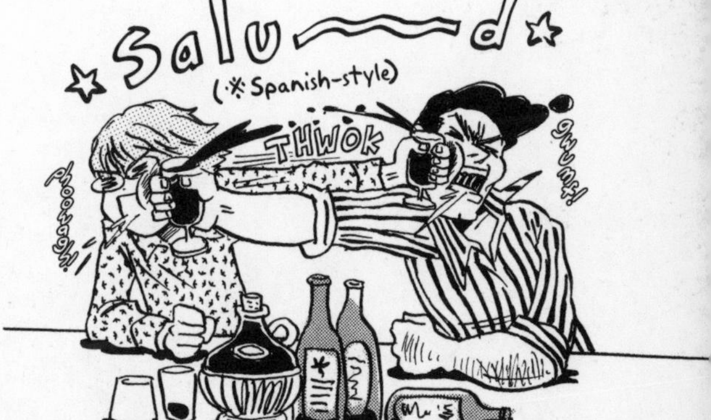
☆Salu——d☆
(※Spanish-style)
THWOK
gwumf!
phooowagh!
Our two cozy drinking amigos.☆

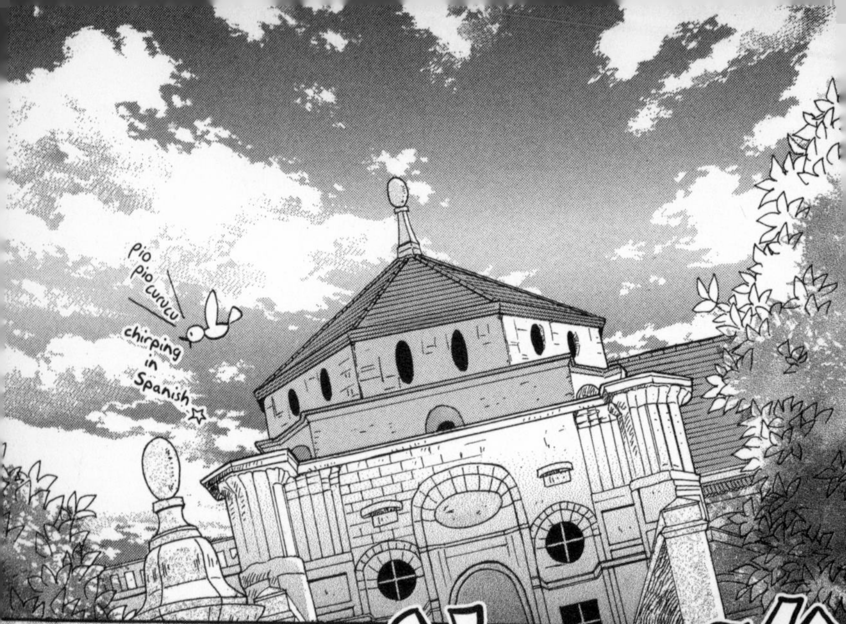
Pio pio curucu
chirping in Spanish

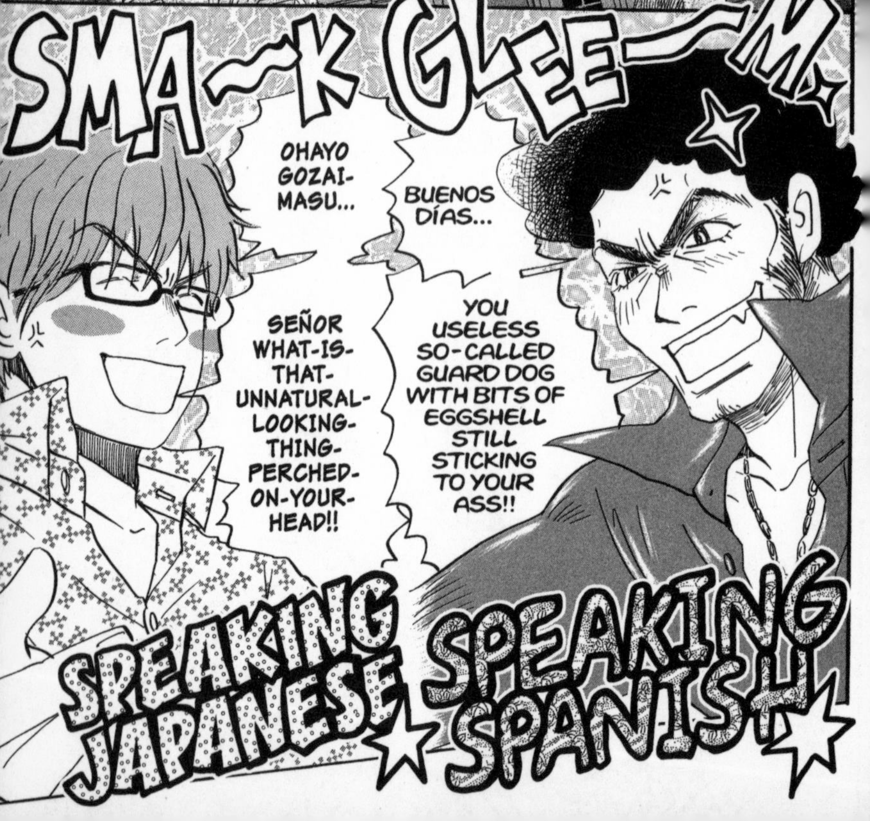
SMA~K GLEE~M.
BUENOS DÍAS...
OHAYO GOZAI-MASU...
YOU USELESS SO-CALLED GUARD DOG WITH BITS OF EGGSHELL STILL STICKING TO YOUR ASS!!
SEÑOR WHAT-IS-THAT-UNNATURAL-LOOKING-THING-PERCHED-ON-YOUR-HEAD!!
SPEAKING SPANISH
SPEAKING JAPANESE

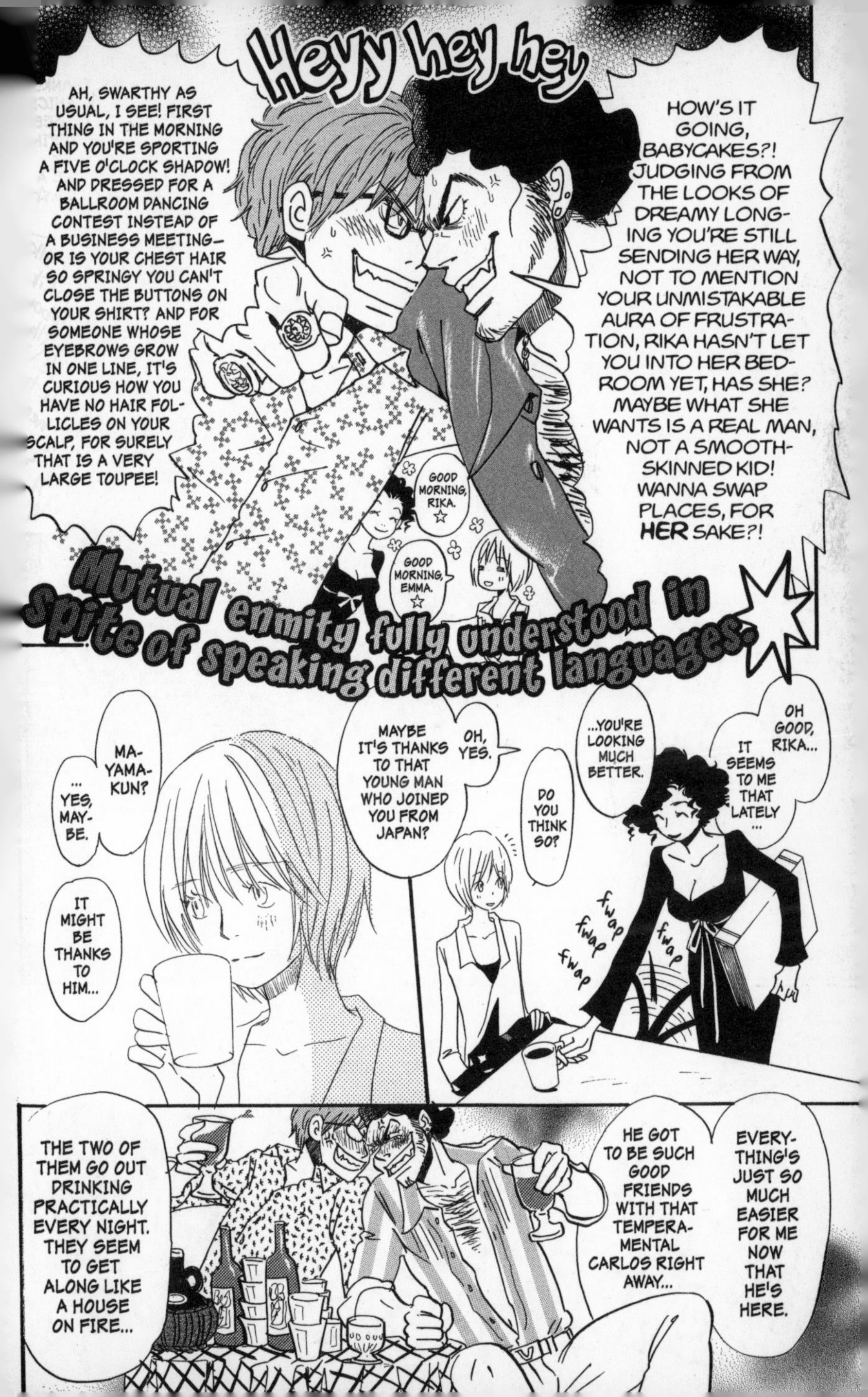
Heyy hey hey
HOW'S IT GOING, BABYCAKES?! JUDGING FROM THE LOOKS OF DREAMY LONGING YOU'RE STILL SENDING HER WAY, NOT TO MENTION YOUR UNMISTAKABLE AURA OF FRUSTRATION, RIKA HASN'T LET YOU INTO HER BEDROOM YET, HAS SHE? MAYBE WHAT SHE WANTS IS A REAL MAN, NOT A SMOOTH-SKINNED KID! WANNA SWAP PLACES, FOR HER SAKE?!
AH, SWARTHY AS USUAL, I SEE! FIRST THING IN THE MORNING AND YOU'RE SPORTING A FIVE O'CLOCK SHADOW! AND DRESSED FOR A BALLROOM DANCING CONTEST INSTEAD OF A BUSINESS MEETING—OR IS YOUR CHEST HAIR SO SPRINGY YOU CAN'T CLOSE THE BUTTONS ON YOUR SHIRT? AND FOR SOMEONE WHOSE EYEBROWS GROW IN ONE LINE, IT'S CURIOUS HOW YOU HAVE NO HAIR FOLLICLES ON YOUR SCALP, FOR SURELY THAT IS A VERY LARGE TOUPEE!
GOOD MORNING, RIKA. ☆
GOOD MORNING, EMMA. ☆
Mutual enmity fully understood in spite of speaking different languages.
OH GOOD, RIKA... IT SEEMS TO ME THAT LATELY...
...YOU'RE LOOKING MUCH BETTER.
fwap fwap fwap fwap
DO YOU THINK SO?
OH, YES.
MAYBE IT'S THANKS TO THAT YOUNG MAN WHO JOINED YOU FROM JAPAN?
MAYAMA-KUN?
...YES, MAYBE.
IT MIGHT BE THANKS TO HIM...
EVERYTHING'S JUST SO MUCH EASIER FOR ME NOW THAT HE'S HERE.
HE GOT TO BE SUCH GOOD FRIENDS WITH THAT TEMPERAMENTAL CARLOS RIGHT AWAY...
THE TWO OF THEM GO OUT DRINKING PRACTICALLY EVERY NIGHT. THEY SEEM TO GET ALONG LIKE A HOUSE ON FIRE...

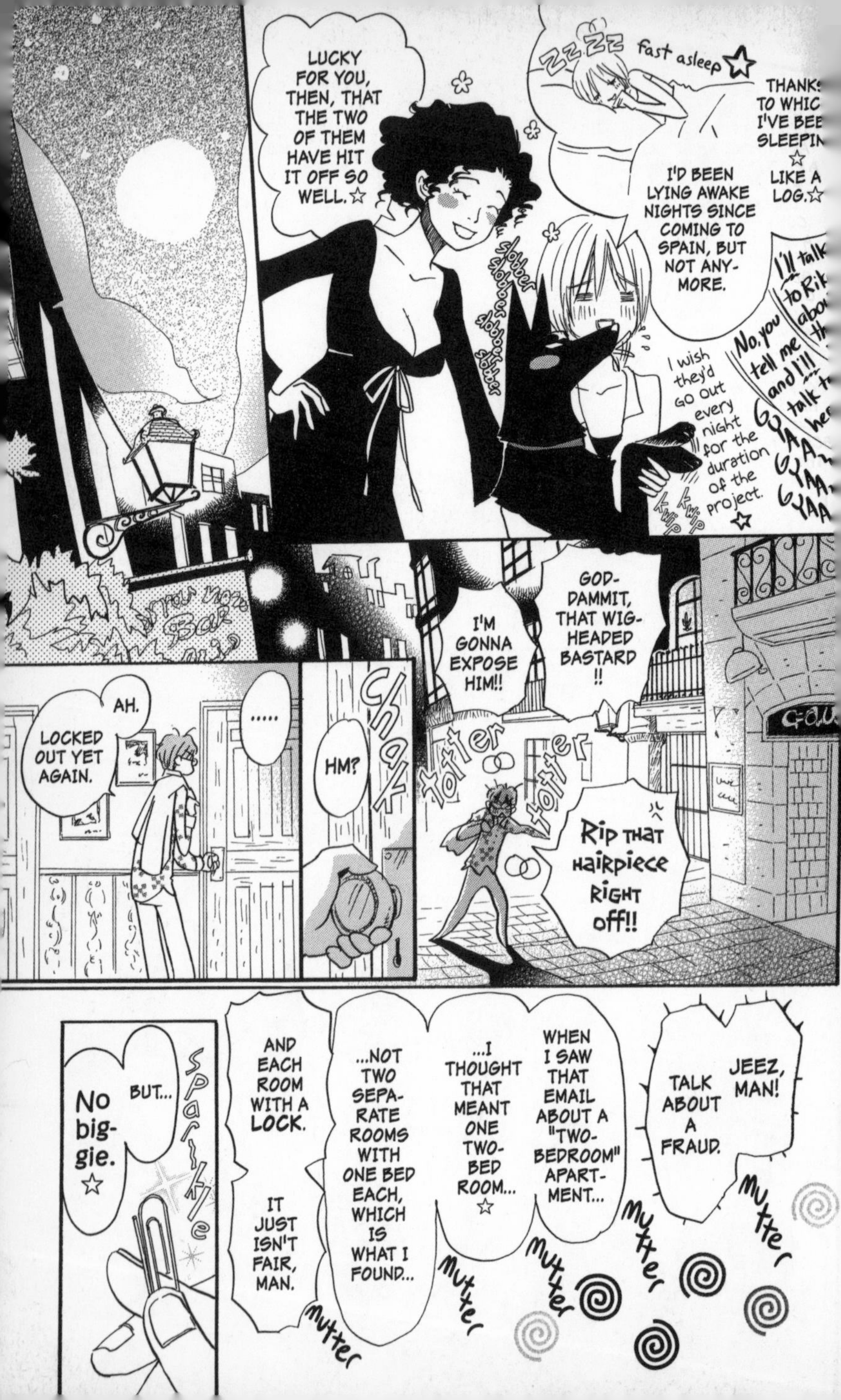
ZZZZ fast asleep ☆
THANKS TO WHIC I'VE BEE SLEEPIN ☆ LIKE A LOG.☆
I'D BEEN LYING AWAKE NIGHTS SINCE COMING TO SPAIN, BUT NOT ANY-MORE.
I'll talk to Rik abo th
No, you tell me and I'll talk t he
YAA YAA YAA
I wish they'd go out every night for the duration of the project. ☆
kwip kwip
slobber slobber slobber slobber
LUCKY FOR YOU, THEN, THAT THE TWO OF THEM HAVE HIT IT OFF SO WELL.☆
GOD-DAMMIT, THAT WIG-HEADED BASTARD !!
I'M GONNA EXPOSE HIM!!
totter totter
Rip THAT HAiRPiECE RiGHT off!!
Chak
HM?
.....
AH.
LOCKED OUT YET AGAIN.
JEEZ, MAN!
TALK ABOUT A FRAUD.
WHEN I SAW THAT EMAIL ABOUT A "TWO-BEDROOM" APART-MENT...
...I THOUGHT THAT MEANT ONE TWO-BED ROOM...☆
...NOT TWO SEPA-RATE ROOMS WITH ONE BED EACH, WHICH IS WHAT I FOUND...
AND EACH ROOM WITH A LOCK.
IT JUST ISN'T FAIR, MAN.
mutter mutter mutter mutter mutter
BUT...
No big-gie. ☆
spar~kle

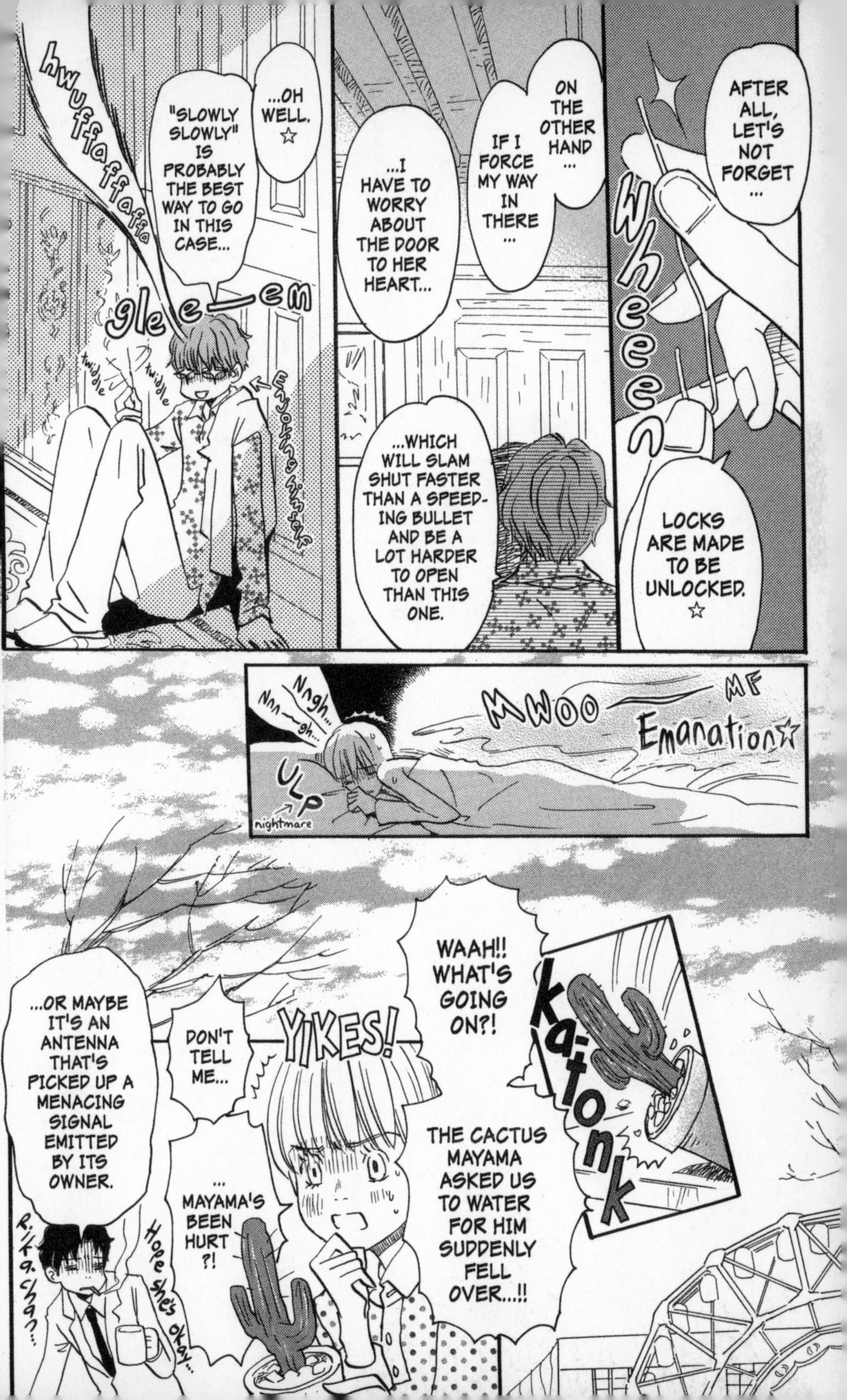
AFTER ALL, LET'S NOT FORGET...
Wheeen
LOCKS ARE MADE TO BE UNLOCKED. ☆
ON THE OTHER HAND...
IF I FORCE MY WAY IN THERE...
...I HAVE TO WORRY ABOUT THE DOOR TO HER HEART...
...WHICH WILL SLAM SHUT FASTER THAN A SPEEDING BULLET AND BE A LOT HARDER TO OPEN THAN THIS ONE.
...OH WELL. ☆
"SLOWLY SLOWLY" IS PROBABLY THE BEST WAY TO GO IN THIS CASE...
hwuffaffaffaffa
gle-e-em
twiddle twiddle
Enjoying himself
MWOO—MF
Emanation☆
Nngh...
Nnn—gh...
ULP
nightmare
WAAH!! WHAT'S GOING ON?!
ka-tonk
THE CACTUS MAYAMA ASKED US TO WATER FOR HIM SUDDENLY FELL OVER...!!
YIKES!
DON'T TELL ME...
...MAYAMA'S BEEN HURT?!
...OR MAYBE IT'S AN ANTENNA THAT'S PICKED UP A MENACING SIGNAL EMITTED BY ITS OWNER.
Hope she's okay...
Rika-chan...

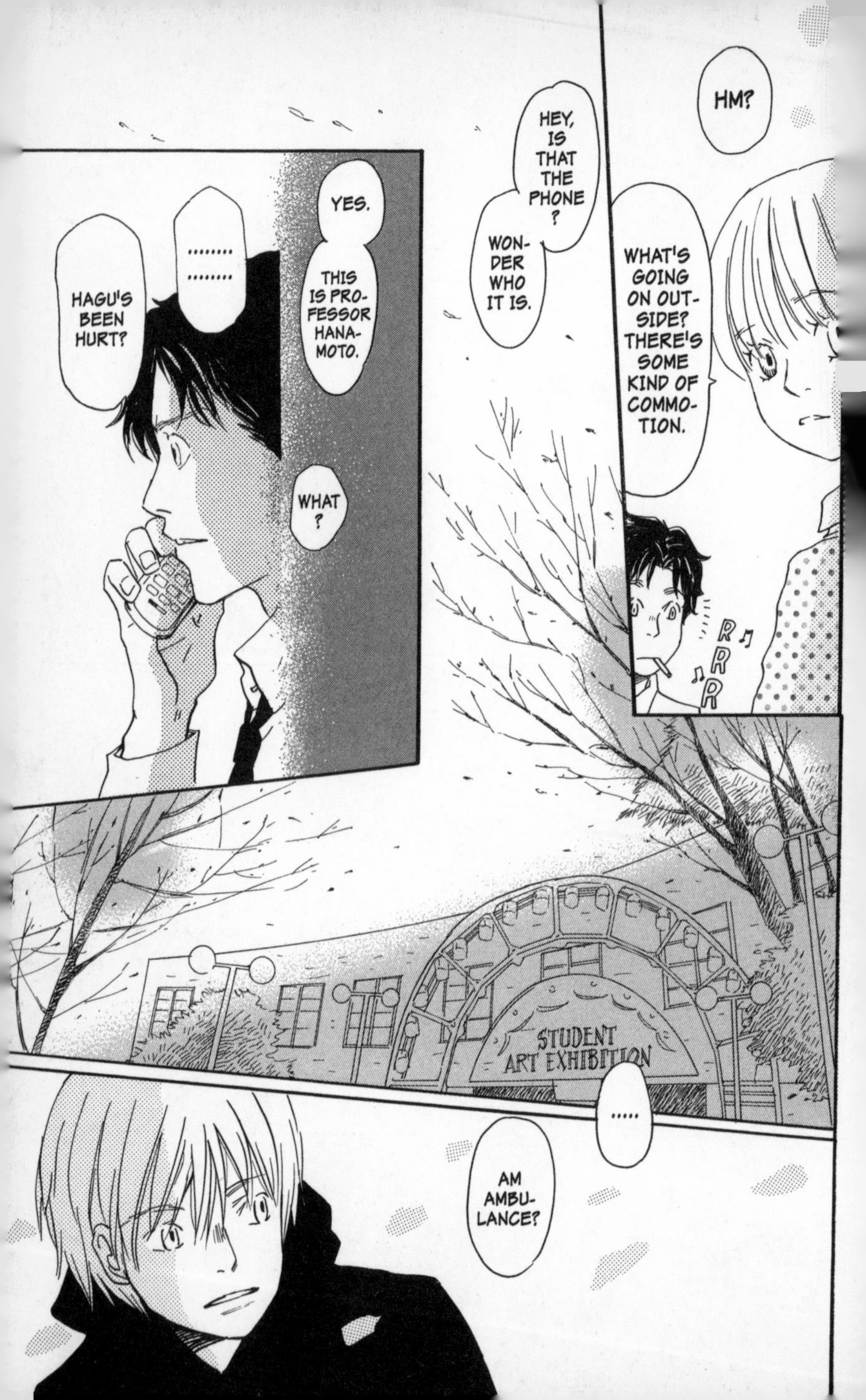
HM?
WHAT'S GOING ON OUTSIDE? THERE'S SOME KIND OF COMMOTION.
RRR
HEY, IS THAT THE PHONE?
WONDER WHO IT IS.
YES.
THIS IS PROFESSOR HANAMOTO.
....
HAGU'S BEEN HURT?
WHAT?
STUDENT ART EXHIBITION
.....
AM AMBULANCE?

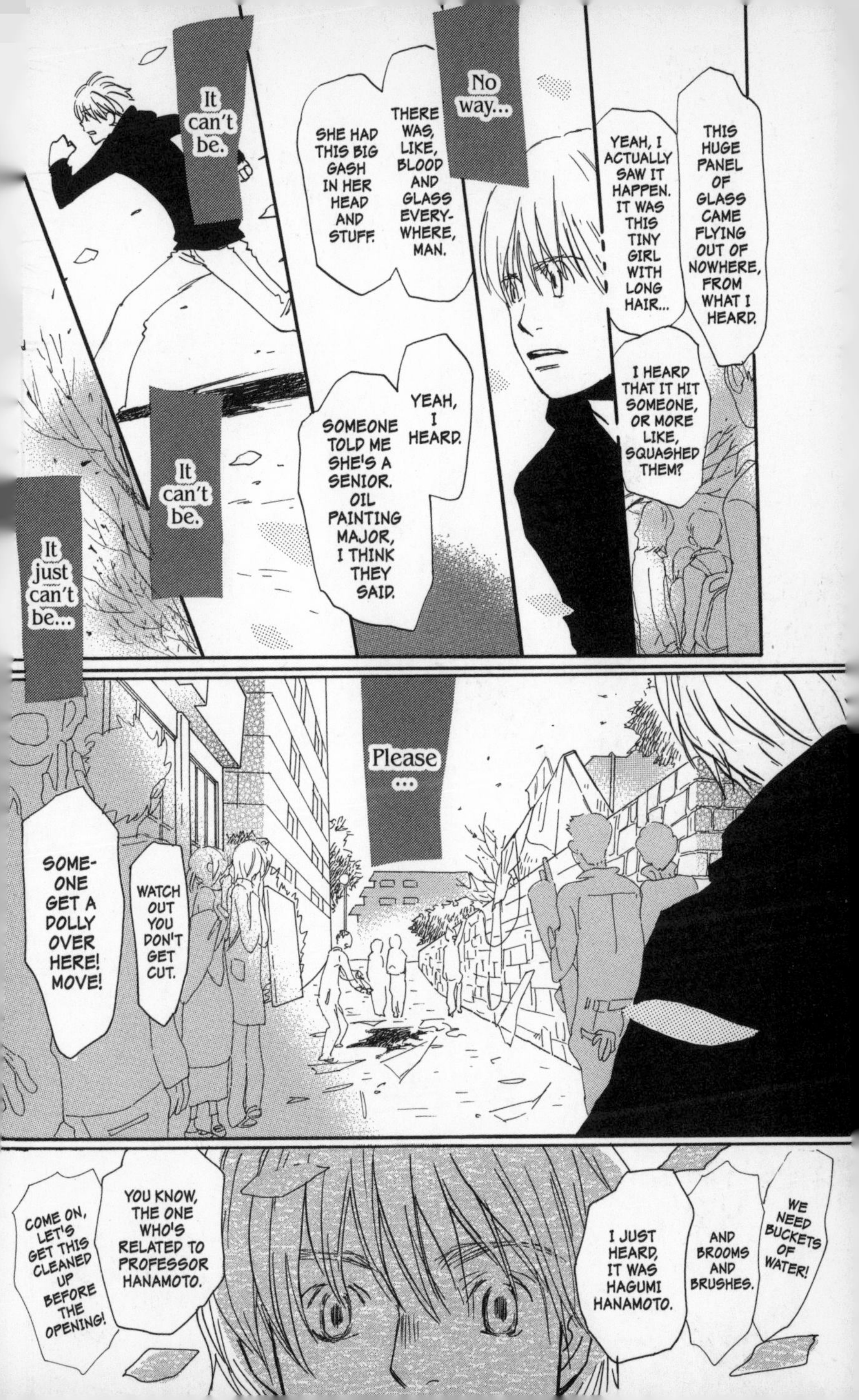
THIS HUGE PANEL OF GLASS CAME FLYING OUT OF NOWHERE, FROM WHAT I HEARD.
YEAH, I ACTUALLY SAW IT HAPPEN. IT WAS THIS TINY GIRL WITH LONG HAIR...
I HEARD THAT IT HIT SOMEONE, OR MORE LIKE, SQUASHED THEM?
No way...
THERE WAS, LIKE, BLOOD AND GLASS EVERY-WHERE, MAN.
SHE HAD THIS BIG GASH IN HER HEAD AND STUFF.
YEAH, I HEARD.
SOMEONE TOLD ME SHE'S A SENIOR. OIL PAINTING MAJOR, I THINK THEY SAID.
It can't be.
It can't be.
It just can't be...
Please ...
WATCH OUT YOU DON'T GET CUT.
SOME-ONE GET A DOLLY OVER HERE! MOVE!
WE NEED BUCKETS OF WATER!
AND BROOMS AND BRUSHES.
I JUST HEARD, IT WAS HAGUMI HANAMOTO.
YOU KNOW, THE ONE WHO'S RELATED TO PROFESSOR HANAMOTO.
COME ON, LET'S GET THIS CLEANED UP BEFORE THE OPENING!

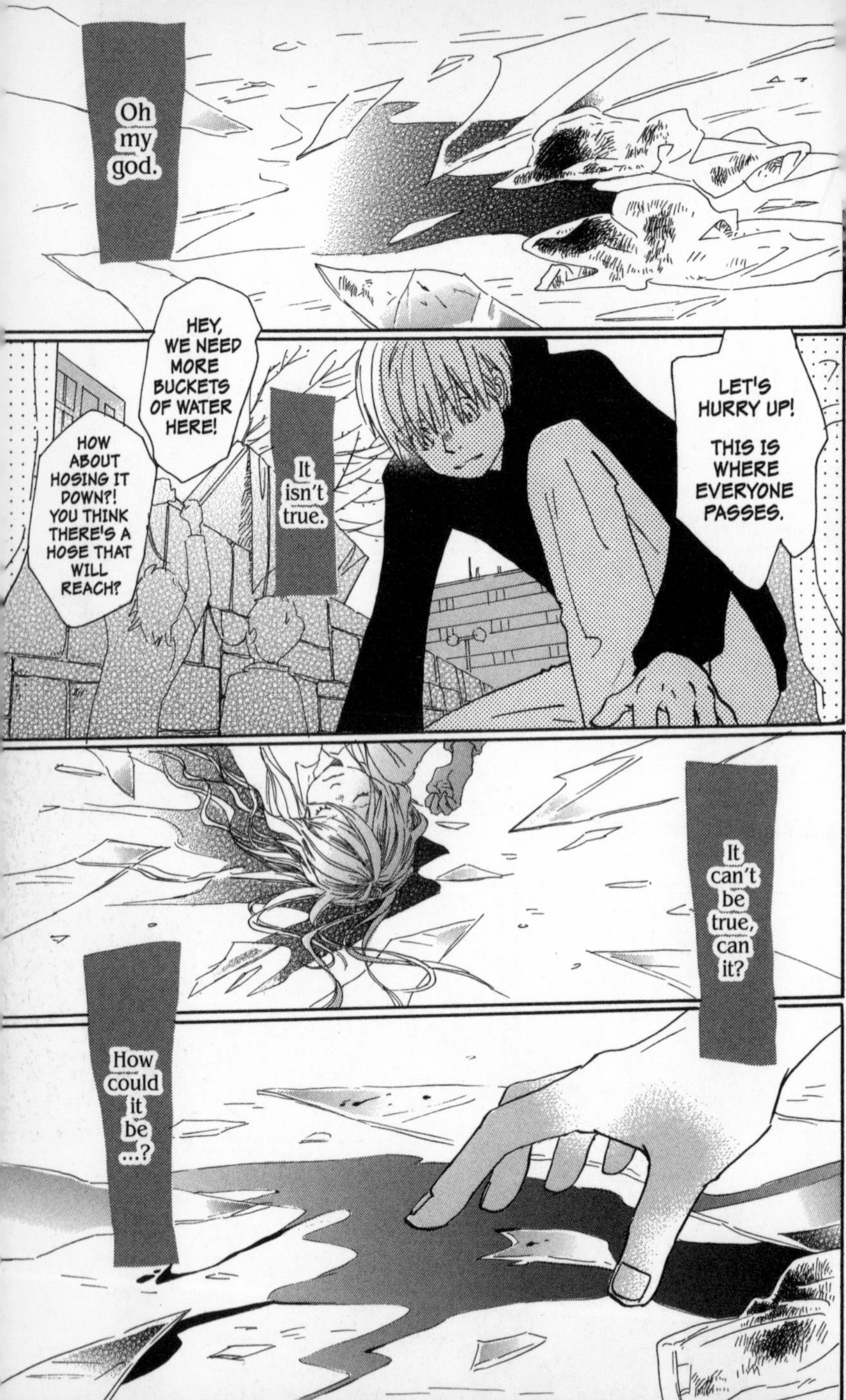
Oh my god.
LET'S HURRY UP!
THIS IS WHERE EVERYONE PASSES.
It isn't true.
HEY, WE NEED MORE BUCKETS OF WATER HERE!
HOW ABOUT HOSING IT DOWN?! YOU THINK THERE'S A HOSE THAT WILL REACH?
It can't be true, can it?
How could it be ...?

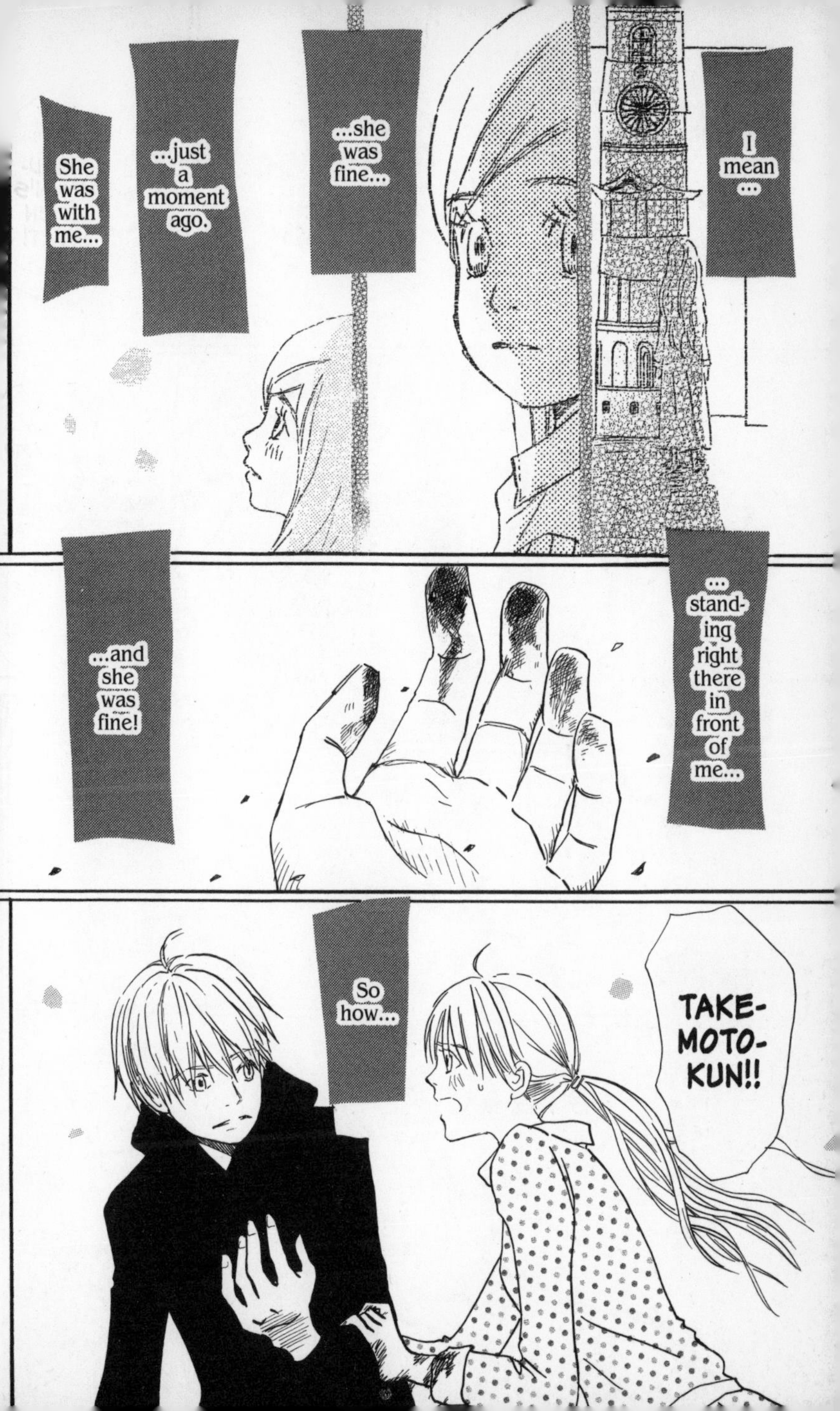
I mean...
...she was fine...
...just a moment ago.
She was with me...
...standing right there in front of me...
...and she was fine!
TAKEMOTO-KUN!!
So how...

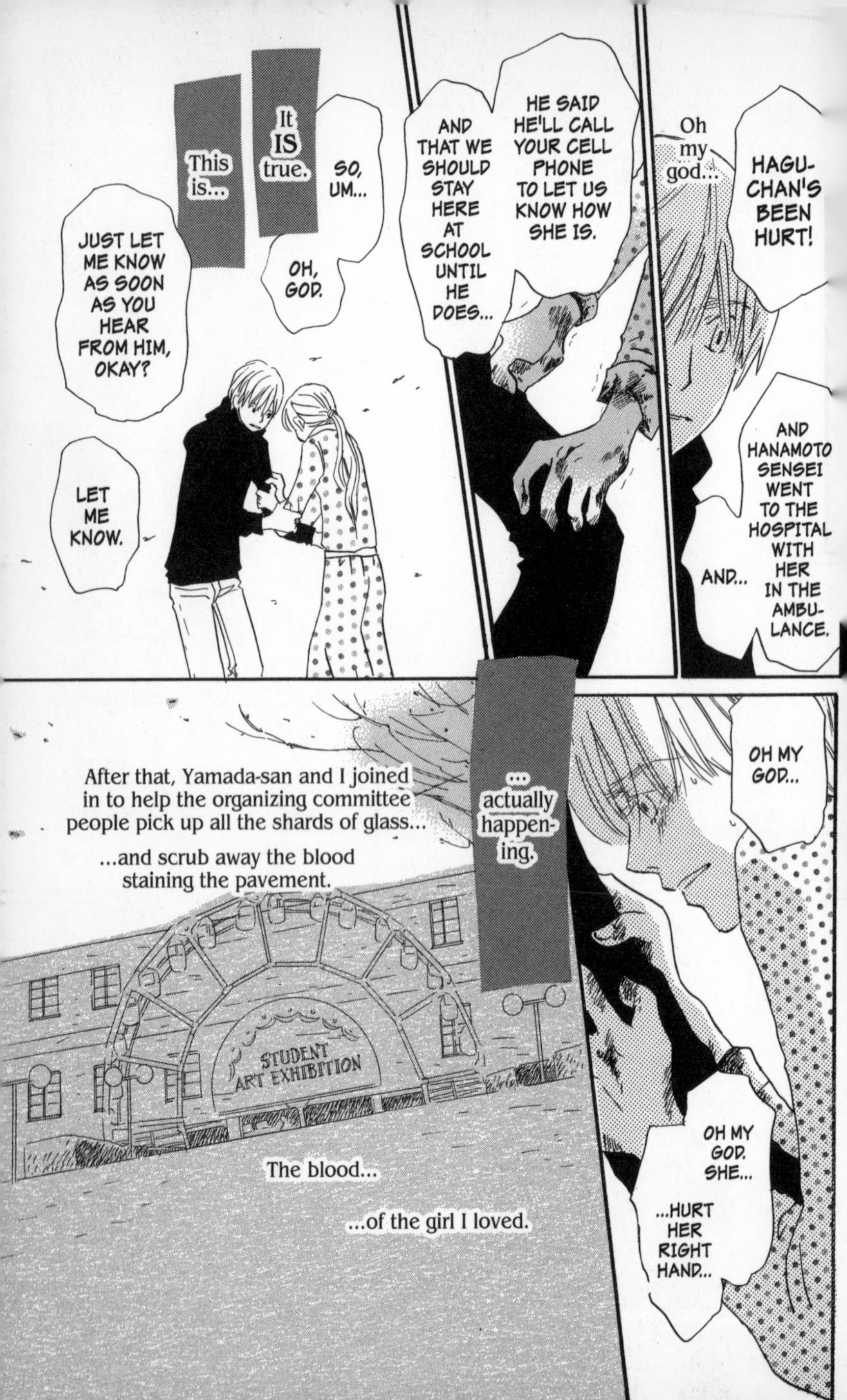
HAGU-CHAN'S BEEN HURT!
Oh my god...
AND HANAMOTO SENSEI WENT TO THE HOSPITAL WITH HER IN THE AMBULANCE.
AND...
HE SAID HE'LL CALL YOUR CELL PHONE TO LET US KNOW HOW SHE IS.
AND THAT WE SHOULD STAY HERE AT SCHOOL UNTIL HE DOES...
It IS true.
This is...
SO, UM...
OH, GOD.
JUST LET ME KNOW AS SOON AS YOU HEAR FROM HIM, OKAY?
LET ME KNOW.
OH MY GOD...
OH MY GOD. SHE...
...HURT HER RIGHT HAND...
...actually happening.
After that, Yamada-san and I joined in to help the organizing committee people pick up all the shards of glass...
...and scrub away the blood staining the pavement.
STUDENT ART EXHIBITION
The blood...
...of the girl I loved.

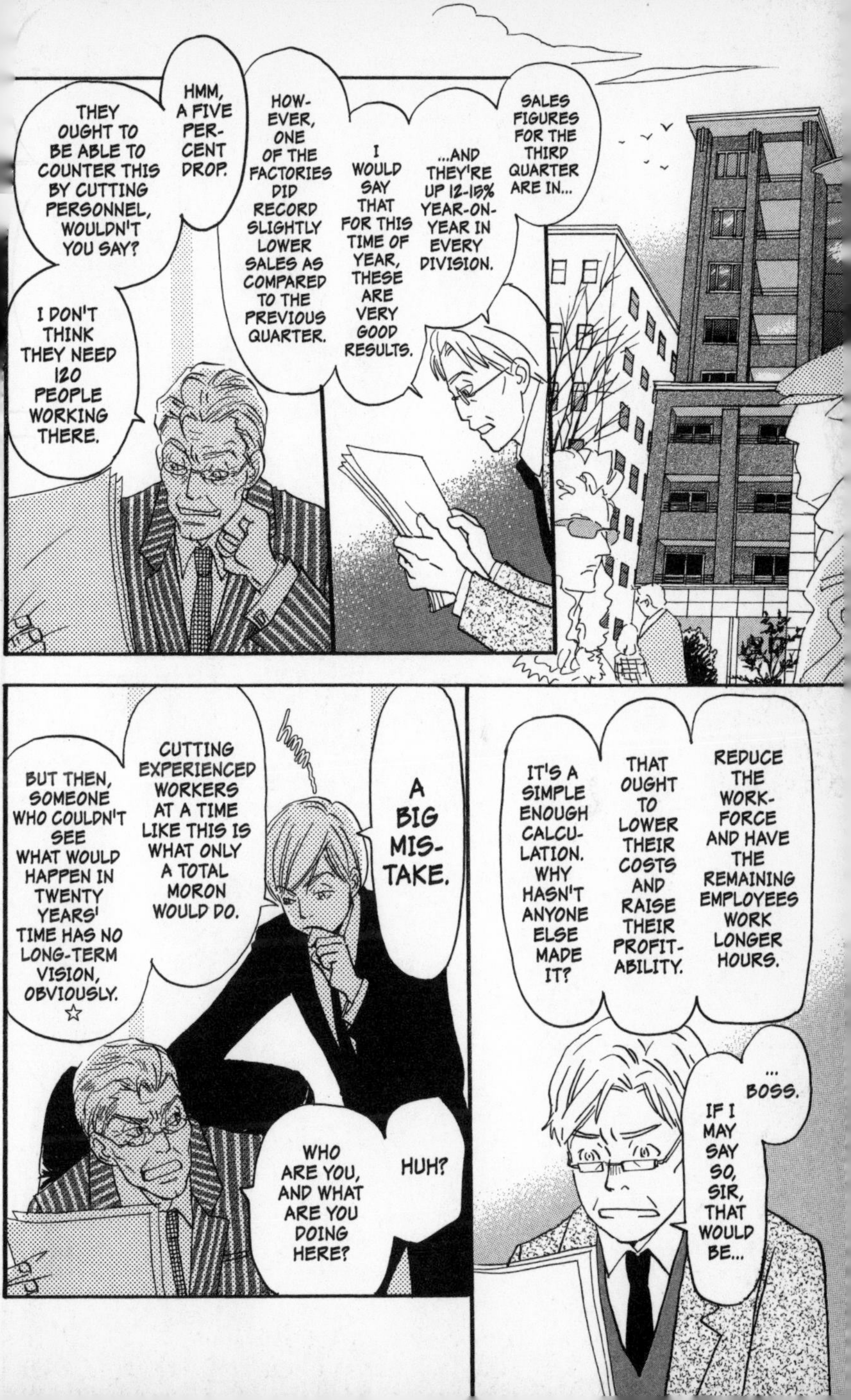
SALES FIGURES FOR THE THIRD QUARTER ARE IN...
...AND THEY'RE UP 12-15% YEAR-ON-YEAR IN EVERY DIVISION.
I WOULD SAY THAT FOR THIS TIME OF YEAR, THESE ARE VERY GOOD RESULTS.
HOW-EVER, ONE OF THE FACTORIES DID RECORD SLIGHTLY LOWER SALES AS COMPARED TO THE PREVIOUS QUARTER.
HMM, A FIVE PER-CENT DROP.
THEY OUGHT TO BE ABLE TO COUNTER THIS BY CUTTING PERSONNEL, WOULDN'T YOU SAY?
I DON'T THINK THEY NEED 120 PEOPLE WORKING THERE.
REDUCE THE WORK-FORCE AND HAVE THE REMAINING EMPLOYEES WORK LONGER HOURS.
THAT OUGHT TO LOWER THEIR COSTS AND RAISE THEIR PROFIT-ABILITY.
IT'S A SIMPLE ENOUGH CALCU-LATION. WHY HASN'T ANYONE ELSE MADE IT?
... BOSS.
IF I MAY SAY SO, SIR, THAT WOULD BE...
A BIG MIS-TAKE.
hmm~
CUTTING EXPERIENCED WORKERS AT A TIME LIKE THIS IS WHAT ONLY A TOTAL MORON WOULD DO.
BUT THEN, SOMEONE WHO COULDN'T SEE WHAT WOULD HAPPEN IN TWENTY YEARS' TIME HAS NO LONG-TERM VISION, OBVIOUSLY. ☆
HUH?
WHO ARE YOU, AND WHAT ARE YOU DOING HERE?

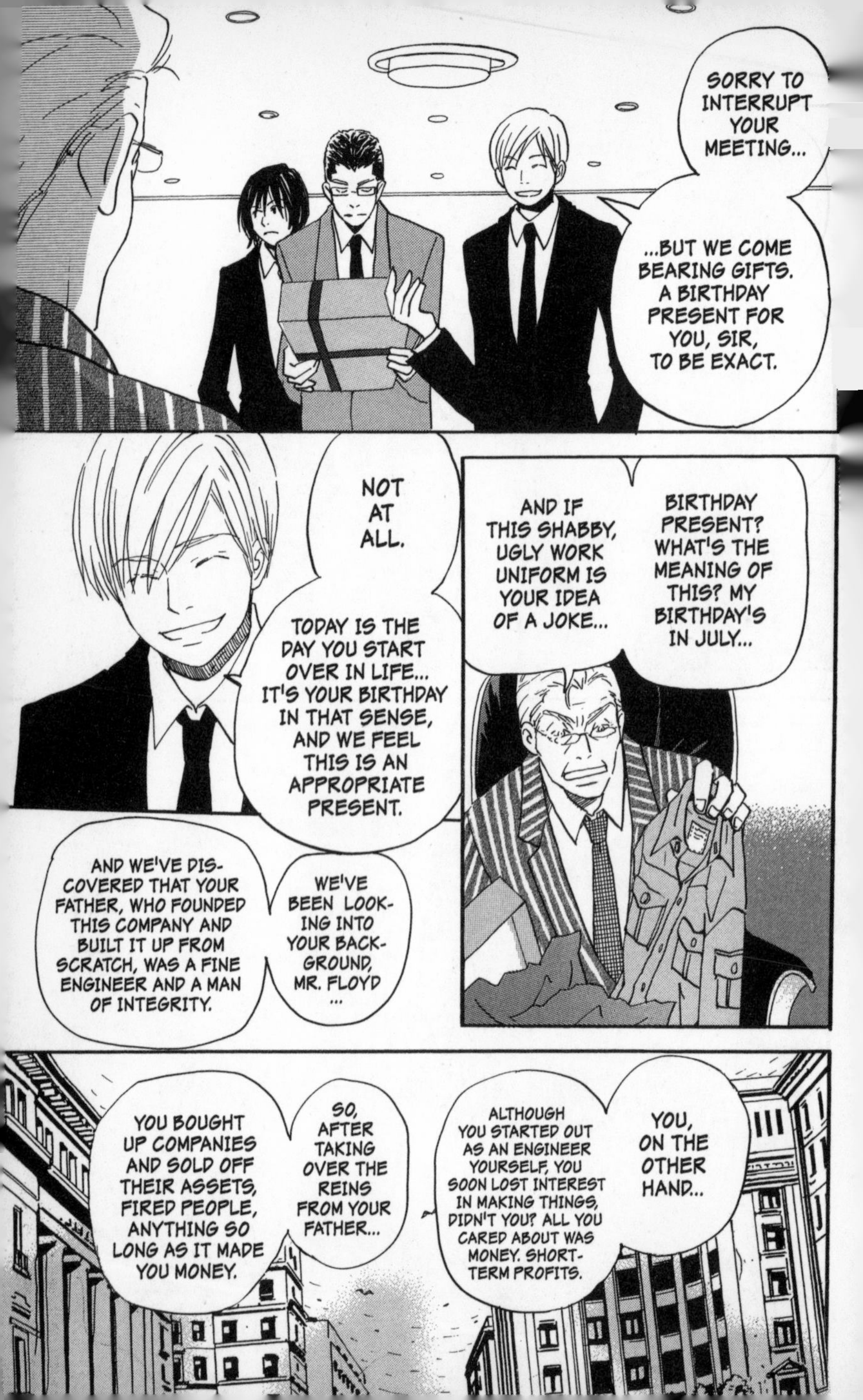
SORRY TO INTERRUPT YOUR MEETING...
...BUT WE COME BEARING GIFTS. A BIRTHDAY PRESENT FOR YOU, SIR, TO BE EXACT.
BIRTHDAY PRESENT? WHAT'S THE MEANING OF THIS? MY BIRTHDAY'S IN JULY...
AND IF THIS SHABBY, UGLY WORK UNIFORM IS YOUR IDEA OF A JOKE...
NOT AT ALL.
TODAY IS THE DAY YOU START OVER IN LIFE... IT'S YOUR BIRTHDAY IN THAT SENSE, AND WE FEEL THIS IS AN APPROPRIATE PRESENT.
WE'VE BEEN LOOKING INTO YOUR BACKGROUND, MR. FLOYD...
AND WE'VE DISCOVERED THAT YOUR FATHER, WHO FOUNDED THIS COMPANY AND BUILT IT UP FROM SCRATCH, WAS A FINE ENGINEER AND A MAN OF INTEGRITY.
YOU, ON THE OTHER HAND...
ALTHOUGH YOU STARTED OUT AS AN ENGINEER YOURSELF, YOU SOON LOST INTEREST IN MAKING THINGS, DIDN'T YOU? ALL YOU CARED ABOUT WAS MONEY. SHORT-TERM PROFITS.
SO, AFTER TAKING OVER THE REINS FROM YOUR FATHER...
YOU BOUGHT UP COMPANIES AND SOLD OFF THEIR ASSETS, FIRED PEOPLE, ANYTHING SO LONG AS IT MADE YOU MONEY.

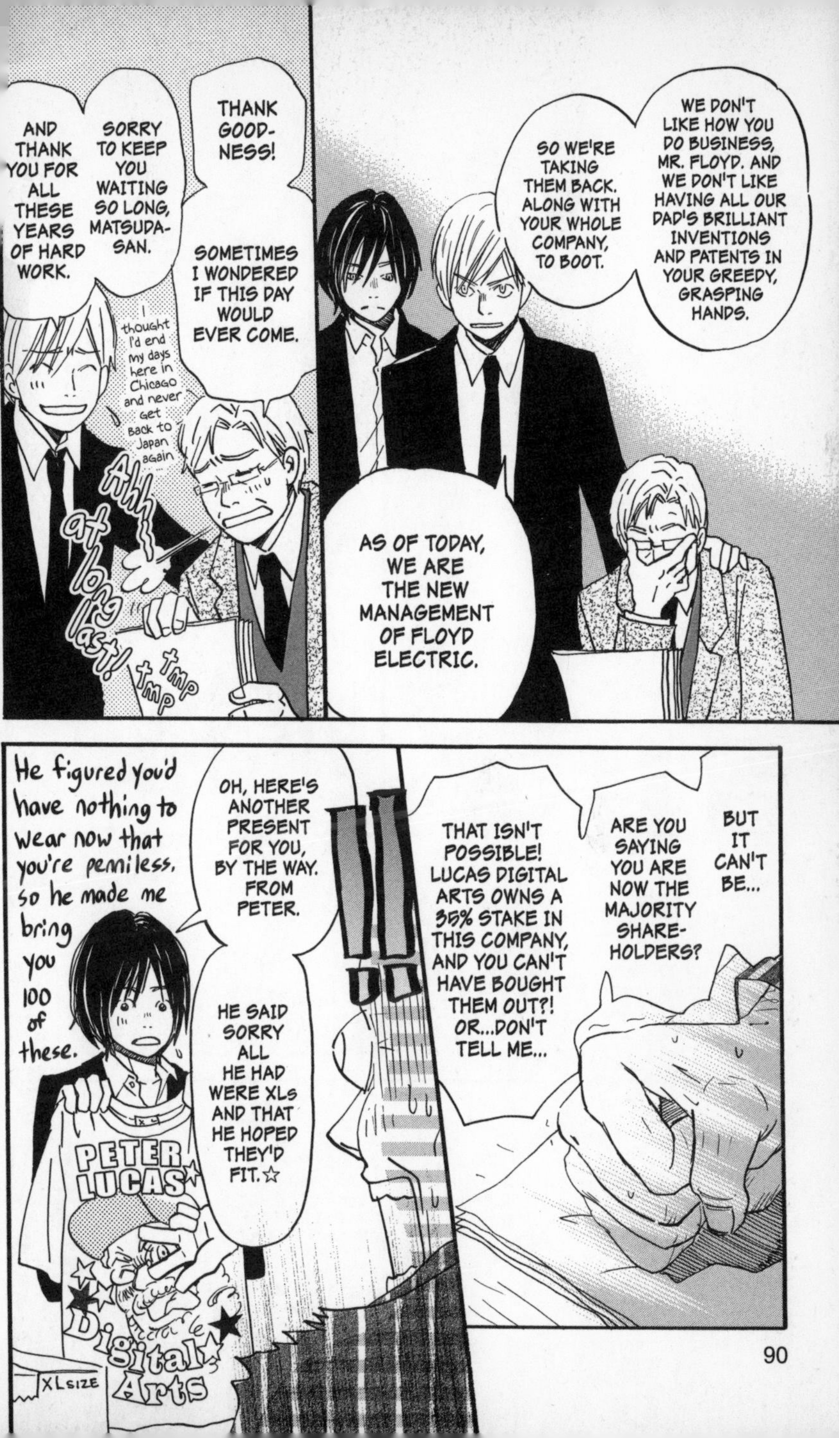
WE DON'T LIKE HOW YOU DO BUSINESS, MR. FLOYD. AND WE DON'T LIKE HAVING ALL OUR DAD'S BRILLIANT INVENTIONS AND PATENTS IN YOUR GREEDY, GRASPING HANDS.
SO WE'RE TAKING THEM BACK. ALONG WITH YOUR WHOLE COMPANY, TO BOOT.
AS OF TODAY, WE ARE THE NEW MANAGEMENT OF FLOYD ELECTRIC.
THANK GOODNESS!
SOMETIMES I WONDERED IF THIS DAY WOULD EVER COME.
I thought I'd end my days here in Chicago and never get back to Japan again...
SORRY TO KEEP YOU WAITING SO LONG, MATSUDA-SAN.
AND THANK YOU FOR ALL THESE YEARS OF HARD WORK.
Ahh~ at long last!
tmp tmp
BUT IT CAN'T BE...
ARE YOU SAYING YOU ARE NOW THE MAJORITY SHARE-HOLDERS?
THAT ISN'T POSSIBLE! LUCAS DIGITAL ARTS OWNS A 35% STAKE IN THIS COMPANY, AND YOU CAN'T HAVE BOUGHT THEM OUT?! OR...DON'T TELL ME...
OH, HERE'S ANOTHER PRESENT FOR YOU, BY THE WAY. FROM PETER.
HE SAID SORRY ALL HE HAD WERE XLs AND THAT HE HOPED THEY'D FIT.☆
He figured you'd have nothing to wear now that you're penniless, so he made me bring you 100 of these.
PETER LUCAS☆
Digital☆ Arts
XL SIZE

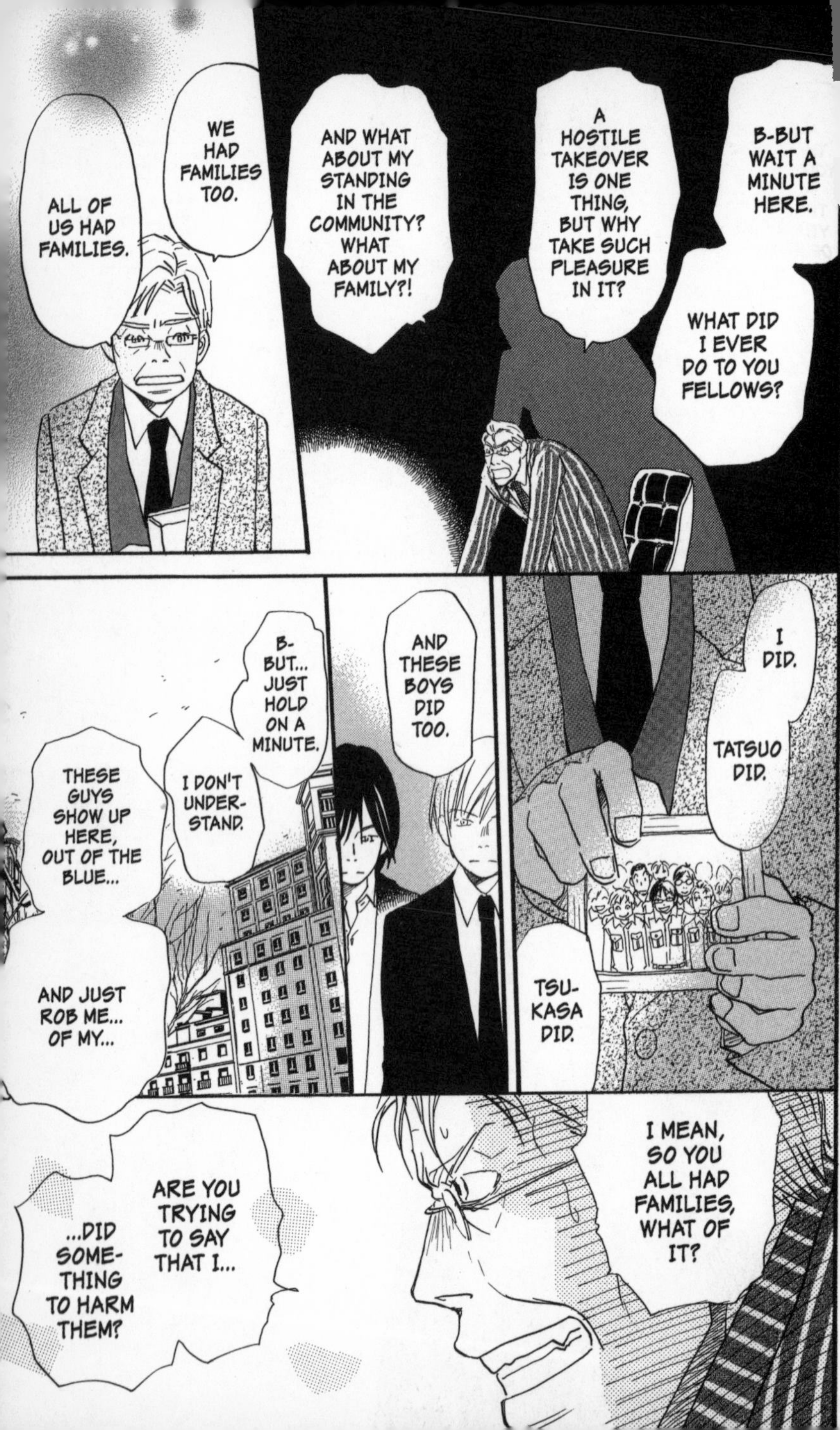
B-BUT WAIT A MINUTE HERE.
A HOSTILE TAKEOVER IS ONE THING, BUT WHY TAKE SUCH PLEASURE IN IT?
WHAT DID I EVER DO TO YOU FELLOWS?
AND WHAT ABOUT MY STANDING IN THE COMMUNITY? WHAT ABOUT MY FAMILY?!
WE HAD FAMILIES TOO.
ALL OF US HAD FAMILIES.
I DID.
TATSUO DID.
TSUKASA DID.
AND THESE BOYS DID TOO.
B-BUT... JUST HOLD ON A MINUTE.
I DON'T UNDERSTAND.
THESE GUYS SHOW UP HERE, OUT OF THE BLUE...
AND JUST ROB ME... OF MY...
I MEAN, SO YOU ALL HAD FAMILIES, WHAT OF IT?
ARE YOU TRYING TO SAY THAT I...
...DID SOMETHING TO HARM THEM?

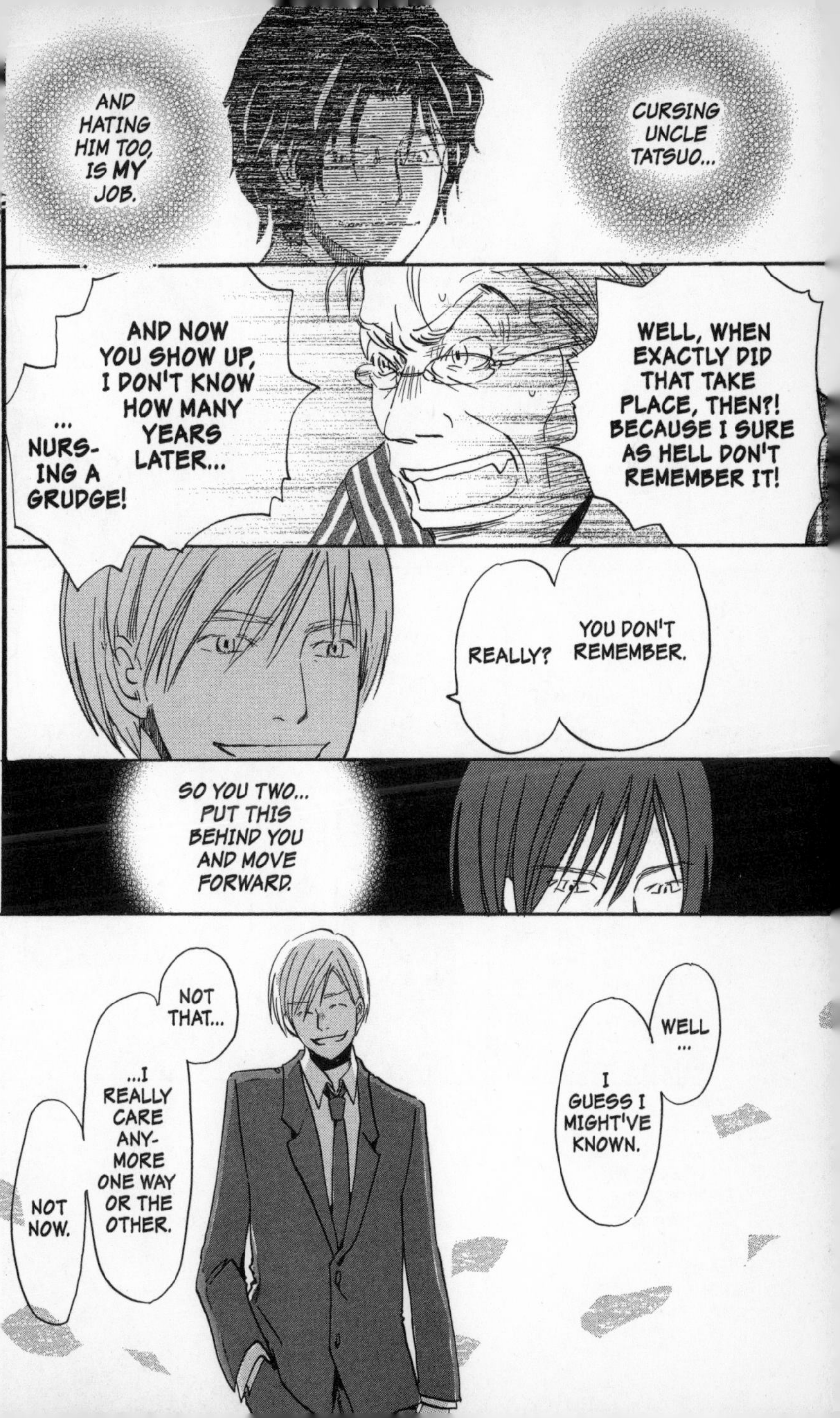
CURSING UNCLE TATSUO...
AND HATING HIM TOO, IS MY JOB.
WELL, WHEN EXACTLY DID THAT TAKE PLACE, THEN?! BECAUSE I SURE AS HELL DON'T REMEMBER IT!
AND NOW YOU SHOW UP, I DON'T KNOW HOW MANY YEARS LATER...
... NURS-ING A GRUDGE!
YOU DON'T REMEMBER.
REALLY?
SO YOU TWO... PUT THIS BEHIND YOU AND MOVE FORWARD.
WELL ...
I GUESS I MIGHT'VE KNOWN.
NOT THAT...
...I REALLY CARE ANY-MORE ONE WAY OR THE OTHER.
NOT NOW.

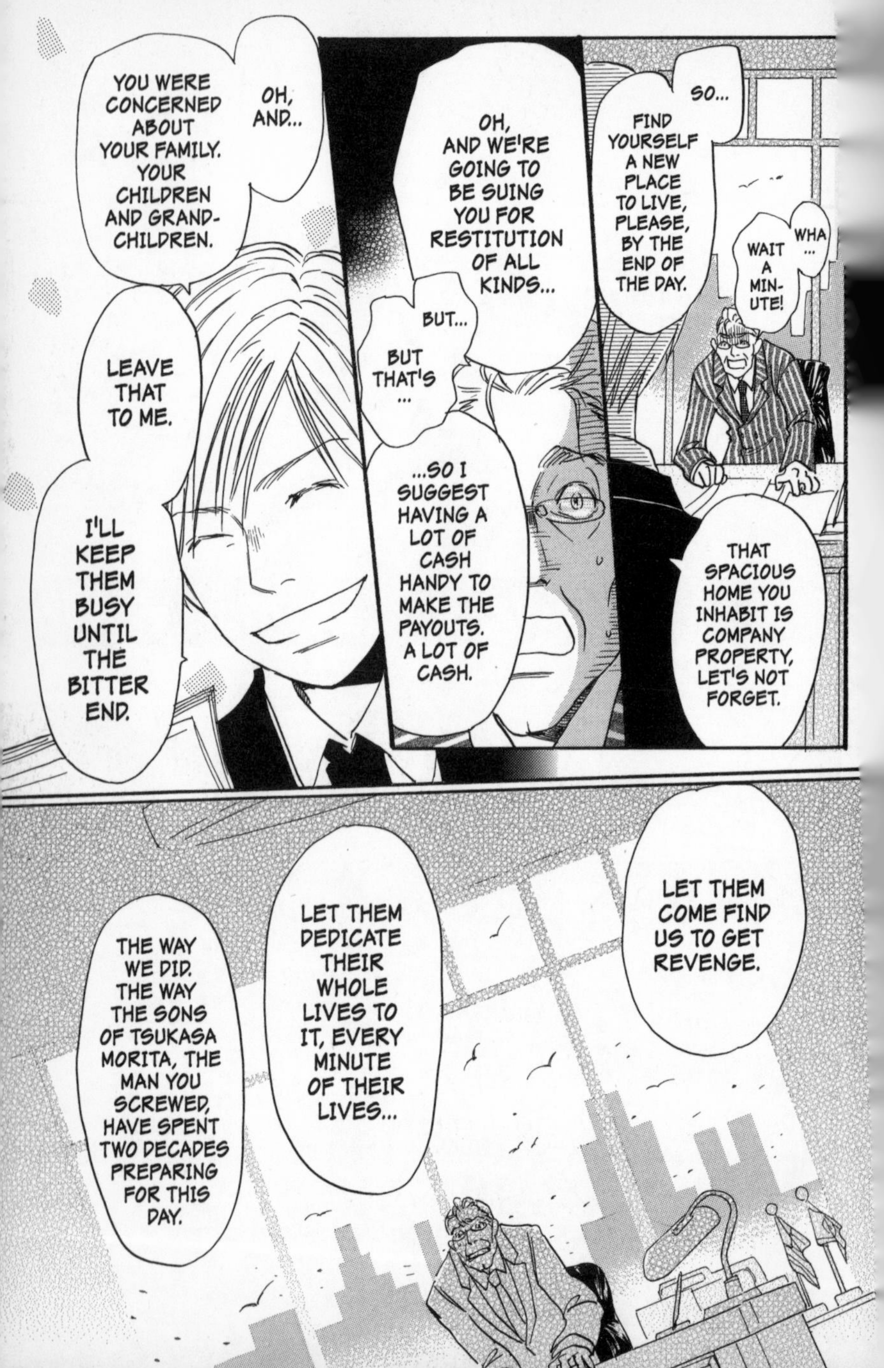
SO...
FIND YOURSELF A NEW PLACE TO LIVE, PLEASE, BY THE END OF THE DAY.
WHA...
WAIT A MINUTE!
THAT SPACIOUS HOME YOU INHABIT IS COMPANY PROPERTY, LET'S NOT FORGET.
OH, AND WE'RE GOING TO BE SUING YOU FOR RESTITUTION OF ALL KINDS...
BUT...
BUT THAT'S ...
...SO I SUGGEST HAVING A LOT OF CASH HANDY TO MAKE THE PAYOUTS. A LOT OF CASH.
OH, AND...
YOU WERE CONCERNED ABOUT YOUR FAMILY. YOUR CHILDREN AND GRANDCHILDREN.
LEAVE THAT TO ME.
I'LL KEEP THEM BUSY UNTIL THE BITTER END.
LET THEM COME FIND US TO GET REVENGE.
LET THEM DEDICATE THEIR WHOLE LIVES TO IT, EVERY MINUTE OF THEIR LIVES...
THE WAY WE DID. THE WAY THE SONS OF TSUKASA MORITA, THE MAN YOU SCREWED, HAVE SPENT TWO DECADES PREPARING FOR THIS DAY.

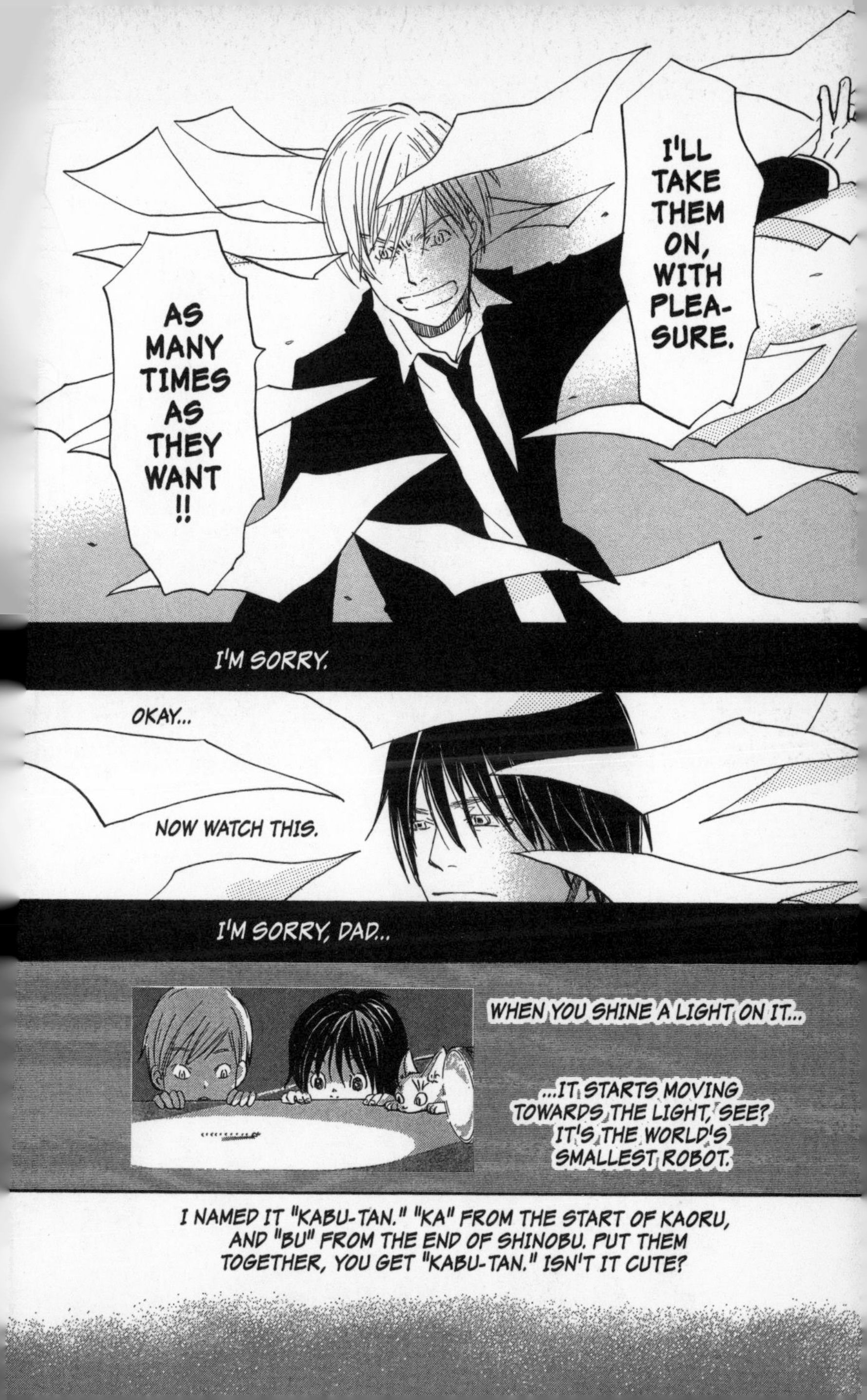
I'LL TAKE THEM ON, WITH PLEASURE.
AS MANY TIMES AS THEY WANT!!
I'M SORRY.
OKAY...
NOW WATCH THIS.
I'M SORRY, DAD...
WHEN YOU SHINE A LIGHT ON IT...
...IT STARTS MOVING TOWARDS THE LIGHT, SEE? IT'S THE WORLD'S SMALLEST ROBOT.
I NAMED IT "KABU-TAN." "KA" FROM THE START OF KAORU, AND "BU" FROM THE END OF SHINOBU. PUT THEM TOGETHER, YOU GET "KABU-TAN." ISN'T IT CUTE?

FOR NOT KEEPING MY PROMISE.

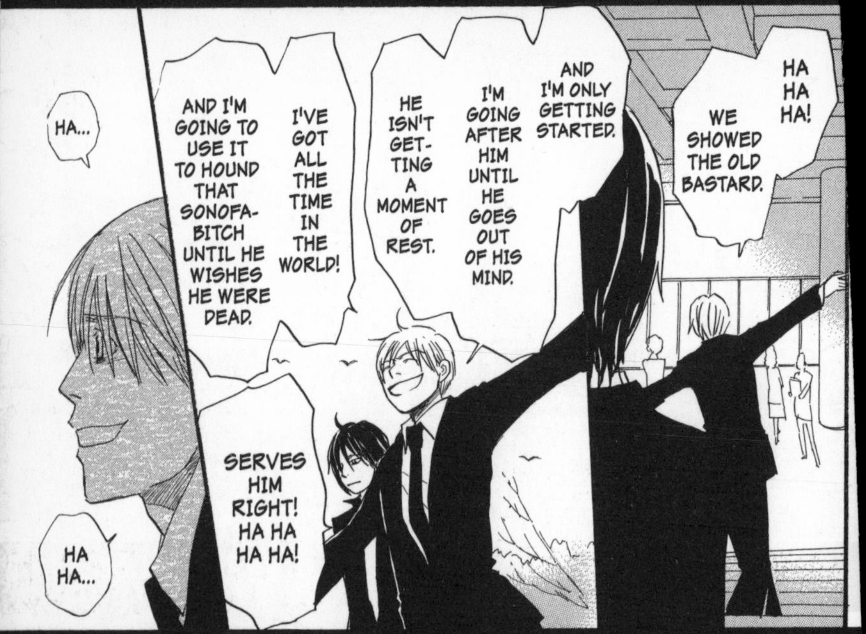
HA HA HA!
WE SHOWED THE OLD BASTARD.
AND I'M ONLY GETTING STARTED.
I'M GOING AFTER HIM UNTIL HE GOES OUT OF HIS MIND.
HE ISN'T GET-TING A MOMENT OF REST.
I'VE GOT ALL THE TIME IN THE WORLD!
AND I'M GOING TO USE IT TO HOUND THAT SONOFA-BITCH UNTIL HE WISHES HE WERE DEAD.
SERVES HIM RIGHT! HA HA HA HA!
HA...
HA HA...

FOR NOT LOOKING AFTER WHAT REALLY MATTERS.

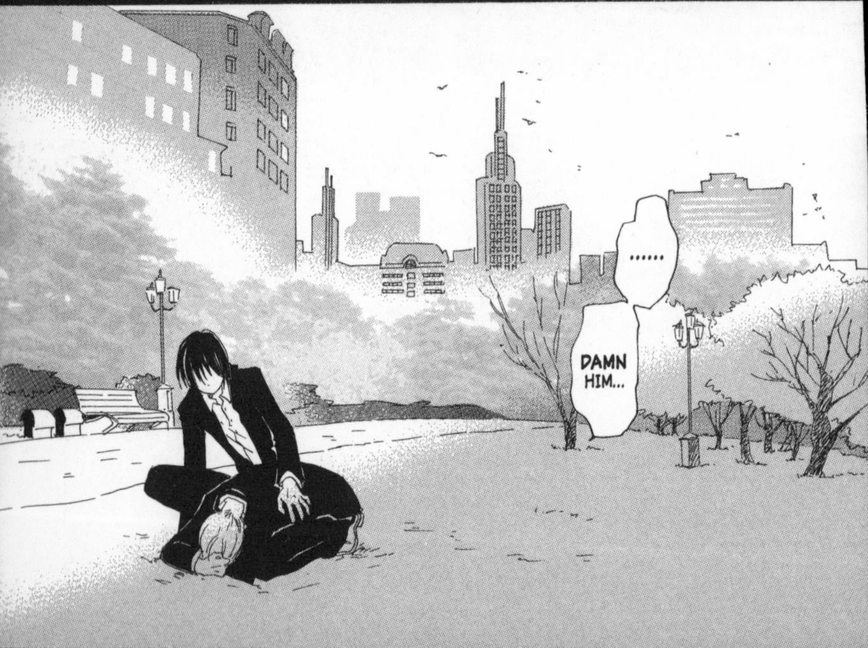
......
DAMN HIM...

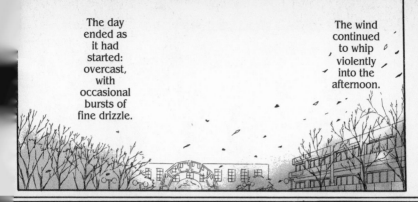

The wind continued to whip violently into the afternoon.
The day ended as it had started: overcast, with occasional bursts of fine drizzle.
We waited in front of Hagu-chan's exhibit—
A large folding screen painted with a row of ngko trees blazing up gold into an infinite blue sky.
We waited, but there was no word from Sensei.
By the time my cell phone rang, it was already early evening and getting dark outside.
Hagu-chan's injuries...
...were to her head (10 stitches)...
...and to her right hand (13 stitches).

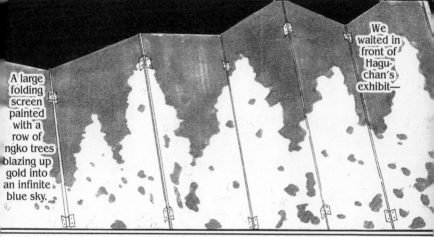

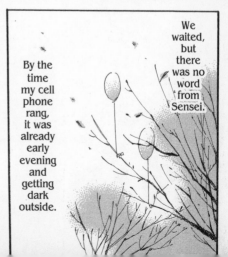

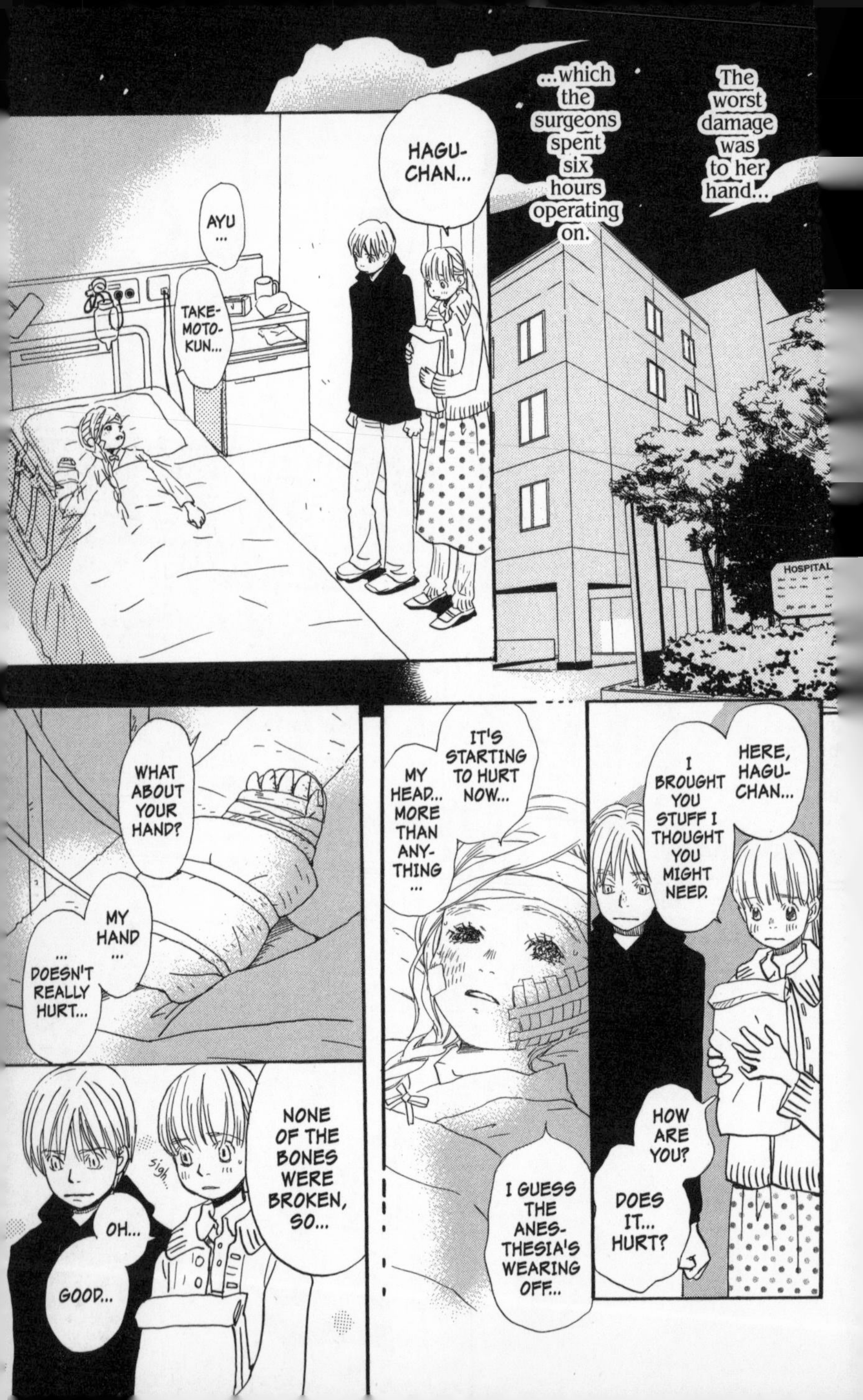
The worst damage was to her hand...
...which the surgeons spent six hours operating on.
HOSPITAL
HAGU-CHAN...
AYU...
TAKE-MOTO-KUN...
HERE, HAGU-CHAN...
I BROUGHT YOU STUFF I THOUGHT YOU MIGHT NEED.
HOW ARE YOU?
DOES IT... HURT?
IT'S STARTING TO HURT NOW...
MY HEAD... MORE THAN ANY-THING...
I GUESS THE ANES-THESIA'S WEARING OFF...
WHAT ABOUT YOUR HAND?
MY HAND...
... DOESN'T REALLY HURT...
NONE OF THE BONES WERE BROKEN, SO...
sigh...
OH...
GOOD...

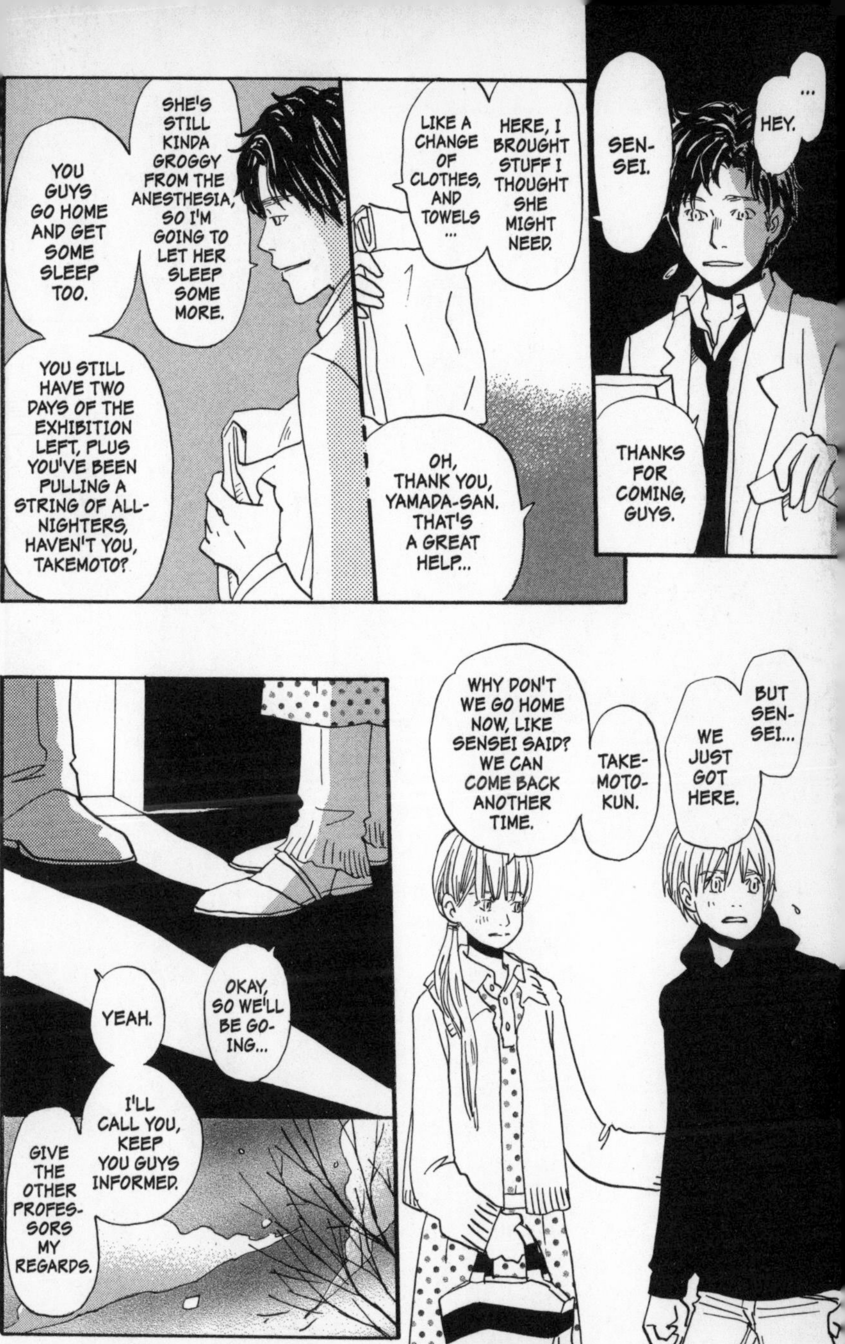
...
HEY.
SENSEI.
THANKS FOR COMING, GUYS.
HERE, I BROUGHT STUFF I THOUGHT SHE MIGHT NEED.
LIKE A CHANGE OF CLOTHES, AND TOWELS ...
OH, THANK YOU, YAMADA-SAN. THAT'S A GREAT HELP...
SHE'S STILL KINDA GROGGY FROM THE ANESTHESIA, SO I'M GOING TO LET HER SLEEP SOME MORE.
YOU GUYS GO HOME AND GET SOME SLEEP TOO.
YOU STILL HAVE TWO DAYS OF THE EXHIBITION LEFT, PLUS YOU'VE BEEN PULLING A STRING OF ALL-NIGHTERS, HAVEN'T YOU, TAKEMOTO?
BUT SENSEI...
WE JUST GOT HERE.
TAKEMOTO-KUN.
WHY DON'T WE GO HOME NOW, LIKE SENSEI SAID? WE CAN COME BACK ANOTHER TIME.
OKAY, SO WE'LL BE GOING...
YEAH.
I'LL CALL YOU, KEEP YOU GUYS INFORMED.
GIVE THE OTHER PROFESSORS MY REGARDS.

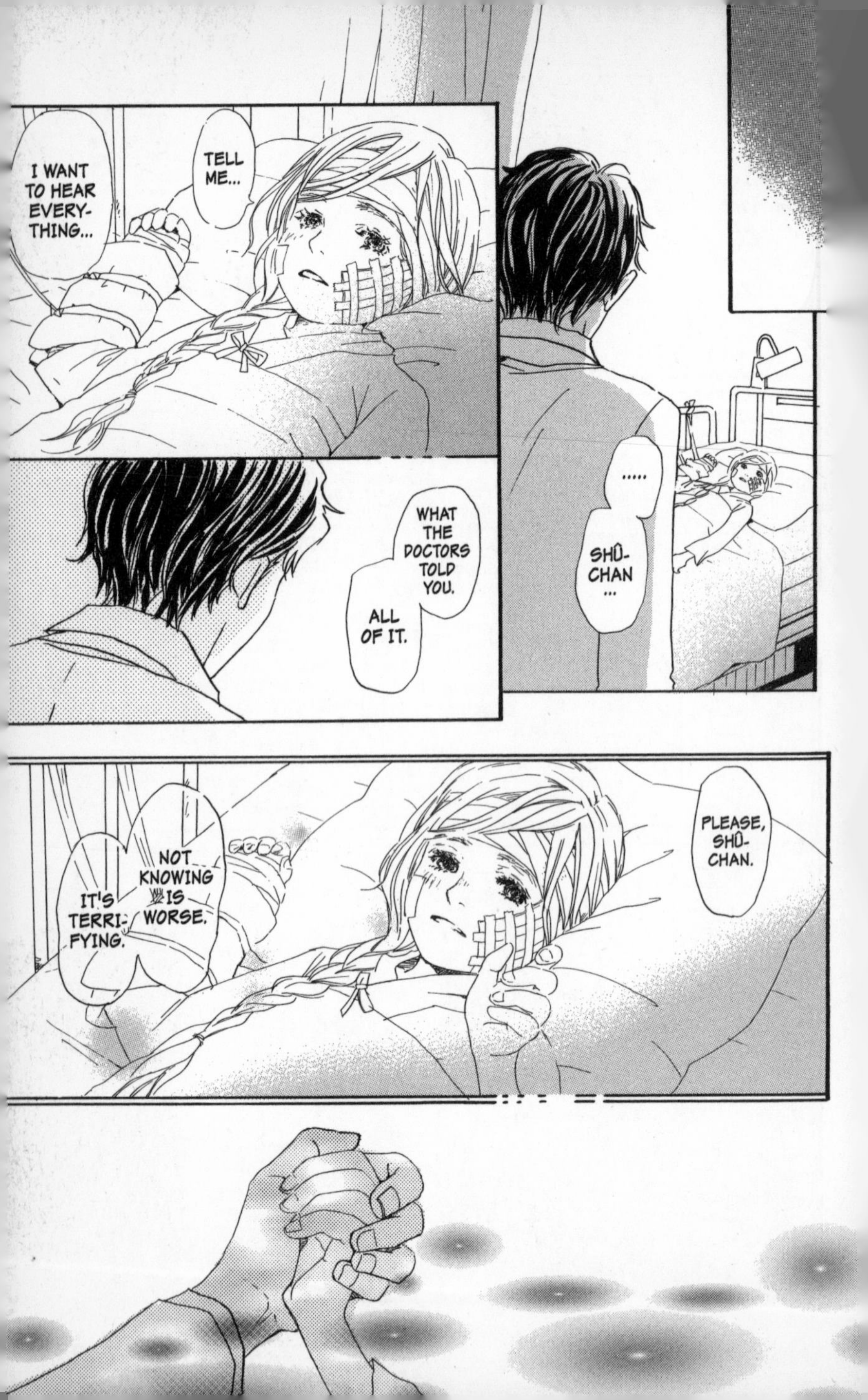

.....
SHÛ-CHAN ...
TELL ME...
I WANT TO HEAR EVERYTHING...
WHAT THE DOCTORS TOLD YOU.
ALL OF IT.
PLEASE, SHÛ-CHAN.
NOT KNOWING IS WORSE.
IT'S TERRIFYING.

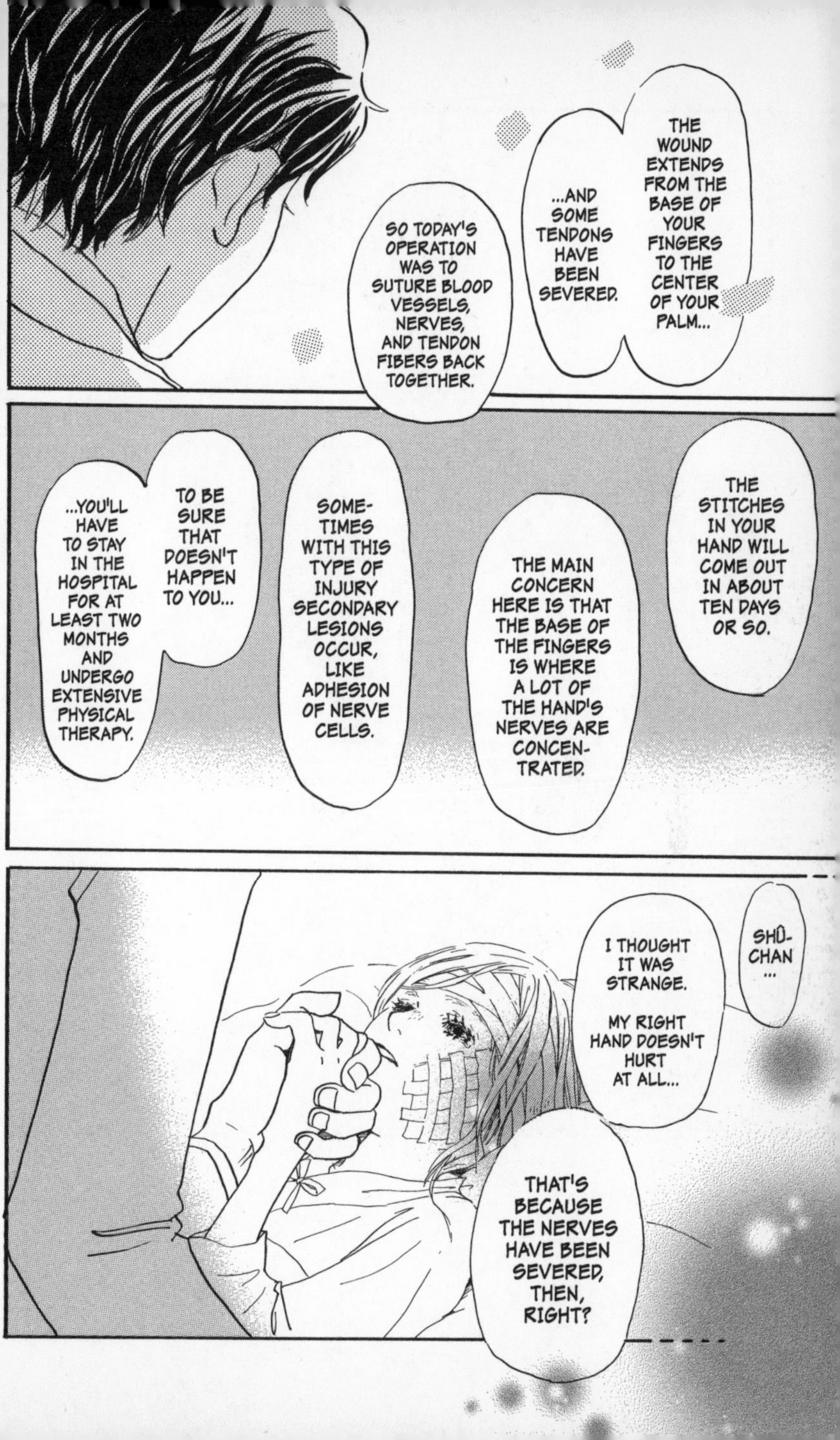
THE WOUND EXTENDS FROM THE BASE OF YOUR FINGERS TO THE CENTER OF YOUR PALM...
...AND SOME TENDONS HAVE BEEN SEVERED.
SO TODAY'S OPERATION WAS TO SUTURE BLOOD VESSELS, NERVES, AND TENDON FIBERS BACK TOGETHER.
THE STITCHES IN YOUR HAND WILL COME OUT IN ABOUT TEN DAYS OR SO.
THE MAIN CONCERN HERE IS THAT THE BASE OF THE FINGERS IS WHERE A LOT OF THE HAND'S NERVES ARE CONCEN-TRATED.
SOME-TIMES WITH THIS TYPE OF INJURY SECONDARY LESIONS OCCUR, LIKE ADHESION OF NERVE CELLS.
TO BE SURE THAT DOESN'T HAPPEN TO YOU...
...YOU'LL HAVE TO STAY IN THE HOSPITAL FOR AT LEAST TWO MONTHS AND UNDERGO EXTENSIVE PHYSICAL THERAPY.
SHŪ-CHAN...
I THOUGHT IT WAS STRANGE. MY RIGHT HAND DOESN'T HURT AT ALL...
THAT'S BECAUSE THE NERVES HAVE BEEN SEVERED, THEN, RIGHT?

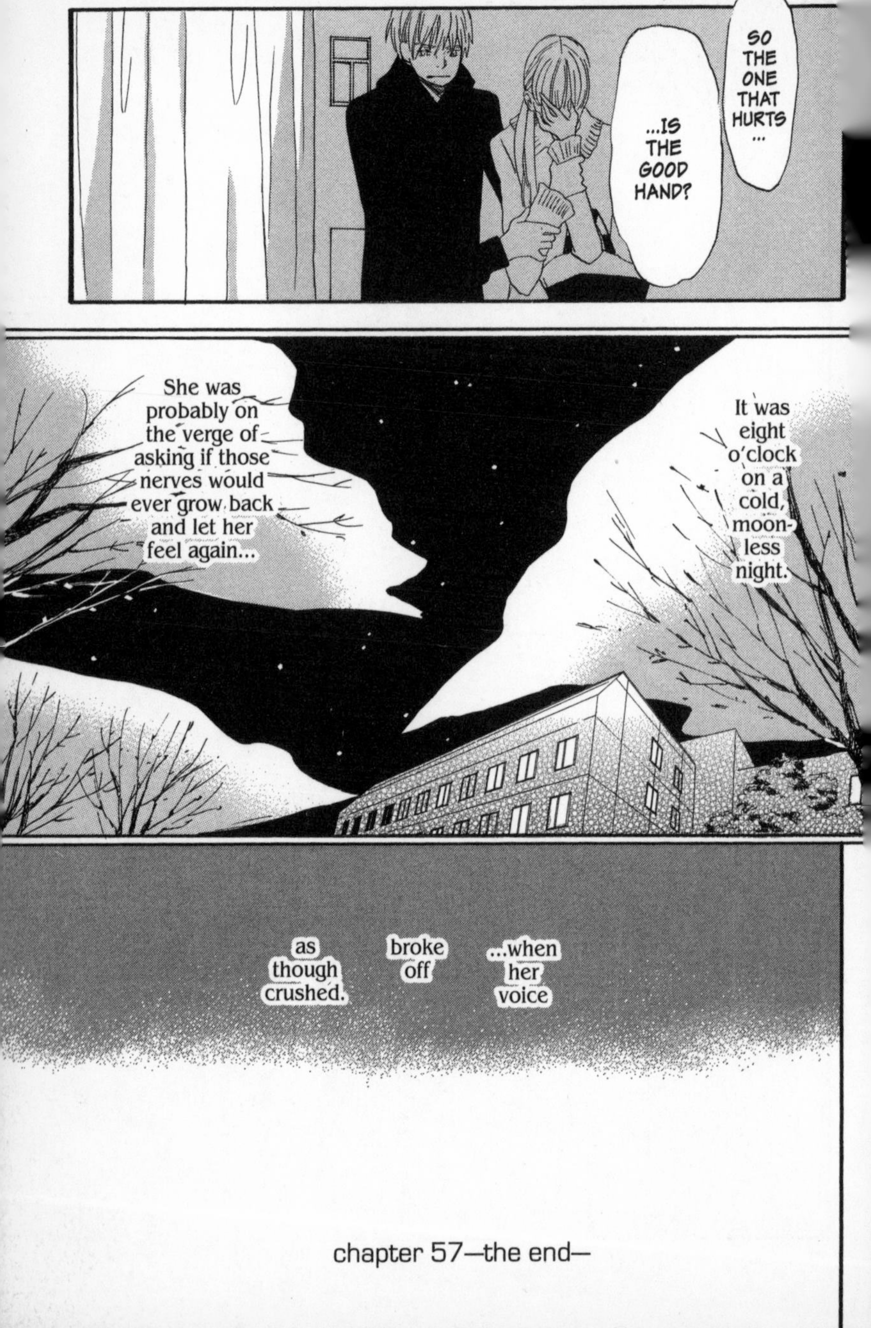
SO THE ONE THAT HURTS...
...IS THE GOOD HAND?
It was eight o'clock on a cold, moonless night.
She was probably on the verge of asking if those nerves would ever grow back and let her feel again...
...when her voice
broke off
as though crushed.
chapter 57—the end—

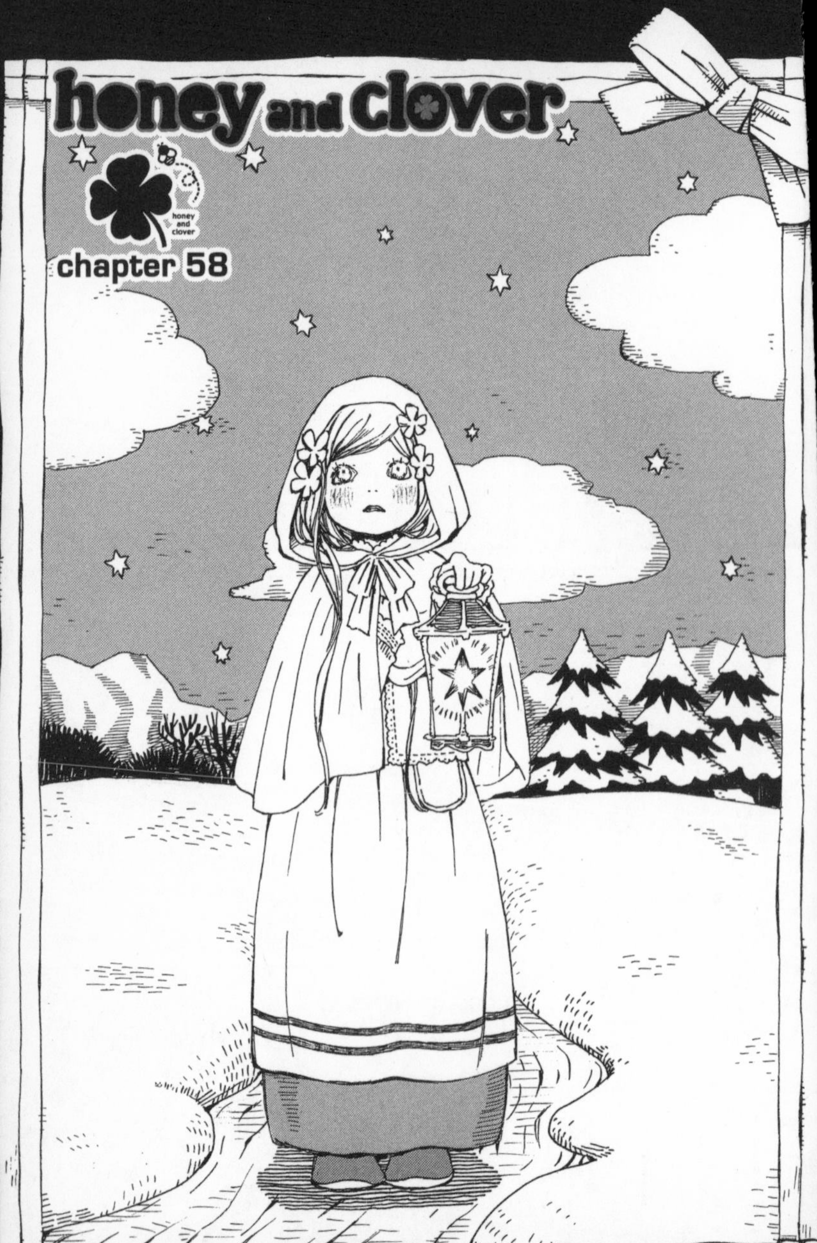
honey and clover
honey and clover
chapter 58

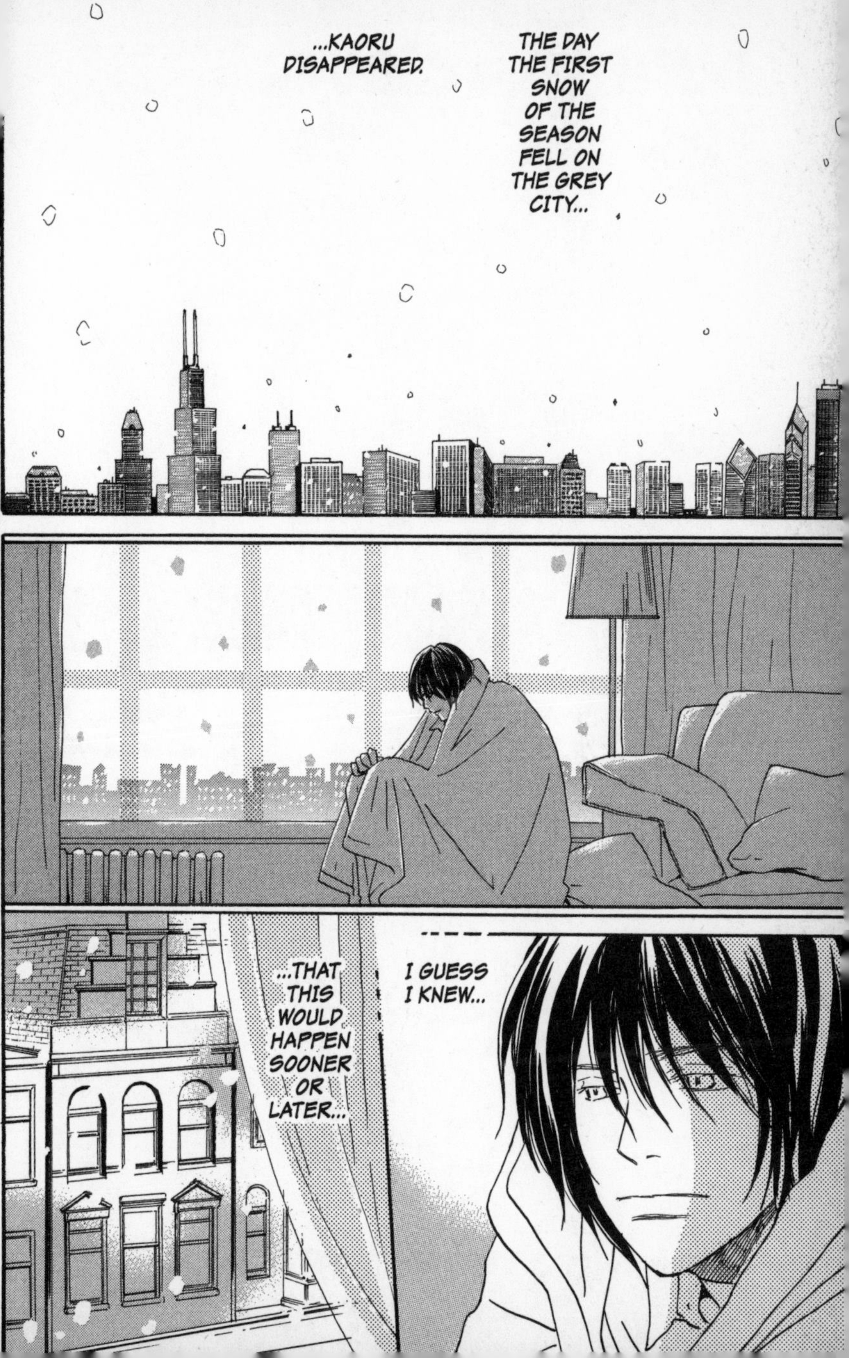
THE DAY THE FIRST SNOW OF THE SEASON FELL ON THE GREY CITY...
...KAORU DISAPPEARED.
I GUESS I KNEW...
...THAT THIS WOULD HAPPEN SOONER OR LATER...

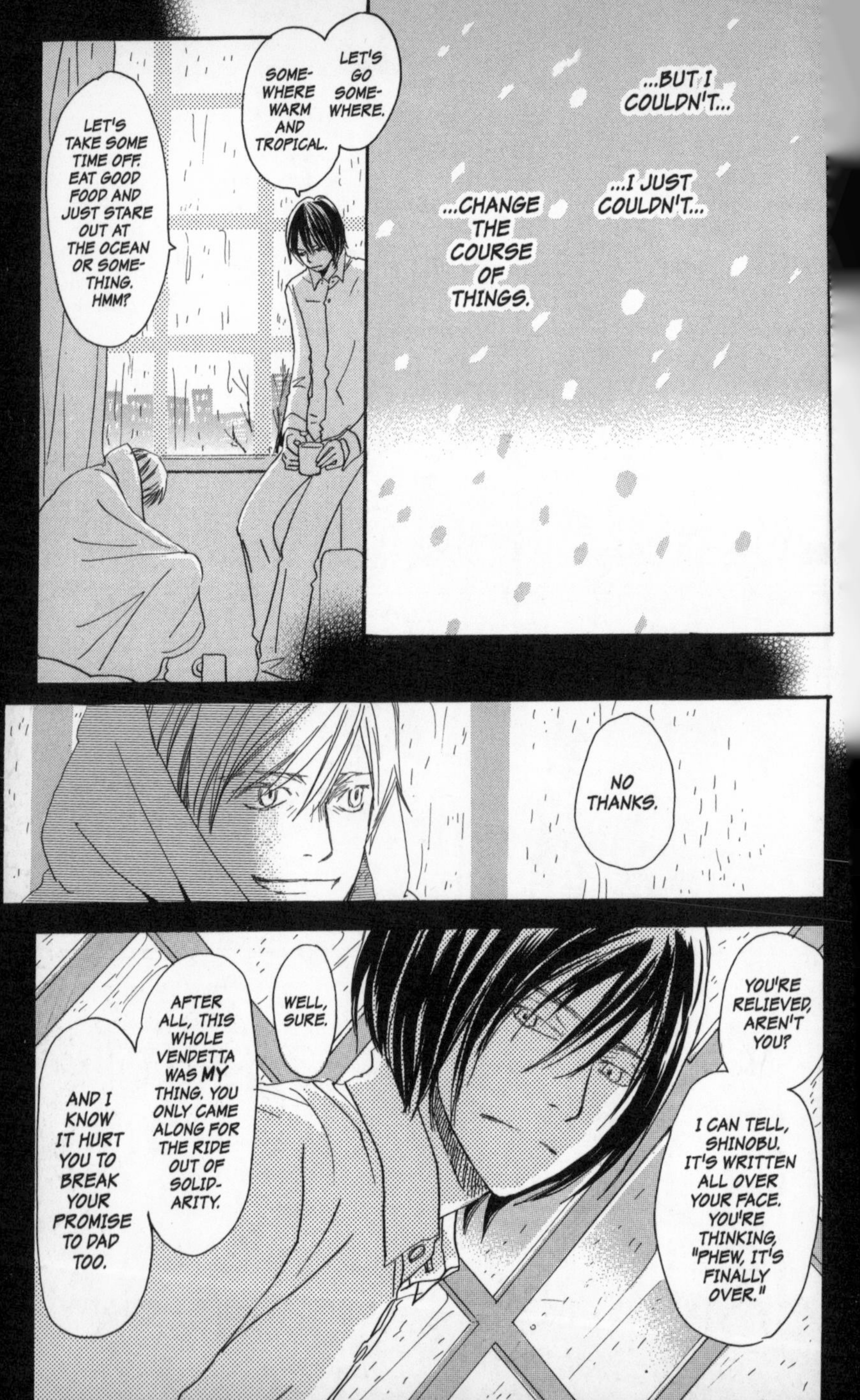
...BUT I COULDN'T...
...I JUST COULDN'T...
...CHANGE THE COURSE OF THINGS.
LET'S GO SOMEWHERE.
SOMEWHERE WARM AND TROPICAL.
LET'S TAKE SOME TIME OFF. EAT GOOD FOOD AND JUST STARE OUT AT THE OCEAN OR SOMETHING. HMM?
NO THANKS.
YOU'RE RELIEVED, AREN'T YOU?
I CAN TELL, SHINOBU. IT'S WRITTEN ALL OVER YOUR FACE. YOU'RE THINKING, "PHEW, IT'S FINALLY OVER."
WELL, SURE.
AFTER ALL, THIS WHOLE VENDETTA WAS MY THING. YOU ONLY CAME ALONG FOR THE RIDE OUT OF SOLIDARITY.
AND I KNOW IT HURT YOU TO BREAK YOUR PROMISE TO DAD TOO.

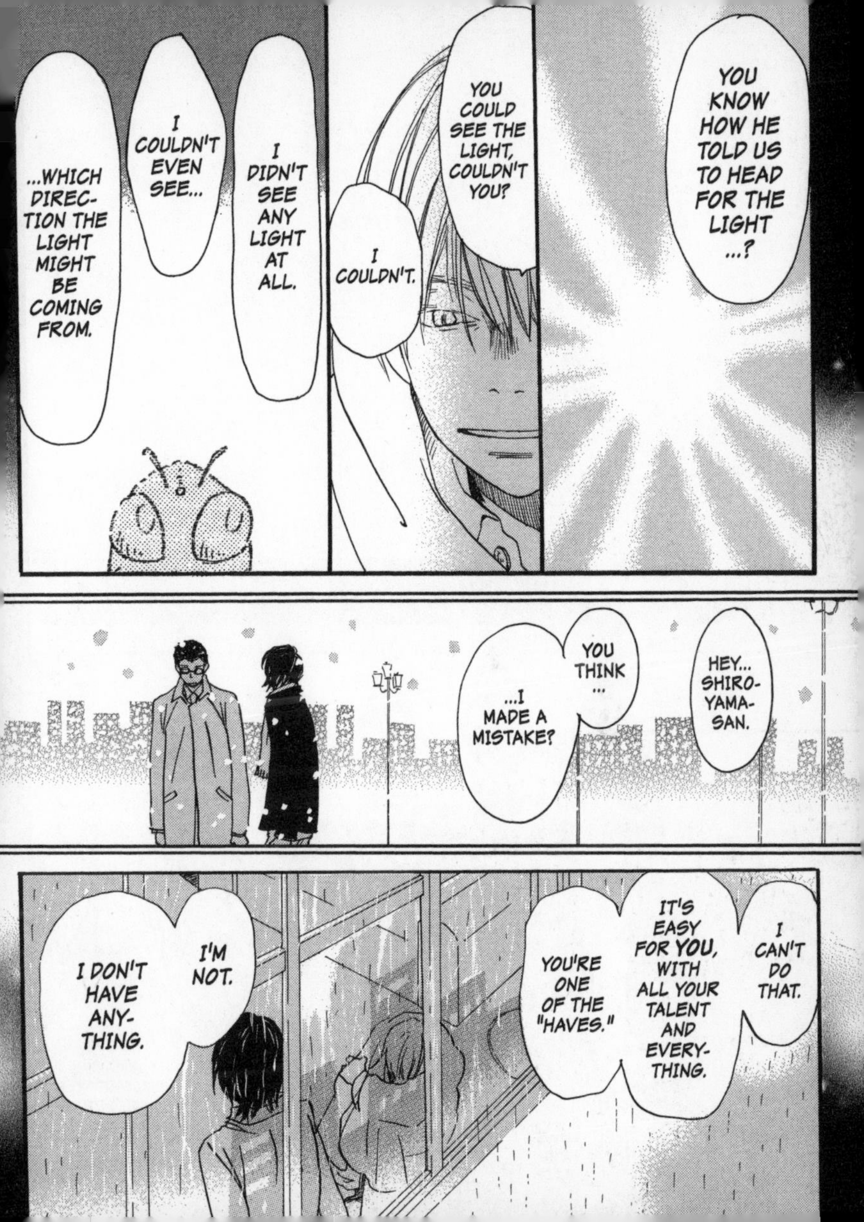

YOU KNOW HOW HE TOLD US TO HEAD FOR THE LIGHT ...?
YOU COULD SEE THE LIGHT, COULDN'T YOU?
I COULDN'T.
I DIDN'T SEE ANY LIGHT AT ALL.
I COULDN'T EVEN SEE...
...WHICH DIRECTION THE LIGHT MIGHT BE COMING FROM.
HEY... SHIROYAMA-SAN.
YOU THINK ...
...I MADE A MISTAKE?
I CAN'T DO THAT.
IT'S EASY FOR **YOU**, WITH ALL YOUR TALENT AND EVERYTHING.
YOU'RE ONE OF THE "HAVES."
I'M NOT.
I DON'T HAVE ANYTHING.

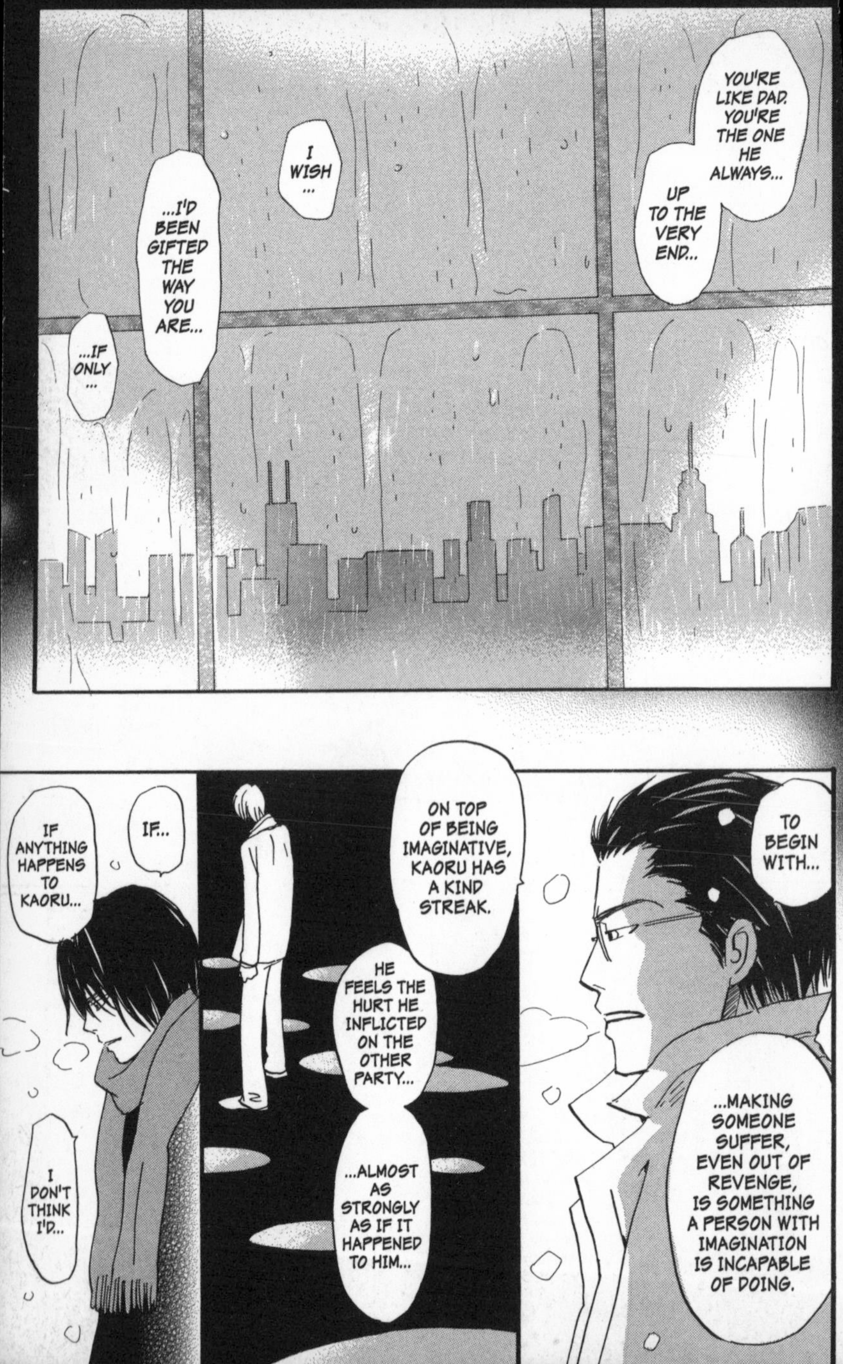
YOU'RE LIKE DAD. YOU'RE THE ONE HE ALWAYS...
UP TO THE VERY END...
I WISH...
...I'D BEEN GIFTED THE WAY YOU ARE...
...IF ONLY...
TO BEGIN WITH...
...MAKING SOMEONE SUFFER, EVEN OUT OF REVENGE, IS SOMETHING A PERSON WITH IMAGINATION IS INCAPABLE OF DOING.
ON TOP OF BEING IMAGINATIVE, KAORU HAS A KIND STREAK.
HE FEELS THE HURT HE INFLICTED ON THE OTHER PARTY...
...ALMOST AS STRONGLY AS IF IT HAPPENED TO HIM...
IF...
IF ANYTHING HAPPENS TO KAORU...
I DON'T THINK I'D...

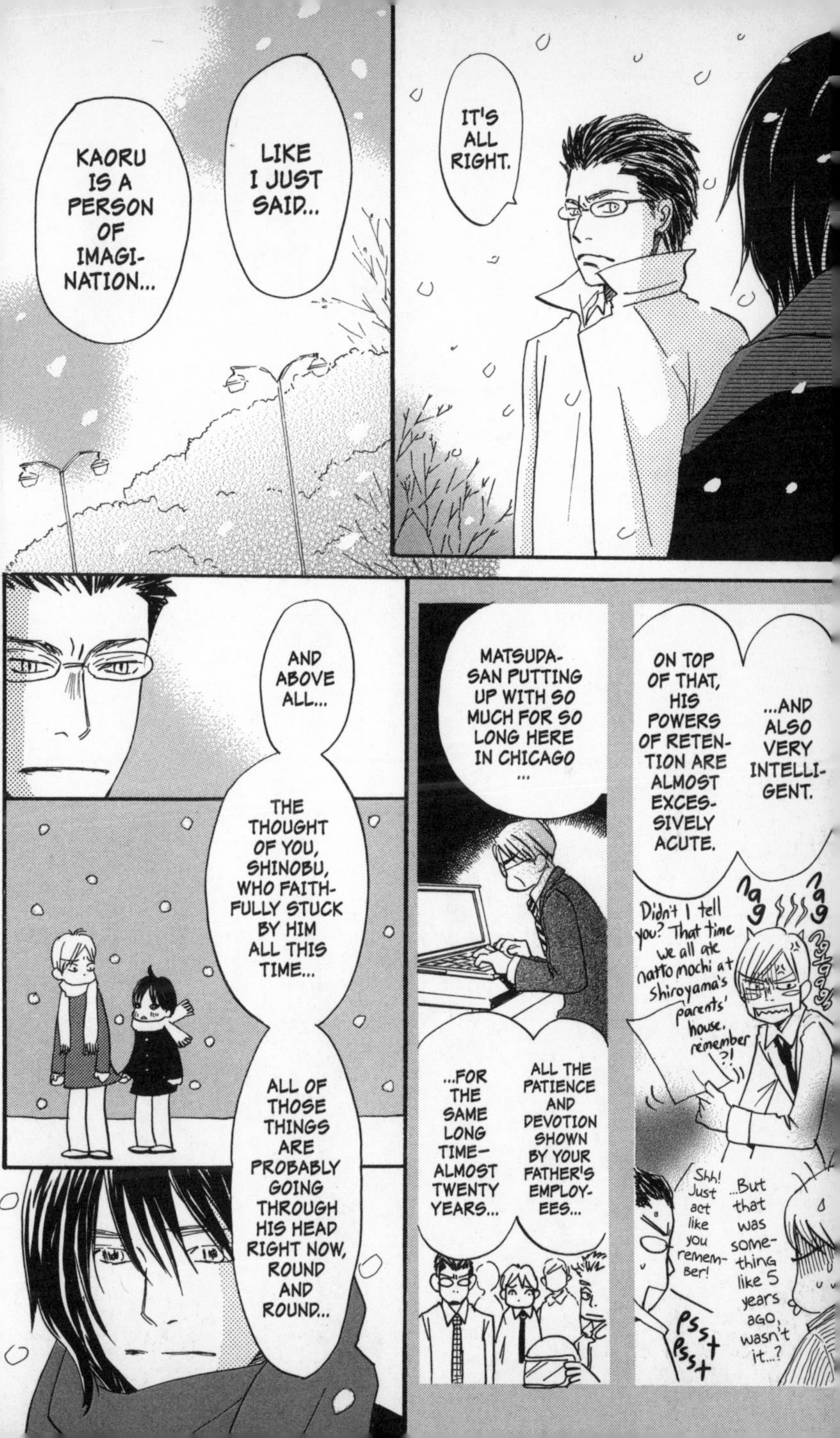
IT'S ALL RIGHT.
LIKE I JUST SAID...
KAORU IS A PERSON OF IMAGINATION...
...AND ALSO VERY INTELLIGENT.
ON TOP OF THAT, HIS POWERS OF RETENTION ARE ALMOST EXCESSIVELY ACUTE.
nag nag
Didn't I tell you? That time we all ate natto mochi at Shiroyama's parents' house, remember?!
...But that was something like 5 years ago, wasn't it...?
Shh! Just act like you remember!
psst psst
MATSUDA-SAN PUTTING UP WITH SO MUCH FOR SO LONG HERE IN CHICAGO...
ALL THE PATIENCE AND DEVOTION SHOWN BY YOUR FATHER'S EMPLOYEES...
...FOR THE SAME LONG TIME—ALMOST TWENTY YEARS...
AND ABOVE ALL...
THE THOUGHT OF YOU, SHINOBU, WHO FAITHFULLY STUCK BY HIM ALL THIS TIME...
ALL OF THOSE THINGS ARE PROBABLY GOING THROUGH HIS HEAD RIGHT NOW, ROUND AND ROUND...

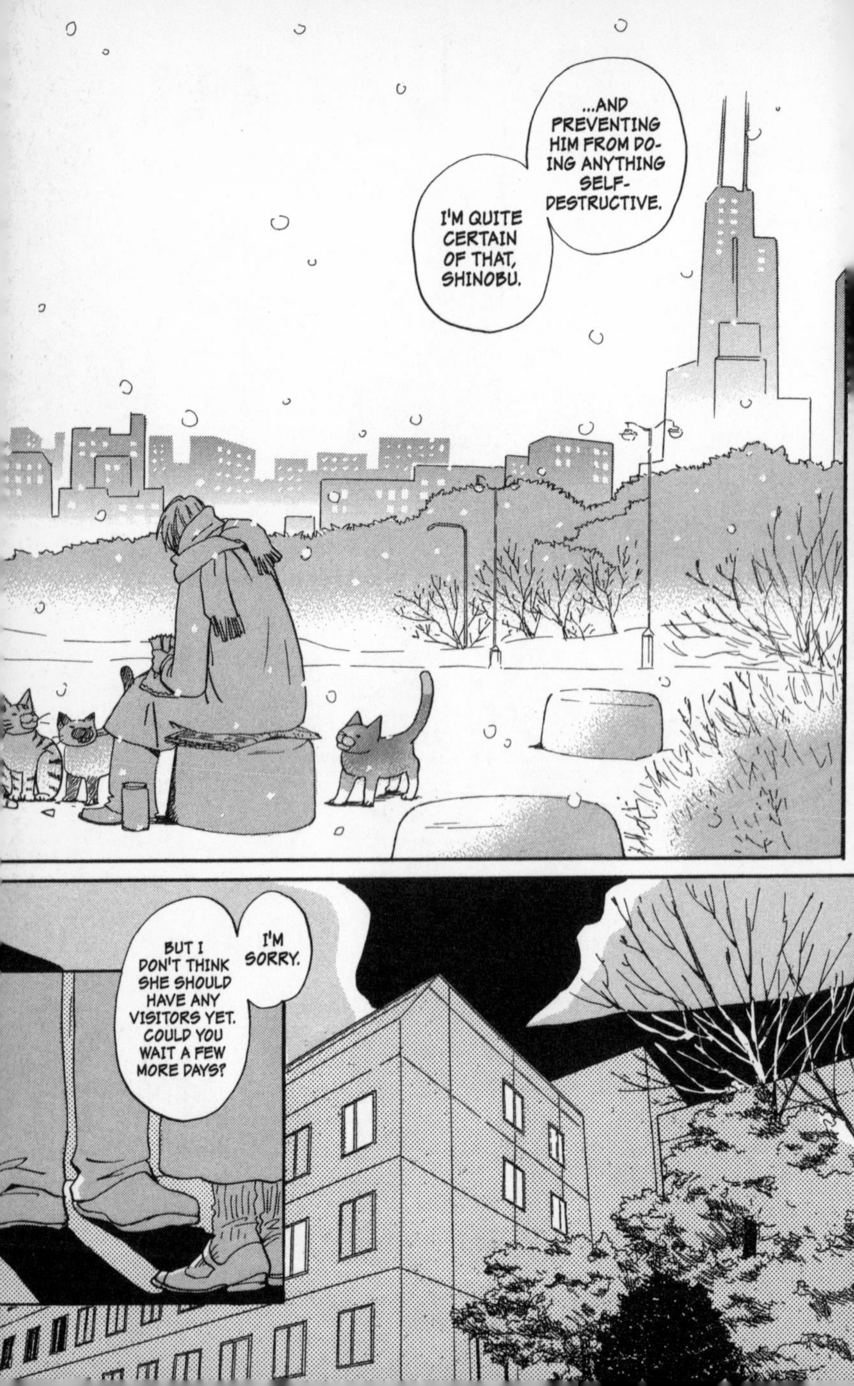
...AND PREVENTING HIM FROM DOING ANYTHING SELF-DESTRUCTIVE.
I'M QUITE CERTAIN OF THAT, SHINOBU.
I'M SORRY.
BUT I DON'T THINK SHE SHOULD HAVE ANY VISITORS YET. COULD YOU WAIT A FEW MORE DAYS?

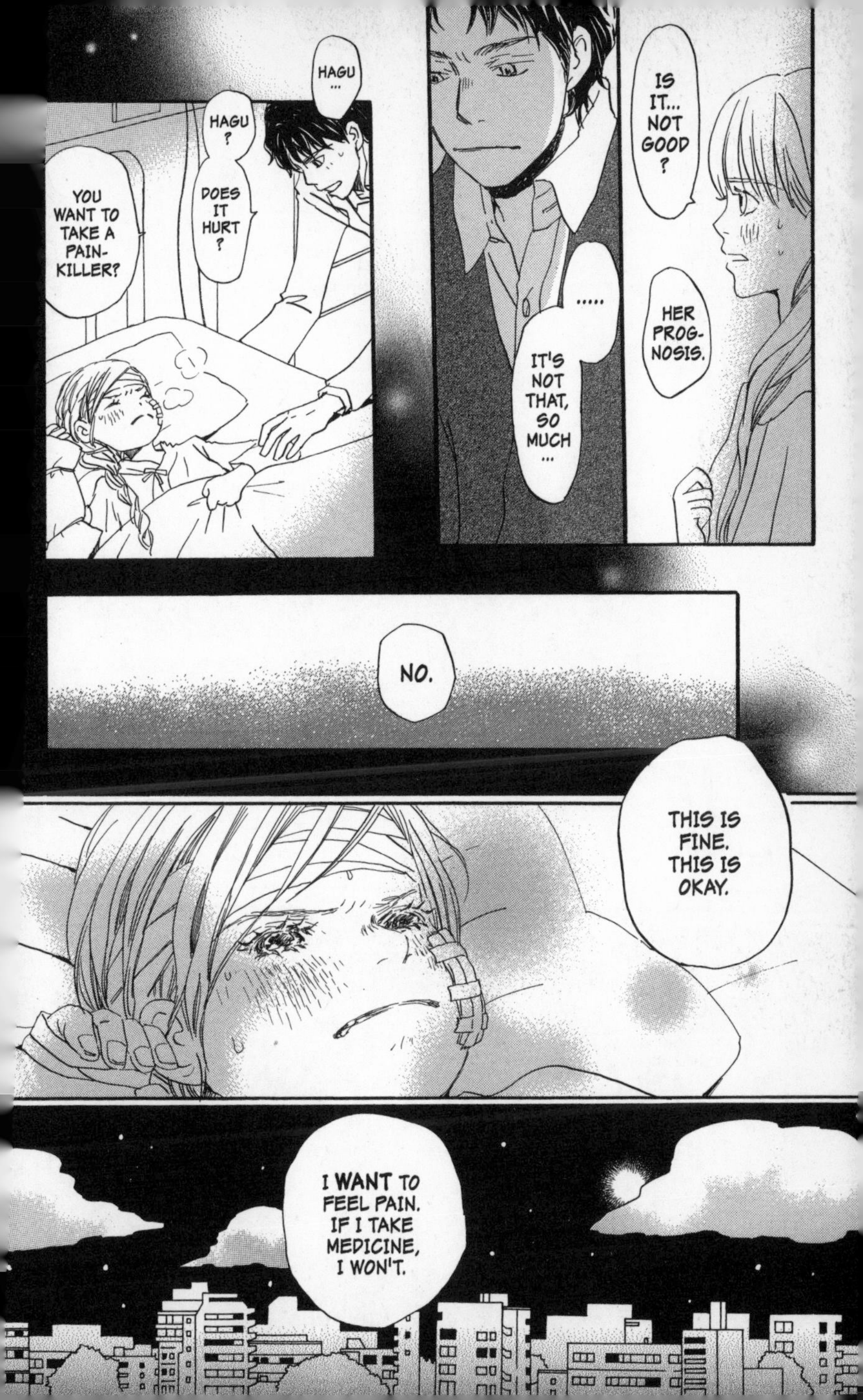
IS IT... NOT GOOD?
HER PROGNOSIS.
.....
IT'S NOT THAT, SO MUCH...
HAGU...
HAGU?
DOES IT HURT?
YOU WANT TO TAKE A PAIN-KILLER?
NO.
THIS IS FINE. THIS IS OKAY.
I WANT TO FEEL PAIN. IF I TAKE MEDICINE, I WON'T.

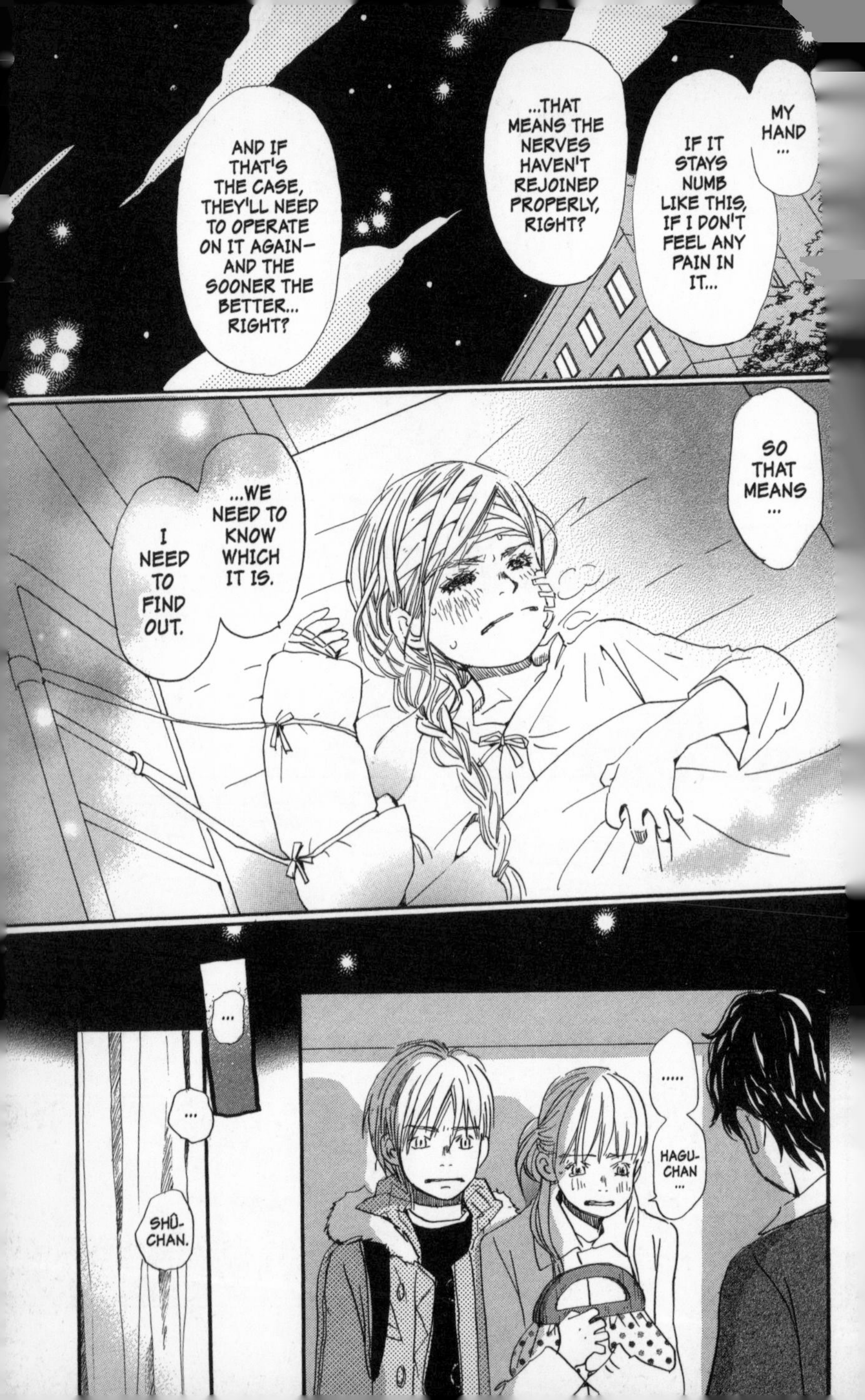
MY HAND...
IF IT STAYS NUMB LIKE THIS, IF I DON'T FEEL ANY PAIN IN IT...
...THAT MEANS THE NERVES HAVEN'T REJOINED PROPERLY, RIGHT?
AND IF THAT'S THE CASE, THEY'LL NEED TO OPERATE ON IT AGAIN— AND THE SOONER THE BETTER... RIGHT?
SO THAT MEANS...
...WE NEED TO KNOW WHICH IT IS.
I NEED TO FIND OUT.
......
HAGU-CHAN...
...
...
SHŪ-CHAN.

IT
CAME.

HAGU?

I'M HERE, WHAT IS IT?!

MY HAND...

IT'S HERE...

THE PAIN.

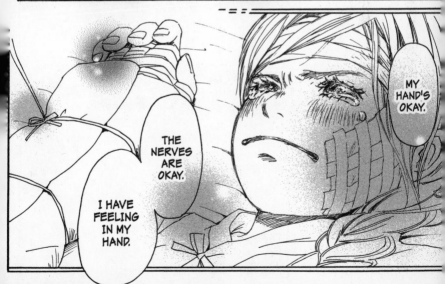

THE NERVES ARE OKAY.

I HAVE FEELING IN MY HAND.

MY HAND'S OKAY.

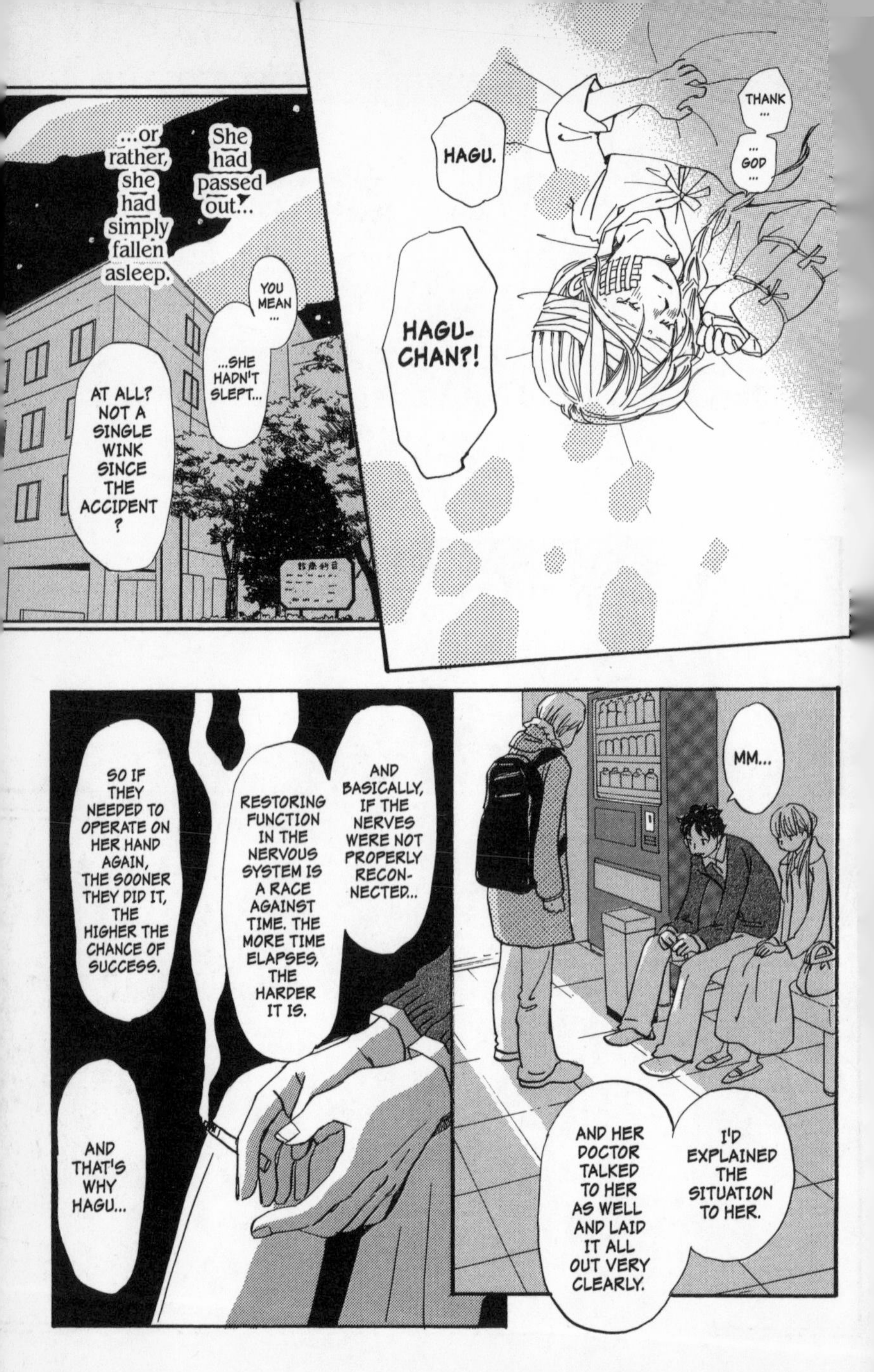
THANK ... ... GOD ...
HAGU.
HAGU-CHAN?!
She had passed out...
...or rather, she had simply fallen asleep.
YOU MEAN ...
...SHE HADN'T SLEPT...
AT ALL? NOT A SINGLE WINK SINCE THE ACCIDENT?
MM...
I'D EXPLAINED THE SITUATION TO HER.
AND HER DOCTOR TALKED TO HER AS WELL AND LAID IT ALL OUT VERY CLEARLY.
AND BASICALLY, IF THE NERVES WERE NOT PROPERLY RECONNECTED...
RESTORING FUNCTION IN THE NERVOUS SYSTEM IS A RACE AGAINST TIME. THE MORE TIME ELAPSES, THE HARDER IT IS.
SO IF THEY NEEDED TO OPERATE ON HER HAND AGAIN, THE SOONER THEY DID IT, THE HIGHER THE CHANCE OF SUCCESS.
AND THAT'S WHY HAGU...

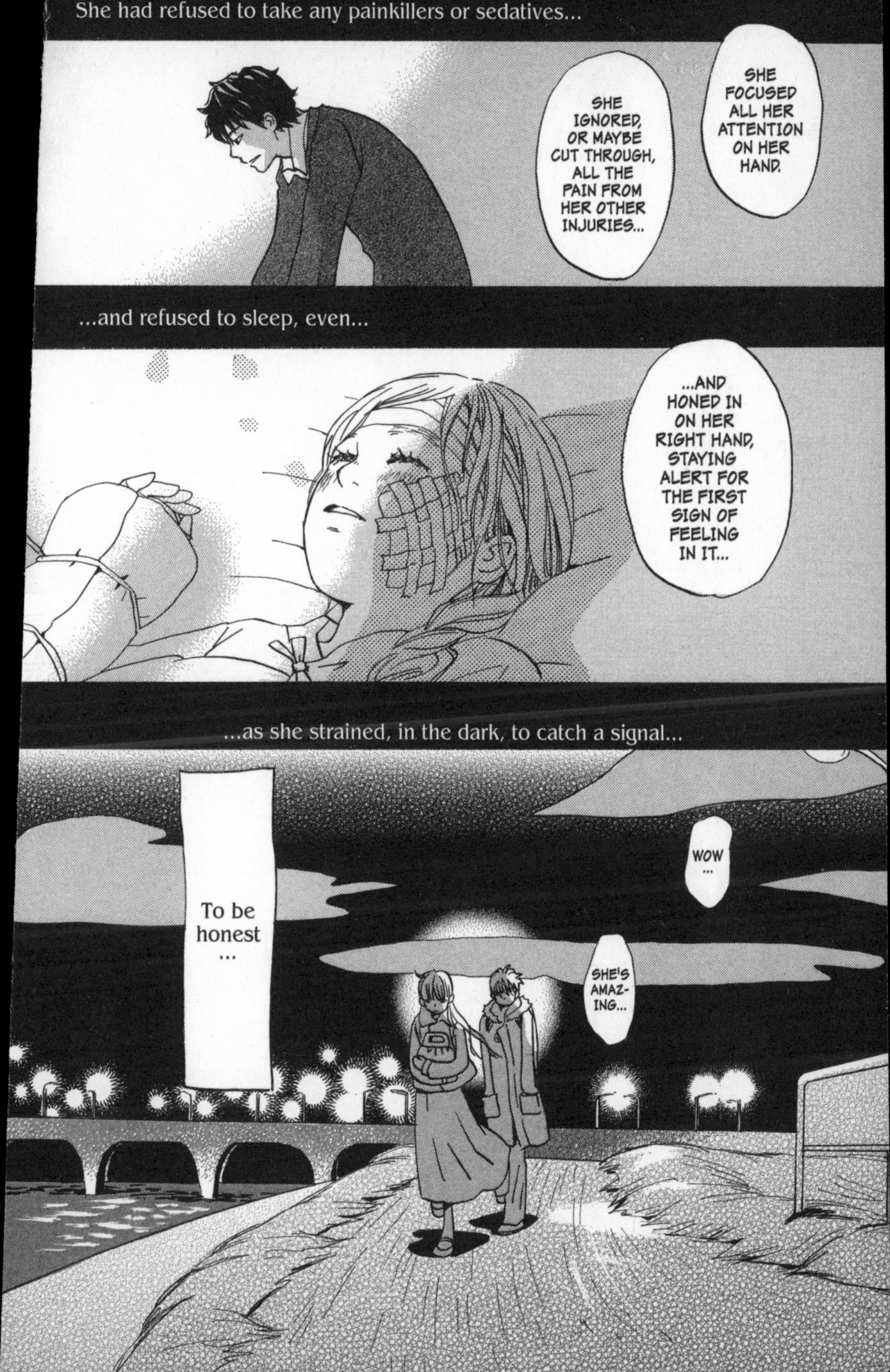
She had refused to take any painkillers or sedatives...
SHE FOCUSED ALL HER ATTENTION ON HER HAND.
SHE IGNORED, OR MAYBE CUT THROUGH, ALL THE PAIN FROM HER OTHER INJURIES...
...and refused to sleep, even...
...AND HONED IN ON HER RIGHT HAND, STAYING ALERT FOR THE FIRST SIGN OF FEELING IN IT...
...as she strained, in the dark, to catch a signal...
WOW...
SHE'S AMAZ-ING...
To be honest...

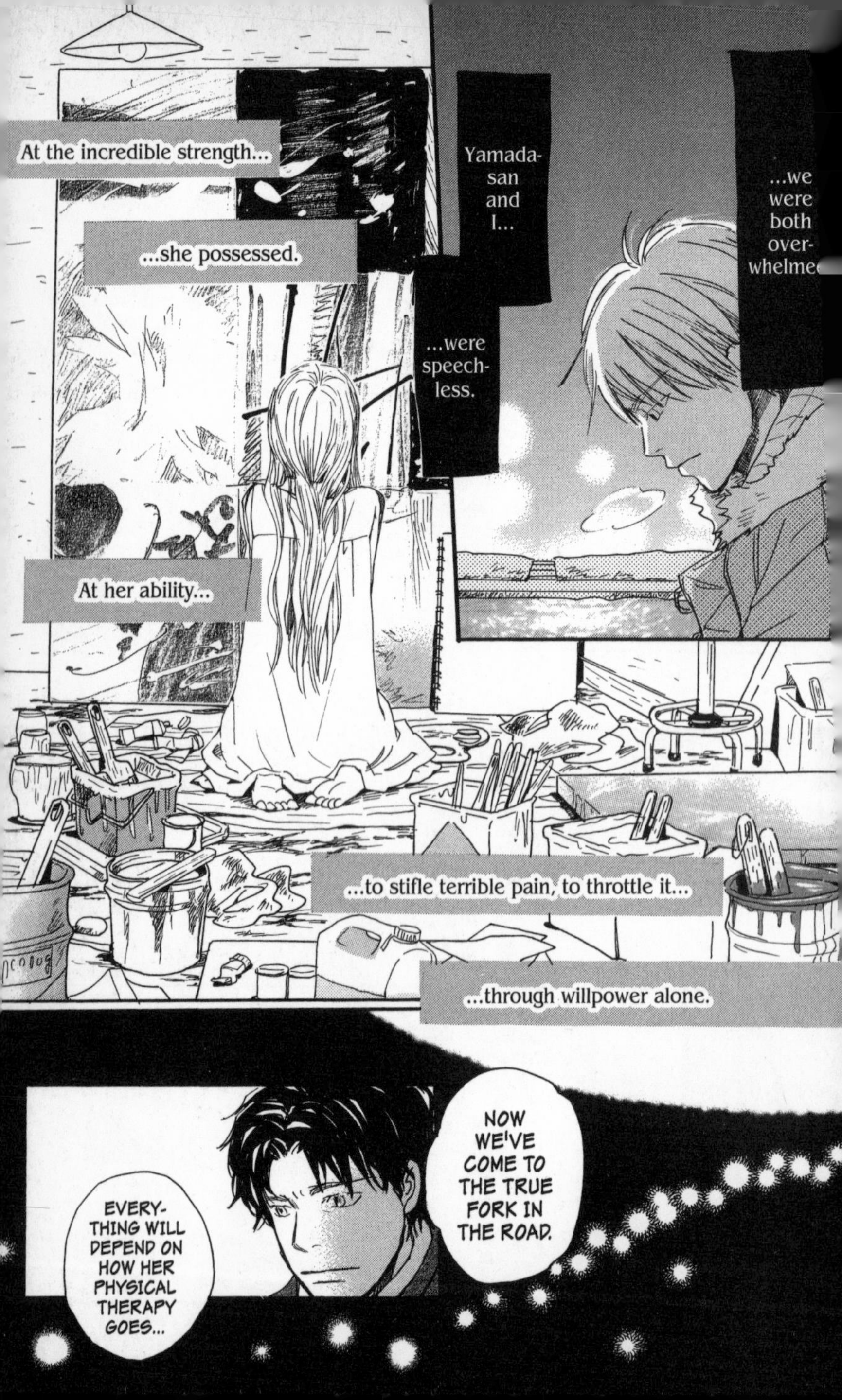
...we were both over-whelme
Yamada-san and I...
...were speechless.
At the incredible strength...
...she possessed.
At her ability...
...to stifle terrible pain, to throttle it...
...through willpower alone.
NOW WE'VE COME TO THE TRUE FORK IN THE ROAD.
EVERY-THING WILL DEPEND ON HOW HER PHYSICAL THERAPY GOES...

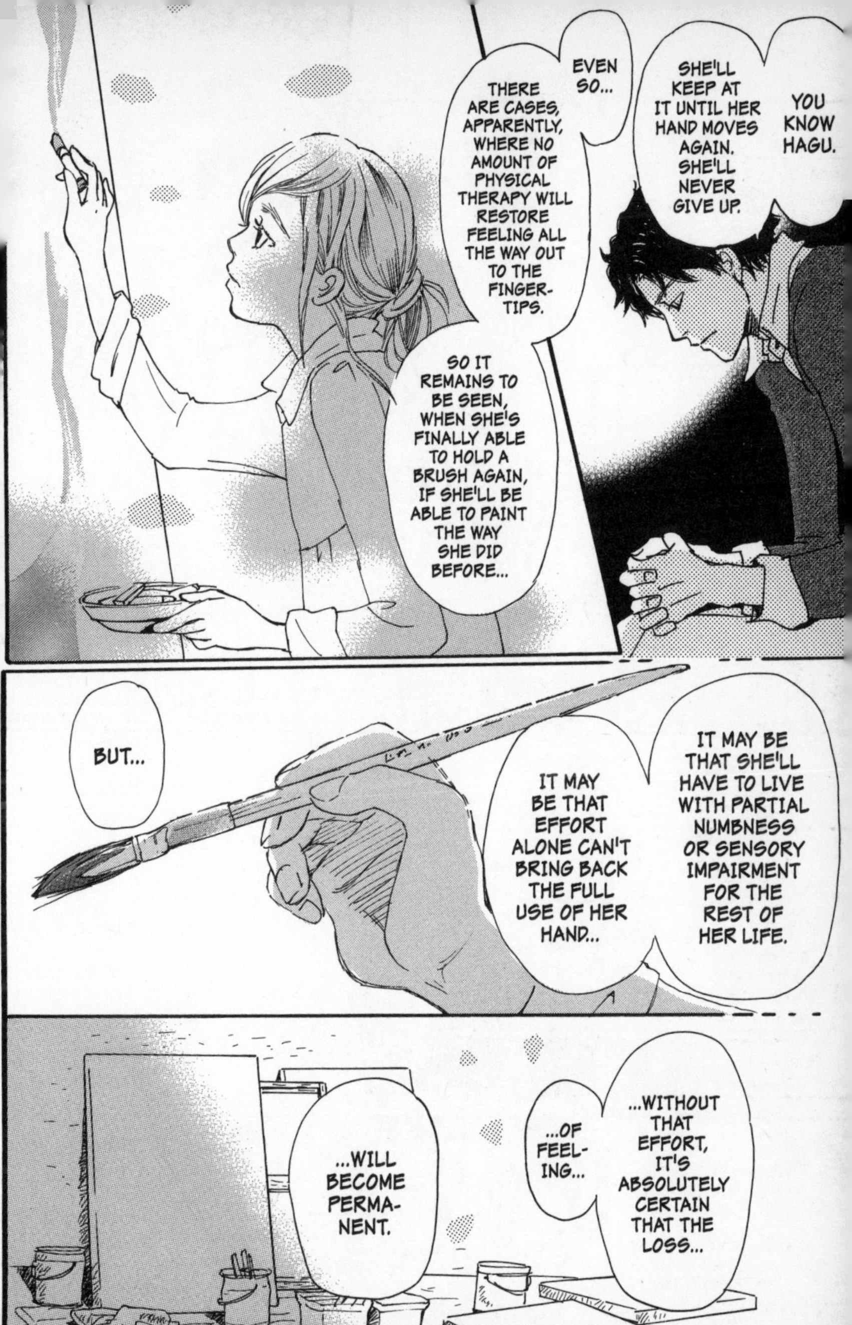
YOU KNOW HAGU.
SHE'LL KEEP AT IT UNTIL HER HAND MOVES AGAIN. SHE'LL NEVER GIVE UP.
EVEN SO...
THERE ARE CASES, APPARENTLY, WHERE NO AMOUNT OF PHYSICAL THERAPY WILL RESTORE FEELING ALL THE WAY OUT TO THE FINGERTIPS.
SO IT REMAINS TO BE SEEN, WHEN SHE'S FINALLY ABLE TO HOLD A BRUSH AGAIN, IF SHE'LL BE ABLE TO PAINT THE WAY SHE DID BEFORE...
IT MAY BE THAT SHE'LL HAVE TO LIVE WITH PARTIAL NUMBNESS OR SENSORY IMPAIRMENT FOR THE REST OF HER LIFE.
IT MAY BE THAT EFFORT ALONE CAN'T BRING BACK THE FULL USE OF HER HAND...
BUT...
...WITHOUT THAT EFFORT, IT'S ABSOLUTELY CERTAIN THAT THE LOSS...
...OF FEELING...
...WILL BECOME PERMANENT.

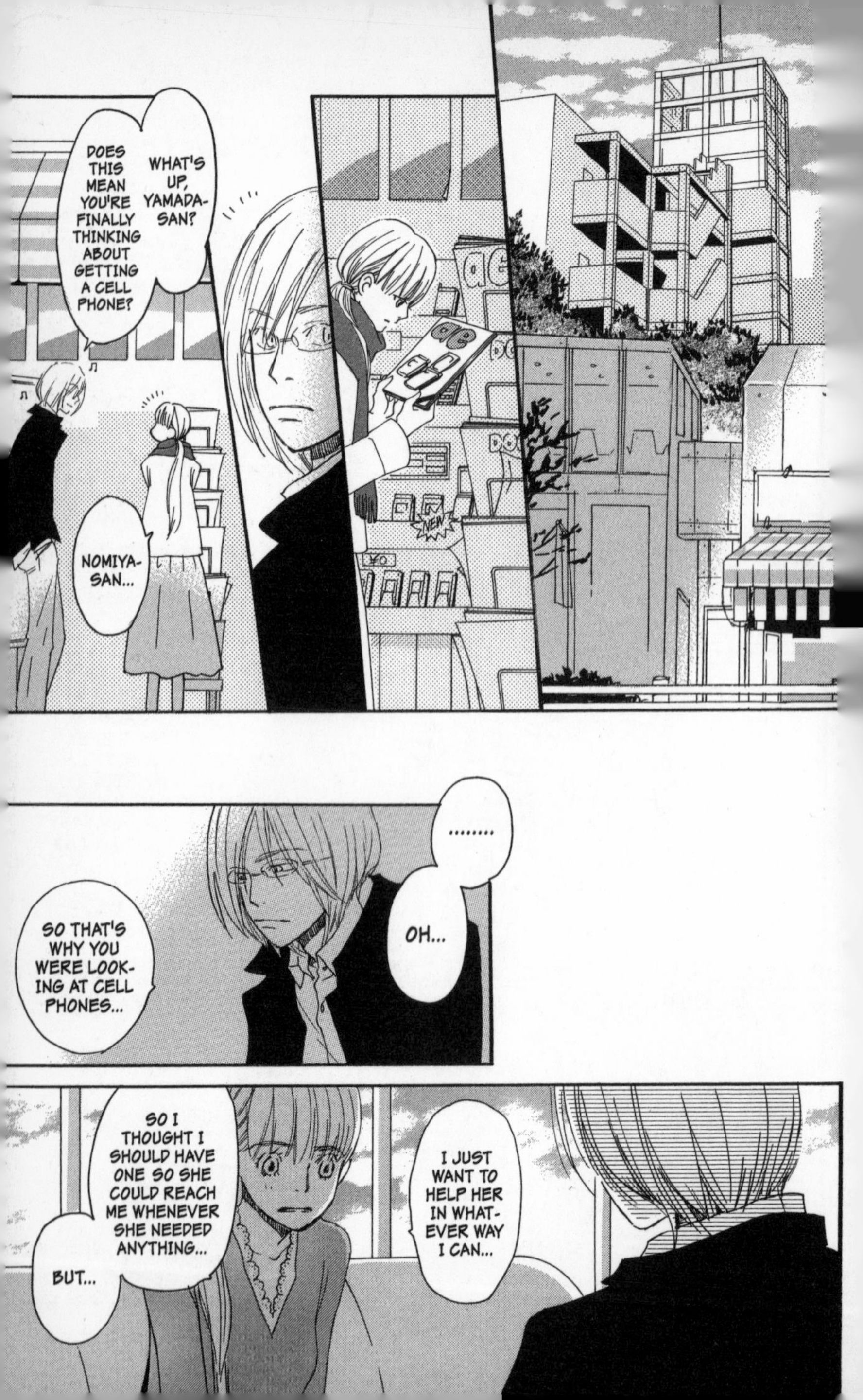
WHAT'S UP, YAMADA-SAN?
DOES THIS MEAN YOU'RE FINALLY THINKING ABOUT GETTING A CELL PHONE?
NOMIYA-SAN...
NEW
....
OH...
SO THAT'S WHY YOU WERE LOOK-ING AT CELL PHONES...
I JUST WANT TO HELP HER IN WHAT-EVER WAY I CAN...
SO I THOUGHT I SHOULD HAVE ONE SO SHE COULD REACH ME WHENEVER SHE NEEDED ANYTHING...
BUT...

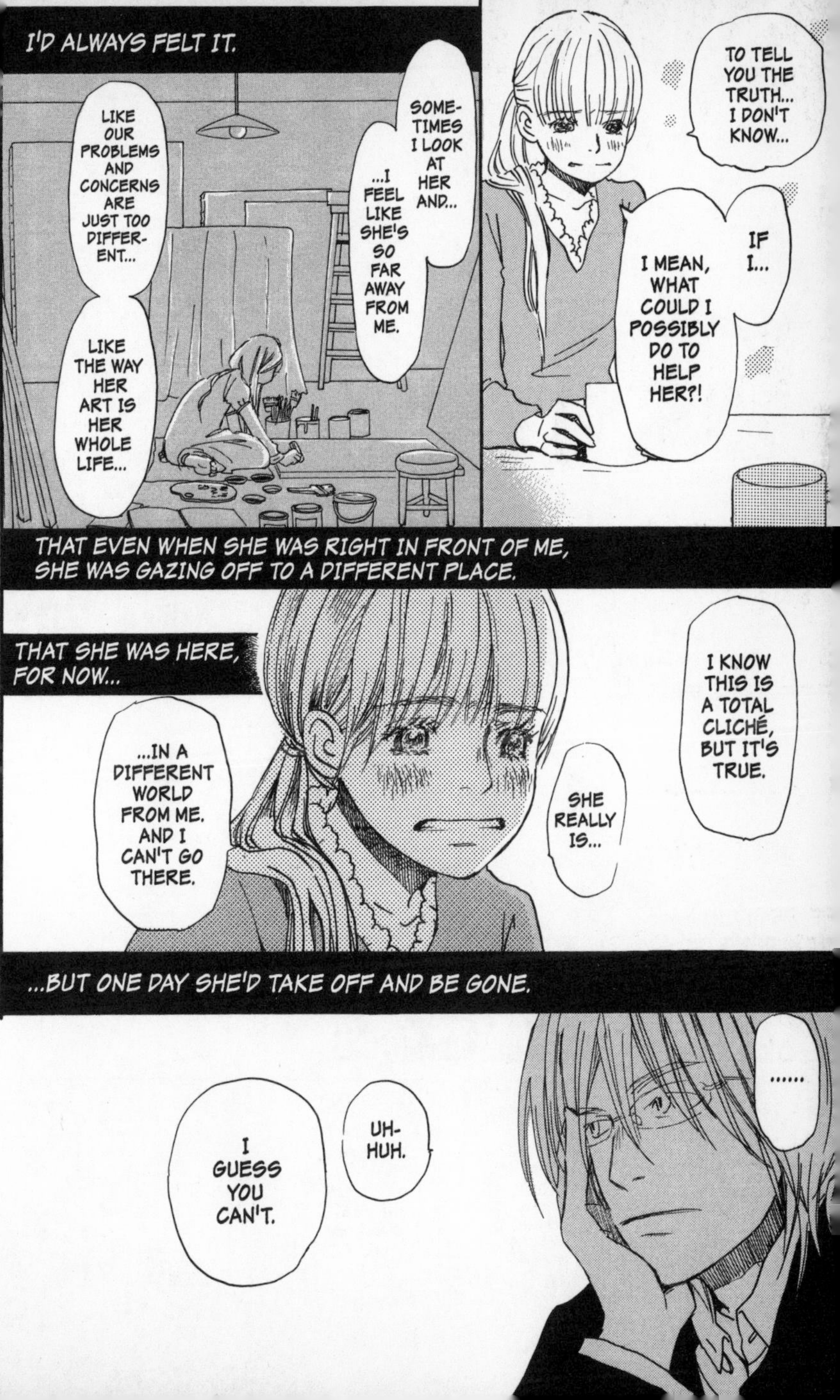
TO TELL YOU THE TRUTH... I DON'T KNOW...
IF I...
I MEAN, WHAT COULD I POSSIBLY DO TO HELP HER?!
I'D ALWAYS FELT IT.
SOMETIMES I LOOK AT HER AND...
...I FEEL LIKE SHE'S SO FAR AWAY FROM ME.
LIKE OUR PROBLEMS AND CONCERNS ARE JUST TOO DIFFERENT...
LIKE THE WAY HER ART IS HER WHOLE LIFE...
THAT EVEN WHEN SHE WAS RIGHT IN FRONT OF ME, SHE WAS GAZING OFF TO A DIFFERENT PLACE.
I KNOW THIS IS A TOTAL CLICHÉ, BUT IT'S TRUE.
SHE REALLY IS...
THAT SHE WAS HERE, FOR NOW...
...IN A DIFFERENT WORLD FROM ME. AND I CAN'T GO THERE.
...BUT ONE DAY SHE'D TAKE OFF AND BE GONE.
......
UH-HUH.
I GUESS YOU CAN'T.

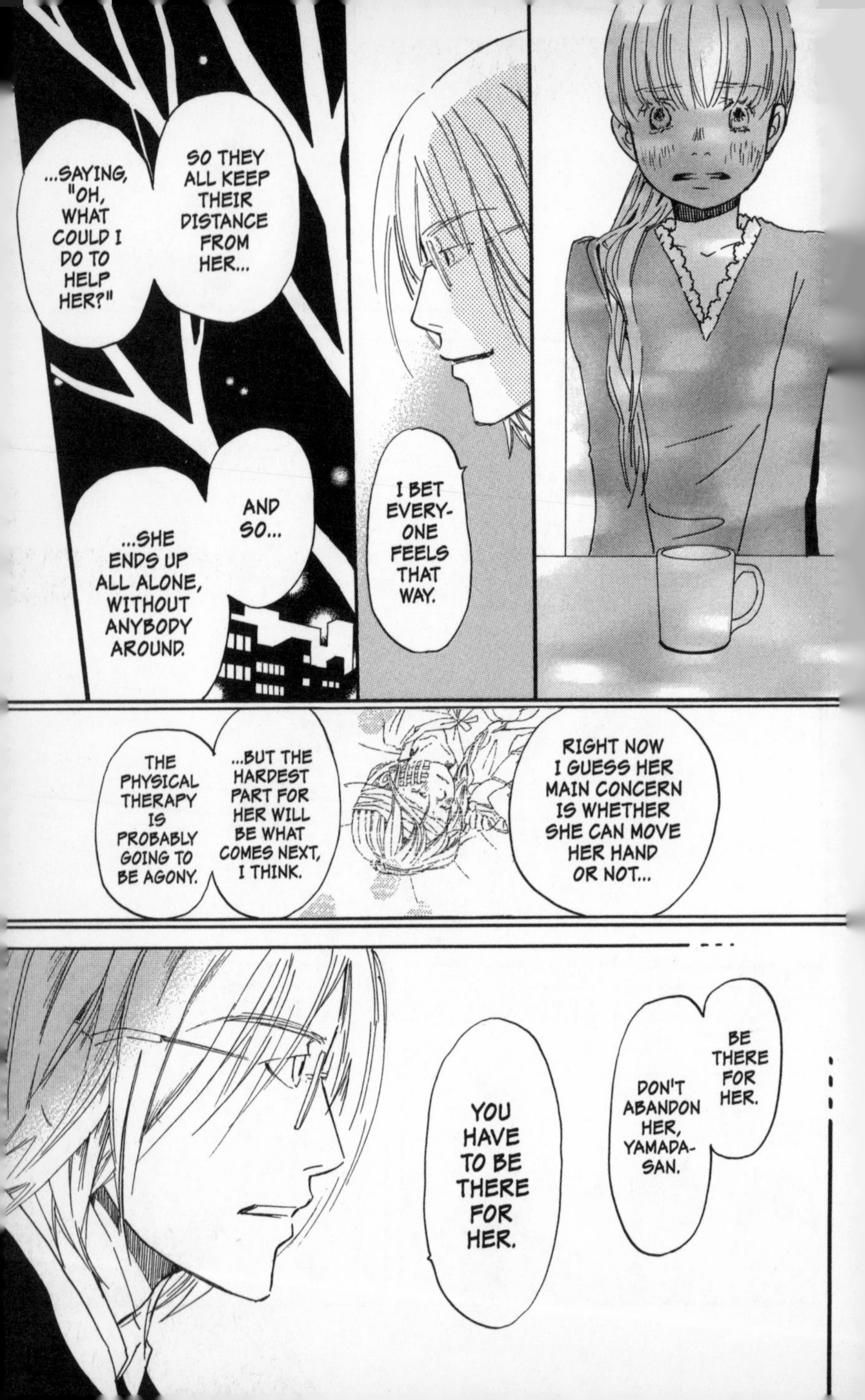
I BET EVERYONE FEELS THAT WAY.
SO THEY ALL KEEP THEIR DISTANCE FROM HER...
...SAYING, "OH, WHAT COULD I DO TO HELP HER?"
AND SO...
...SHE ENDS UP ALL ALONE, WITHOUT ANYBODY AROUND.
RIGHT NOW I GUESS HER MAIN CONCERN IS WHETHER SHE CAN MOVE HER HAND OR NOT...
...BUT THE HARDEST PART FOR HER WILL BE WHAT COMES NEXT, I THINK.
THE PHYSICAL THERAPY IS PROBABLY GOING TO BE AGONY.
BE THERE FOR HER.
DON'T ABANDON HER, YAMADA-SAN.
YOU HAVE TO BE THERE FOR HER.

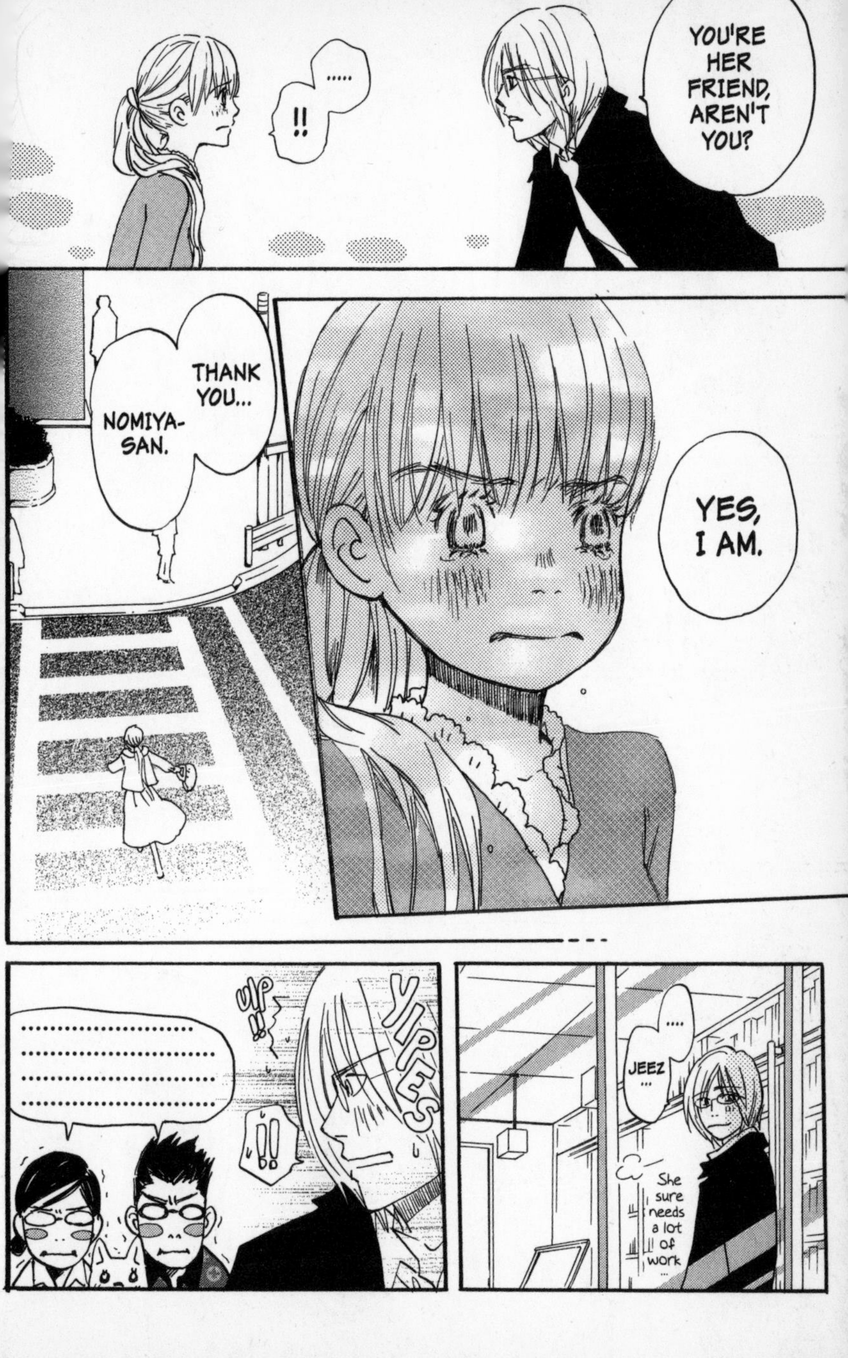
YOU'RE HER FRIEND, AREN'T YOU?
.....
!!
YES, I AM.
THANK YOU... NOMIYA-SAN.
.... JEEZ ...
She sure needs a lot of work ...
YIPES
UP!!
!!
....

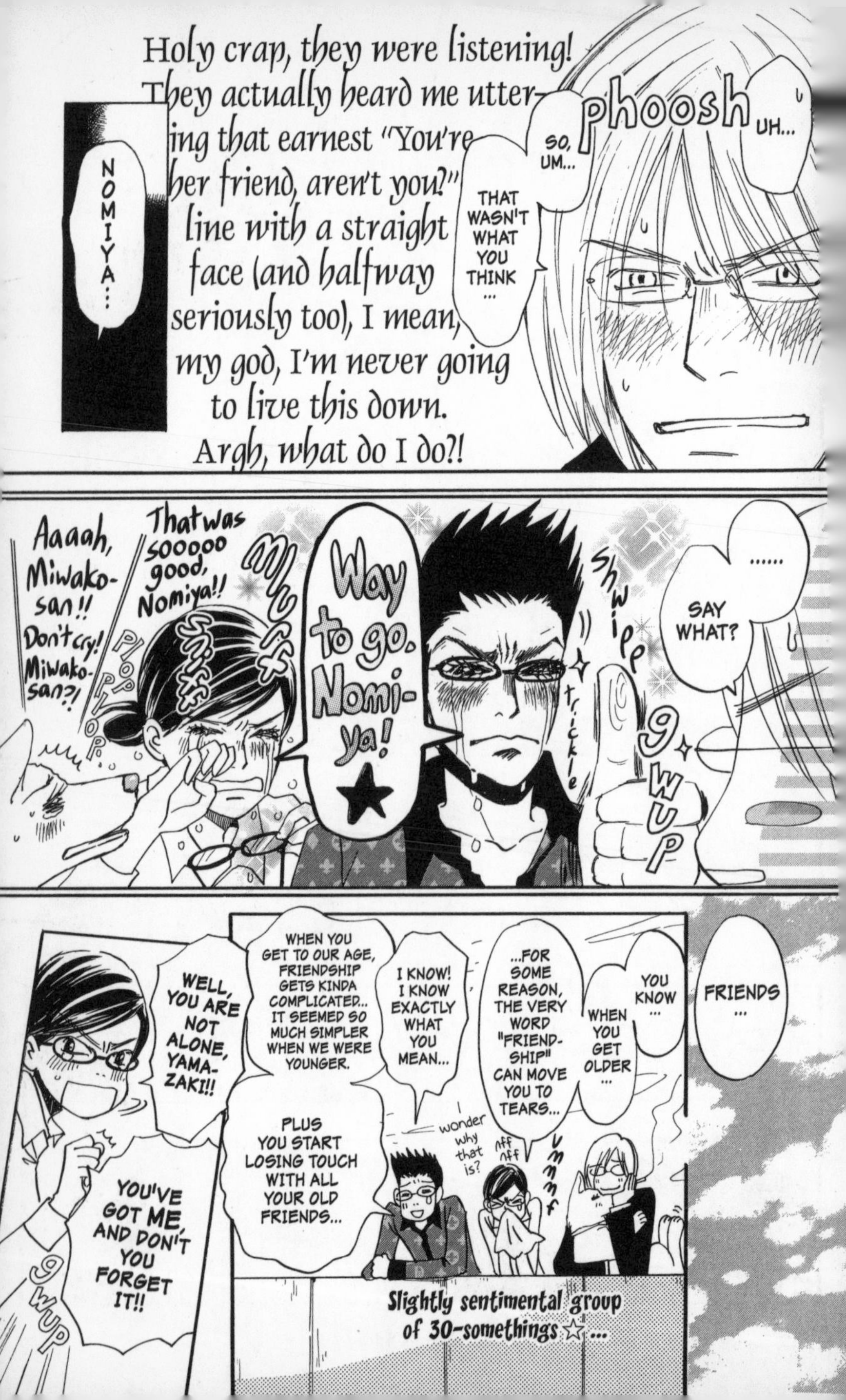
Phoosh
UH...
SO, UM...
THAT WASN'T WHAT YOU THINK ...
Holy crap, they were listening! They actually heard me uttering that earnest "You're her friend, aren't you?" line with a straight face (and halfway seriously too), I mean, my god, I'm never going to live this down. Argh, what do I do?!
NOMIYA...
......
SAY WHAT?
Shwipp
trickle
gwup
Way to go, Nomi-ya! ★
Murf
sniff
That was soooooo good, Nomiya!!
Aaaah, Miwako-san!! Don't cry! Miwako-san?!
FRIENDS ...
YOU KNOW ...
WHEN YOU GET OLDER ...
...FOR SOME REASON, THE VERY WORD "FRIENDSHIP" CAN MOVE YOU TO TEARS...
I KNOW! I KNOW EXACTLY WHAT YOU MEAN...
WHEN YOU GET TO OUR AGE, FRIENDSHIP GETS KINDA COMPLICATED... IT SEEMED SO MUCH SIMPLER WHEN WE WERE YOUNGER.
PLUS YOU START LOSING TOUCH WITH ALL YOUR OLD FRIENDS...
I wonder why that is?
nff nff
WELL, YOU ARE NOT ALONE, YAMAZAKI!!
YOU'VE GOT ME, AND DON'T YOU FORGET IT!!
gwup
Slightly sentimental group of 30-somethings ☆ ...

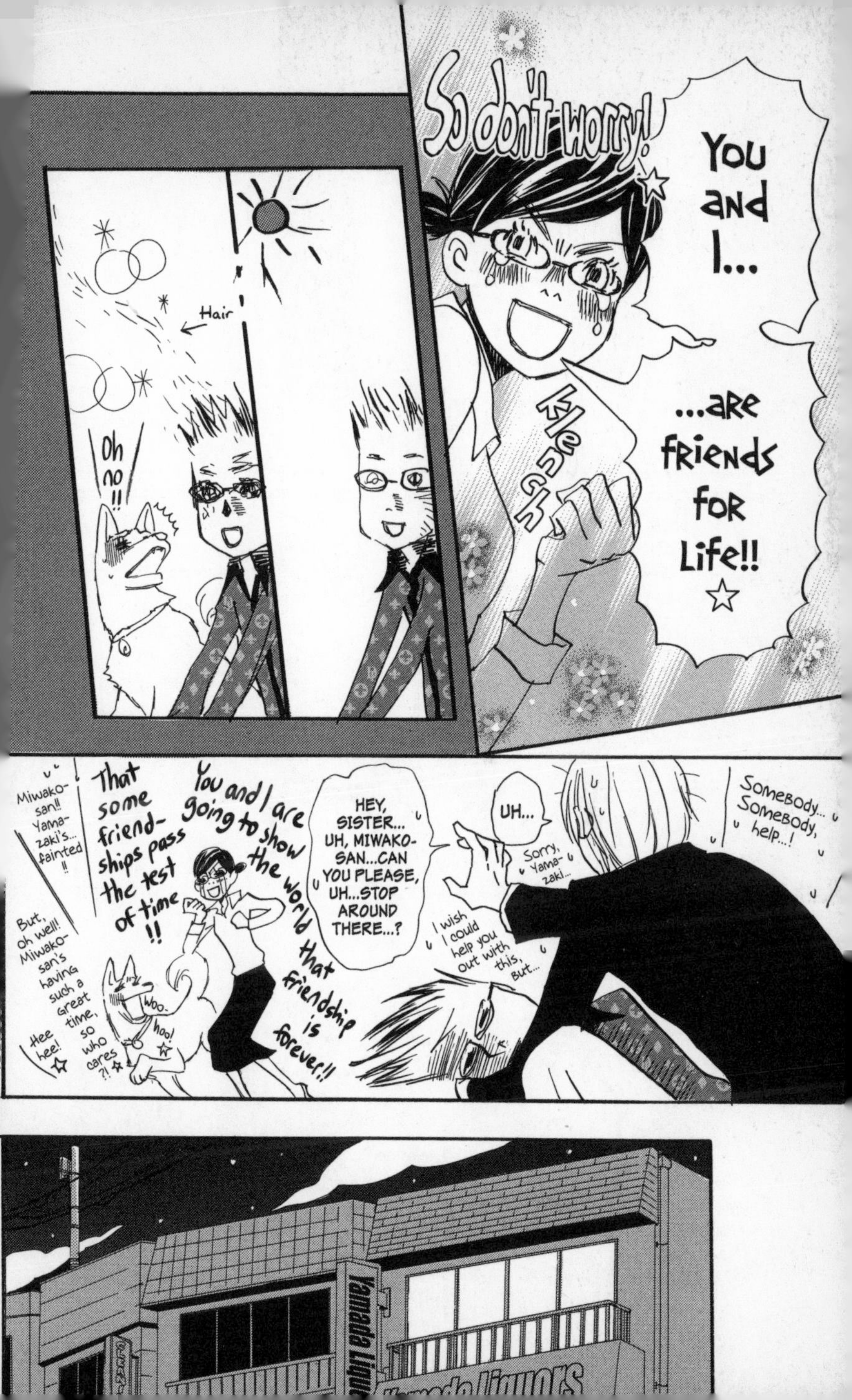
So don't worry!
You and I...
...are friends for Life!! ☆
Klench
Hair
Oh no!!
Somebody... Somebody, help...!
UH...
Sorry, Yamazaki...
I wish I could help you out with this, But...
HEY, SISTER... UH, MIWAKO-SAN...CAN YOU PLEASE, UH...STOP AROUND THERE...?
You and I are going to show the world that friendship is forever!!
That some friendships pass the test of time!!
Woo-hoo! ☆
Miwako-san!! Yamazaki's... fainted!!
But, oh well! Miwako-san's having such a great time, so who cares?! ☆
Hee hee! ☆

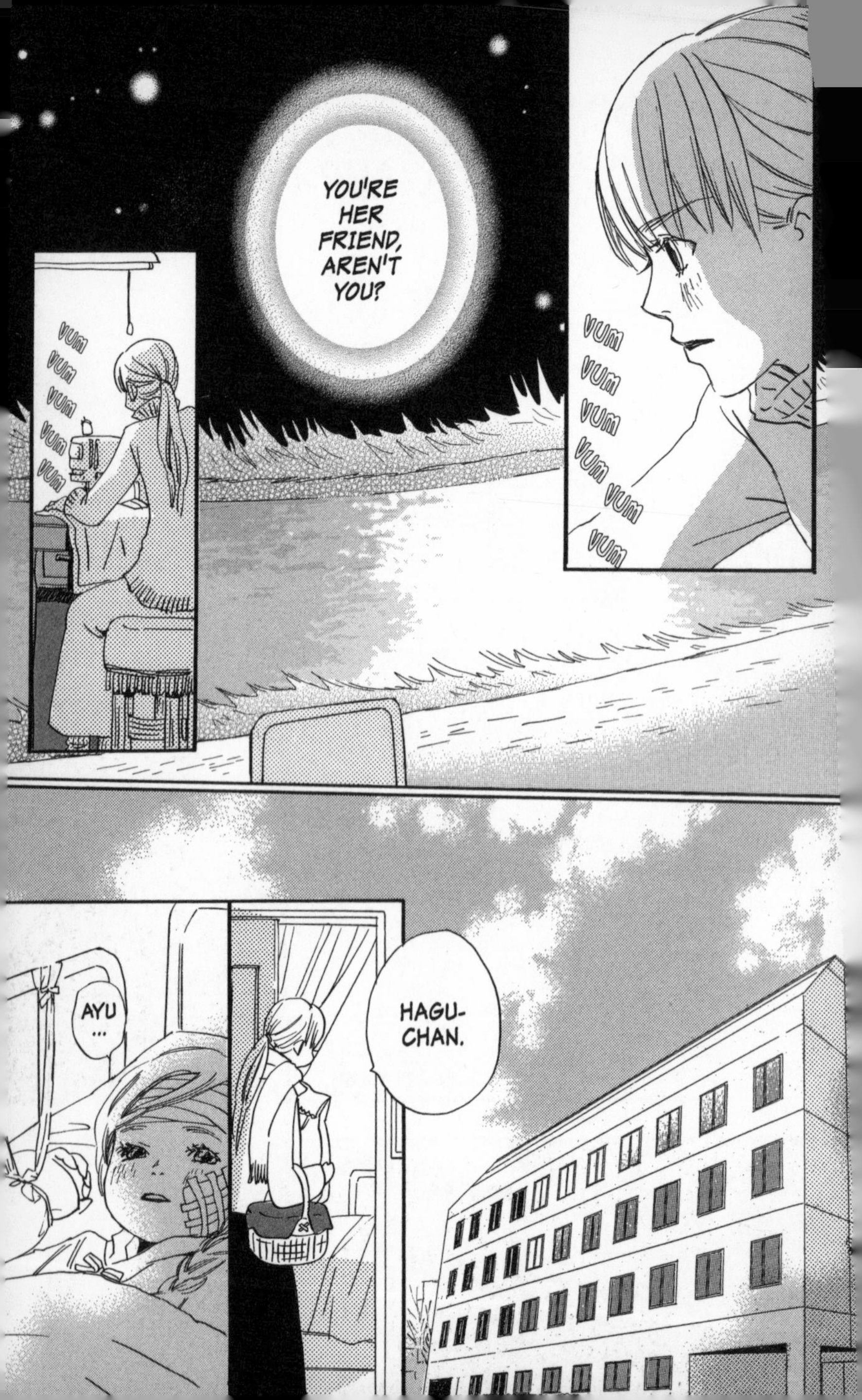
VUM VUM VUM VUM VUM VUM VUM
YOU'RE HER FRIEND, AREN'T YOU?
VUM VUM VUM VUM VUM VUM
HAGU-CHAN.
AYU ...

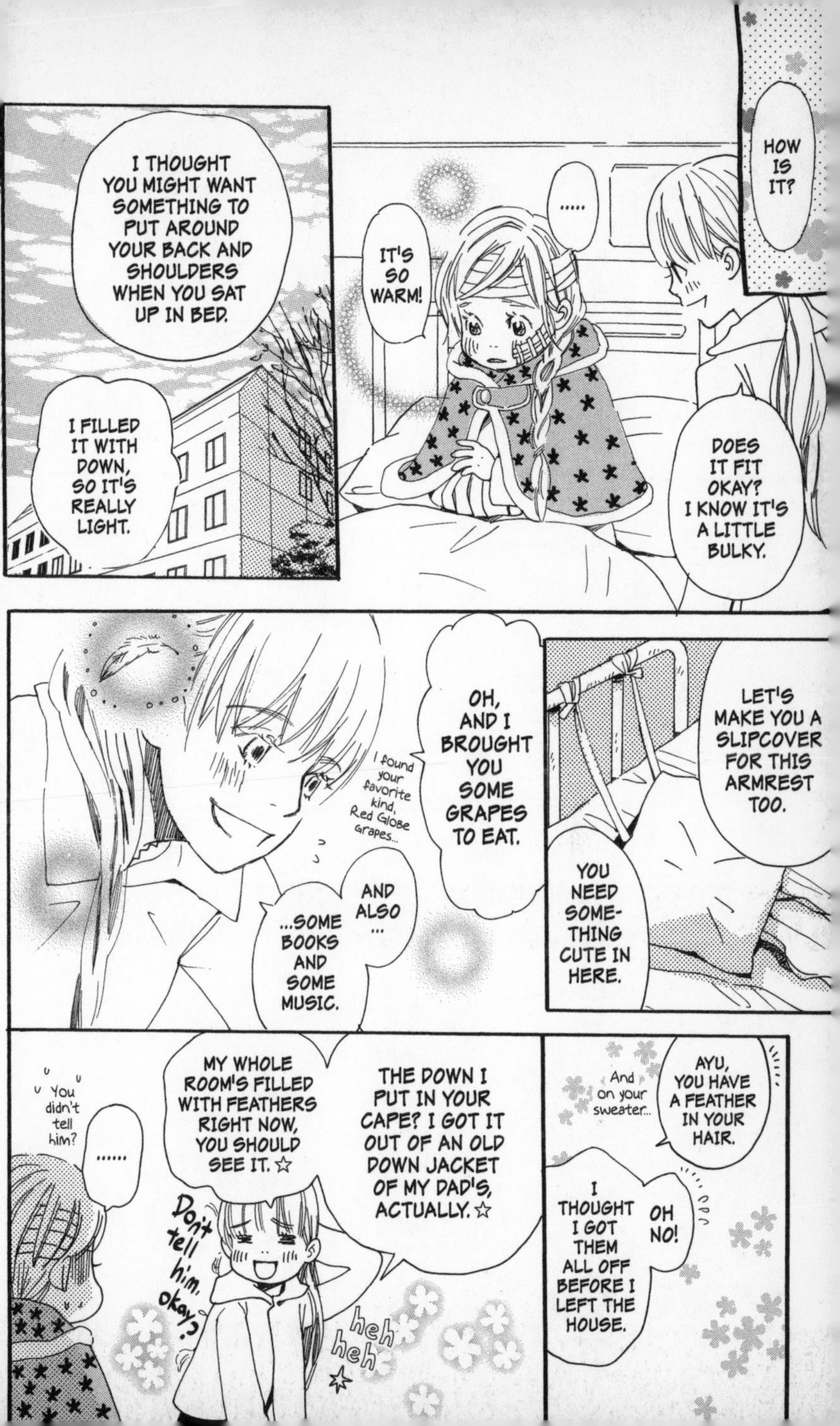
HOW IS IT?
DOES IT FIT OKAY? I KNOW IT'S A LITTLE BULKY.
.....
IT'S SO WARM!
I THOUGHT YOU MIGHT WANT SOMETHING TO PUT AROUND YOUR BACK AND SHOULDERS WHEN YOU SAT UP IN BED.
I FILLED IT WITH DOWN, SO IT'S REALLY LIGHT.
LET'S MAKE YOU A SLIPCOVER FOR THIS ARMREST TOO.
YOU NEED SOMETHING CUTE IN HERE.
OH, AND I BROUGHT YOU SOME GRAPES TO EAT.
I found your favorite kind, Red Globe Grapes...
AND ALSO...
...SOME BOOKS AND SOME MUSIC.
AYU, YOU HAVE A FEATHER IN YOUR HAIR.
And on your sweater...
OH NO!
I THOUGHT I GOT THEM ALL OFF BEFORE I LEFT THE HOUSE.
THE DOWN I PUT IN YOUR CAPE? I GOT IT OUT OF AN OLD DOWN JACKET OF MY DAD'S, ACTUALLY. ☆
MY WHOLE ROOM'S FILLED WITH FEATHERS RIGHT NOW, YOU SHOULD SEE IT. ☆
Don't tell him, okay?
heh heh ☆
You didn't tell him?
......

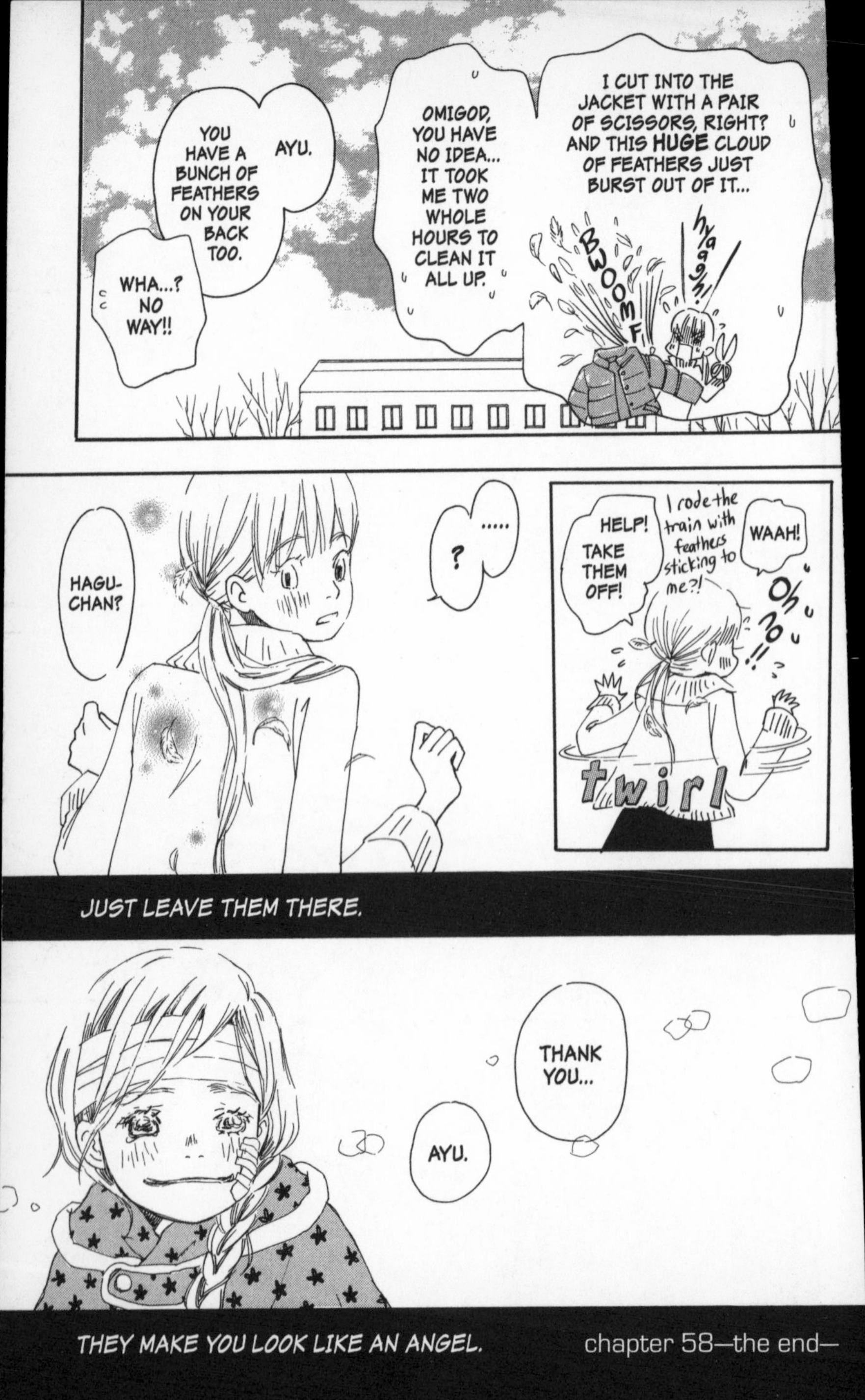
I CUT INTO THE JACKET WITH A PAIR OF SCISSORS, RIGHT? AND THIS **HUGE** CLOUD OF FEATHERS JUST BURST OUT OF IT...
hyaagh!
BWOOMF
OMIGOD, YOU HAVE NO IDEA... IT TOOK ME TWO WHOLE HOURS TO CLEAN IT ALL UP.
AYU.
YOU HAVE A BUNCH OF FEATHERS ON YOUR BACK TOO.
WHA...? NO WAY!!
WAAH!
Oh no!!
I rode the train with feathers sticking to me?!
HELP! TAKE THEM OFF!
twirl
.....
?
HAGU-CHAN?
JUST LEAVE THEM THERE.
THANK YOU...
AYU.
THEY MAKE YOU LOOK LIKE AN ANGEL.
chapter 58—the end—

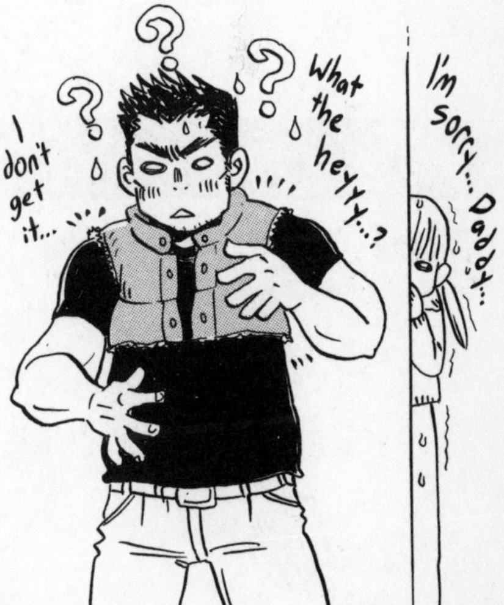
I'm sorry... Daddy...
What the heyyy...?
I don't get it...

honey and clover

chapter 59

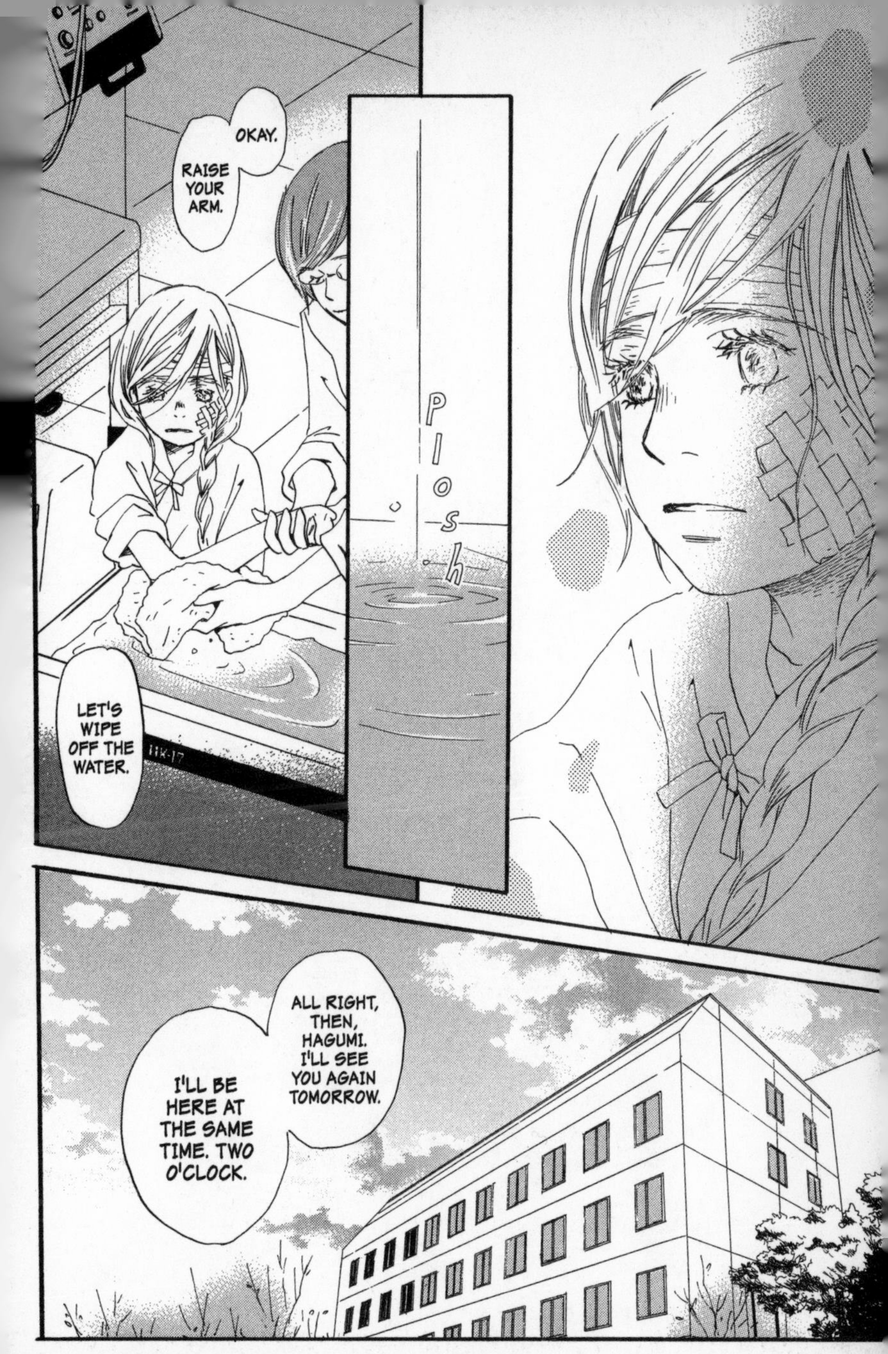
Plosh
OKAY.
RAISE YOUR ARM.
LET'S WIPE OFF THE WATER.
ALL RIGHT, THEN, HAGUMI. I'LL SEE YOU AGAIN TOMORROW.
I'LL BE HERE AT THE SAME TIME. TWO O'CLOCK.

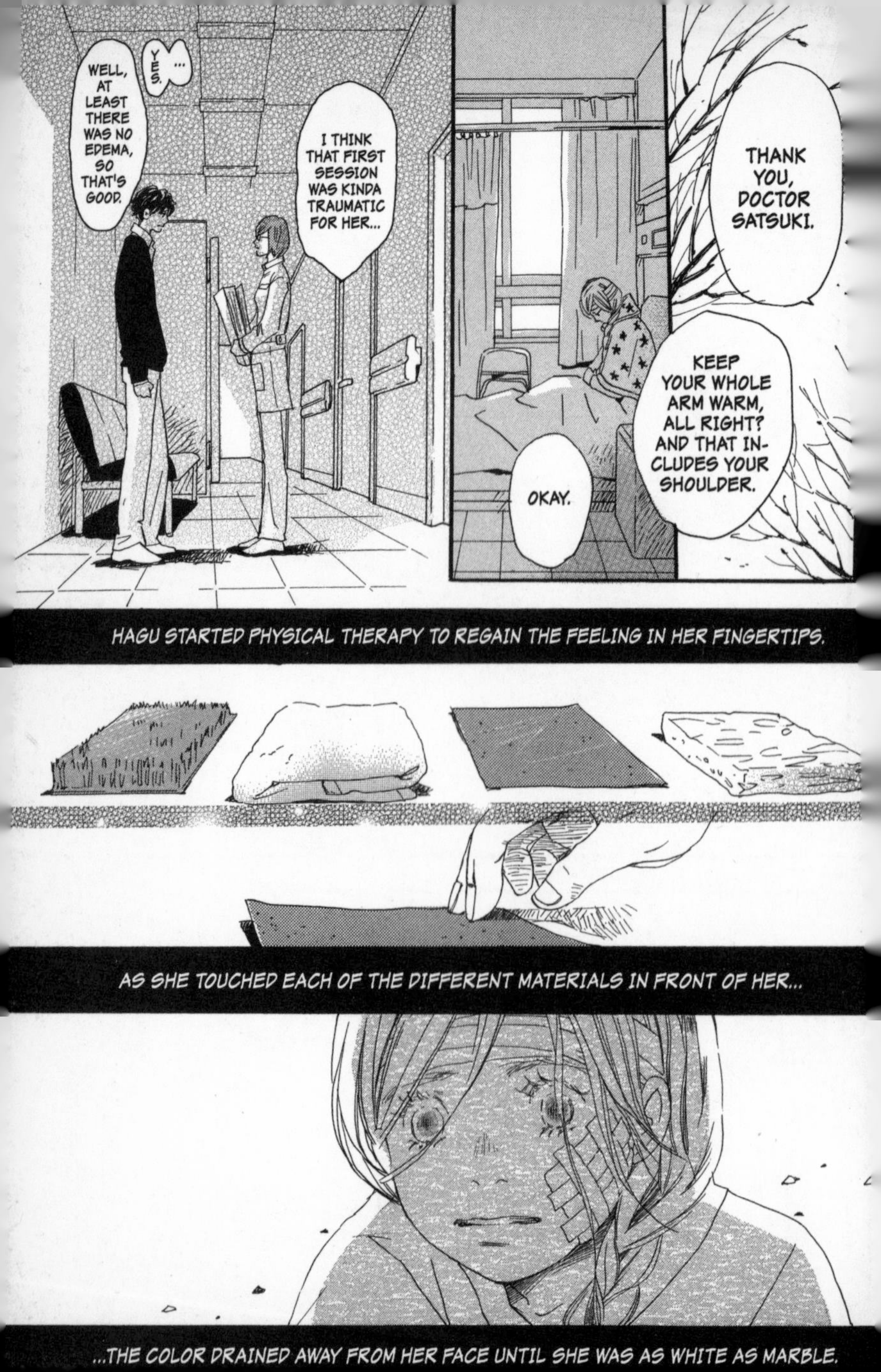
THANK YOU, DOCTOR SATSUKI.
KEEP YOUR WHOLE ARM WARM, ALL RIGHT? AND THAT IN-CLUDES YOUR SHOULDER.
OKAY.
I THINK THAT FIRST SESSION WAS KINDA TRAUMATIC FOR HER...
YES. ...
WELL, AT LEAST THERE WAS NO EDEMA, SO THAT'S GOOD.
HAGU STARTED PHYSICAL THERAPY TO REGAIN THE FEELING IN HER FINGERTIPS.
AS SHE TOUCHED EACH OF THE DIFFERENT MATERIALS IN FRONT OF HER...
...THE COLOR DRAINED AWAY FROM HER FACE UNTIL SHE WAS AS WHITE AS MARBLE.

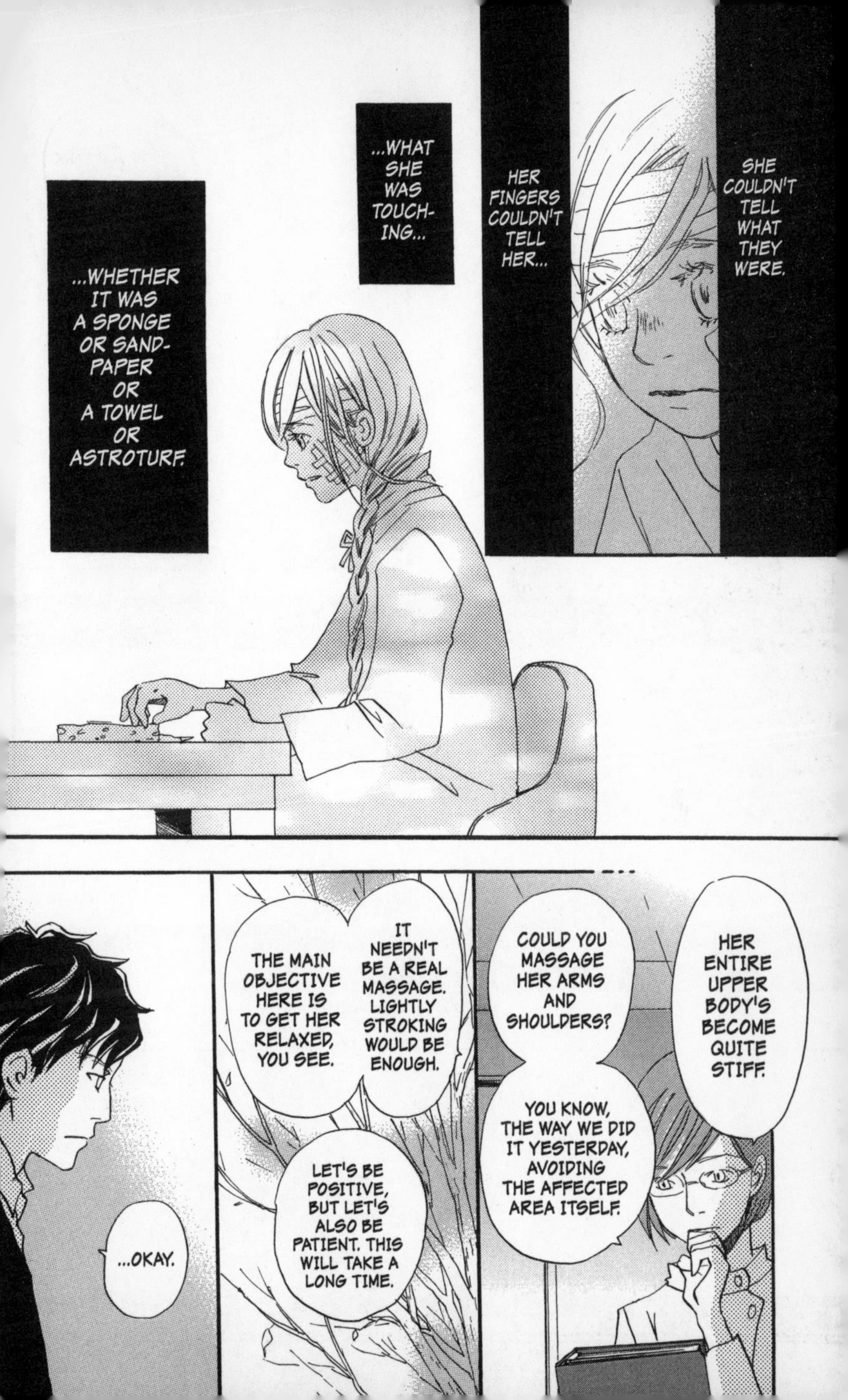
SHE COULDN'T TELL WHAT THEY WERE.
HER FINGERS COULDN'T TELL HER...
...WHAT SHE WAS TOUCHING...
...WHETHER IT WAS A SPONGE OR SANDPAPER OR A TOWEL OR ASTROTURF.
HER ENTIRE UPPER BODY'S BECOME QUITE STIFF.
COULD YOU MASSAGE HER ARMS AND SHOULDERS?
YOU KNOW, THE WAY WE DID IT YESTERDAY, AVOIDING THE AFFECTED AREA ITSELF.
IT NEEDN'T BE A REAL MASSAGE. LIGHTLY STROKING WOULD BE ENOUGH.
THE MAIN OBJECTIVE HERE IS TO GET HER RELAXED, YOU SEE.
LET'S BE POSITIVE, BUT LET'S ALSO BE PATIENT. THIS WILL TAKE A LONG TIME.
...OKAY.

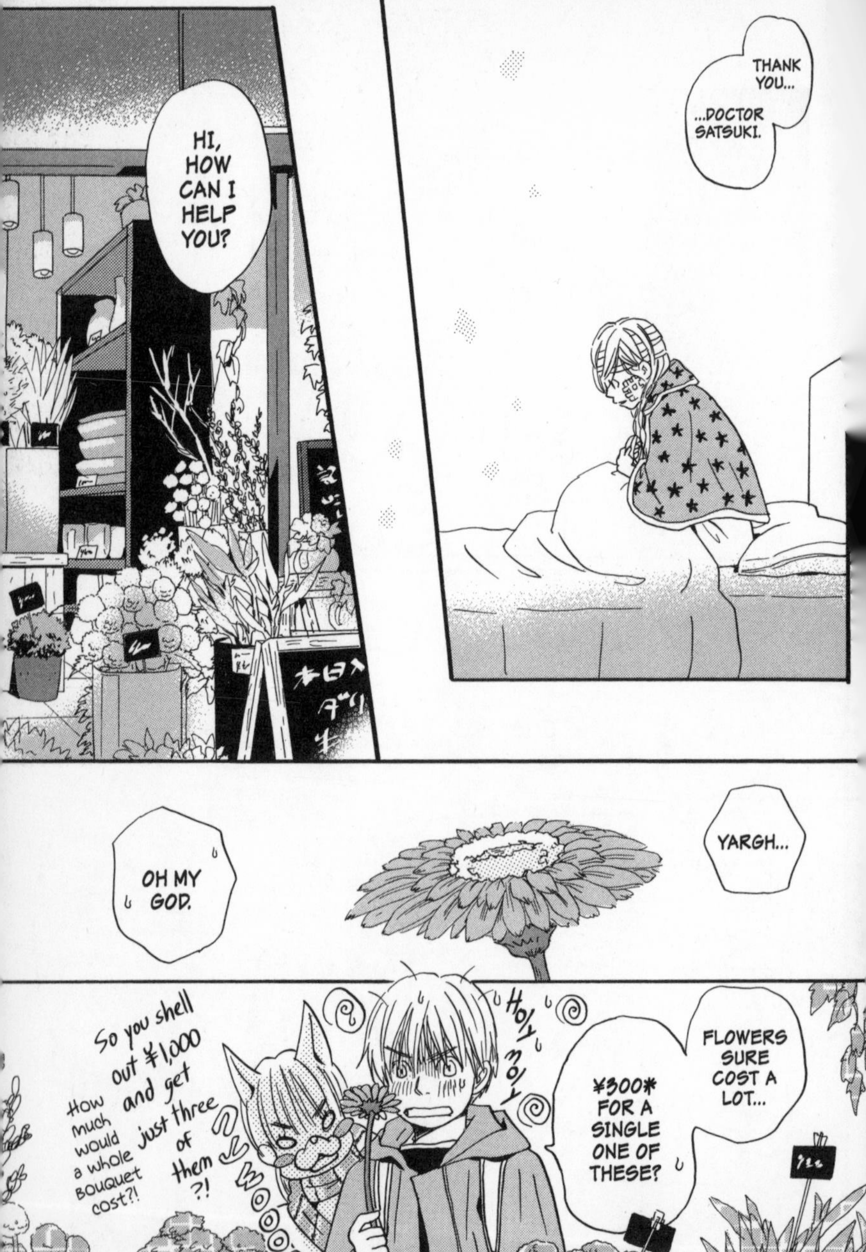
THANK YOU...
...DOCTOR SATSUKI.
HI, HOW CAN I HELP YOU?
YARGH...
OH MY GOD.
FLOWERS SURE COST A LOT...
¥300* FOR A SINGLE ONE OF THESE?
Holy moly
So you shell out ¥1,000 and get just three of them?!
How much would a whole bouquet cost?!

*about $2.87

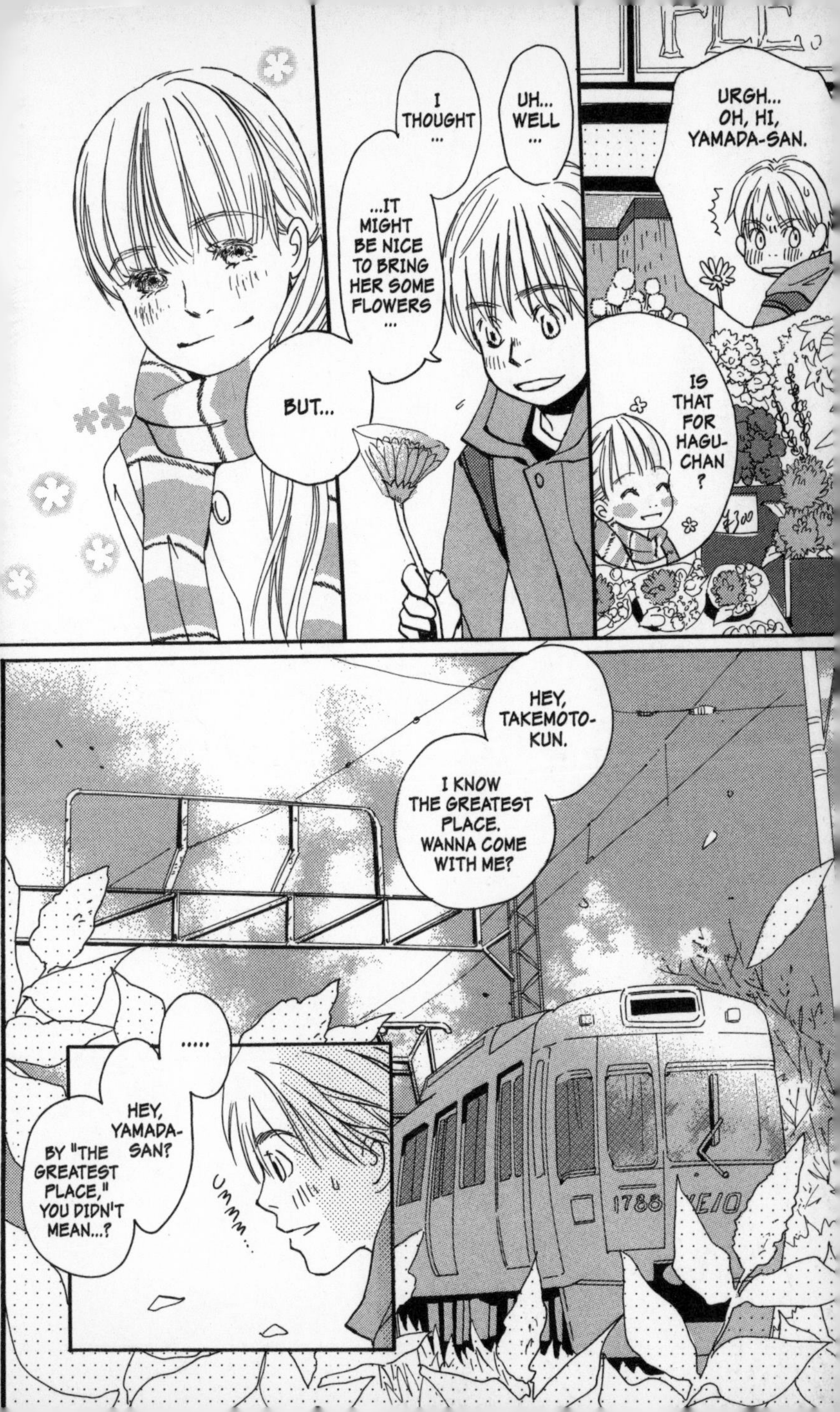
URGH... OH, HI, YAMADA-SAN.
IS THAT FOR HAGU-CHAN?
UH... WELL...
I THOUGHT...
...IT MIGHT BE NICE TO BRING HER SOME FLOWERS...
BUT...
HEY, TAKEMOTO-KUN.
I KNOW THE GREATEST PLACE. WANNA COME WITH ME?
......
HEY, YAMADA-SAN?
BY "THE GREATEST PLACE," YOU DIDN'T MEAN...?
UMMM...
1788
KEIO

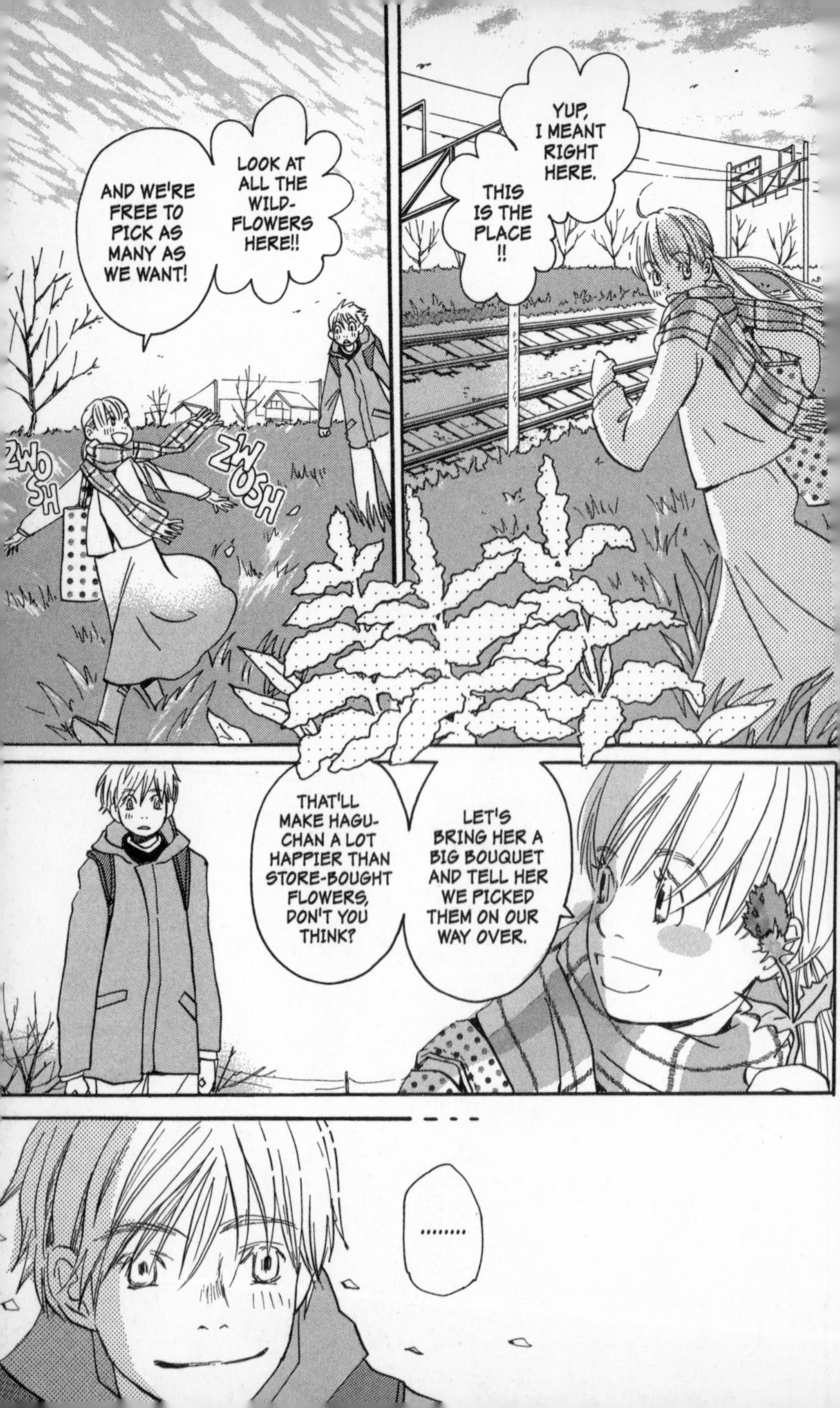
YUP, I MEANT RIGHT HERE.
THIS IS THE PLACE !!
LOOK AT ALL THE WILD-FLOWERS HERE!!
AND WE'RE FREE TO PICK AS MANY AS WE WANT!
ZWOSH
ZWOSH
LET'S BRING HER A BIG BOUQUET AND TELL HER WE PICKED THEM ON OUR WAY OVER.
THAT'LL MAKE HAGU-CHAN A LOT HAPPIER THAN STORE-BOUGHT FLOWERS, DON'T YOU THINK?
....

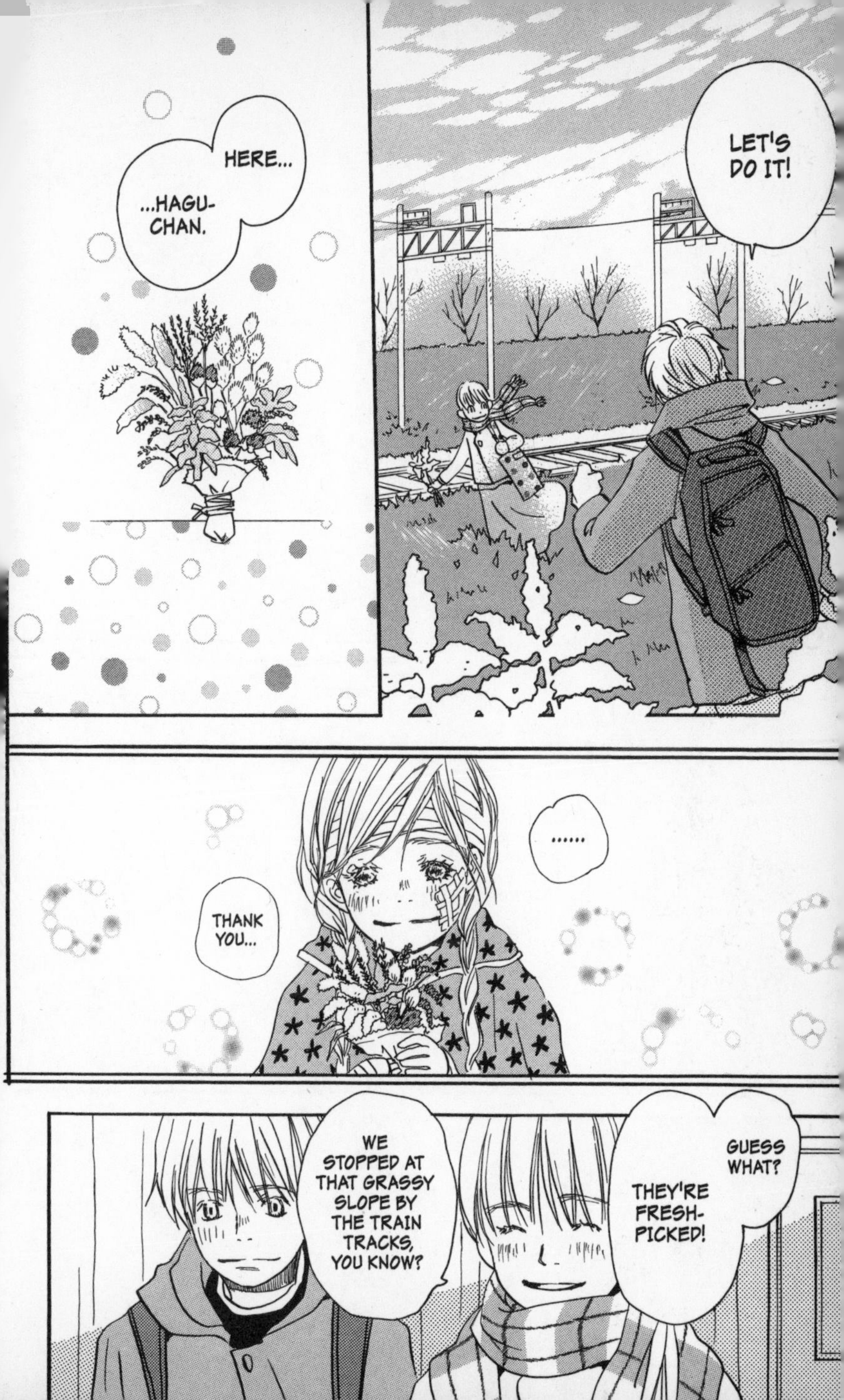
LET'S DO IT!
HERE...
...HAGU-CHAN.
......
THANK YOU...
GUESS WHAT?
THEY'RE FRESH-PICKED!
WE STOPPED AT THAT GRASSY SLOPE BY THE TRAIN TRACKS, YOU KNOW?

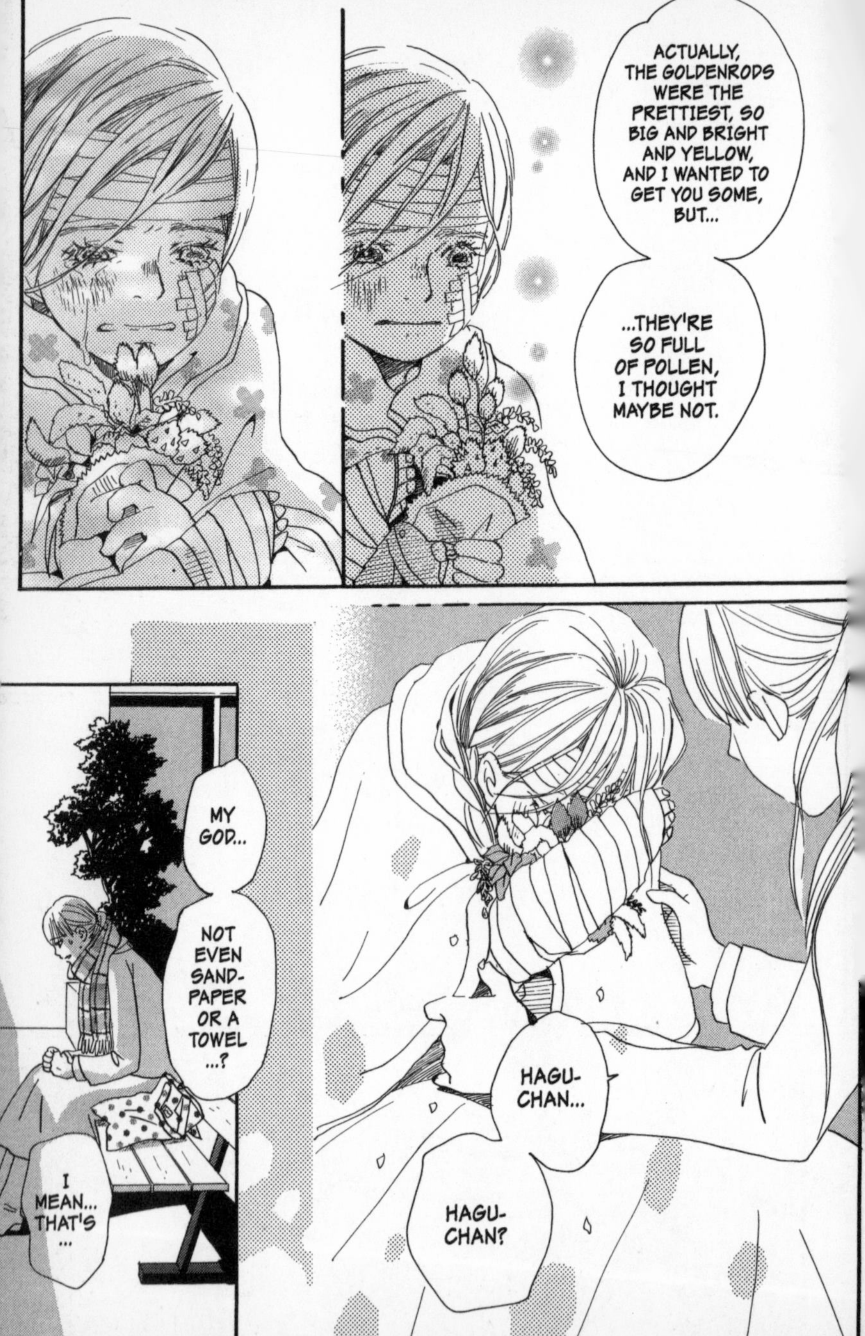
ACTUALLY, THE GOLDENRODS WERE THE PRETTIEST, SO BIG AND BRIGHT AND YELLOW, AND I WANTED TO GET YOU SOME, BUT...
...THEY'RE SO FULL OF POLLEN, I THOUGHT MAYBE NOT.
HAGU-CHAN...
HAGU-CHAN?
MY GOD...
NOT EVEN SAND-PAPER OR A TOWEL ...?
I MEAN... THAT'S ...

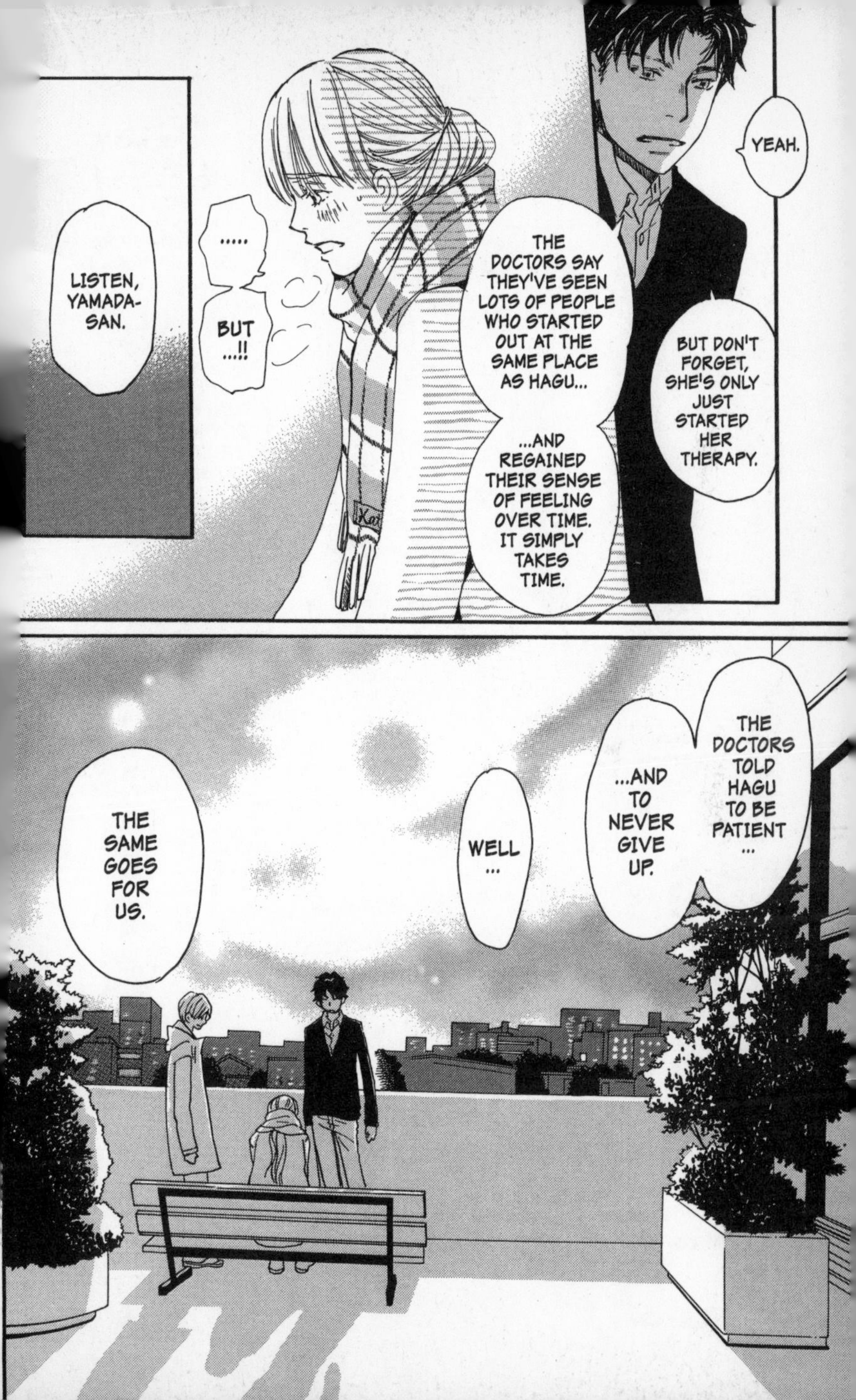
YEAH.
BUT DON'T FORGET, SHE'S ONLY JUST STARTED HER THERAPY.
THE DOCTORS SAY THEY'VE SEEN LOTS OF PEOPLE WHO STARTED OUT AT THE SAME PLACE AS HAGU...
...AND REGAINED THEIR SENSE OF FEELING OVER TIME. IT SIMPLY TAKES TIME.
.....
BUT ...!!
LISTEN, YAMADA-SAN.
THE DOCTORS TOLD HAGU TO BE PATIENT ...
...AND TO NEVER GIVE UP.
WELL ...
THE SAME GOES FOR US.

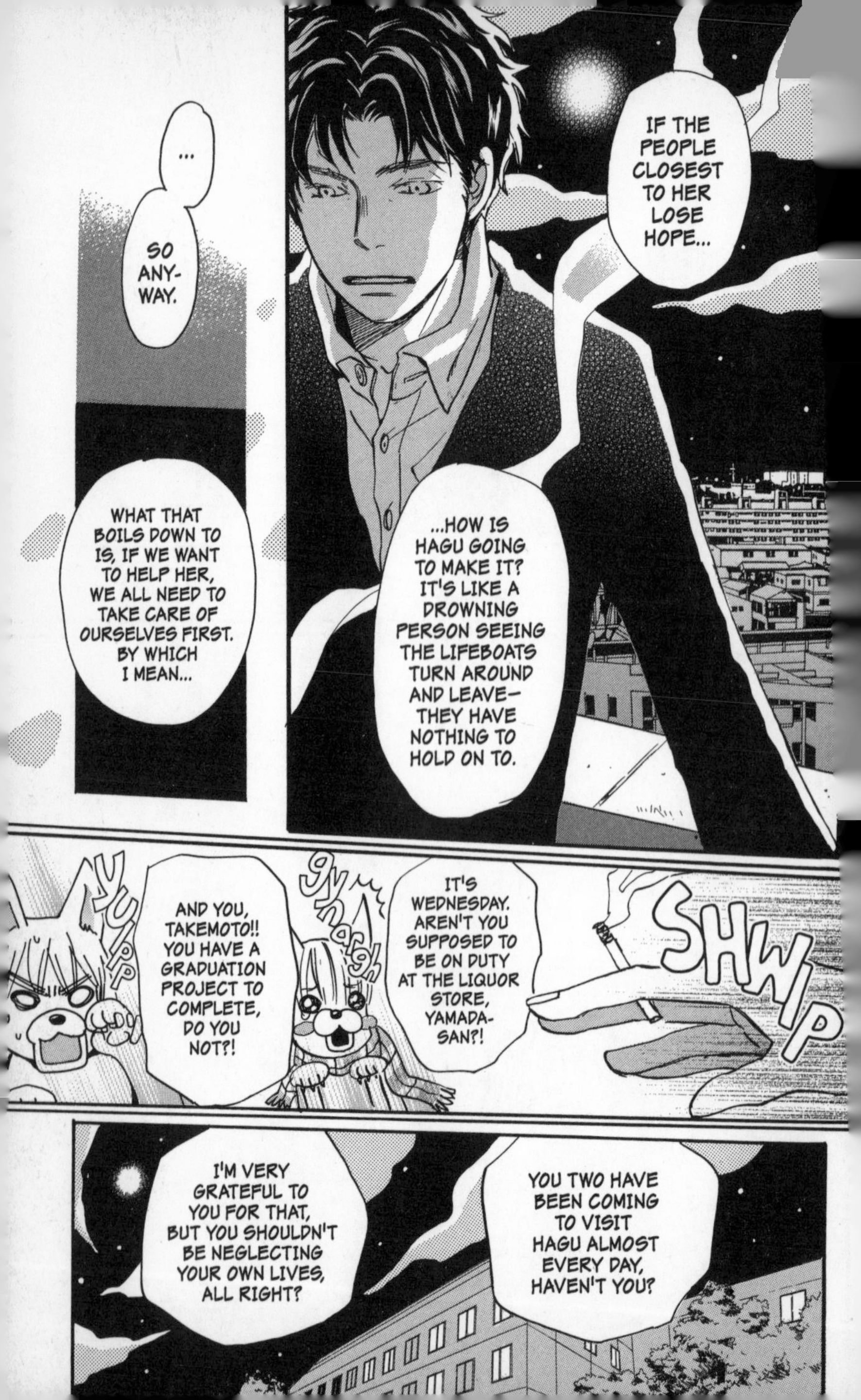
IF THE PEOPLE CLOSEST TO HER LOSE HOPE...
...HOW IS HAGU GOING TO MAKE IT? IT'S LIKE A DROWNING PERSON SEEING THE LIFEBOATS TURN AROUND AND LEAVE— THEY HAVE NOTHING TO HOLD ON TO.
...
SO ANY-WAY.
WHAT THAT BOILS DOWN TO IS, IF WE WANT TO HELP HER, WE ALL NEED TO TAKE CARE OF OURSELVES FIRST. BY WHICH I MEAN...
SHWIP
IT'S WEDNESDAY. AREN'T YOU SUPPOSED TO BE ON DUTY AT THE LIQUOR STORE, YAMADA-SAN?!
AND YOU, TAKEMOTO!! YOU HAVE A GRADUATION PROJECT TO COMPLETE, DO YOU NOT?!
YUIPP
YOU TWO HAVE BEEN COMING TO VISIT HAGU ALMOST EVERY DAY, HAVEN'T YOU?
I'M VERY GRATEFUL TO YOU FOR THAT, BUT YOU SHOULDN'T BE NEGLECTING YOUR OWN LIVES, ALL RIGHT?

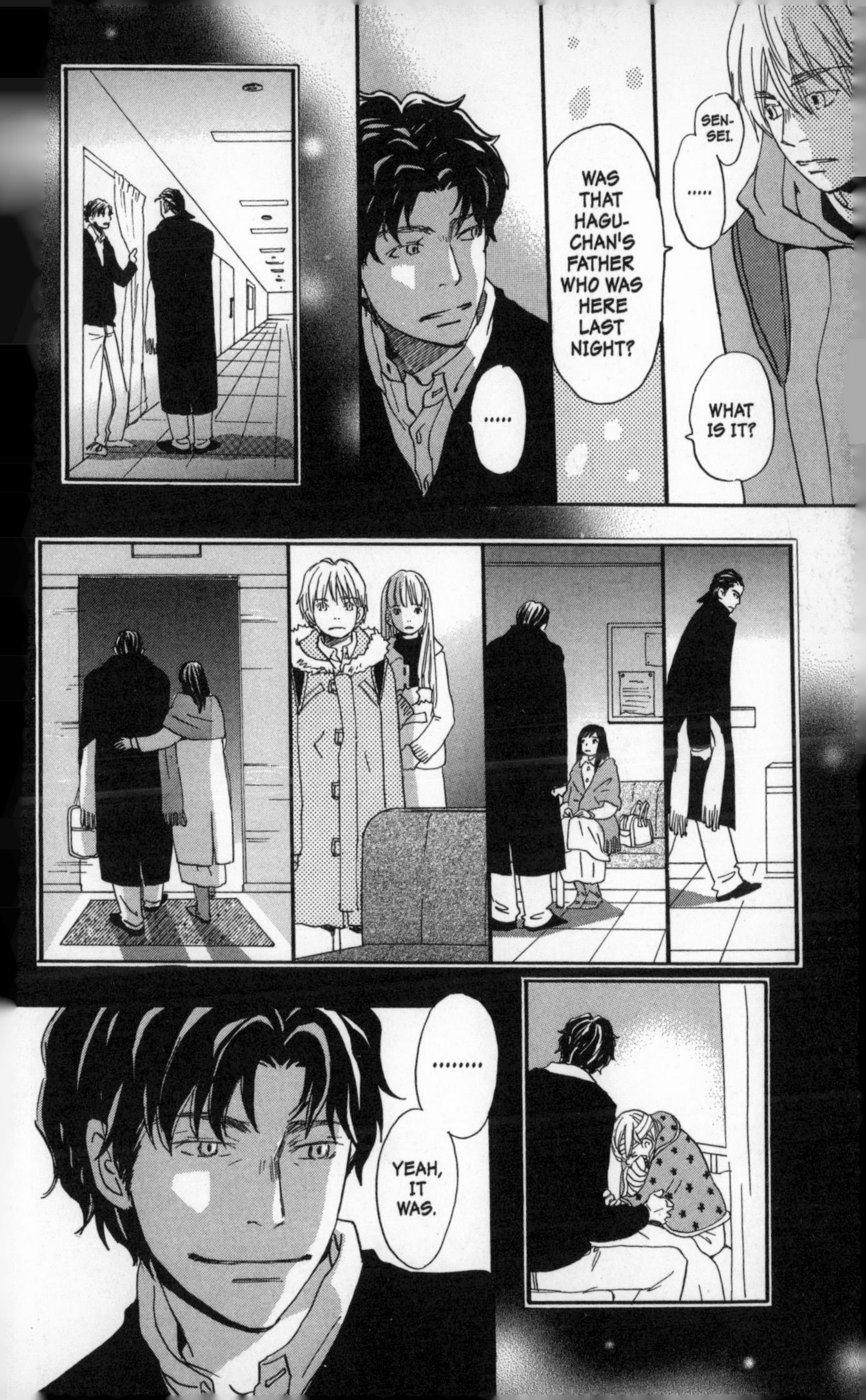
SEN-SEI.
.....
WHAT IS IT?
WAS THAT HAGU-CHAN'S FATHER WHO WAS HERE LAST NIGHT?
.....
....
YEAH, IT WAS.

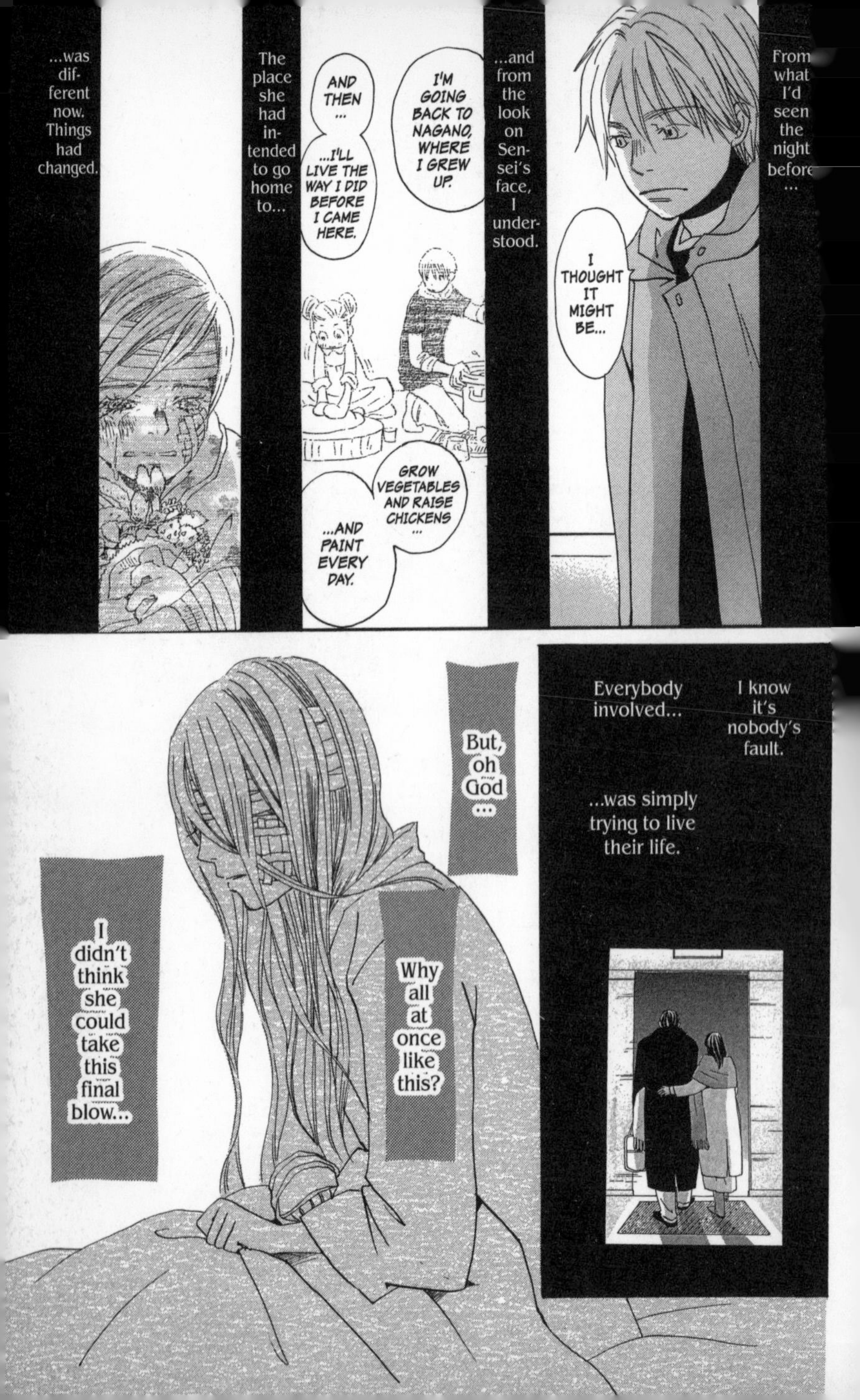
From what I'd seen the night before...
I thought it might be...
...and from the look on Sensei's face, I understood.
I'm going back to Nagano, where I grew up.
And then...
...I'll live the way I did before I came here.
Grow vegetables and raise chickens...
...and paint every day.
The place she had intended to go home to...
...was different now. Things had changed.
I know it's nobody's fault.
Everybody involved...
...was simply trying to live their life.
But, oh God...
Why all at once like this?
I didn't think she could take this final blow...

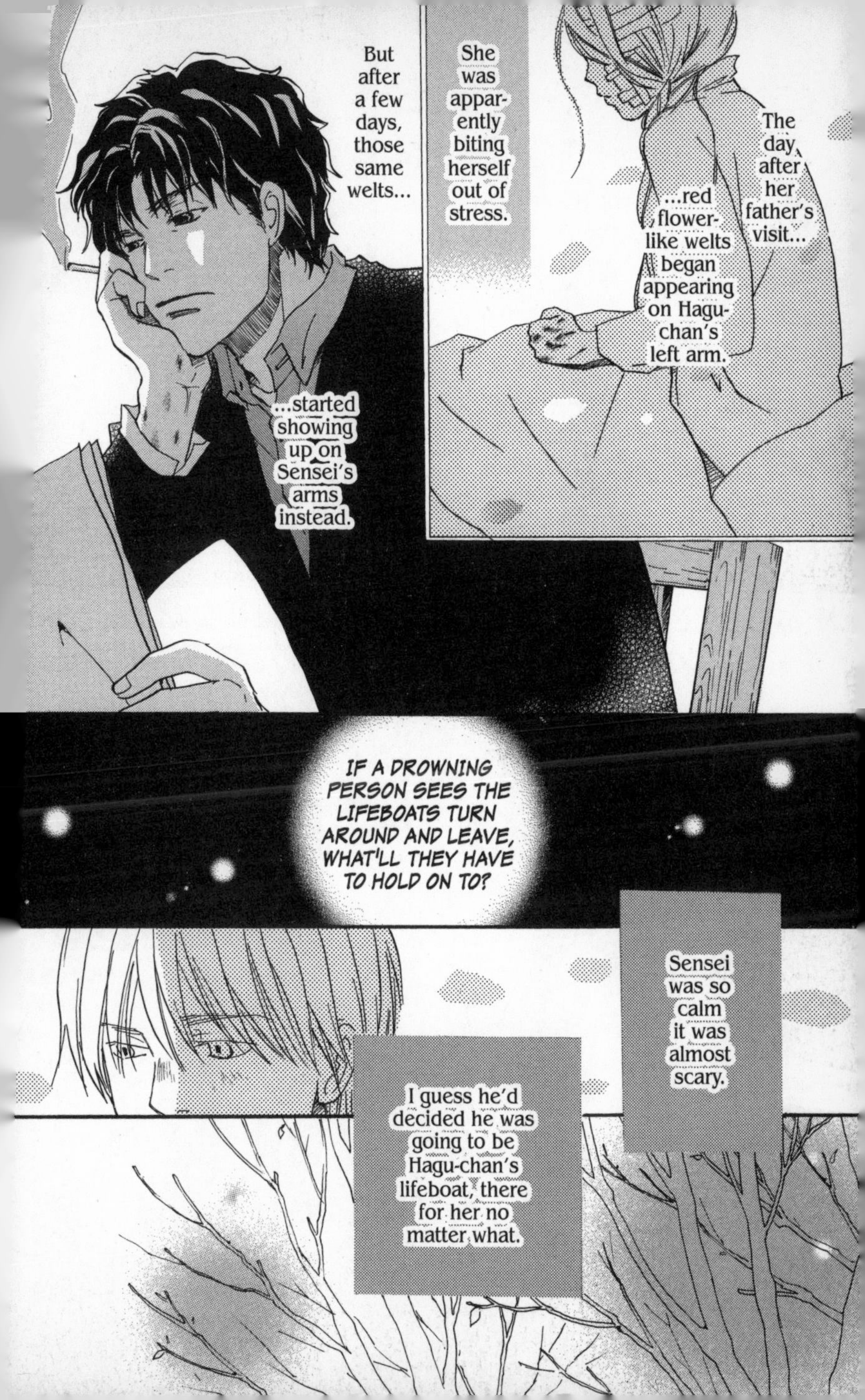
The day after her father's visit...
...red flower-like welts began appearing on Hagu-chan's left arm.
She was apparently biting herself out of stress.
But after a few days, those same welts...
...started showing up on Sensei's arms instead.
IF A DROWNING PERSON SEES THE LIFEBOATS TURN AROUND AND LEAVE, WHAT'LL THEY HAVE TO HOLD ON TO?
Sensei was so calm it was almost scary.
I guess he'd decided he was going to be Hagu-chan's lifeboat, there for her no matter what.

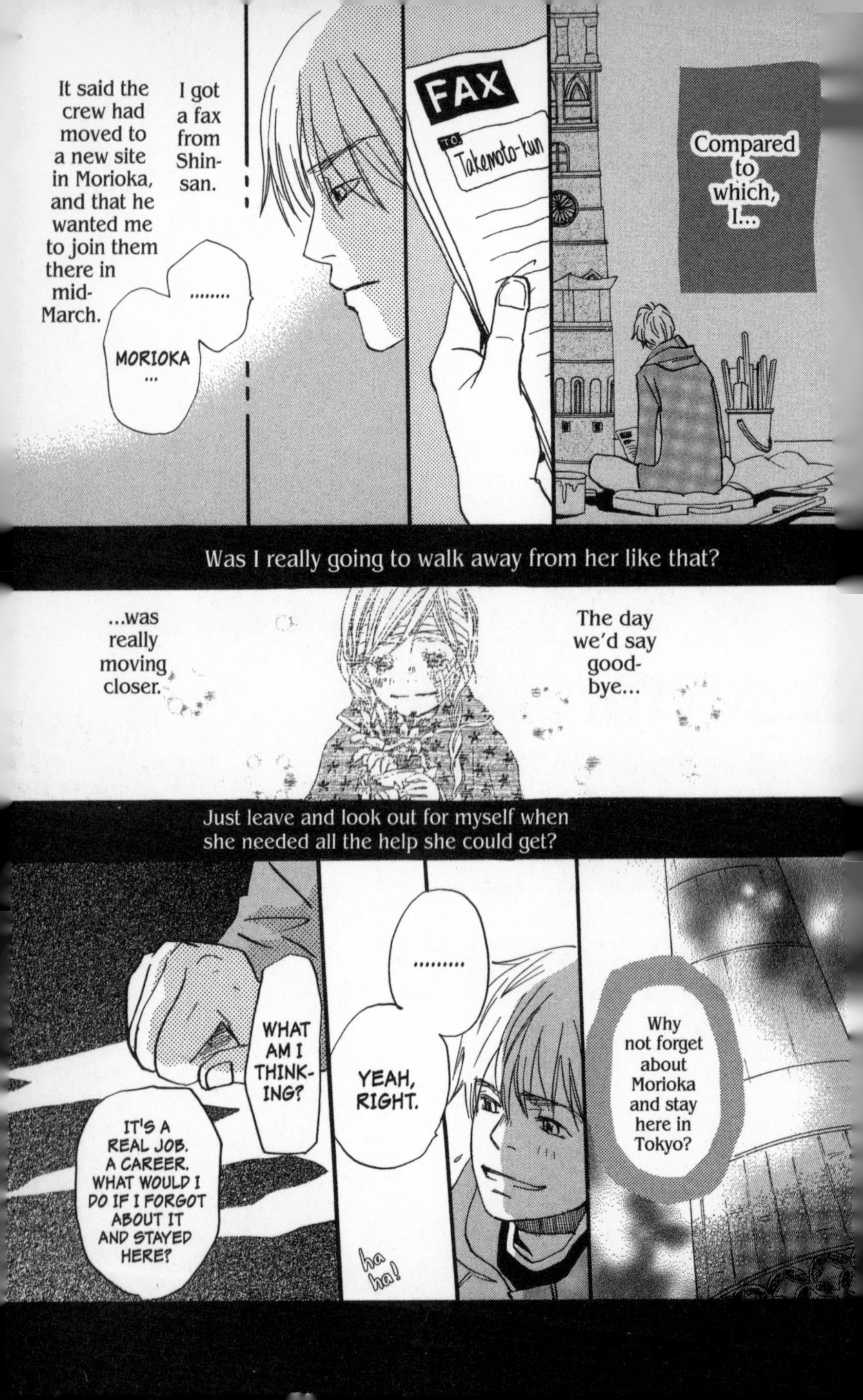
Compared to which, I...
FAX
TO: Takemoto-kun
I got a fax from Shin-san.
It said the crew had moved to a new site in Morioka, and that he wanted me to join them there in mid-March.
....
MORIOKA ...
Was I really going to walk away from her like that?
The day we'd say good-bye...
...was really moving closer.
Just leave and look out for myself when she needed all the help she could get?
Why not forget about Morioka and stay here in Tokyo?
....
YEAH, RIGHT.
ha ha!
WHAT AM I THINK-ING?
IT'S A REAL JOB. A CAREER. WHAT WOULD I DO IF I FORGOT ABOUT IT AND STAYED HERE?

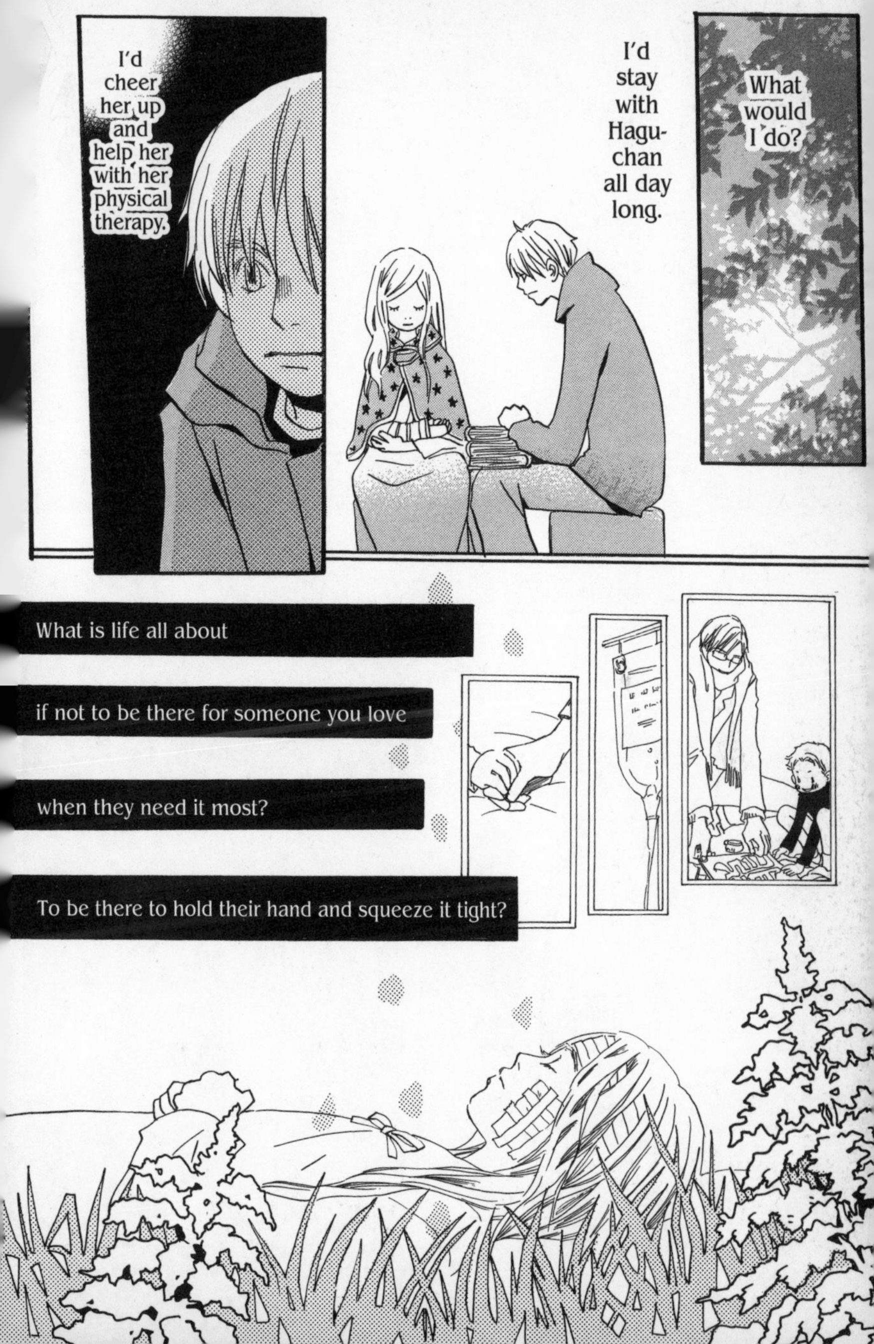
What would I do?
I'd stay with Hagu-chan all day long.
I'd cheer her up and help her with her physical therapy.
What is life all about
if not to be there for someone you love
when they need it most?
To be there to hold their hand and squeeze it tight?

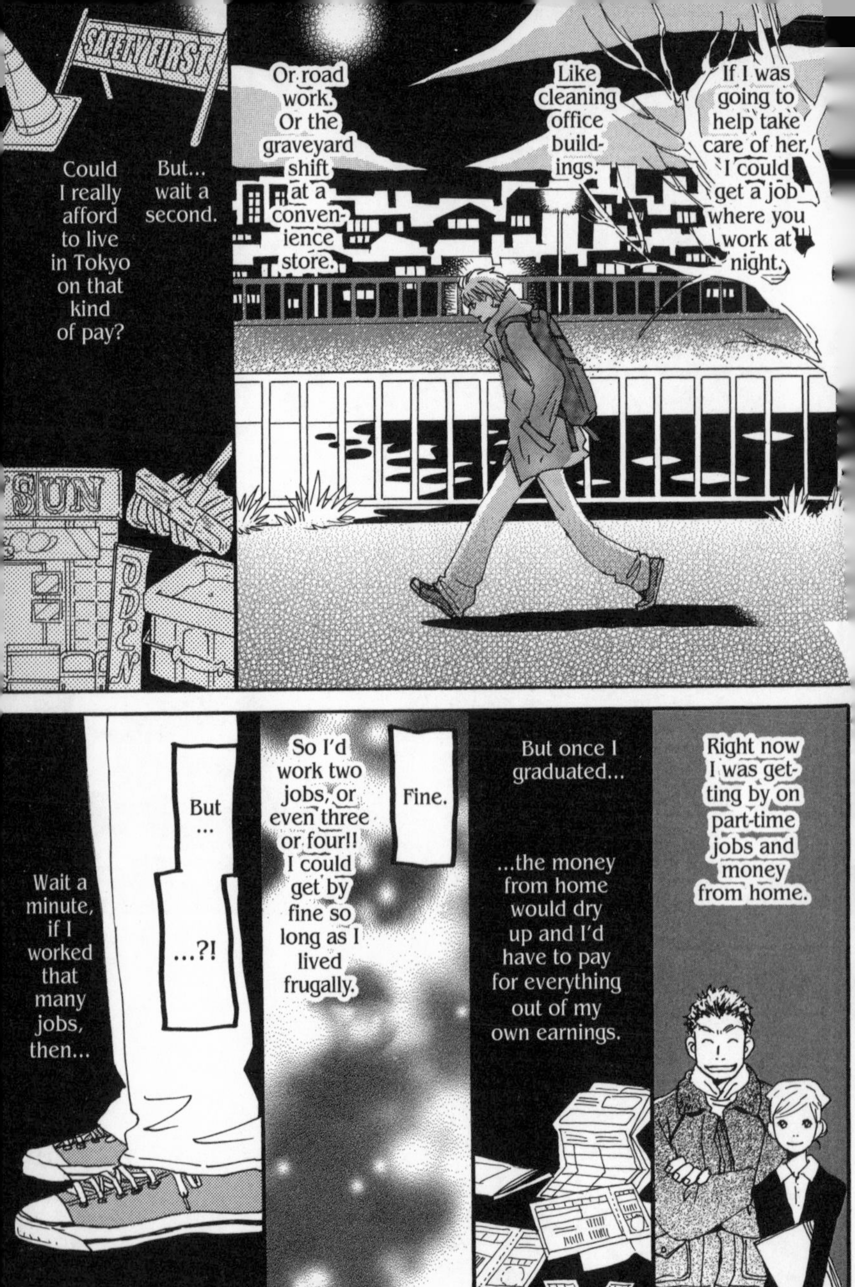
If I was going to help take care of her, I could get a job where you work at night.
Like cleaning office buildings.
Or road work. Or the graveyard shift at a convenience store.
SAFETY FIRST
But... wait a second.
Could I really afford to live in Tokyo on that kind of pay?
SUN
Right now I was getting by on part-time jobs and money from home.
But once I graduated...
...the money from home would dry up and I'd have to pay for everything out of my own earnings.
Fine.
So I'd work two jobs, or even three or four!! I could get by fine so long as I lived frugally.
But...
...?!
Wait a minute, if I worked that many jobs, then...

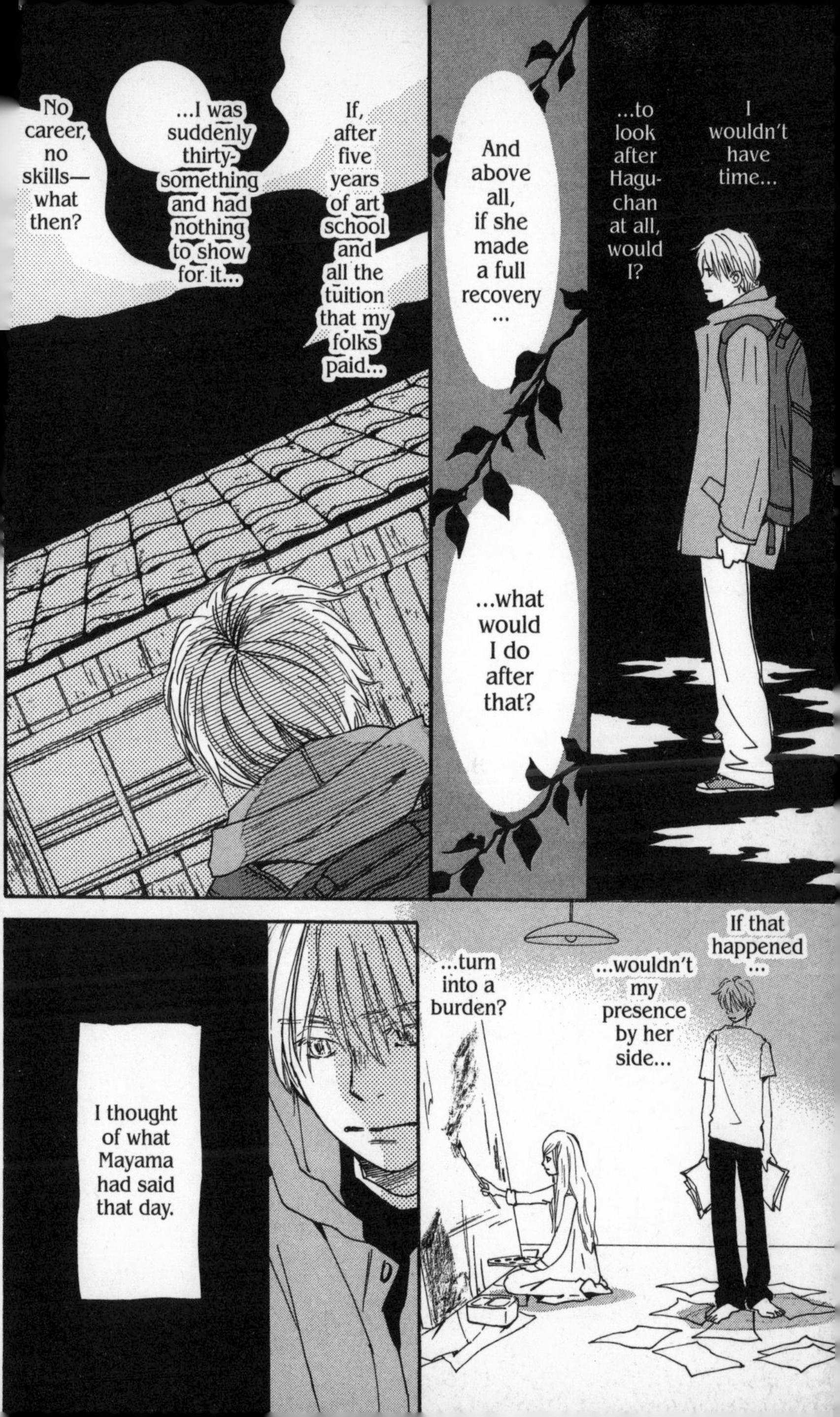
I wouldn't have time...
...to look after Hagu-chan at all, would I?
And above all, if she made a full recovery...
...what would I do after that?
If, after five years of art school and all the tuition that my folks paid...
...I was suddenly thirty-something and had nothing to show for it...
No career, no skills—what then?
If that happened...
...wouldn't my presence by her side...
...turn into a burden?
I thought of what Mayama had said that day.

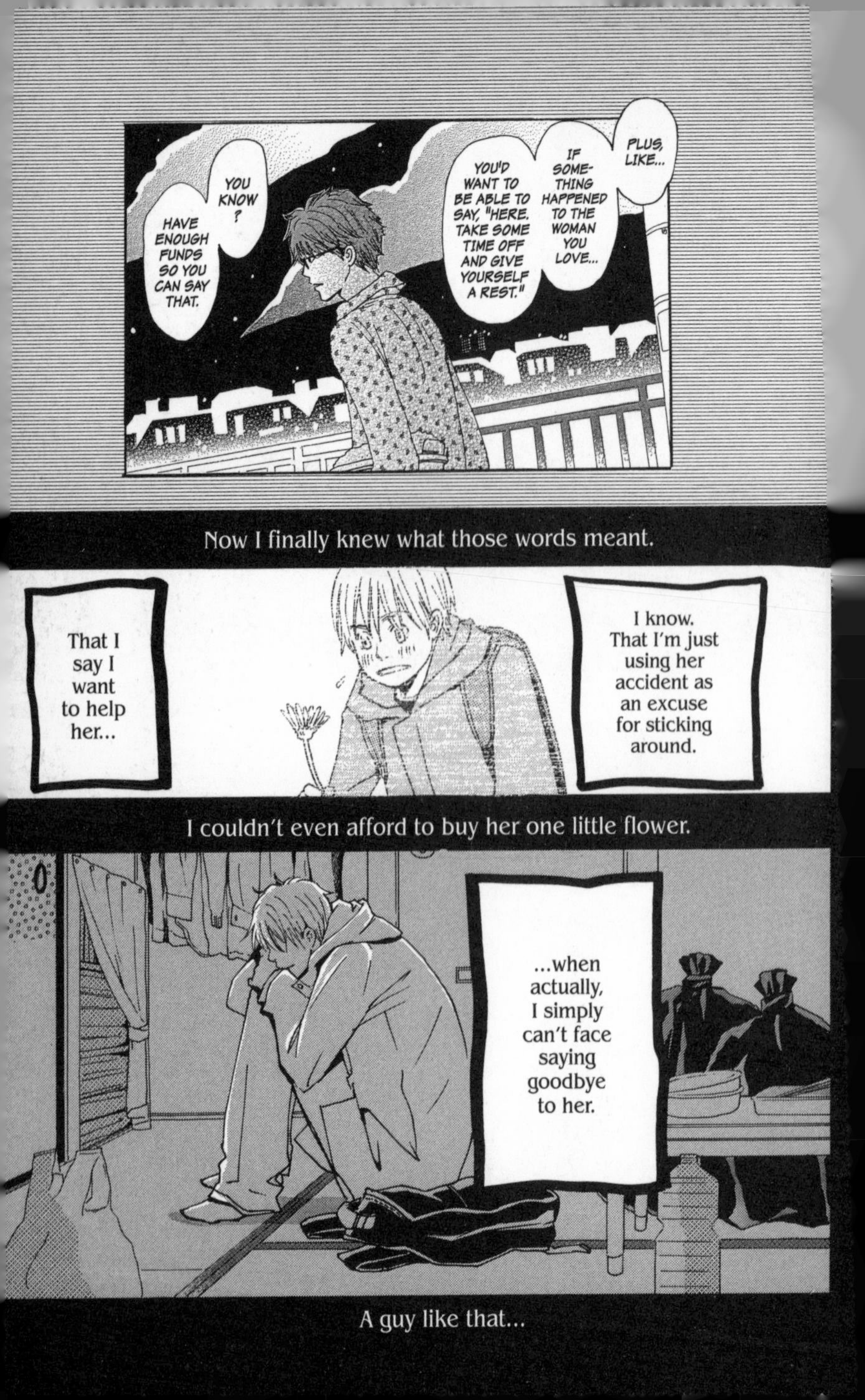
PLUS, LIKE...
IF SOMETHING HAPPENED TO THE WOMAN YOU LOVE...
YOU'D WANT TO BE ABLE TO SAY, "HERE. TAKE SOME TIME OFF AND GIVE YOURSELF A REST."
YOU KNOW?
HAVE ENOUGH FUNDS SO YOU CAN SAY THAT.
Now I finally knew what those words meant.
I know. That I'm just using her accident as an excuse for sticking around.
That I say I want to help her...
I couldn't even afford to buy her one little flower.
...when actually, I simply can't face saying goodbye to her.
A guy like that...

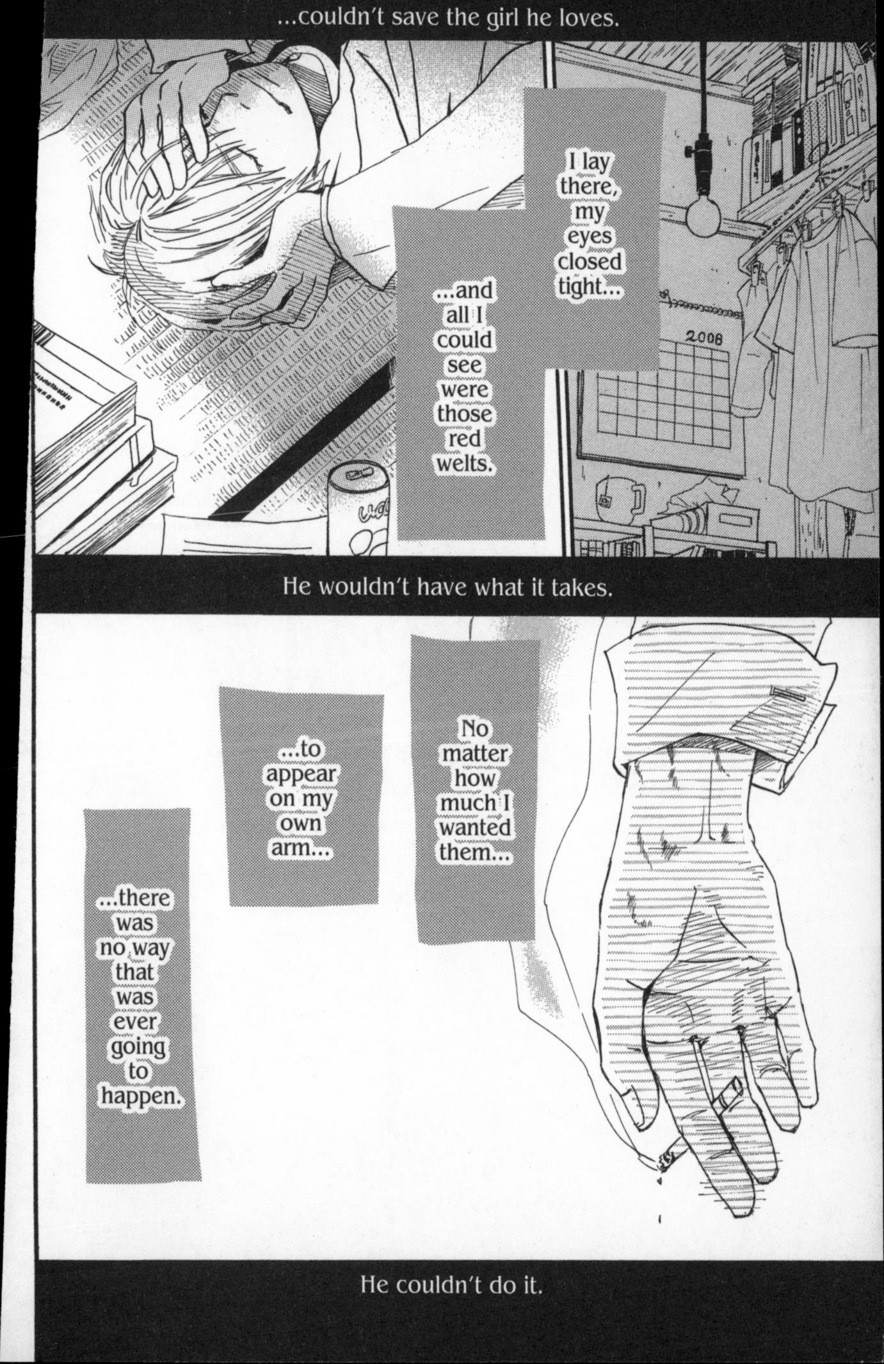
...couldn't save the girl he loves.
I lay there, my eyes closed tight...
...and all I could see were those red welts.
He wouldn't have what it takes.
No matter how much I wanted them...
...to appear on my own arm...
...there was no way that was ever going to happen.
He couldn't do it.

honey and clover

chapter 60

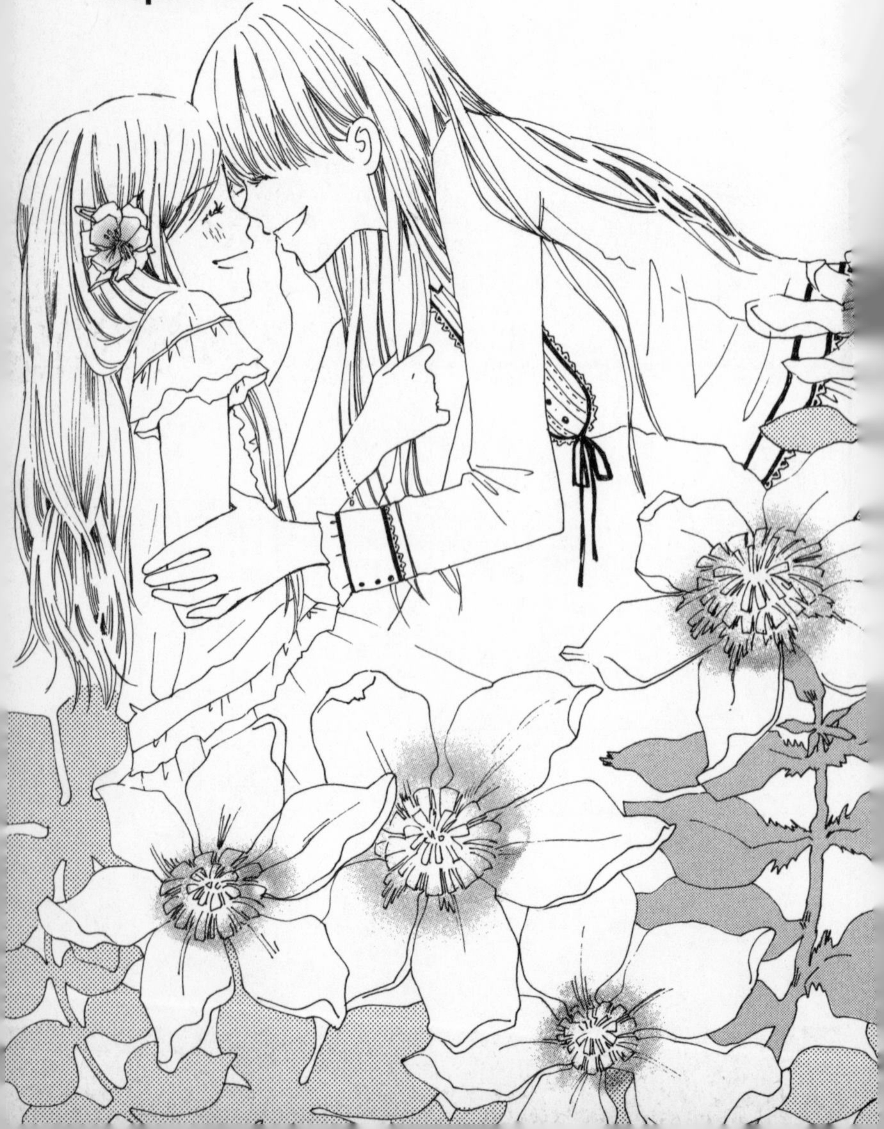

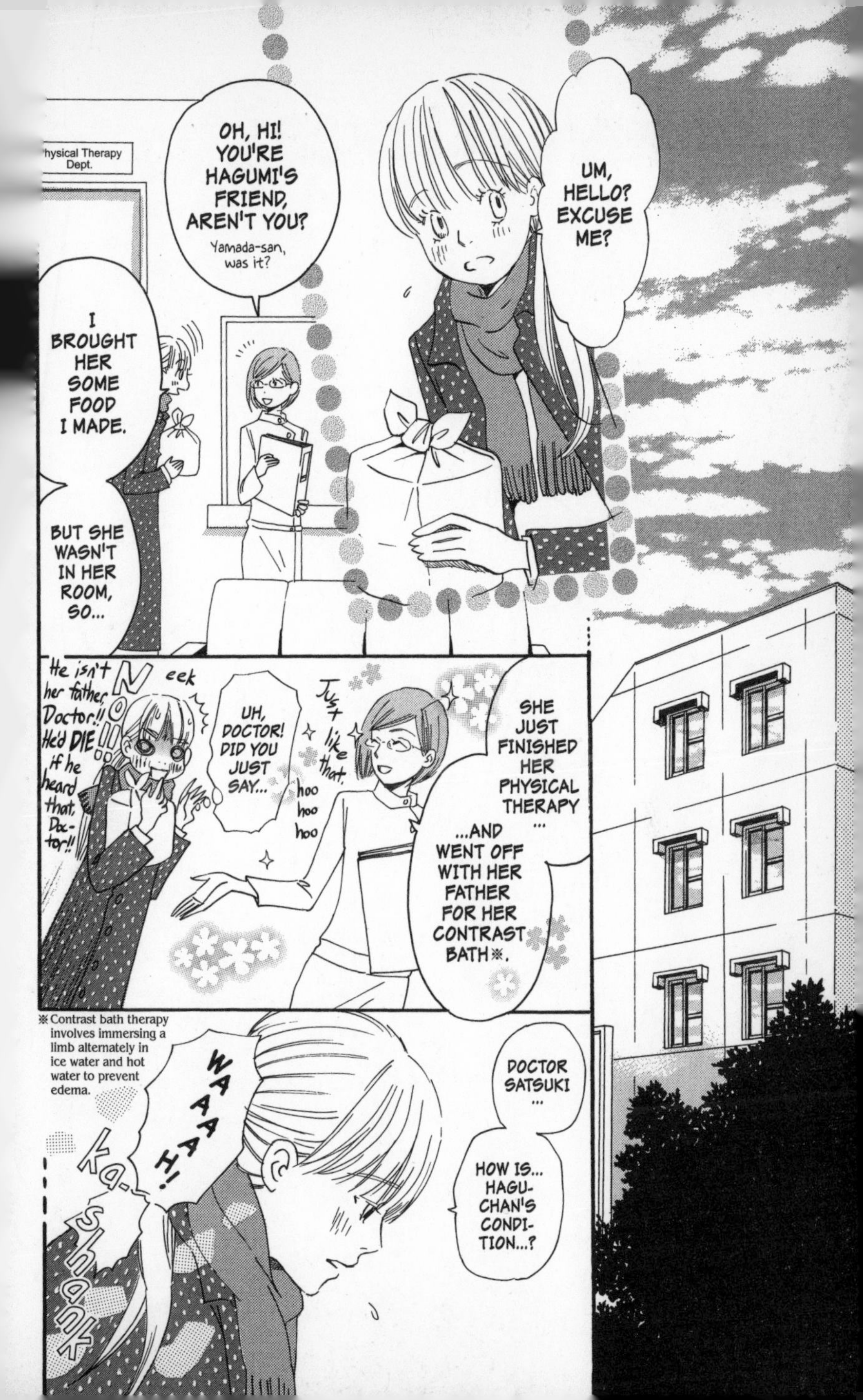
UM, HELLO? EXCUSE ME?
Physical Therapy Dept.
OH, HI! YOU'RE HAGUMI'S FRIEND, AREN'T YOU?
Yamada-san, was it?
I BROUGHT HER SOME FOOD I MADE.
BUT SHE WASN'T IN HER ROOM, SO...
SHE JUST FINISHED HER PHYSICAL THERAPY...
...AND WENT OFF WITH HER FATHER FOR HER CONTRAST BATH※.
Just like that.
hoo hoo hoo
UH, DOCTOR! DID YOU JUST SAY...
eek
NO!!
He isn't her father, Doctor!! He'd DIE if he heard that, Doctor!!
DOCTOR SATSUKI...
HOW IS... HAGU-CHAN'S CONDITION...?
WAAAAH!
ka-shak

※Contrast bath therapy involves immersing a limb alternately in ice water and hot water to prevent edema.

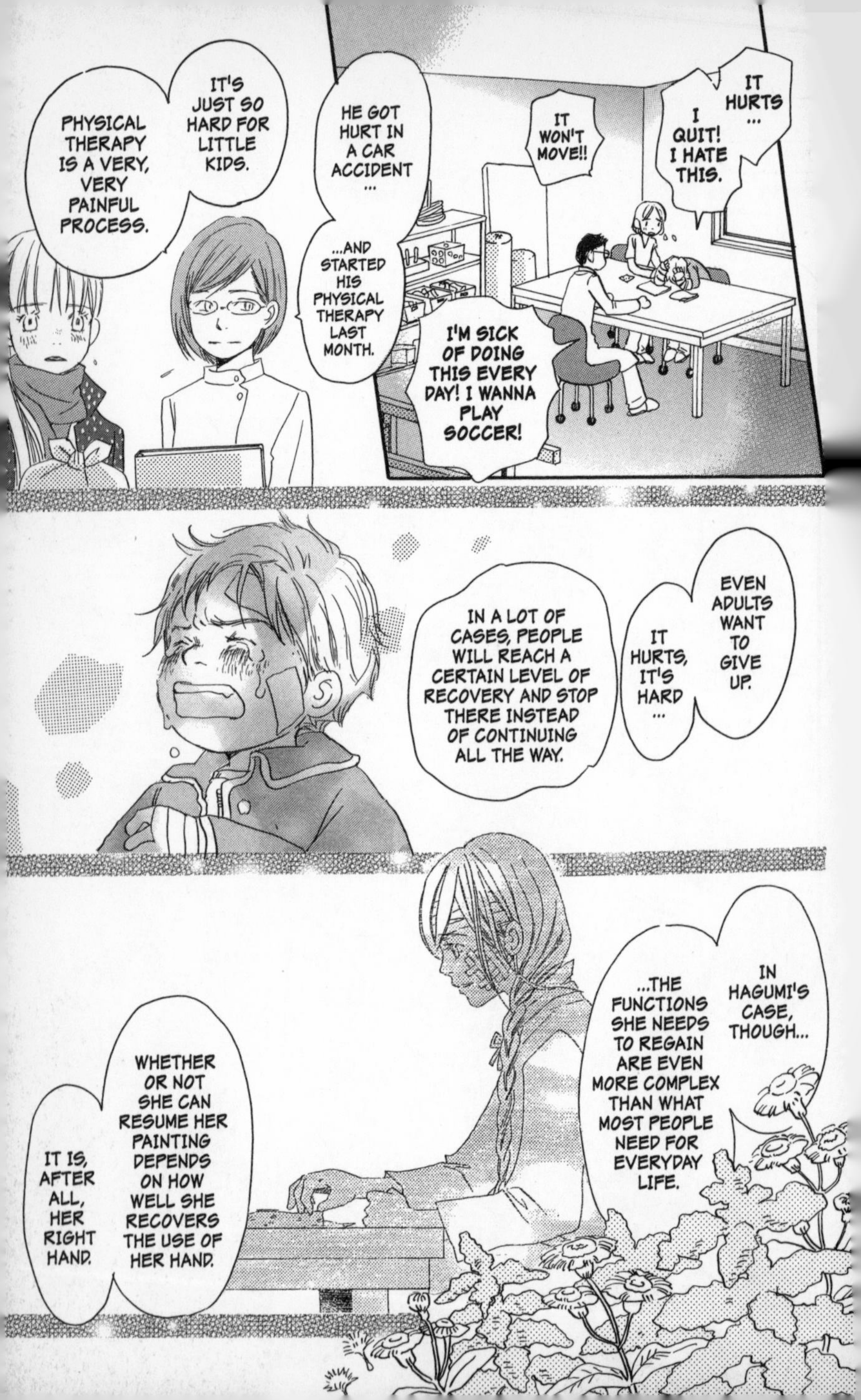
IT HURTS...
I QUIT! I HATE THIS.
IT WON'T MOVE!!
I'M SICK OF DOING THIS EVERY DAY! I WANNA PLAY SOCCER!
HE GOT HURT IN A CAR ACCIDENT...
...AND STARTED HIS PHYSICAL THERAPY LAST MONTH.
IT'S JUST SO HARD FOR LITTLE KIDS.
PHYSICAL THERAPY IS A VERY, VERY PAINFUL PROCESS.
EVEN ADULTS WANT TO GIVE UP.
IT HURTS, IT'S HARD...
IN A LOT OF CASES, PEOPLE WILL REACH A CERTAIN LEVEL OF RECOVERY AND STOP THERE INSTEAD OF CONTINUING ALL THE WAY.
IN HAGUMI'S CASE, THOUGH...
...THE FUNCTIONS SHE NEEDS TO REGAIN ARE EVEN MORE COMPLEX THAN WHAT MOST PEOPLE NEED FOR EVERYDAY LIFE.
WHETHER OR NOT SHE CAN RESUME HER PAINTING DEPENDS ON HOW WELL SHE RECOVERS THE USE OF HER HAND.
IT IS, AFTER ALL, HER RIGHT HAND.

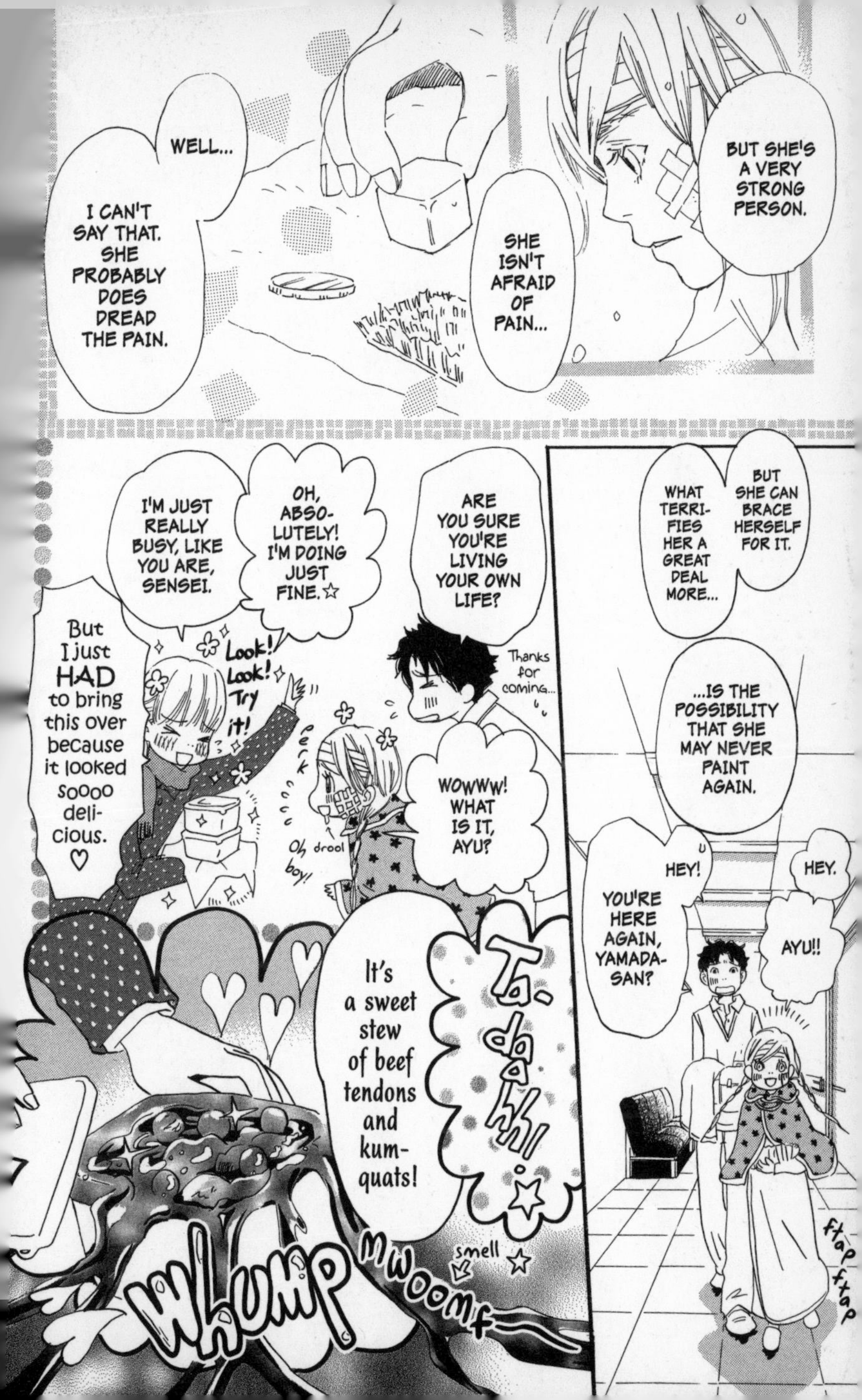
BUT SHE'S A VERY STRONG PERSON.
SHE ISN'T AFRAID OF PAIN...
WELL...
I CAN'T SAY THAT. SHE PROBABLY DOES DREAD THE PAIN.
BUT SHE CAN BRACE HERSELF FOR IT.
WHAT TERRI-FIES HER A GREAT DEAL MORE...
...IS THE POSSIBILITY THAT SHE MAY NEVER PAINT AGAIN.
HEY.
AYU!!
HEY!
YOU'RE HERE AGAIN, YAMADA-SAN?
ftap ftap
ARE YOU SURE YOU'RE LIVING YOUR OWN LIFE?
OH, ABSO-LUTELY! I'M DOING JUST FINE. ☆
I'M JUST REALLY BUSY, LIKE YOU ARE, SENSEI.
Thanks for coming...
WOWWW! WHAT IS IT, AYU?
perk
Look! Look! Try it!
drool
Oh boy!
But I just HAD to bring this over because it looked soooo deli-cious. ♡
Ta-daahh! ☆
It's a sweet stew of beef tendons and kum-quats!
smell ☆
mwoomf
WHUMP

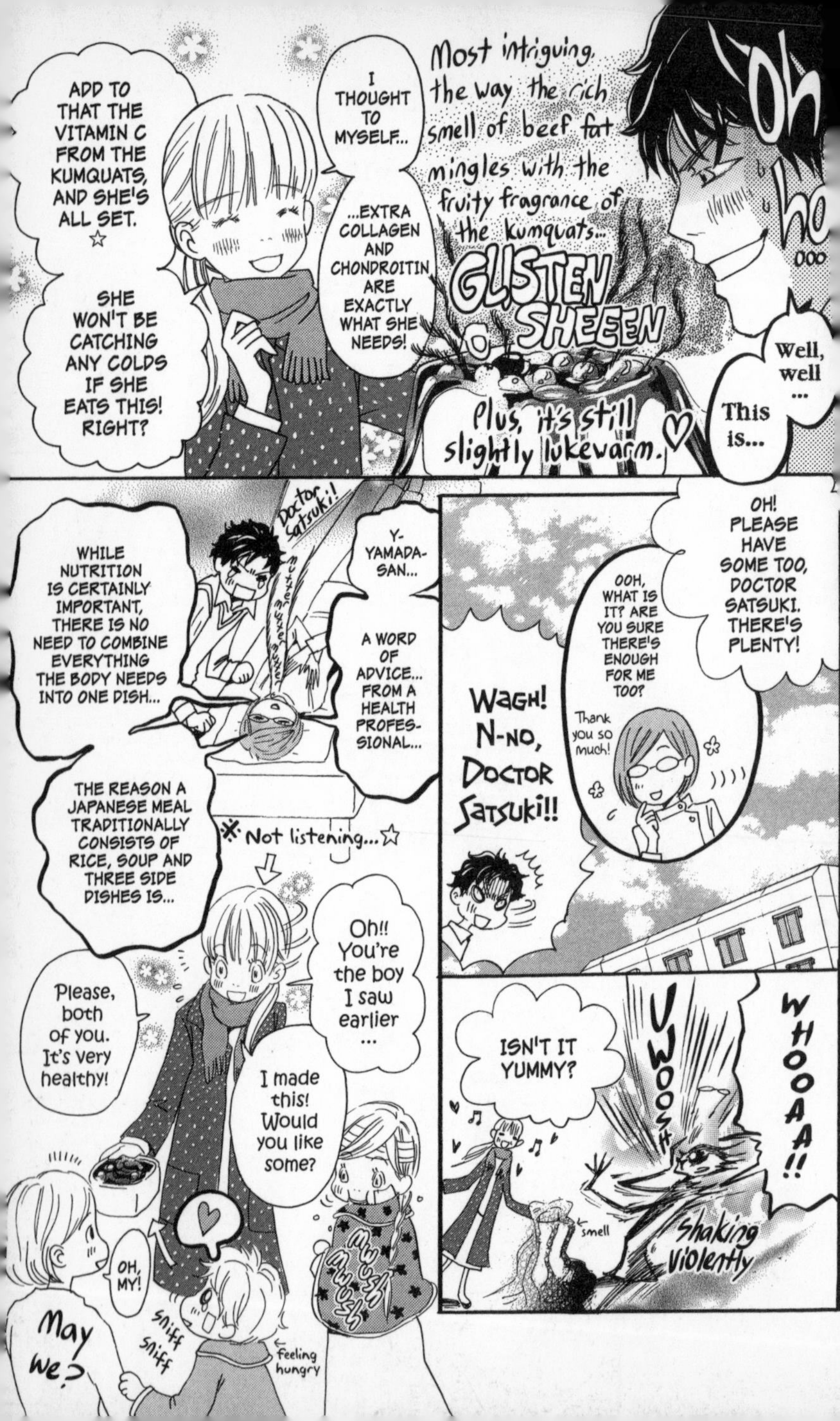

Oh hohooo
Well, well ...
This is...
Most intriguing, the way the rich smell of beef fat mingles with the fruity fragrance of the kumquats...
GLISTEN SHEEEN
Plus, it's still slightly lukewarm. ♡
I THOUGHT TO MYSELF...
...EXTRA COLLAGEN AND CHONDROITIN ARE EXACTLY WHAT SHE NEEDS!
ADD TO THAT THE VITAMIN C FROM THE KUMQUATS, AND SHE'S ALL SET. ☆
SHE WON'T BE CATCHING ANY COLDS IF SHE EATS THIS! RIGHT?
OH! PLEASE HAVE SOME TOO, DOCTOR SATSUKI. THERE'S PLENTY!
OOH, WHAT IS IT? ARE YOU SURE THERE'S ENOUGH FOR ME TOO?
Thank you so much!
WAGH! N-NO, DOCTOR SATSUKI!!
WHOOOAA!!
UWOOSH
ISN'T IT YUMMY?
smell
Shaking violently
Doctor Satsuki!
Y-YAMADA-SAN...
A WORD OF ADVICE... FROM A HEALTH PROFESSIONAL...
mutter mutter mutter
WHILE NUTRITION IS CERTAINLY IMPORTANT, THERE IS NO NEED TO COMBINE EVERYTHING THE BODY NEEDS INTO ONE DISH...
THE REASON A JAPANESE MEAL TRADITIONALLY CONSISTS OF RICE, SOUP AND THREE SIDE DISHES IS...
※Not listening...☆
Oh!! You're the boy I saw earlier ...
I made this! Would you like some?
Please, both of you. It's very healthy!
OH, MY!
Feeling hungry
sniff sniff
May we?

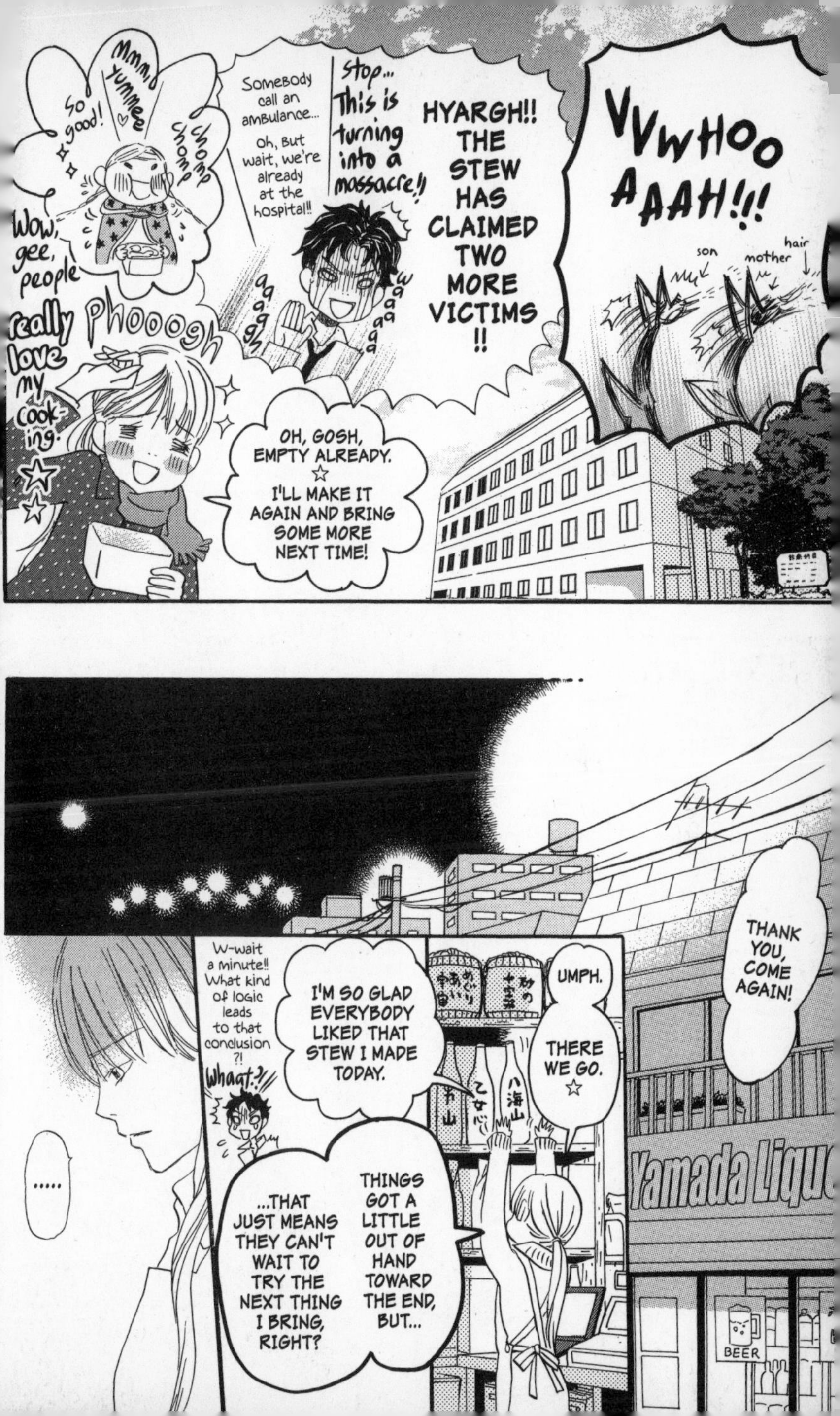
VVWHOO AAAH!!!
hair
mother
son
HYARGH!! THE STEW HAS CLAIMED TWO MORE VICTIMS!!
stop... This is turning into a massacre!!
aaaggh
waaaaaa
Somebody call an ambulance... Oh, But wait, we're already at the hospital!!
Mmm, yummee
chomp chomp
So good!
Wow, gee, people really love my cooking.
Phooogh
OH, GOSH, EMPTY ALREADY. ☆ I'LL MAKE IT AGAIN AND BRING SOME MORE NEXT TIME!
THANK YOU, COME AGAIN!
Yamada Liqu
BEER
UMPH.
THERE WE GO. ☆
I'M SO GLAD EVERYBODY LIKED THAT STEW I MADE TODAY.
W-wait a minute!! What kind of logic leads to that conclusion?!
Whaat?!
THINGS GOT A LITTLE OUT OF HAND TOWARD THE END, BUT...
...THAT JUST MEANS THEY CAN'T WAIT TO TRY THE NEXT THING I BRING, RIGHT?
......

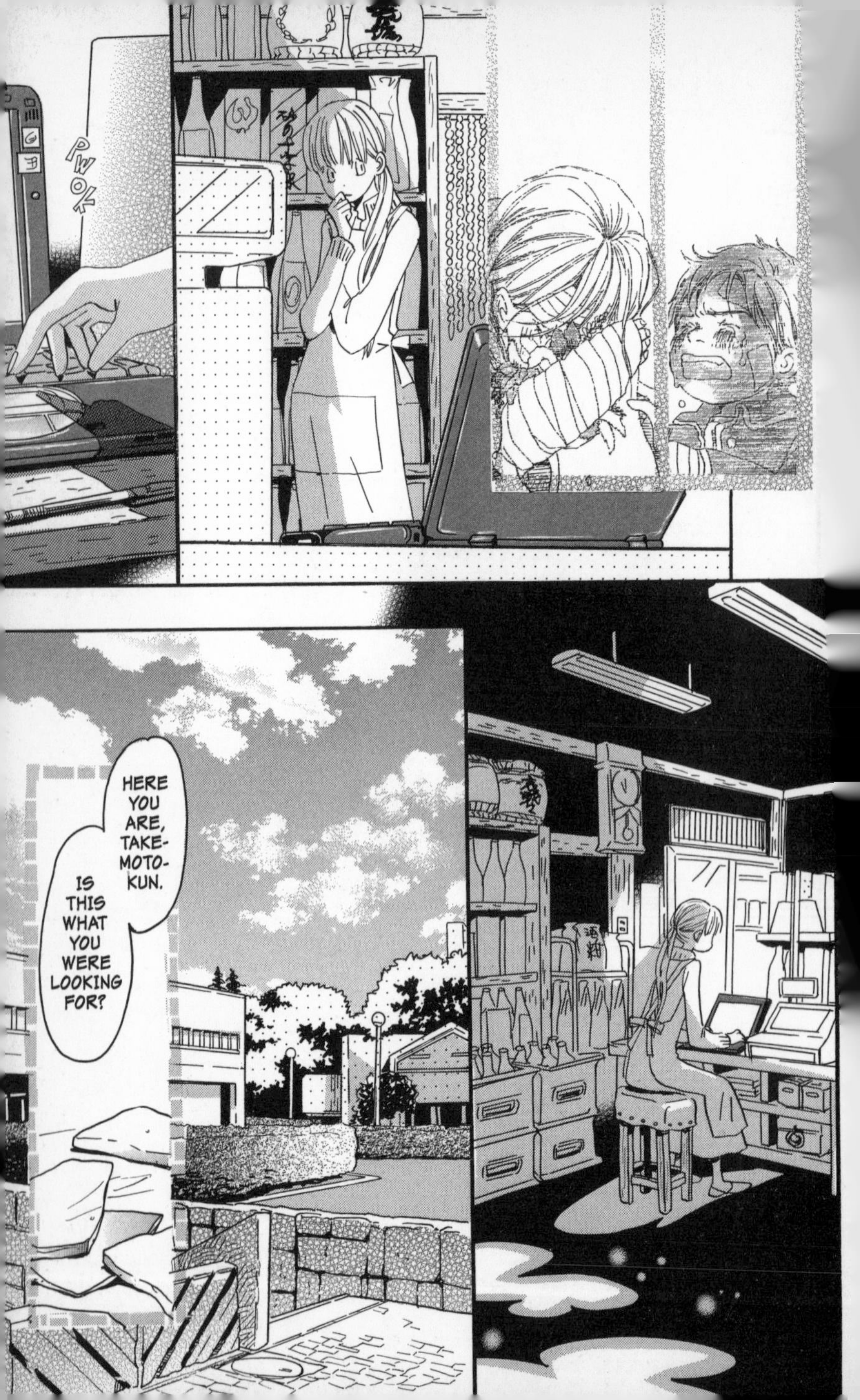
PWOK
HERE YOU ARE, TAKE-MOTO-KUN.
IS THIS WHAT YOU WERE LOOKING FOR?

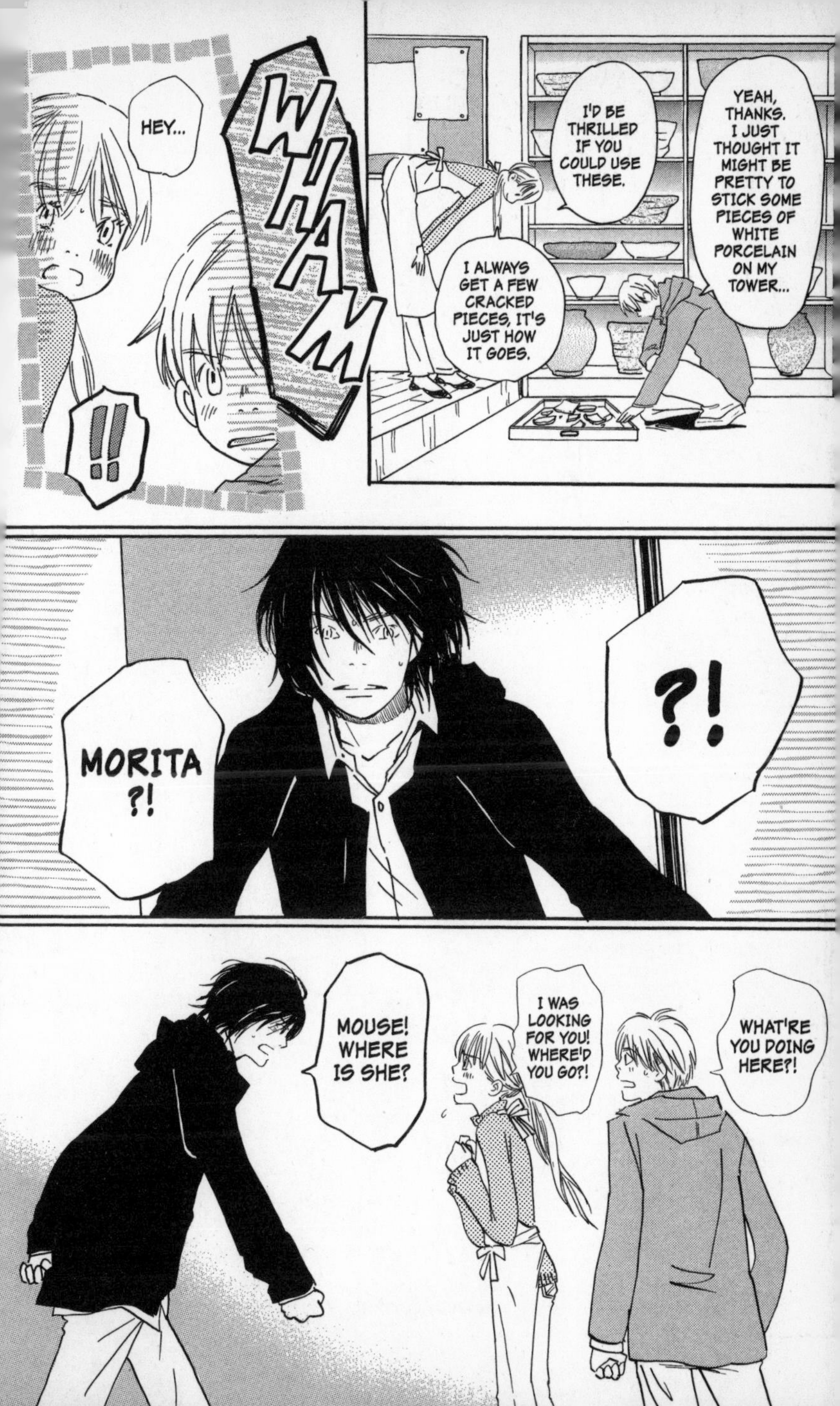
YEAH, THANKS. I JUST THOUGHT IT MIGHT BE PRETTY TO STICK SOME PIECES OF WHITE PORCELAIN ON MY TOWER...
I'D BE THRILLED IF YOU COULD USE THESE.
I ALWAYS GET A FEW CRACKED PIECES, IT'S JUST HOW IT GOES.
WHAM
HEY...
!!
?!
MORITA ?!
WHAT'RE YOU DOING HERE?!
I WAS LOOKING FOR YOU! WHERE'D YOU GO?!
MOUSE! WHERE IS SHE?

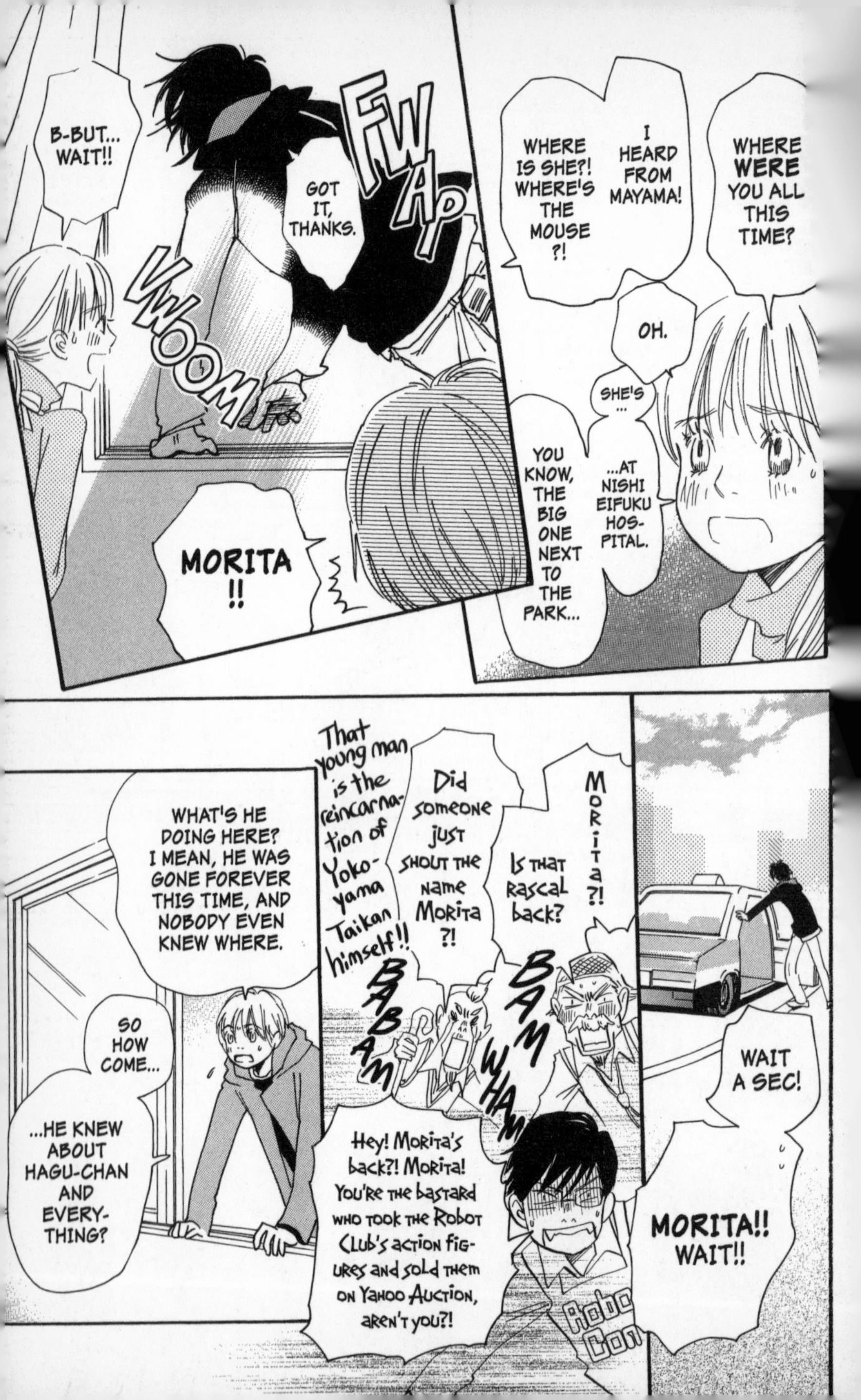
WHERE WERE YOU ALL THIS TIME?
I HEARD FROM MAYAMA!
WHERE IS SHE?! WHERE'S THE MOUSE?!
OH.
SHE'S ...
...AT NISHI EIFUKU HOS-PITAL.
YOU KNOW, THE BIG ONE NEXT TO THE PARK...
FWAP
GOT IT, THANKS.
VWOOM
B-BUT... WAIT!!
MORITA!!
WAIT A SEC!
MORITA!! WAIT!!
MORITA?!
Is that rascal back?
Did someone just shout the name Morita?!
That young man is the reincarnation of Yokoyama Taikan himself!!
BAM
BABAM
WHAM
Hey! Morita's back?! Morita! You're the bastard who took the Robot Club's action figures and sold them on Yahoo Auction, aren't you?!
RoboCon
WHAT'S HE DOING HERE? I MEAN, HE WAS GONE FOREVER THIS TIME, AND NOBODY EVEN KNEW WHERE.
SO HOW COME...
...HE KNEW ABOUT HAGU-CHAN AND EVERYTHING?

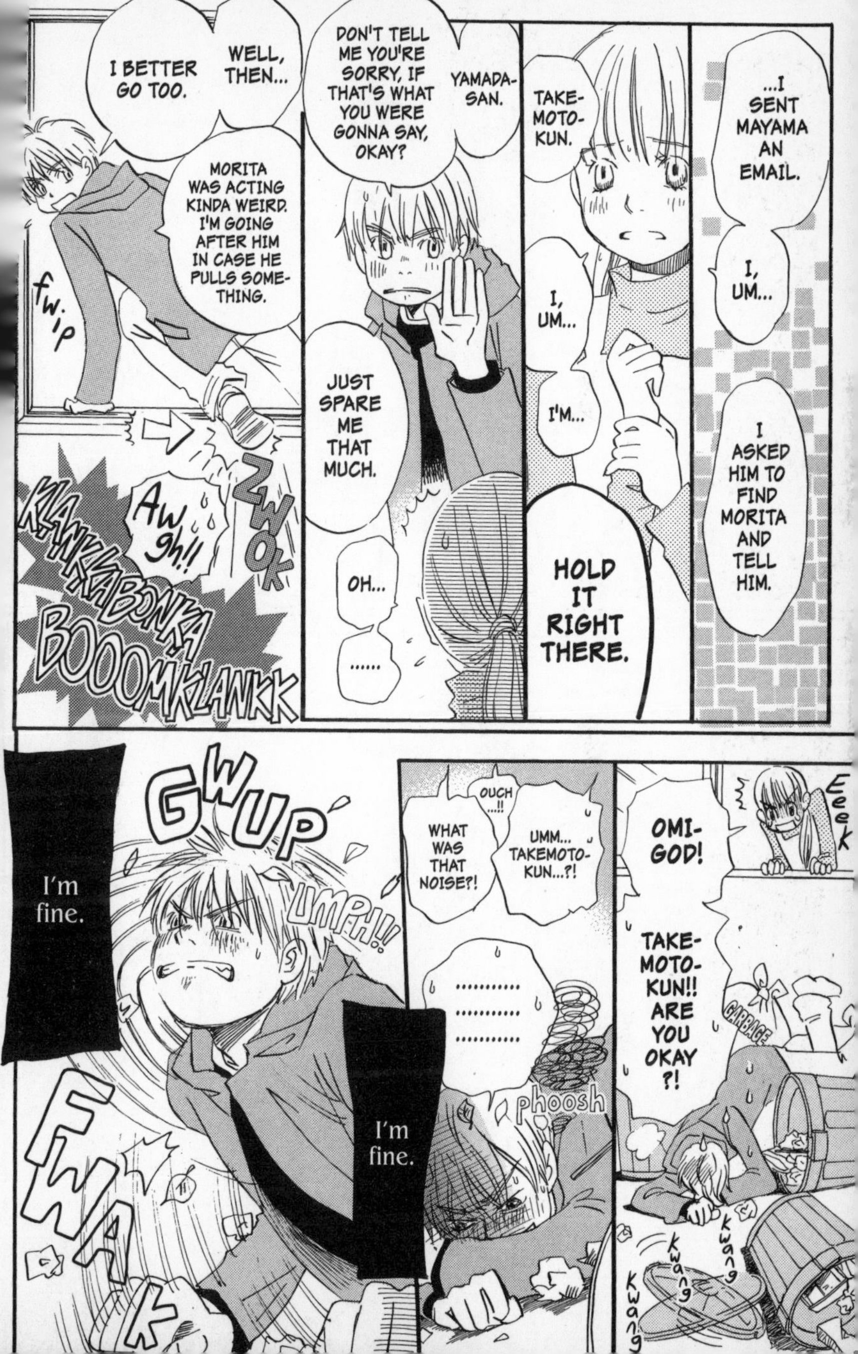
...I SENT MAYAMA AN EMAIL.
I, UM...
I ASKED HIM TO FIND MORITA AND TELL HIM.
TAKE-MOTO-KUN.
I, UM...
I'M...
HOLD IT RIGHT THERE.
YAMADA-SAN.
DON'T TELL ME YOU'RE SORRY, IF THAT'S WHAT YOU WERE GONNA SAY, OKAY?
JUST SPARE ME THAT MUCH.
OH...
......
WELL, THEN...
I BETTER GO TOO.
MORITA WAS ACTING KINDA WEIRD. I'M GOING AFTER HIM IN CASE HE PULLS SOME-THING.
fwip
ZWOK
Awgh!!
KLANKKABONKKA BOOOOMKLANKK
Eeeek
OMI-GOD!
TAKE-MOTO-KUN!! ARE YOU OKAY?!
GARBAGE
kwang
kwang
kwang
OUCH...!!
WHAT WAS THAT NOISE?!
UMM... TAKEMOTO-KUN...?!
....
....
....
phoosh
GWUP
UMPH!!
I'm fine.
I'm fine.
FWAK

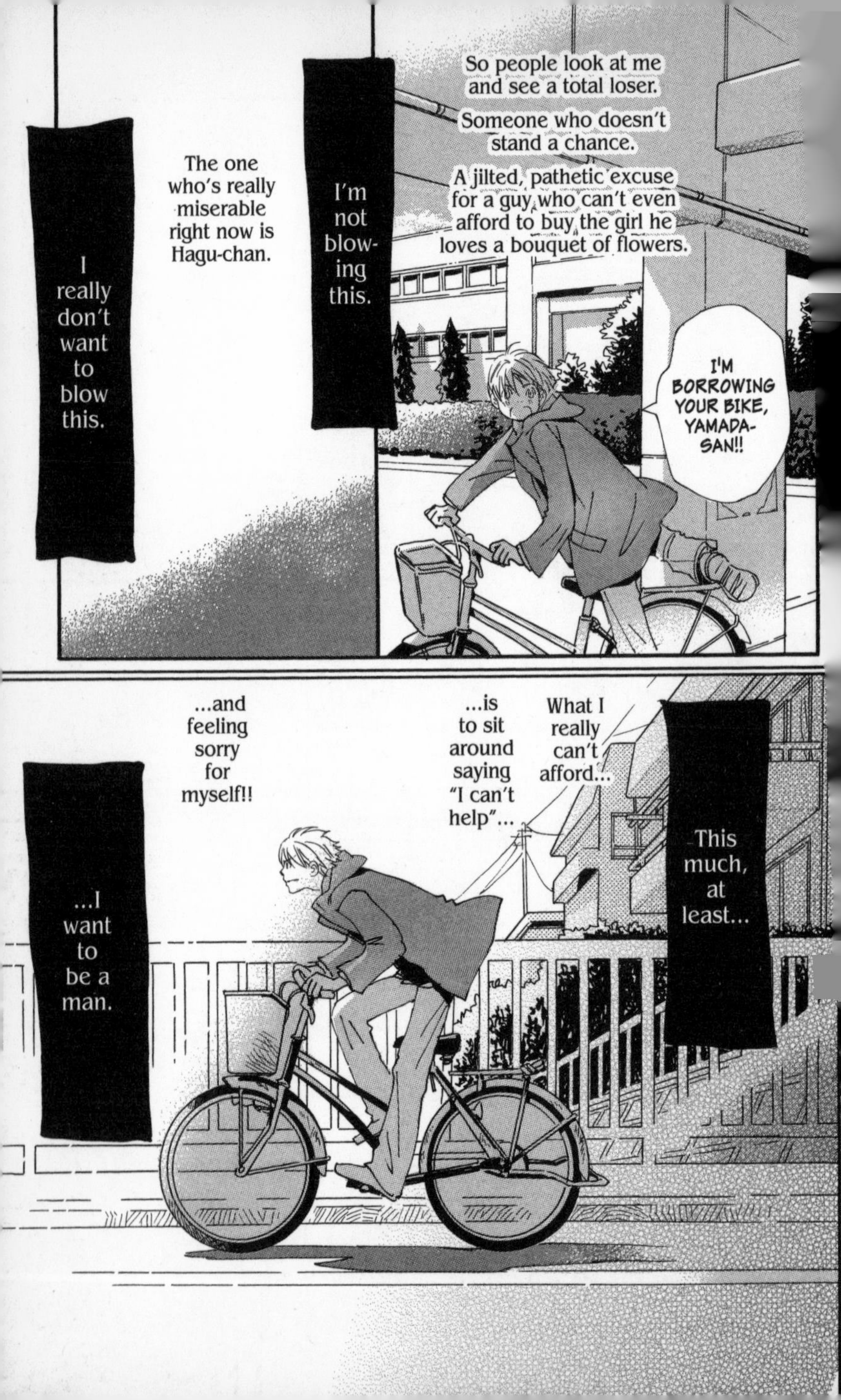
So people look at me and see a total loser.
Someone who doesn't stand a chance.
A jilted, pathetic excuse for a guy who can't even afford to buy the girl he loves a bouquet of flowers.
I'M BORROWING YOUR BIKE, YAMADA-SAN!!
I'm not blowing this.
The one who's really miserable right now is Hagu-chan.
I really don't want to blow this.
This much, at least...
What I really can't afford...
...is to sit around saying "I can't help"...
...and feeling sorry for myself!!
...I want to be a man.

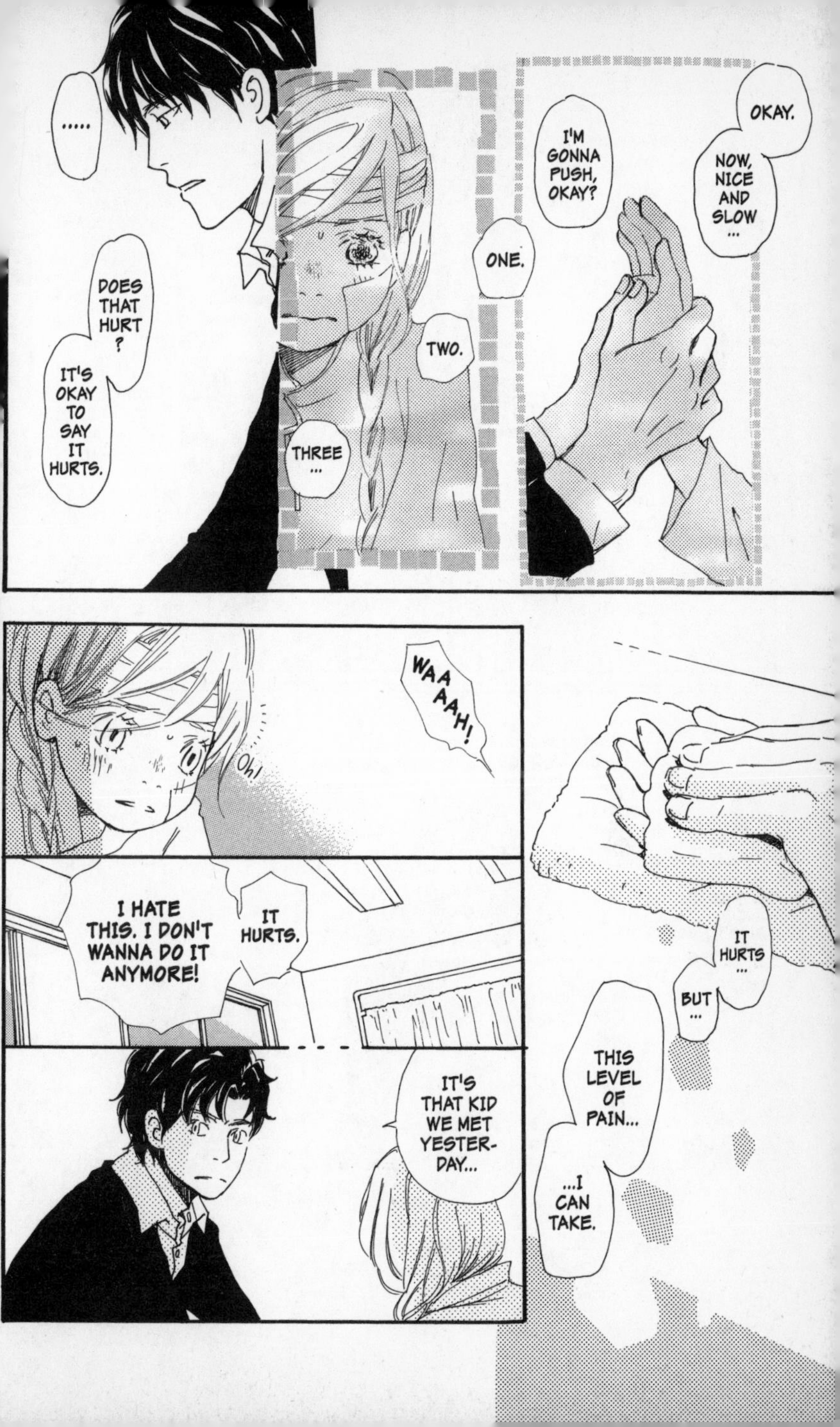
OKAY.
NOW, NICE AND SLOW...
I'M GONNA PUSH, OKAY?
ONE.
TWO.
THREE...
......
DOES THAT HURT?
IT'S OKAY TO SAY IT HURTS.
IT HURTS...
BUT...
THIS LEVEL OF PAIN...
...I CAN TAKE.
WAAAAH!
Oh!
IT HURTS.
I HATE THIS. I DON'T WANNA DO IT ANYMORE!
IT'S THAT KID WE MET YESTERDAY...

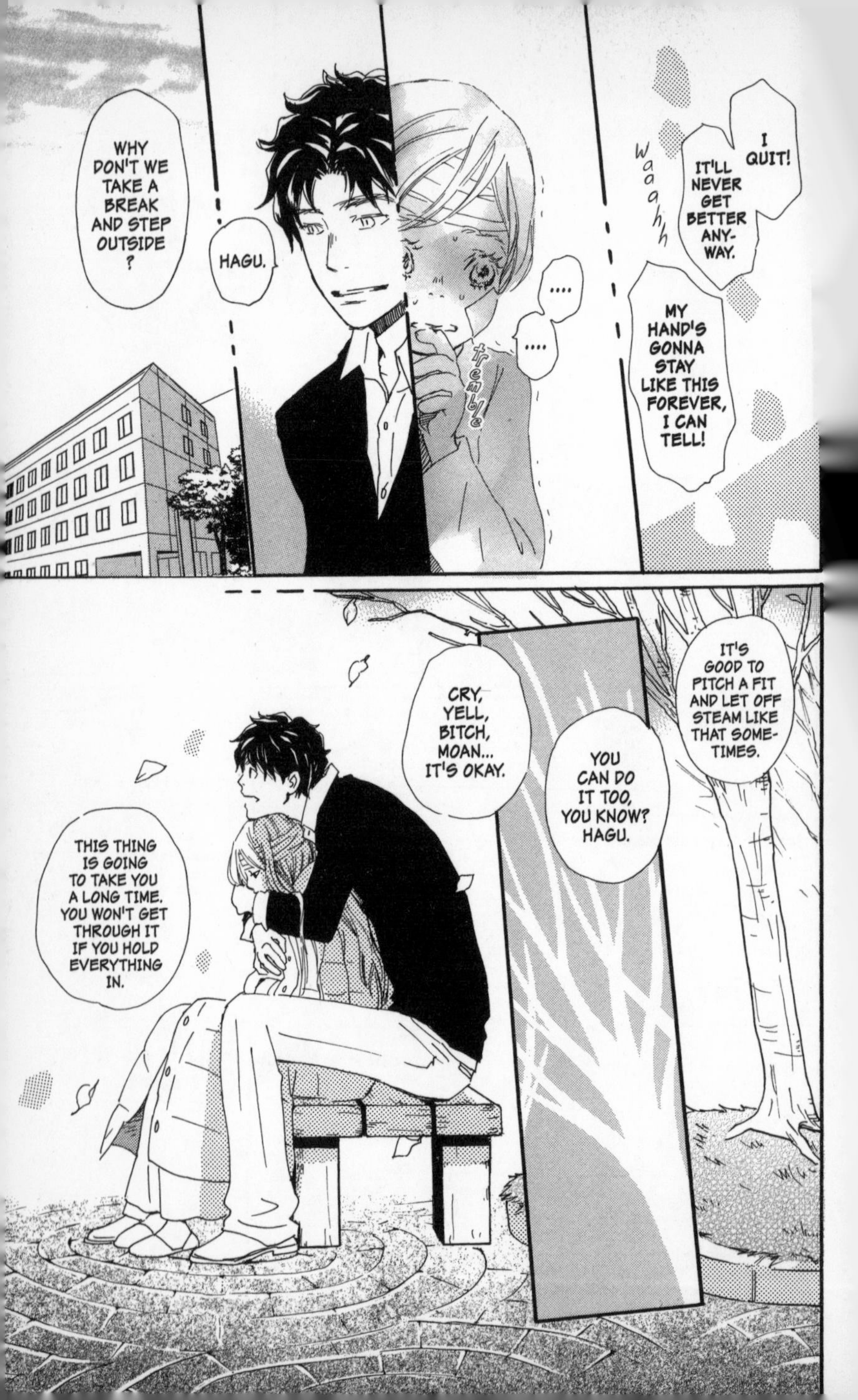
I QUIT!
IT'LL NEVER GET BETTER ANY-WAY.
Waaahh
MY HAND'S GONNA STAY LIKE THIS FOREVER, I CAN TELL!
....
....
tremble
HAGU.
WHY DON'T WE TAKE A BREAK AND STEP OUTSIDE?
IT'S GOOD TO PITCH A FIT AND LET OFF STEAM LIKE THAT SOME-TIMES.
YOU CAN DO IT TOO, YOU KNOW? HAGU.
CRY, YELL, BITCH, MOAN... IT'S OKAY.
THIS THING IS GOING TO TAKE YOU A LONG TIME. YOU WON'T GET THROUGH IT IF YOU HOLD EVERYTHING IN.

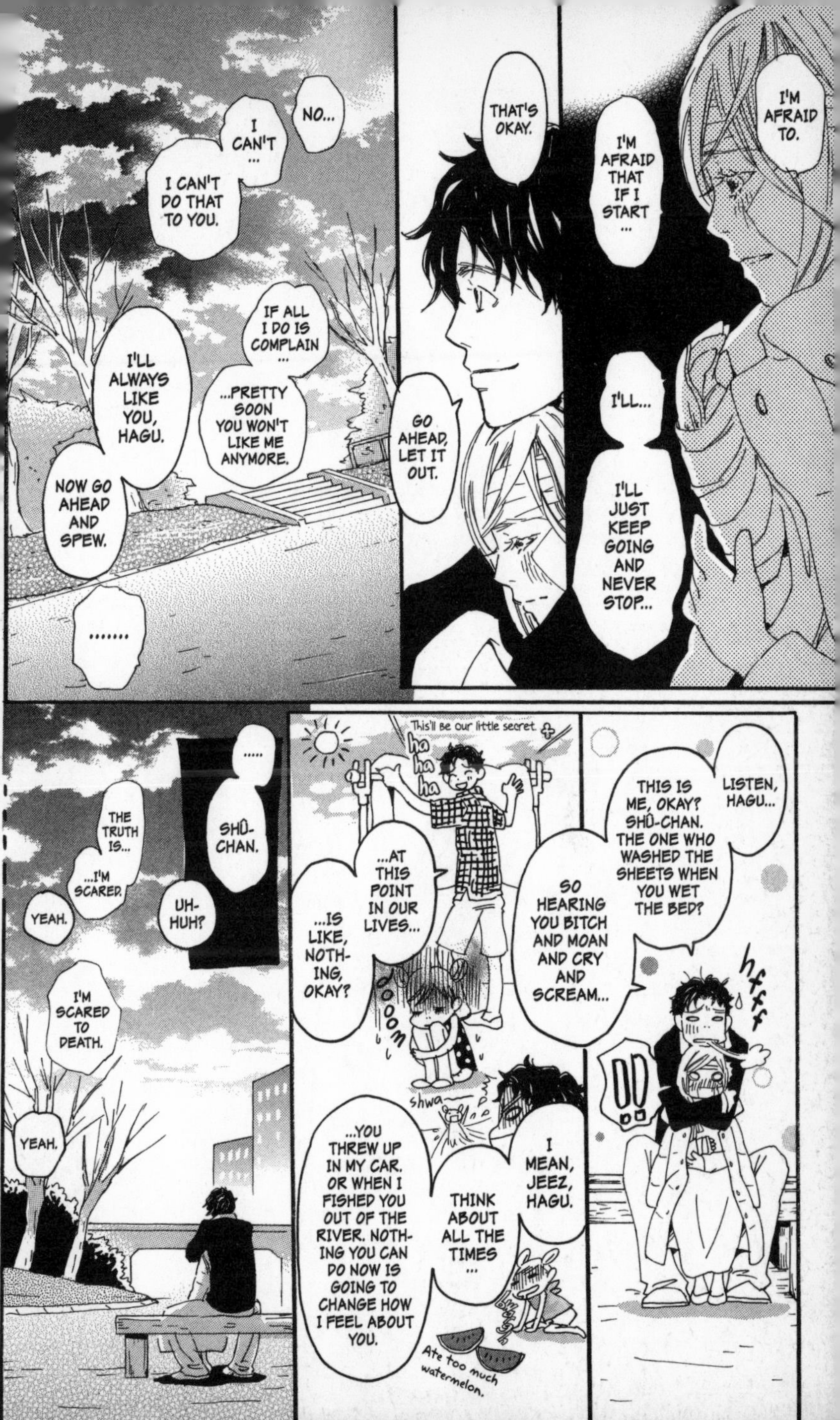
I'M AFRAID TO.
I'M AFRAID THAT IF I START ...
I'LL...
I'LL JUST KEEP GOING AND NEVER STOP...
THAT'S OKAY.
GO AHEAD, LET IT OUT.
NO...
I CAN'T ...
I CAN'T DO THAT TO YOU.
IF ALL I DO IS COMPLAIN ...
...PRETTY SOON YOU WON'T LIKE ME ANYMORE.
I'LL ALWAYS LIKE YOU, HAGU.
NOW GO AHEAD AND SPEW.
....
LISTEN, HAGU...
THIS IS ME, OKAY? SHŪ-CHAN. THE ONE WHO WASHED THE SHEETS WHEN YOU WET THE BED?
hfff
SO HEARING YOU BITCH AND MOAN AND CRY AND SCREAM...
This'll be our little secret.
ha ha ha
...AT THIS POINT IN OUR LIVES...
...IS LIKE, NOTH-ING, OKAY?
dooom
shwa~
I MEAN, JEEZ, HAGU.
THINK ABOUT ALL THE TIMES ...
...YOU THREW UP IN MY CAR. OR WHEN I FISHED YOU OUT OF THE RIVER. NOTH-ING YOU CAN DO NOW IS GOING TO CHANGE HOW I FEEL ABOUT YOU.
Ate too much watermelon.
.....
SHŪ-CHAN.
UH-HUH?
THE TRUTH IS...
...I'M SCARED.
YEAH.
I'M SCARED TO DEATH.
YEAH.

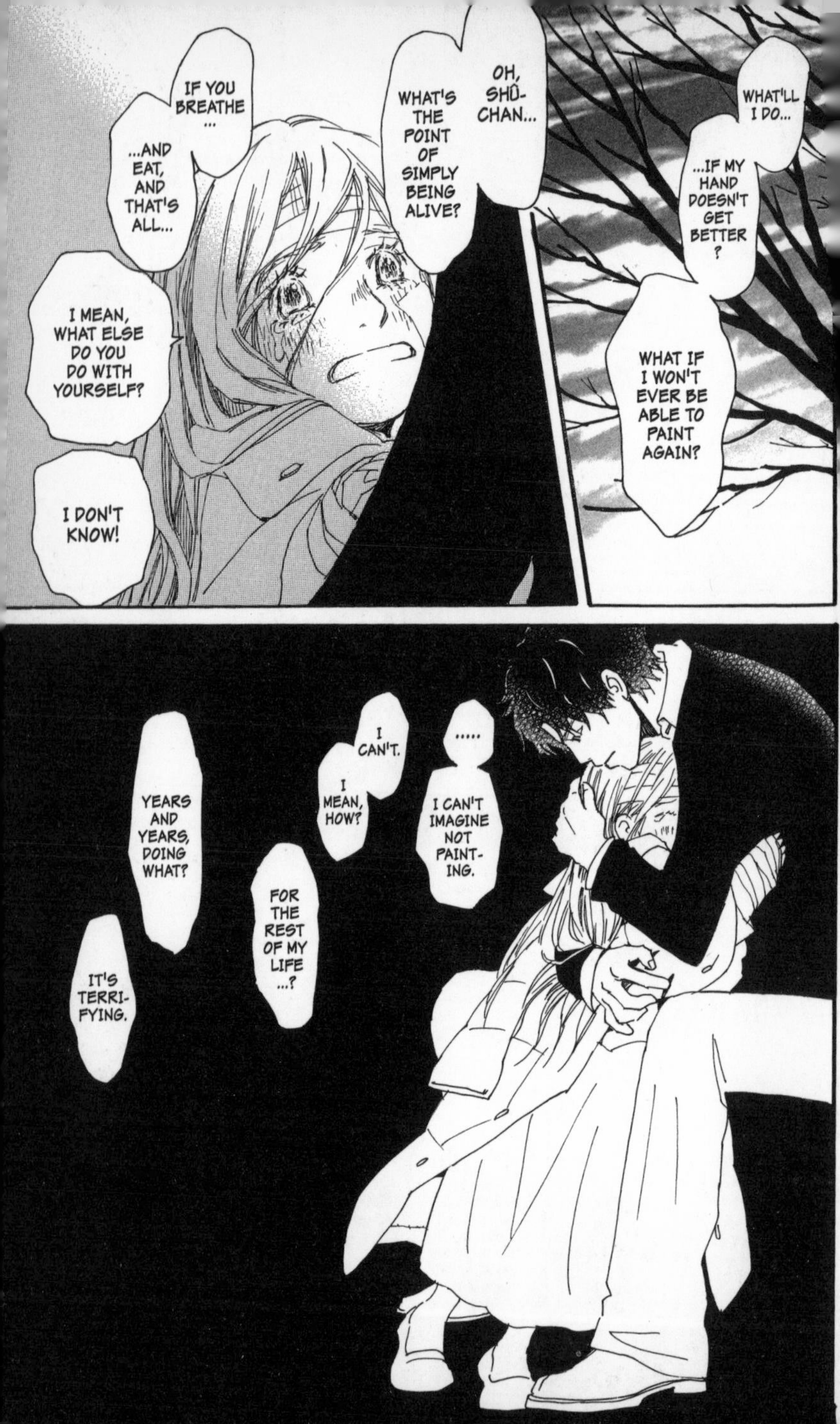
WHAT'LL I DO...
...IF MY HAND DOESN'T GET BETTER?
WHAT IF I WON'T EVER BE ABLE TO PAINT AGAIN?
OH, SHÛ-CHAN...
WHAT'S THE POINT OF SIMPLY BEING ALIVE?
IF YOU BREATHE...
...AND EAT, AND THAT'S ALL...
I MEAN, WHAT ELSE DO YOU DO WITH YOURSELF?
I DON'T KNOW!
.....
I CAN'T.
I MEAN, HOW?
I CAN'T IMAGINE NOT PAINT-ING.
FOR THE REST OF MY LIFE...?
YEARS AND YEARS, DOING WHAT?
IT'S TERRI-FYING.

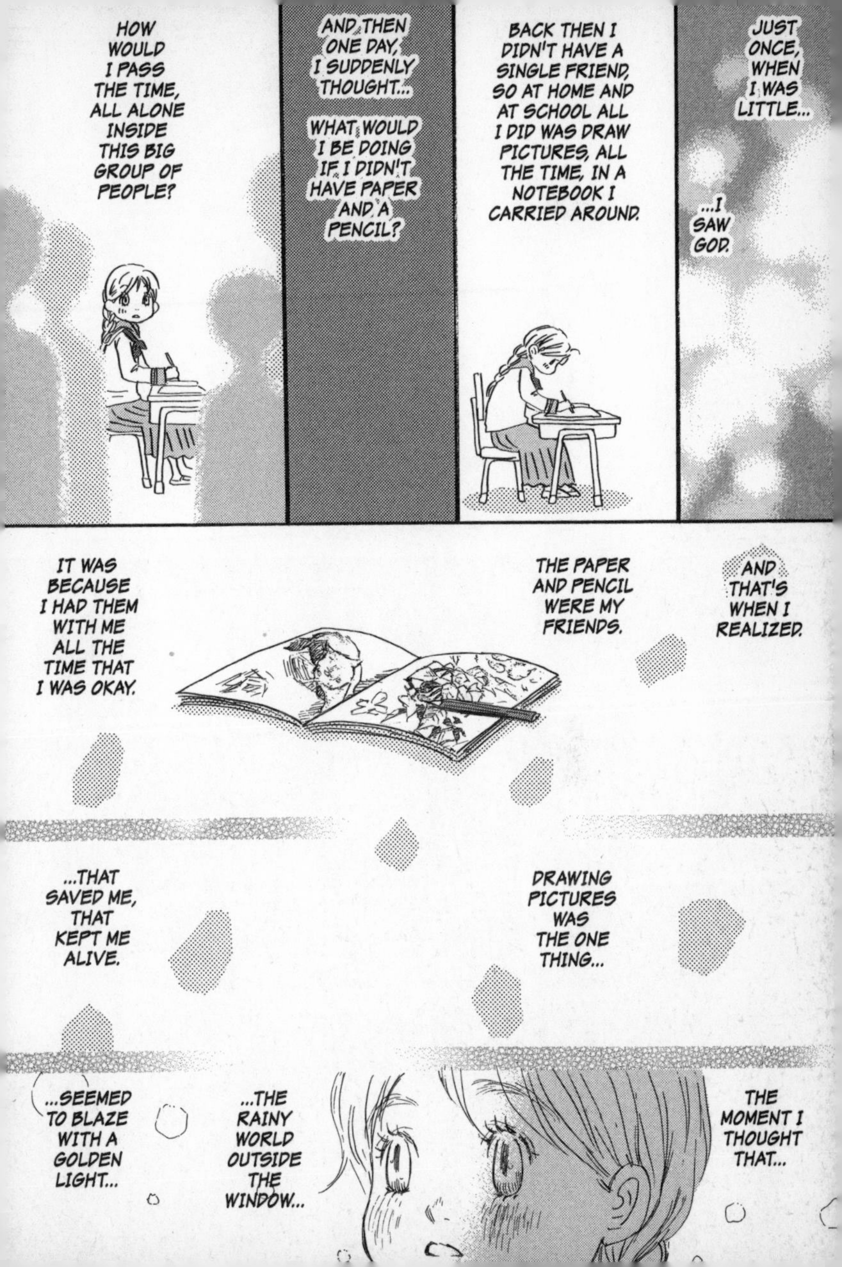
JUST ONCE, WHEN I WAS LITTLE...
...I SAW GOD.
BACK THEN I DIDN'T HAVE A SINGLE FRIEND, SO AT HOME AND AT SCHOOL ALL I DID WAS DRAW PICTURES, ALL THE TIME, IN A NOTEBOOK I CARRIED AROUND.
AND THEN ONE DAY, I SUDDENLY THOUGHT...
WHAT WOULD I BE DOING IF I DIDN'T HAVE PAPER AND A PENCIL?
HOW WOULD I PASS THE TIME, ALL ALONE INSIDE THIS BIG GROUP OF PEOPLE?
AND THAT'S WHEN I REALIZED.
THE PAPER AND PENCIL WERE MY FRIENDS.
IT WAS BECAUSE I HAD THEM WITH ME ALL THE TIME THAT I WAS OKAY.
DRAWING PICTURES WAS THE ONE THING...
...THAT SAVED ME, THAT KEPT ME ALIVE.
THE MOMENT I THOUGHT THAT...
...THE RAINY WORLD OUTSIDE THE WINDOW...
...SEEMED TO BLAZE WITH A GOLDEN LIGHT...

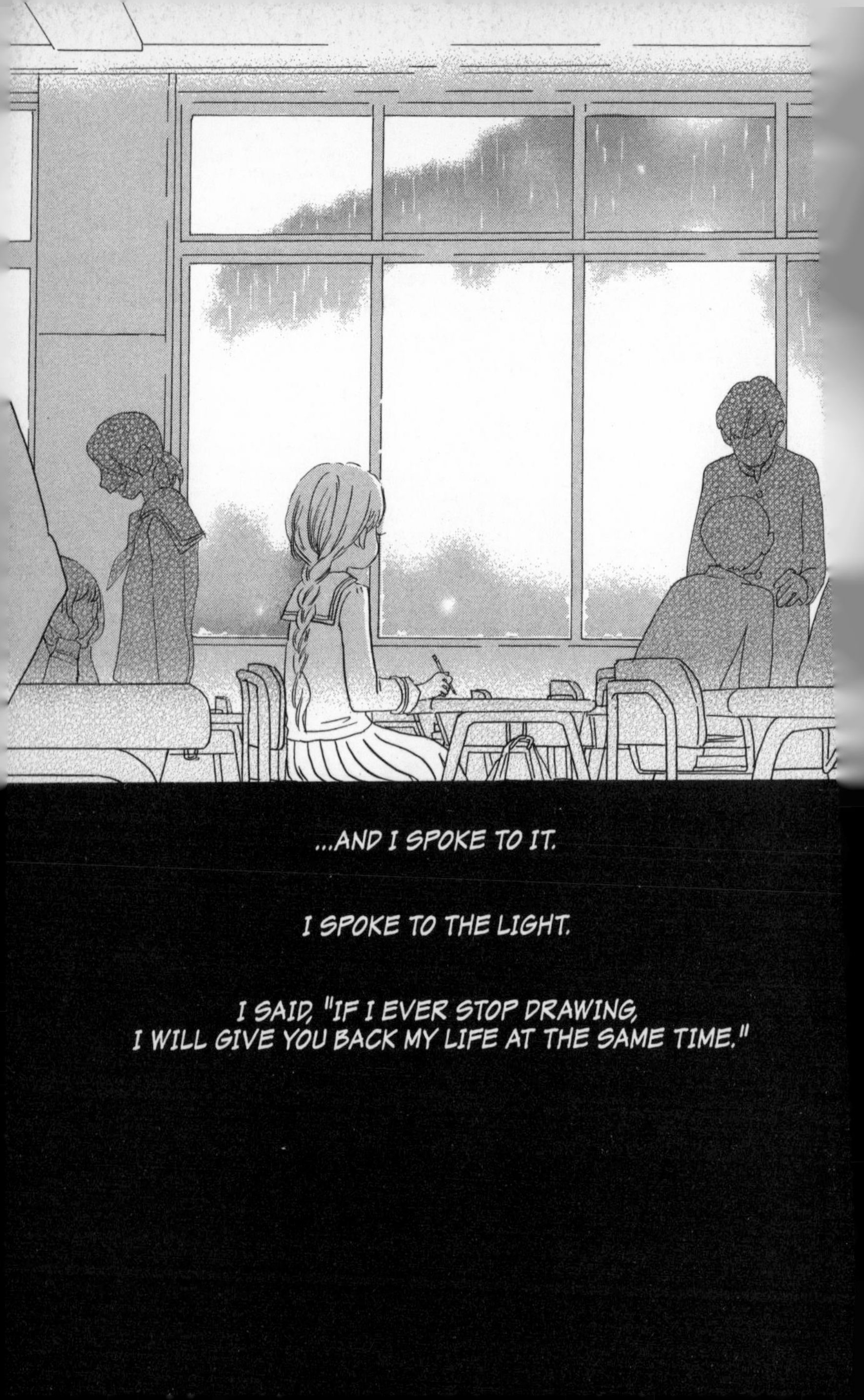

...AND I SPOKE TO IT.

I SPOKE TO THE LIGHT.

I SAID, "IF I EVER STOP DRAWING,
I WILL GIVE YOU BACK MY LIFE AT THE SAME TIME."

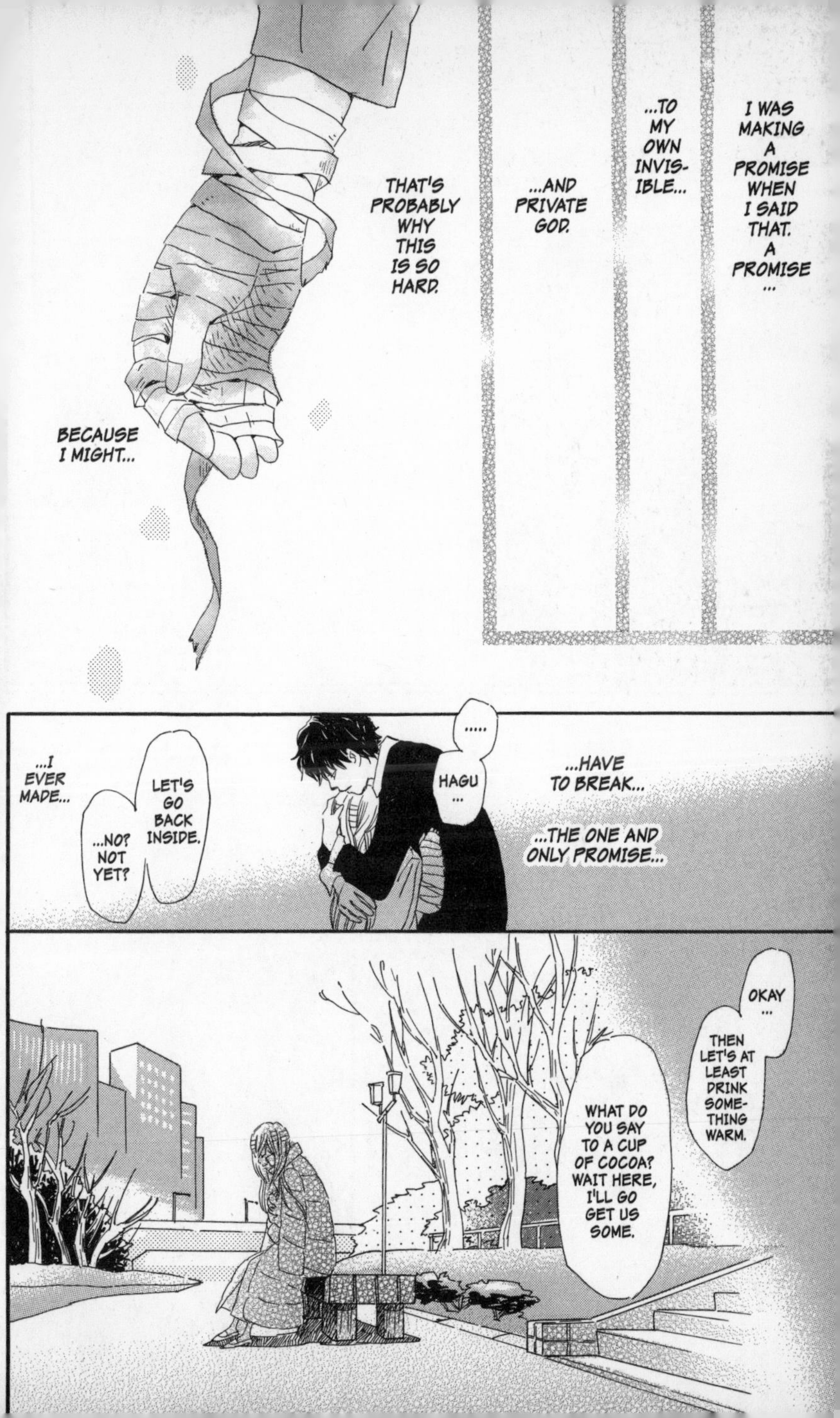
I WAS MAKING A PROMISE WHEN I SAID THAT. A PROMISE...
...TO MY OWN INVISIBLE...
...AND PRIVATE GOD.
THAT'S PROBABLY WHY THIS IS SO HARD.
BECAUSE I MIGHT...
...HAVE TO BREAK...
...THE ONE AND ONLY PROMISE...
.....
HAGU...
LET'S GO BACK INSIDE.
...NO? NOT YET?
...I EVER MADE...
OKAY...
THEN LET'S AT LEAST DRINK SOMETHING WARM.
WHAT DO YOU SAY TO A CUP OF COCOA? WAIT HERE, I'LL GO GET US SOME.

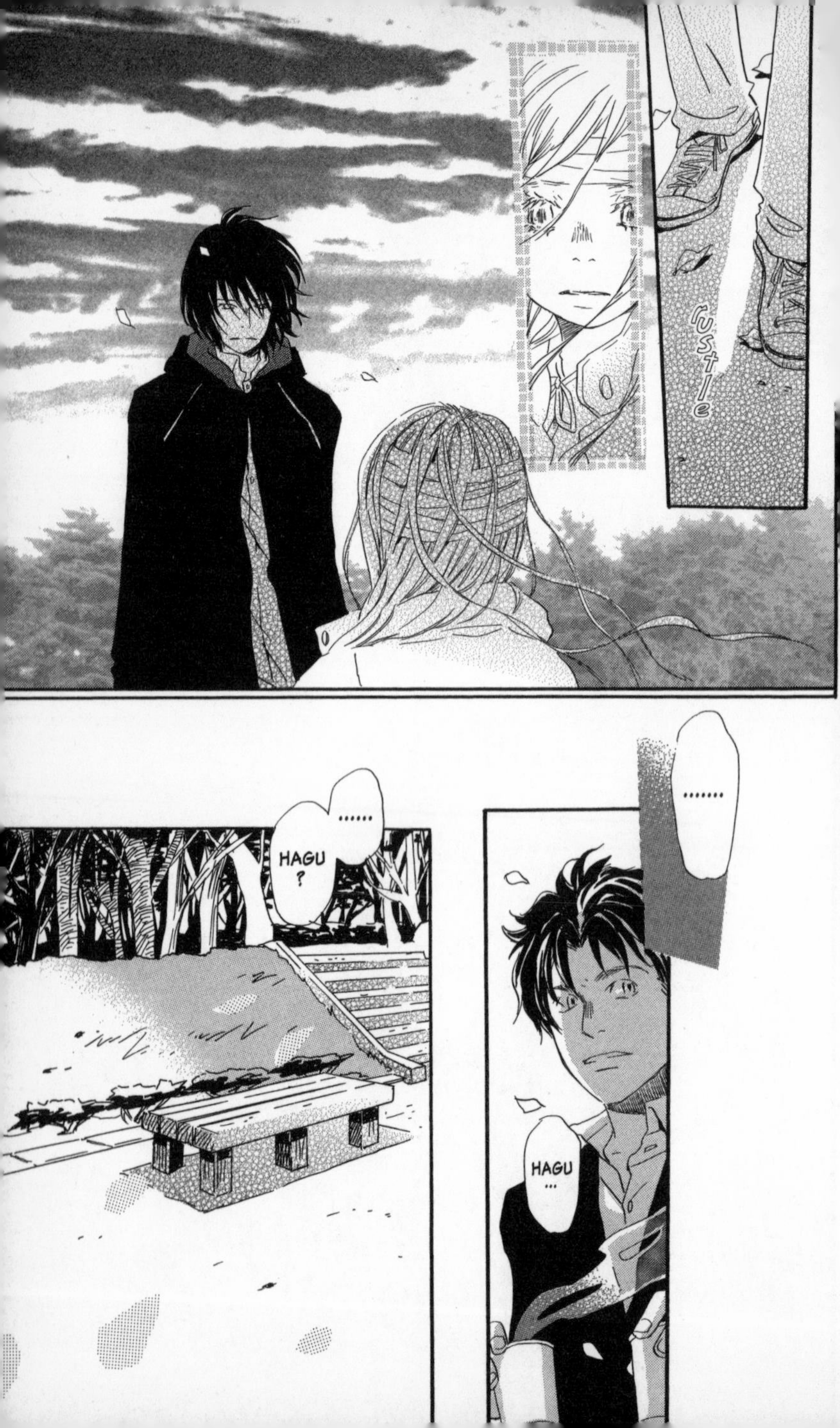
rustle
....
HAGU ...
......
HAGU ?

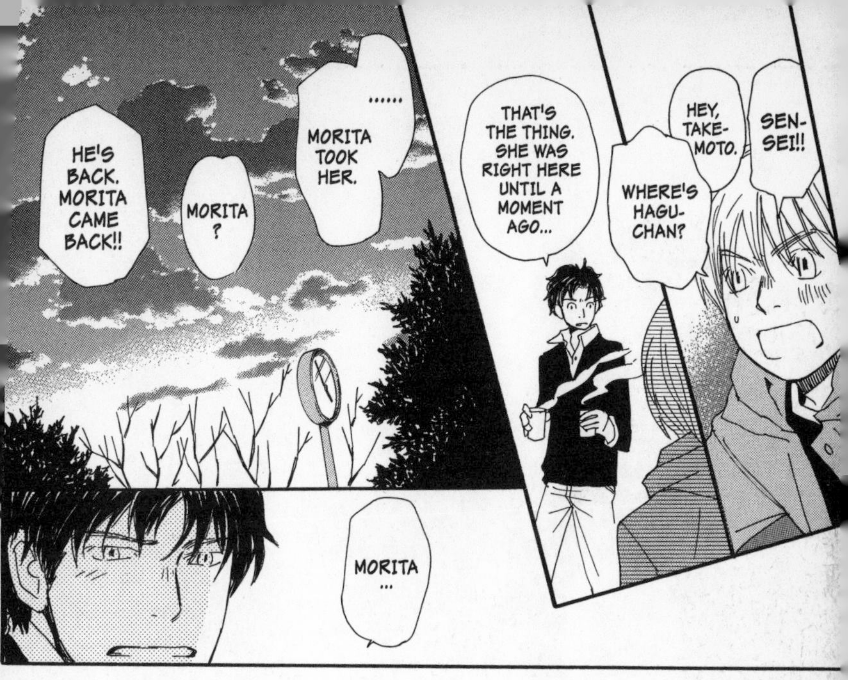
SEN-SEI!!
HEY, TAKE-MOTO.
WHERE'S HAGU-CHAN?
THAT'S THE THING. SHE WAS RIGHT HERE UNTIL A MOMENT AGO...
......
MORITA TOOK HER.
MORITA?
HE'S BACK. MORITA CAME BACK!!
MORITA...
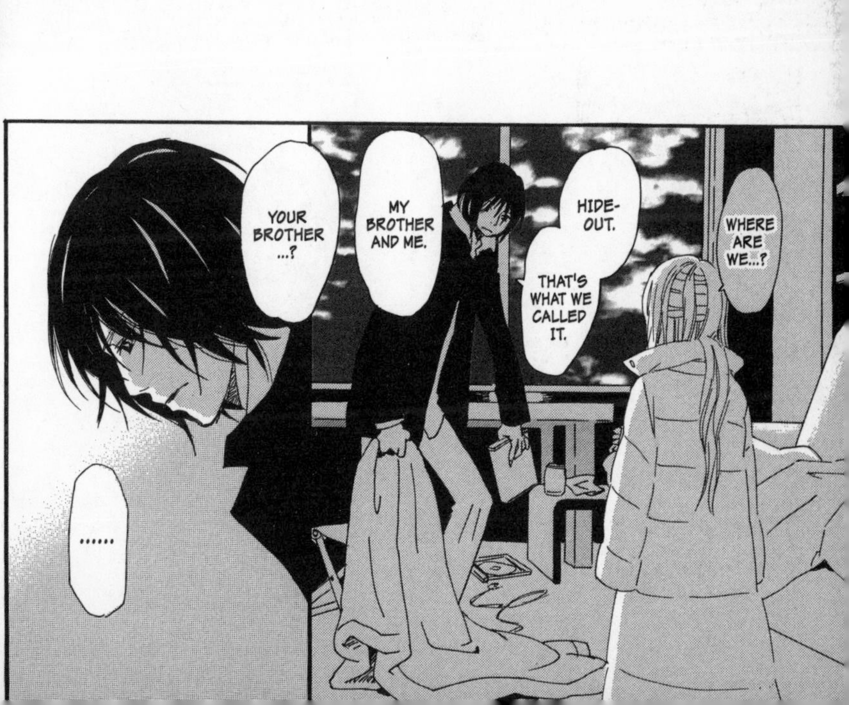
WHERE ARE WE...?
HIDE-OUT.
THAT'S WHAT WE CALLED IT.
MY BROTHER AND ME.
YOUR BROTHER...?
......

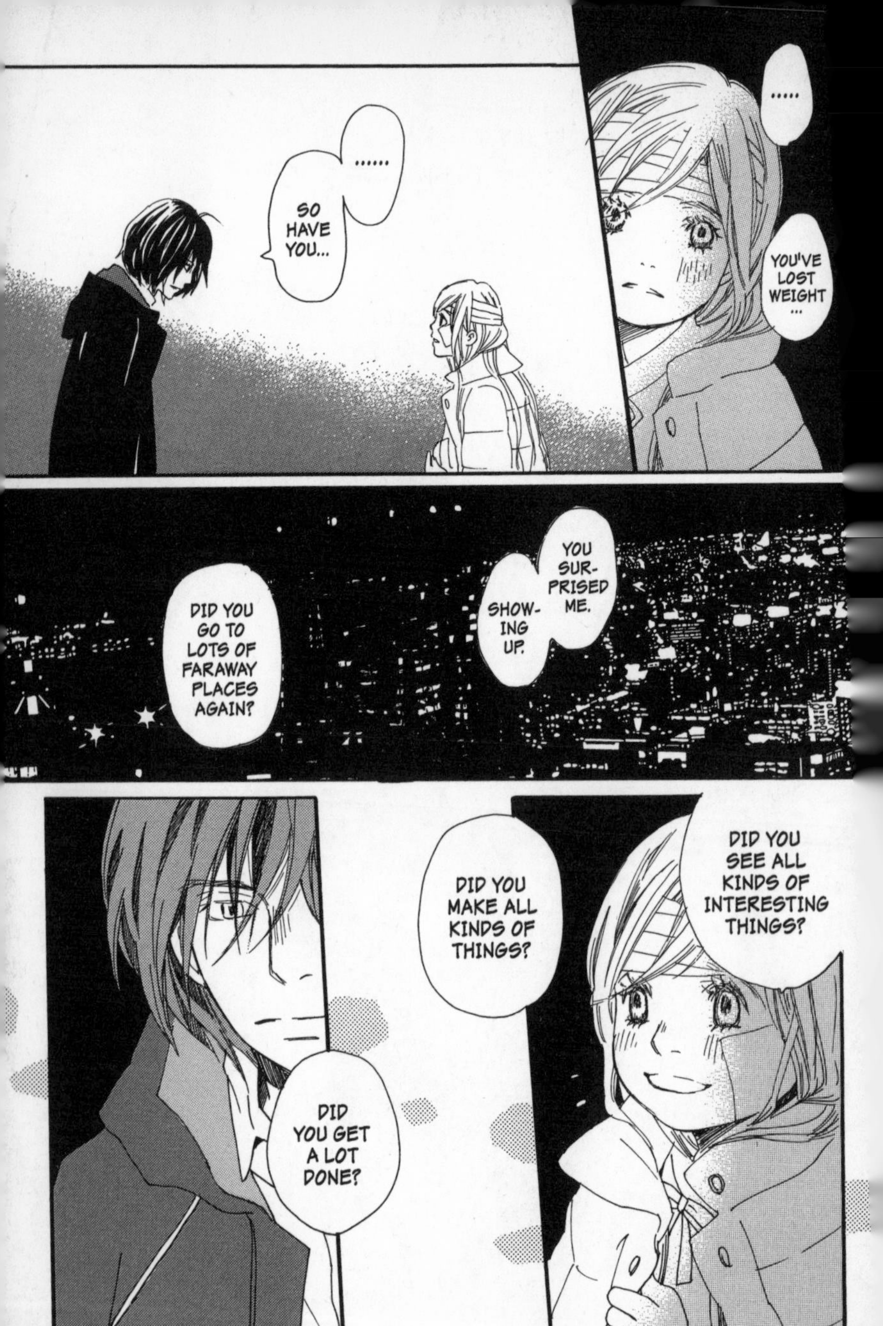
......
YOU'VE LOST WEIGHT ...
......
SO HAVE YOU...
YOU SURPRISED ME.
SHOWING UP.
DID YOU GO TO LOTS OF FARAWAY PLACES AGAIN?
DID YOU SEE ALL KINDS OF INTERESTING THINGS?
DID YOU MAKE ALL KINDS OF THINGS?
DID YOU GET A LOT DONE?

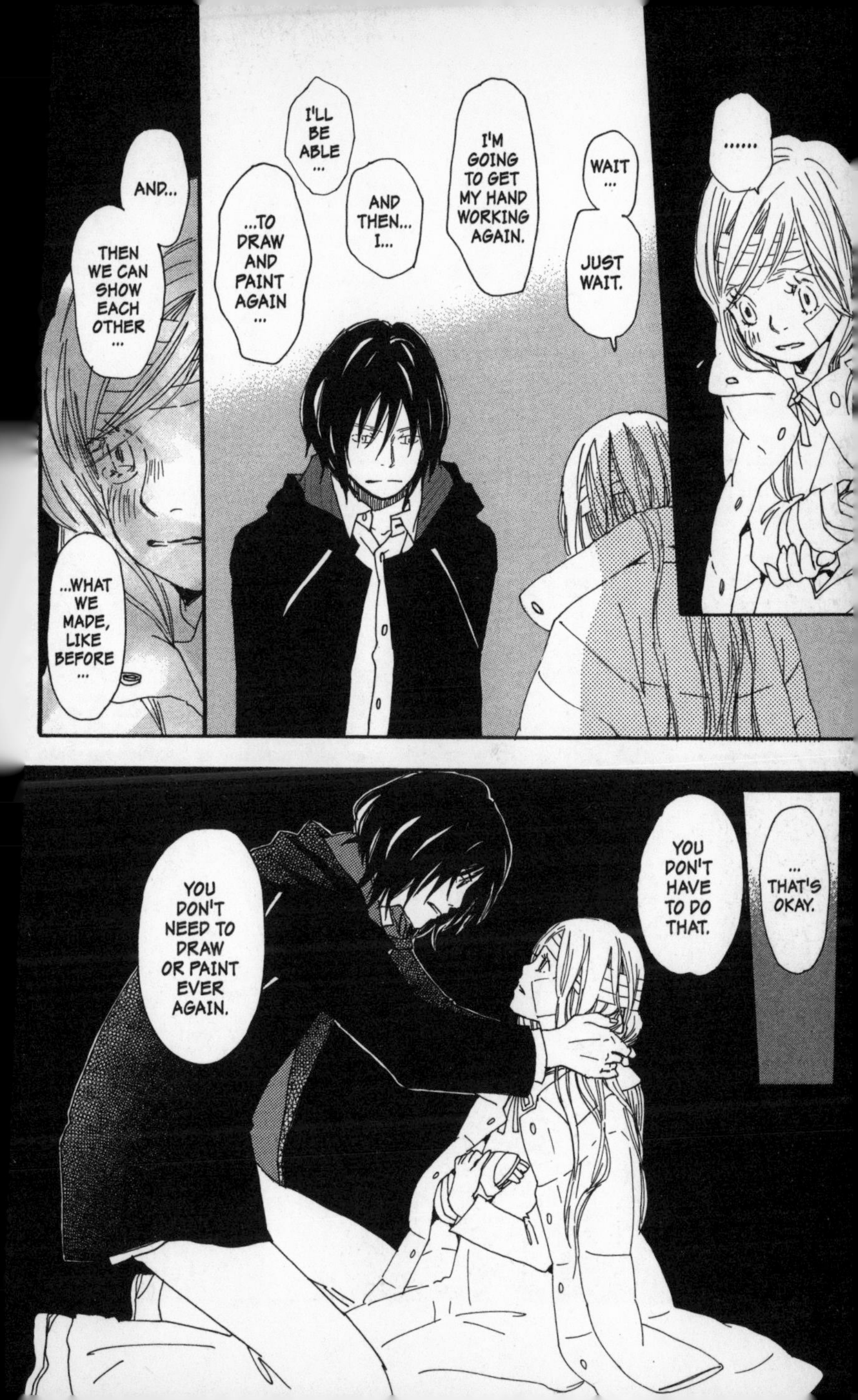
......
WAIT...
JUST WAIT.
I'M GOING TO GET MY HAND WORKING AGAIN.
AND THEN... I...
I'LL BE ABLE...
...TO DRAW AND PAINT AGAIN...
AND...
THEN WE CAN SHOW EACH OTHER...
...WHAT WE MADE, LIKE BEFORE...
...THAT'S OKAY.
YOU DON'T HAVE TO DO THAT.
YOU DON'T NEED TO DRAW OR PAINT EVER AGAIN.

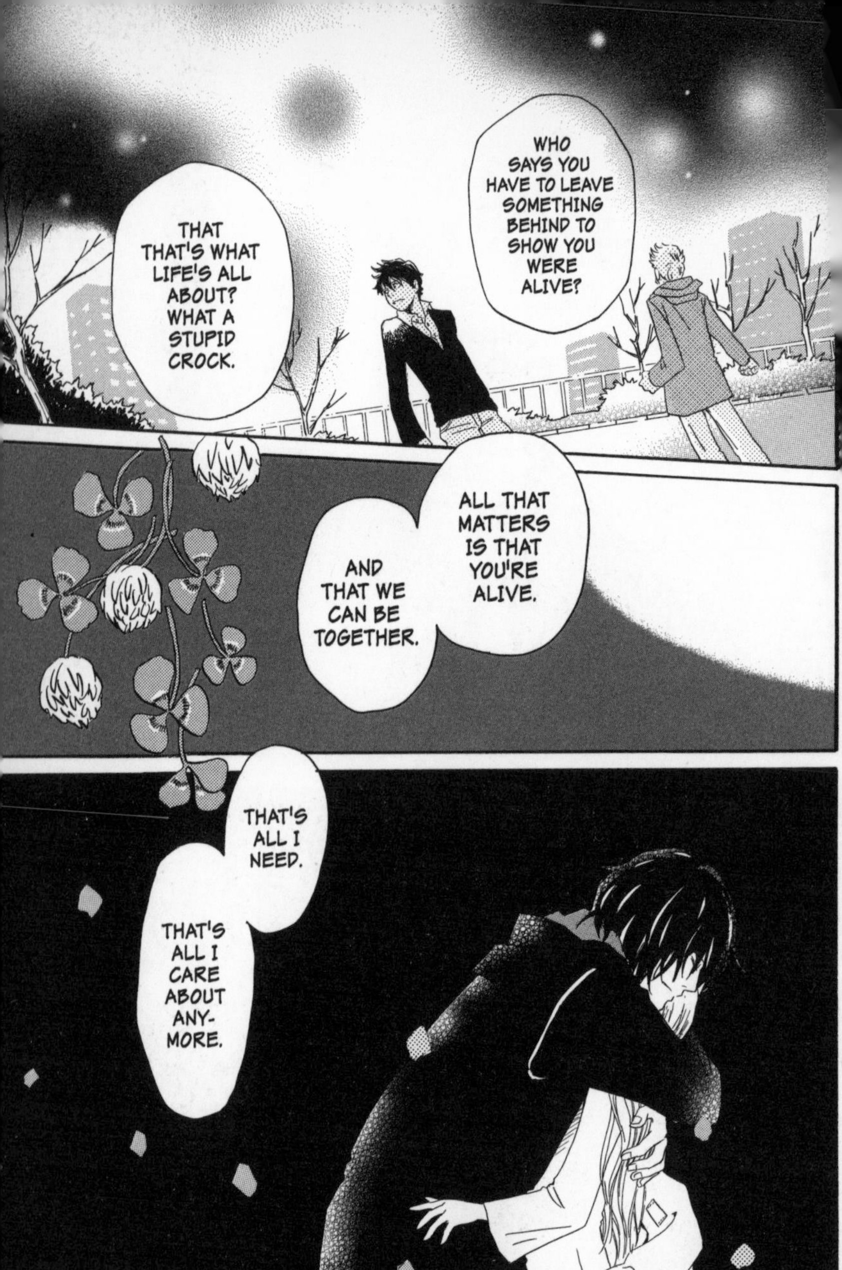
WHO SAYS YOU HAVE TO LEAVE SOMETHING BEHIND TO SHOW YOU WERE ALIVE?
THAT THAT'S WHAT LIFE'S ALL ABOUT? WHAT A STUPID CROCK.
ALL THAT MATTERS IS THAT YOU'RE ALIVE.
AND THAT WE CAN BE TOGETHER.
THAT'S ALL I NEED.
THAT'S ALL I CARE ABOUT ANY-MORE.

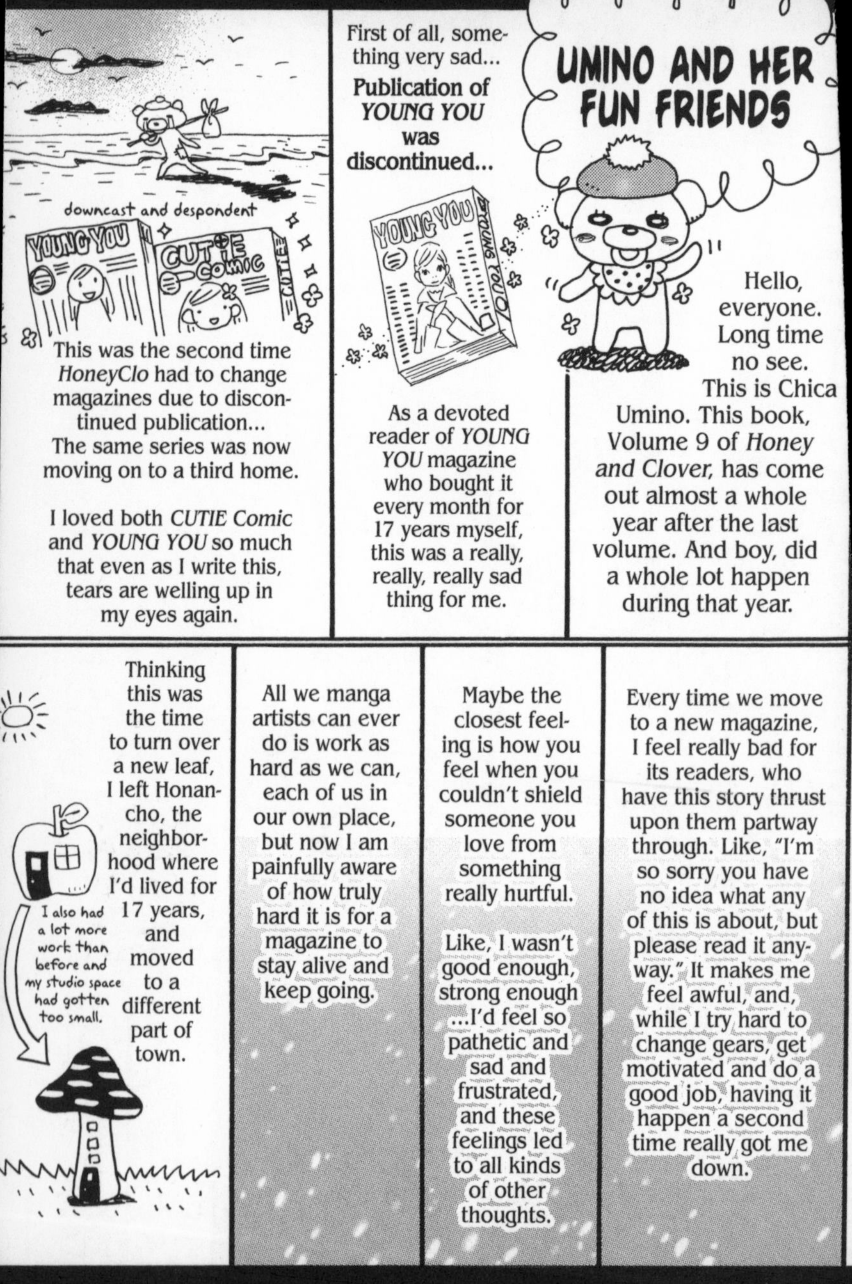
UMINO AND HER FUN FRIENDS
Hello, everyone. Long time no see. This is Chica Umino. This book, Volume 9 of *Honey and Clover,* has come out almost a whole year after the last volume. And boy, did a whole lot happen during that year.
First of all, something very sad...
Publication of *YOUNG YOU* was discontinued...
YOUNG YOU
As a devoted reader of *YOUNG YOU* magazine who bought it every month for 17 years myself, this was a really, really, really sad thing for me.
downcast and despondent
YOUNG YOU
CUTIE Comic
This was the second time *HoneyClo* had to change magazines due to discontinued publication... The same series was now moving on to a third home.
I loved both *CUTIE Comic* and *YOUNG YOU* so much that even as I write this, tears are welling up in my eyes again.
Every time we move to a new magazine, I feel really bad for its readers, who have this story thrust upon them partway through. Like, "I'm so sorry you have no idea what any of this is about, but please read it anyway." It makes me feel awful, and, while I try hard to change gears, get motivated and do a good job, having it happen a second time really got me down.
Maybe the closest feeling is how you feel when you couldn't shield someone you love from something really hurtful.
Like, I wasn't good enough, strong enough ...I'd feel so pathetic and sad and frustrated, and these feelings led to all kinds of other thoughts.
All we manga artists can ever do is work as hard as we can, each of us in our own place, but now I am painfully aware of how truly hard it is for a magazine to stay alive and keep going.
Thinking this was the time to turn over a new leaf, I left Honancho, the neighborhood where I'd lived for 17 years, and moved to a different part of town.
I also had a lot more work than before and my studio space had gotten too small.

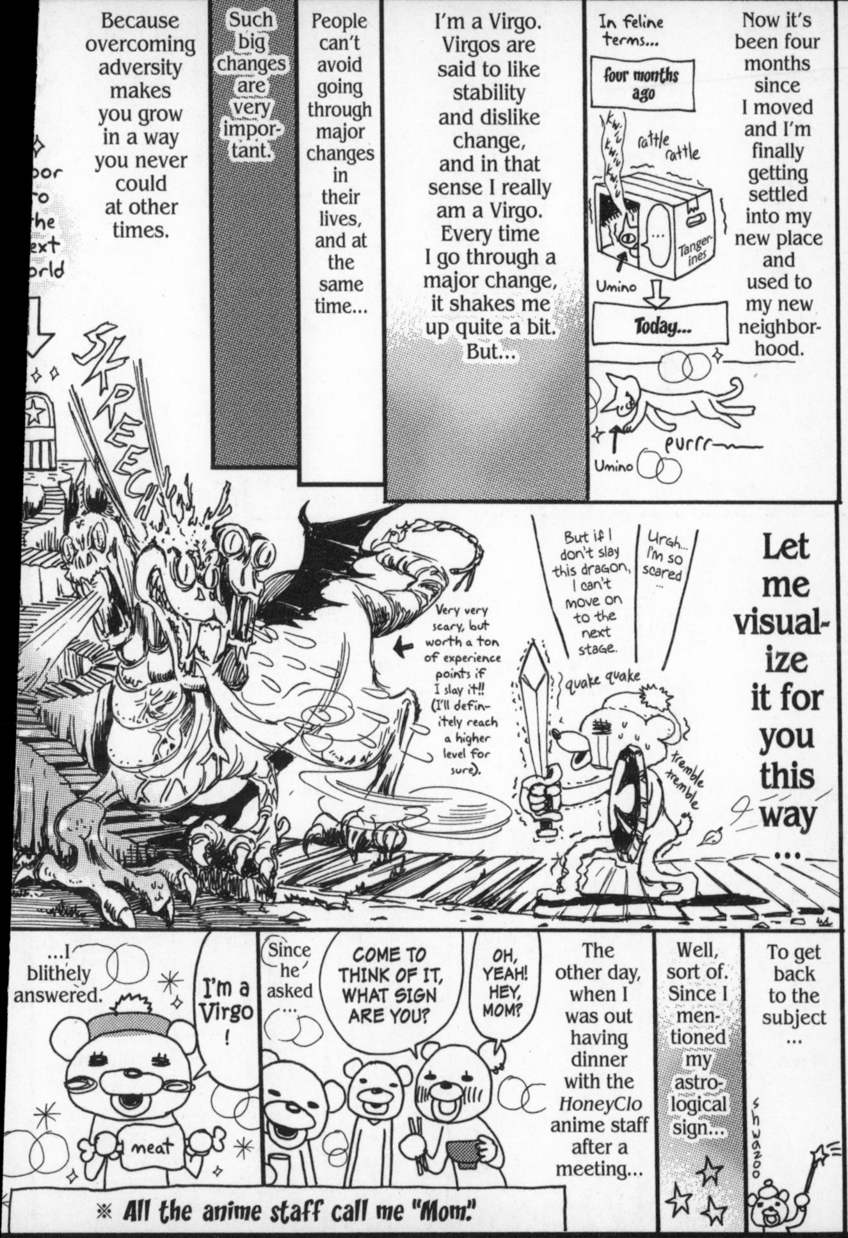
Now it's been four months since I moved and I'm finally getting settled into my new place and used to my new neighborhood.
In feline terms...
four months ago
kwiu kwiu kwiu
rattle rattle
...
Tangerines
Umino
Today...
purrr
Umino
I'm a Virgo. Virgos are said to like stability and dislike change, and in that sense I really am a Virgo. Every time I go through a major change, it shakes me up quite a bit. But...
People can't avoid going through major changes in their lives, and at the same time...
Such big changes are very important.
Because overcoming adversity makes you grow in a way you never could at other times.
Let me visualize it for you this way...
Urgh... I'm so scared...
But if I don't slay this dragon, I can't move on to the next stage.
Very very scary, but worth a ton of experience points if I slay it!! (I'll definitely reach a higher level for sure).
quake quake
tremble tremble
SKREECH
To get back to the subject...
shwazoo
Well, sort of. Since I mentioned my astrological sign...
The other day, when I was out having dinner with the *HoneyClo* anime staff after a meeting...
OH, YEAH! HEY, MOM?
COME TO THINK OF IT, WHAT SIGN ARE YOU?
Since he asked...
I'm a Virgo!
...I blithely answered.
meat
※ All the anime staff call me "Mom."

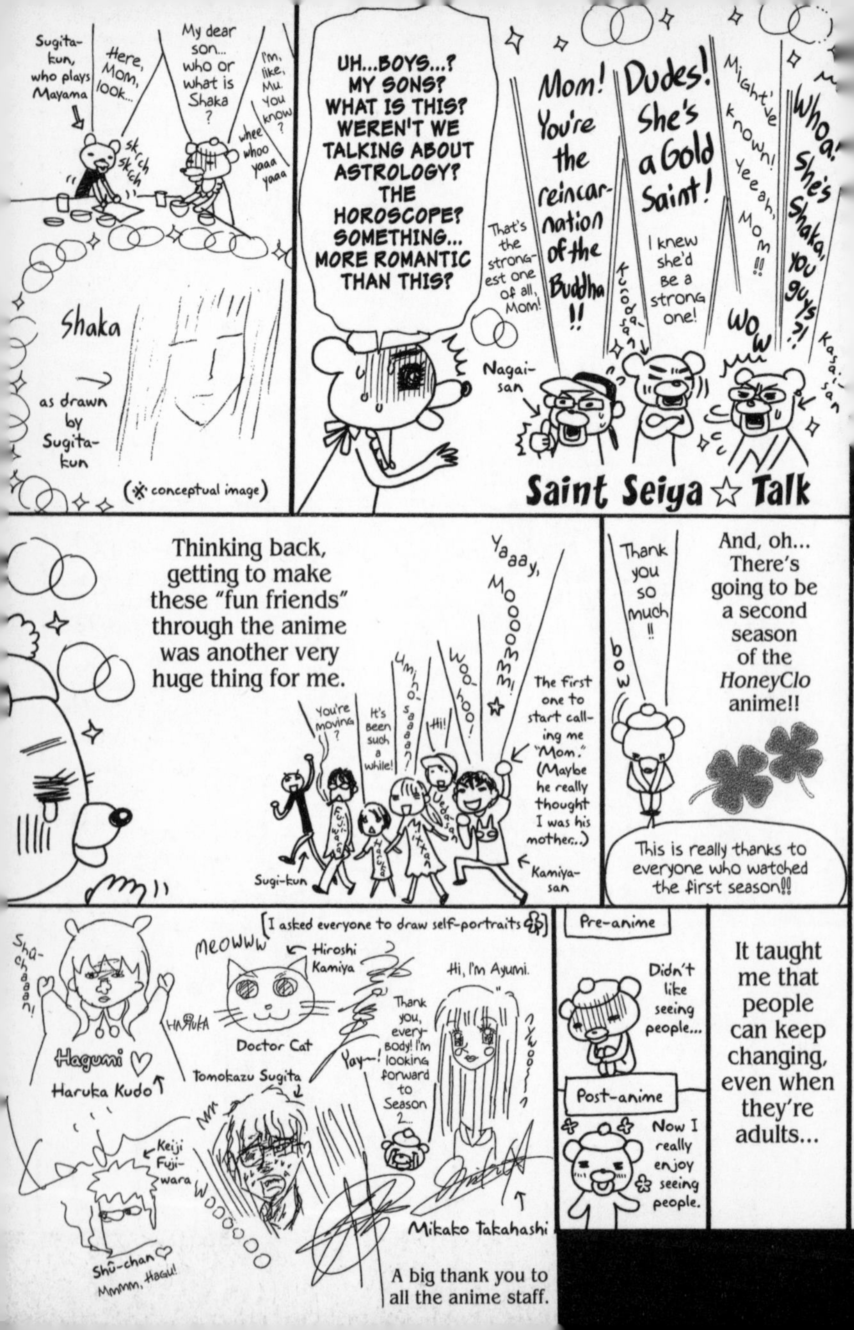

Saint Seiya ☆ Talk
Mom! You're the reincarnation of the Buddha!!
That's the strongest one of all, Mom!
Dudes! She's a Gold Saint!
I knew she'd be a strong one!
Might've known! Yeeeah, Mom!!
Whoa! She's Shaka, you guys?!
WOW
Nagai-san
Kuroda-san
Kasai-san
UH...BOYS...? MY SONS? WHAT IS THIS? WEREN'T WE TALKING ABOUT ASTROLOGY? THE HOROSCOPE? SOMETHING... MORE ROMANTIC THAN THIS?
Sugita-kun, who plays Mayama
Here, Mom, look...
My dear son... who or what is Shaka?
I'm, like, Mu. You know?
skrch skrch
whee whoo yaaa yaaa
Shaka
as drawn by Sugita-kun
(※ conceptual image)
And, oh... There's going to be a second season of the *HoneyClo* anime!!
Thank you so much!!
bow
This is really thanks to everyone who watched the first season!!
Thinking back, getting to make these "fun friends" through the anime was another very huge thing for me.
Yaaay, Mooooommm!
Woo-hoo!
Umino-saaaan!
Hi!
It's been such a while!
You're moving?
The first one to start calling me "Mom." (Maybe he really thought I was his mother...)
Fujiwara
Haruka
Mikitan
Ueda-san
Sugi-kun
Kamiya-san
It taught me that people can keep changing, even when they're adults...
Pre-anime
Didn't like seeing people...
Post-anime
Now I really enjoy seeing people.
[I asked everyone to draw self-portraits]
Shu-chaaaan!
HARUKA
Hagumi ♡
Haruka Kudo
MEOWWW
Hiroshi Kamiya
Doctor Cat
Tomokazu Sugita
Yay~!
Thank you, everybody! I'm looking forward to Season 2...
Hi, I'm Ayumi.
Nyooo~n
Keiji Fujiwara
Shû-chan ♡
Mmmm, Hagu!
Woooooo
Mikako Takahashi
A big thank you to all the anime staff.

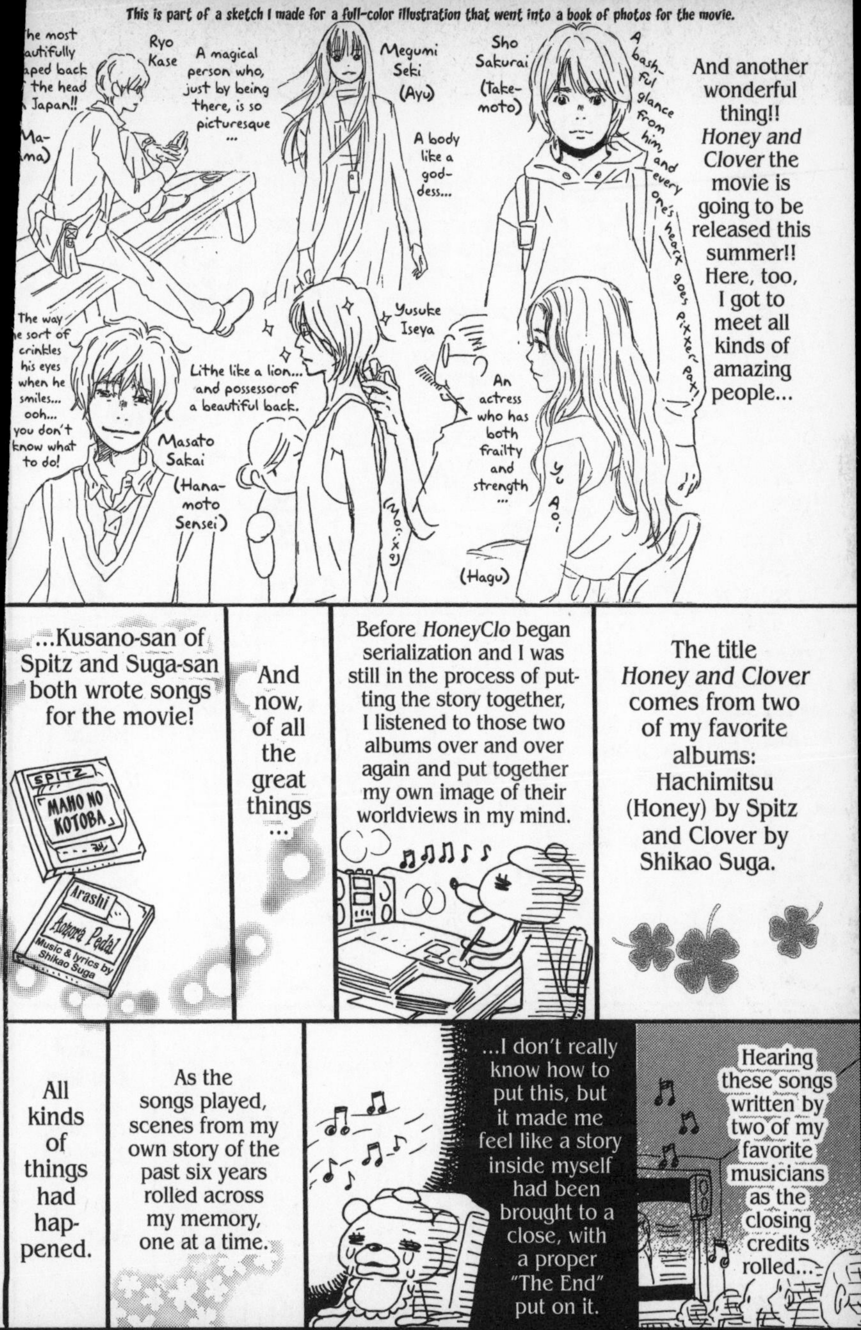
This is part of a sketch I made for a full-color illustration that went into a book of photos for the movie.
And another wonderful thing!! *Honey and Clover* the movie is going to be released this summer!! Here, too, I got to meet all kinds of amazing people...
Sho Sakurai (Take-moto)
A bash-ful glance from him, and every one's heart goes pitter-pat!
Megumi Seki (Ayu)
A body like a god-dess...
Ryo Kase
A magical person who, just by being there, is so picturesque...
Yu Aoi
An actress who has both frailty and strength...
(Hagu)
Yusuke Iseya
Lithe like a lion... and possessorof a beautiful back.
(Morita)
Masato Sakai (Hana-moto Sensei)
The way he sort of crinkles his eyes when he smiles... ooh... you don't know what to do!
The title *Honey and Clover* comes from two of my favorite albums: Hachimitsu (Honey) by Spitz and Clover by Shikao Suga.
Before *HoneyClo* began serialization and I was still in the process of putting the story together, I listened to those two albums over and over again and put together my own image of their worldviews in my mind.
And now, of all the great things...
...Kusano-san of Spitz and Suga-san both wrote songs for the movie!
SPITZ
MAHO NO KOTOBA
Arashi
Aozora Pedal
Music & lyrics by Shikao Suga
Hearing these songs written by two of my favorite musicians as the closing credits rolled...
...I don't really know how to put this, but it made me feel like a story inside myself had been brought to a close, with a proper "The End" put on it.
As the songs played, scenes from my own story of the past six years rolled across my memory, one at a time.
All kinds of things had happened.

※ I am called "Dad" by the residents of Umino Village.

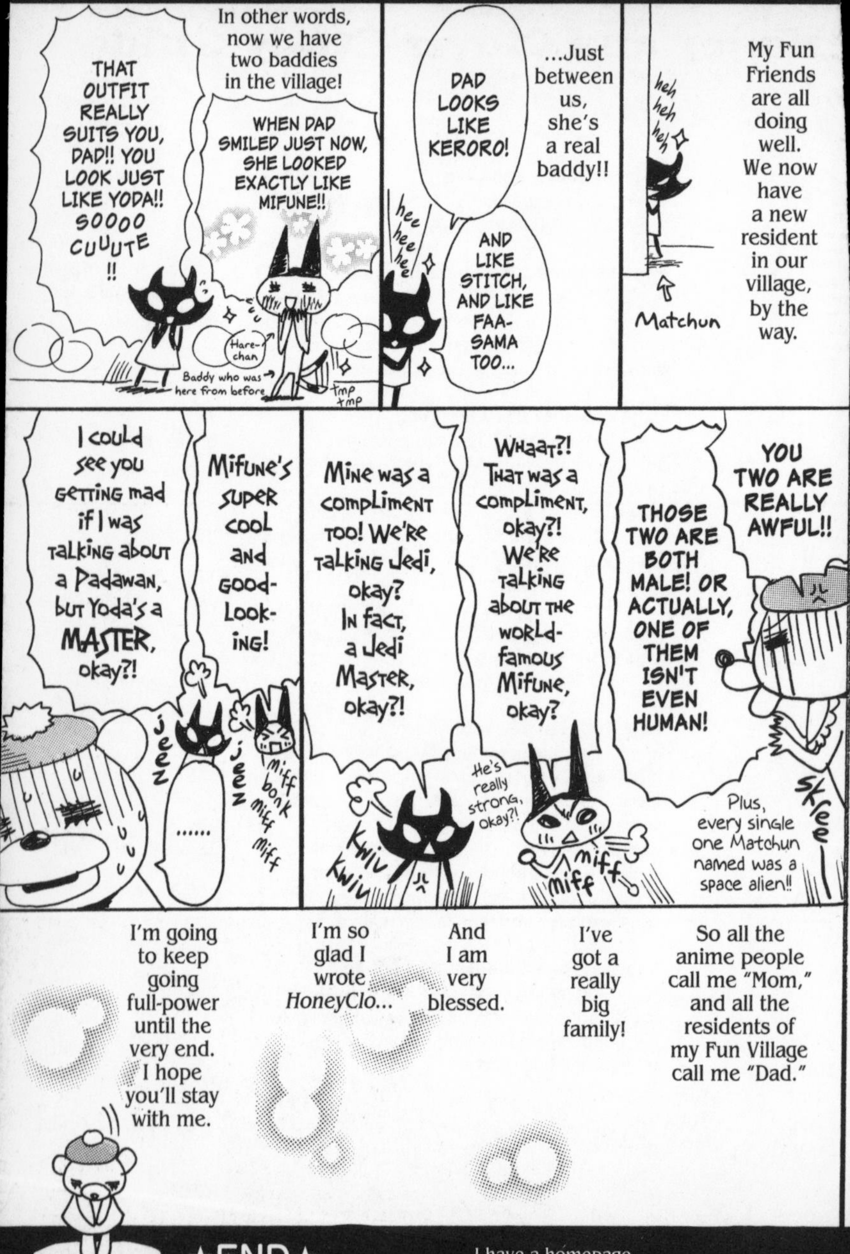
My Fun Friends are all doing well. We now have a new resident in our village, by the way.
heh heh heh
Matchun
...Just between us, she's a real baddy!!
DAD LOOKS LIKE KERORO!
AND LIKE STITCH, AND LIKE FAA-SAMA TOO...
hee hee hee
In other words, now we have two baddies in the village!
WHEN DAD SMILED JUST NOW, SHE LOOKED EXACTLY LIKE MIFUNE!!
THAT OUTFIT REALLY SUITS YOU, DAD!! YOU LOOK JUST LIKE YODA!! SOOOO CUUUTE!!
Hare-chan
Baddy who was here from before
tmp tmp
YOU TWO ARE REALLY AWFUL!!
THOSE TWO ARE BOTH MALE! OR ACTUALLY, ONE OF THEM ISN'T EVEN HUMAN!
Skree
Plus, every single one Matchun named was a space alien!!
Whaat?! That was a compliment, okay?! We're talking about the world-famous Mifune, okay?
Mine was a compliment too! We're talking Jedi, okay? In fact, a Jedi Master, okay?!
He's really strong, okay?!
miff miff
Kwiv Kwiv
Mifune's super cool and good-looking!
I could see you getting mad if I was talking about a Padawan, but Yoda's a MASTER, okay?!
jeez jeez
miff bonk miff miff
......
So all the anime people call me "Mom," and all the residents of my Fun Village call me "Dad."
I've got a really big family!
And I am very blessed.
I'm so glad I wrote *HoneyClo*...
I'm going to keep going full-power until the very end. I hope you'll stay with me.

★END★

I have a homepage.
http://www13.plala.or.jp/umino/

Honey and Clover Study Guide

Page 8, panel 2: Kabu-tan
Tan is baby talk for *chan*, an honorific often used with children's names.

Page 19, panel 3: Katsuobushi, somen
Katsuobushi is a type of fish flake made from dried, fermented and smoked bonito. *Somen* is a type of thin wheat noodle. Somen is often served chilled with a dipping sauce of some kind.

Page 19, panel 3: Shichimi, etc.
Mayama is bringing Rika a care package of Japanese staples. *Shichimi* (seven flavor chili powder) is a spice mixture of red chili powder and other ingredients; *umeboshi* are pickled plums; *nori* is a type of seaweed often used to wrap sushi but also used in other dishes; *yukari* is a seasoning made from the flakes of dried purple shiso left over from making umeboshi; *dashi* is a broth or stock commonly made from *konbu* (kelp) and bonito flakes; and *tsukudani* is seaweed or other ingredients cooked in soy sauce.

Page 108, panel 3: Natto mochi
Mochi is traditionally made by pounding soaked glutinous rice until it forms a sticky mass, although it can also be made of rice flour and water. While some mochi are sweet, it can also be part of a savory dish. *Natto* is made from fermented soybeans and is known for its distinct aroma, texture and flavor. For natto mochi, the mochi is usually toasted and then topped with natto.

Page 155, panel 4: Yokoyama Taikan
An important Japanese artist who helped establish the Nihonga style of painting. He was known for his monochrome ink paintings and his mastery of tones and shades of black.